HANDBOOK OF MARKETING AND FINANCE

Handbook of Marketing and Finance

Edited by

Shankar Ganesan

University of Arizona, USA

Edward Elgar
Cheltenham, UK • Northampton, MA, USA

Published by
Edward Elgar Publishing Limited
The Lypiatts
15 Lansdown Road
Cheltenham
Glos GL50 2JA
UK

Edward Elgar Publishing, Inc.
William Pratt House
9 Dewey Court
Northampton
Massachusetts 01060
USA

A catalogue record for this book
is available from the British Library

Library of Congress Control Number: 2012930574

MIX
Paper from
responsible sources
FSC® C018575
www.fsc.org

ISBN 978 1 84980 272 7

Typeset by Servis Filmsetting Ltd, Stockport, Cheshire
Printed and bound by MPG Books Group, UK

Contents

Figures

Tables

Contributors

Anindita Chakravarty, Assistant Professor, Department of Marketing, Terry College of Business, University of Georgia, Athens, GA, USA

Yubo Chen, Assistant Professor of Marketing, Eller College of Management, University of Arizona, Tucson, AZ, USA

Susan Fournier, Professor of Marketing and Dean's Research Fellow, Boston University School of Management, Boston, MA, USA

Shankar Ganesan, Karl Eller Professor of Marketing, Eller College of Management, University of Arizona, Tucson, AZ, USA

Inge Geyskens, Professor of Marketing, Tilburg School of Economics and Management, Tilburg University, Tilburg, the Netherlands

Katrijn Gielens, Associate Professor of Marketing, Kenan-Flagler Business School, UNC, Chapel Hill, NC, USA

Rajdeep Grewal, Irving & Irene Bard Professor of Marketing, Smeal College of Business, Pennsylvania State University, University Park, PA, USA

Dominique M. Hanssens, Bud Knapp Professor of Marketing, UCLA Anderson School of Management, Los Angeles, CA, USA

Ronald Hess, Associate Professor of Marketing, Mason College of Business, College of William and Mary, Williamsburg, VA, USA

Liwu Hsu, doctoral student, Boston University School of Management, Boston, MA, USA

John Hulland, Robert O. Arnold Professor of Business, University of Georgia, Athens, GA, USA

Michael D. Hutt, Ford Motor Company Distinguished Professor of Marketing, Arizona State University, Tempe, AZ, USA

V. Kumar, Richard and Susan Lenny Distinguished Chair Professor of Marketing, Executive Director of the Center for Excellence in Brand and Customer Management, and Director of the PhD Program in Marketing, J. Mack Robinson College of Business of Georgia State University, Atlanta, GA, USA

Didem Kurt, doctoral candidate, Katz Graduate School of Business, University of Pittsburgh, Pittsburgh, PA, USA

Yong Liu, Associate Professor of Marketing and Gary M. Munsinger Chair in Entrepreneurship and Innovation, Eller College of Management, University of Arizona, Tucson, AZ, USA

Xueming Luo, Eunice and James L. West Distinguished Professor of Marketing, College of Business, University of Texas at Arlington, TX, USA

Natalie Mizik, Gantcher Associate Professor of Business, Columbia Graduate School of Business, Columbia University, New York and Visiting Associate Professor of Marketing, MIT Sloan School of Management, Cambridge, MA, USA

Koen H. Pauwels, Professor, School of Economics and Administrative Sciences, Özyeğin University, Istanbul, Turkey

Joost M.E. Pennings, Professor of Marketing and Finance, Maastricht University, the Netherlands, Professor of Marketing, University of Illinois at Urbana-Champaign, IL, USA and Professor of Marketing and Consumer Behavior, Wageningen University, the Netherlands

Debika Sihi, PhD student in Marketing, Red McCombs School of Business, University of Texas at Austin, Austin, TX, USA

Alina Sorescu, Associate Professor and Mays Fellow, Mays Business School, Texas A&M University, College Station, TX, USA

Raji Srinivasan, Associate Professor of Marketing, Red McCombs School of Business, University of Texas at Austin, Austin, TX, USA

Shuba Srinivasan, Associate Professor of Marketing and Dean's Research Fellow, Boston University School of Management, Boston, MA, USA

Crina O. Tarasi, Assistant Professor of Marketing, Central Michigan University, Mount Pleasant, MI, USA

Nita Umashankar, Assistant Professor of Marketing, J. Mack Robinson College of Business of Georgia State University, Atlanta, GA, USA

Peter C. Verhoef, Professor of Marketing, Faculty of Economics and Business, University of Groningen, Groningen, the Netherlands

Beth A. Walker, State Farm Professor of Marketing, Arizona State University, Tempe, AZ, USA

Introduction
Shankar Ganesan

Demonstrating the value created by the marketing function to business operations and financial performance has become very important in many organizations. Top managers are constantly challenging marketers to document marketing's contribution to the bottom line and link marketing investments and assets to metrics that matter to them. This handbook relates marketing actions to various types of risk and return metrics that are typically used in the domain of finance. This unique handbook provides current knowledge of this marketing–finance interface in a single, authoritative volume and brings together new cutting-edge research by established marketing scholars on a range of topics in the area.

The research on the marketing–finance interface spans tactical and strategic marketing actions related to the creation, communication, delivery, and appropriation of the value proposition. The chapters draw on theoretical developments in economics, accounting, finance, psychology, and cutting-edge statistical and econometric approaches.

This handbook consists of 12 further chapters and is an attempt to bring together state-of-the-art research by established marketing scholars on various topics related to the marketing–finance interface. These chapters are specifically written for this handbook and cover both methodological and substantive issues. They are based on a thorough academic review, including multiple revisions of the initial chapters by the authors.

OVERVIEW OF THE CHAPTERS IN THE HANDBOOK

The chapters are organized into three major parts, labeled Parts I, II, and III. Part I covers the metrics and methods related to the understanding of firm value. Part II covers topics that are in some sense fundamental to the marketing–finance interface. These topics deal with the creation, communication, delivery, sustaining of value and its relationship to firm performance. Part III focuses on marketing actions and the destruction of firm value.

1

Part I   Metrics and Methods

Chapter 1 by Kumar and Umashankar describes the several marketing metrics intended to increase marketing's accountability within the firm and justify spending firm resources on marketing initiatives. In addition, they suggest that there is an increasing shift from product-based metrics to customer-level metrics. They review prominent streams of customer metrics and link them to firm performance. Specifically, the five major domains of customer-based metrics include customer value metrics (what is the worth of the customers), cognitive and affective value metrics (how customers think about the firm), customer satisfaction metrics (the extent to which customers' expectations have been met or exceeded), retention and acquisition metrics (which customers to retain), churn and winback metrics (the customers to leave and the ones to win back), and the referral metrics (the value of customer referrals). This chapter provides insights that allow firms to (1) select the right customers for targeting, (2) understand the behavior and perceptions of their customer base, (3) optimally allocate marketing resources, (4) acquire and retain high-value customers, (5) cultivate customer relationships, (6) invest in building customer-valued brands, and (7) retain customers with valuable social capital.

In Chapter 2, Luo, Pauwels, and Hanssens review various time-series methods as the primary research tool for evaluating the pricing of marketing actions and marketing assets. They argue that since the effects of marketing actions occur over time, the investment community could over-estimate or underestimate the financial impact of a marketing action or marketing metric, resulting in mispricing or departures from full market efficiency. This chapter presents the classification of mispricing and how time-series models can be employed to test it empirically. They show that time-series models can be implemented at the stock portfolio level and at the individual stock/firm level across time periods. Finally, they provide insights on the mispricing of both returns and risk due to marketing.

In Chapter 3, Mizik describes a new approach for valuing branded businesses. In this conditional multiplier valuation method, information about consumer perceptions of the firm's brands is incorporated directly into the valuation of the enterprise. This method was validated using a large sample of US-based publicly traded companies. The results show a significant improvement in predictive accuracy of enterprise valuation – models incorporating brand perceptions show a 16 percent average out-of-sample reduction in mean absolute error of enterprise value estimates. This chapter starts with discussion of the discounted cash flow and multiplier-based valuation analyses and then follows up with how the multiplier-based valuation approach can be implemented and extended to account for the role of brand perceptions. Finally, the chapter applies the conditional multiplier approach to illustrate the valuation of Hewlett-Packard in 2005. Using the estimated parameters from the model, along with HP's actual measures of return on sales and brand perceptions, the author estimates a value multiplier and thus actual value of Hewlett-Packard's enterprise value-to-sales.

In Chapter 4, Hutt, Tarasi, and Walker review the application of financial portfolio theory in marketing and show how this theory provides the basis for identifying the risk–return tradeoffs in both individual customers as well as market segments. In this chapter, they suggest that the risk associated with an individual customer does not arise solely from the probability of defection but is also affected by the variability in their purchases. In addition, they show that individual customer risk influences the risk associated with the entire customer base and thus, the company itself. An important highlight of this chapter is the introduction of a new customer risk metric, the customer reward ratio. The authors show how this measure can be used to assess the reward-on-risk for customers.

Chapter 5, by Srinivasan and Sihi, focuses on marketing information disclosures – any information the firm discloses about its marketing activities and programs, marketing assets, and marketing personnel. Accordingly, marketing information disclosures are disclosures about the firm's products, prices, distribution channels, entry into new markets, marketing alliances, and appointments (departures) of marketing executives. In this chapter, they first discuss the mandatory requirements for disclosure of marketing information by publicly listed firms and subsequently show that there is considerable discretion in how and what managers reveal regarding their marketing programs and spending. In the next section, they discuss the costs and benefits of marketing information disclosures and then propose a conceptual model that examines the antecedents and consequences of marketing information disclosures. Finally, they identify several research questions for marketing scholars to pursue.

Part II   Creating, Communicating, Delivering, and Sustaining Value and Firm Performance

The focus of the next set of chapters is on creating, communicating, delivering, and sustaining the value and how it impacts a firm's performance.

In Chapter 6, Sorescu provides a comprehensive review of how innovation creates shareholder value. First, she discusses the determinants of successful innovation. The author suggests that the returns to innovation are different when (1) innovation is measured using patents versus new products, (2) innovation is radical versus incremental, (3) innovation is generated by the firm alone, or due to an alliance, or is outsourced from another firm or from an open community of inventors. In the next section, the discussion is focused on the metrics used to measure the value of innovation. In the final section, the focus is on how innovation affects shareholder value. Finally, the author provides directions for future research in this area.

In Chapter 7, Srinivasan, Hsu, and Fournier provide a comprehensive review of the literature on branding and shareholder value. They use the insights from this literature and provide a process framework that explains the brand–finance link. The chapter starts off with a discussion of why shareholder value (i.e., stock returns and risk) is an appropriate metric to assess brand performance and brand value. The main metrics discussed include concepts such as Tobin's Q, abnormal returns, and idiosyncratic and systematic risk. The discussion of brand equity includes three distinct perspectives – customer-based, product market-based and finance-based. Next, the chapter provides a nice discussion of two key process mechanisms for how branding affects shareholder value (the brand-as-information and brand-as-asset routes). In the following sections, the authors review the antecedents of brand equity creation and then discuss brand management tools such as advertising and promotion for building brand equity and influencing shareholder value. In the last section, the authors outline key gaps in our understanding in this area. Some of the key research topics include how brands' participation in social media drives shareholder value, the theory of risk as it pertains to brands and brand equity, and value-destroying consequences of brand crisis events.

Chapter 8 by Gielens and Geyskens describes the impact of distribution channel decisions on shareholder value. In the first part of the chapter, the authors provide an overview of the extant literature. They conclude that very little research has been done linking distribution channel decisions to shareholder value despite the long-term nature of the distribution decisions. In addition, their review indicates that the majority of the research has focused on channel design issues whereas channel coordination issues have not been addressed in the marketing–finance interface. In the next section, the authors elaborate on potential research avenues in both the channel design and channel coordination areas. In terms of channel design, the discussion emphasizes both the channel intensity and multichannel decisions and their impact on firm value. In terms of channel coordination, the authors explain how the three main coordination mechanisms (vertical integration, partnerships with distributors, and the use of power) affect shareholder value. Finally, in their summary, they provide different ways in which future research can examine whether and how distribution channel decisions affect shareholder value.

In Chapter 9, Verhoef and Pennings focus on the marketing–finance interface. They start with a detailed review of the extant literature on the marketing–finance interface and then develop potential strategies for improving this link between marketing and finance. They approach this interface from three different perspectives. The first perspective focuses on the power and influence of marketing and finance departments within the firm. The second perspective takes a cross-functional view, while the third perspective examines how the marketing–finance interface affects relationships between marketing and its key stakeholders such as customers and channel partners. In the final analysis, they conclude that it is imperative for marketers to understand the intricacies of finance to improve marketing's role in the domain of finance.

In Chapter 10, Kurt and Hulland examine the interrelationship between marketing strategy, corporate financial policy, and firm value. In the first part of the chapter, they focus on how marketing strategy affects and is affected by corporate financial policy. For example, equity financing plays a crucial role in supporting major increases in marketing spending. Thus, a better understanding of the connection between marketing strategy and firms' acquisition of equity capital through initial public offerings (IPOs) and seasoned equity offerings (SEOs) is critical to longer-term success. In the second part, the authors focus on the interactive effects of marketing decisions (e.g., advertising and promotion) and corporate financial policy on firm value. Specifically, they examine how corporate financial policy decisions of firms and their industry rivals moderate the link between marketing strategy and firm value. In conclusion, this chapter develops a neat contingency theory of the marketing–finance interface that goes beyond examining simple main effect relationships.

Part III   Marketing Actions and Value Destruction

In Chapter 11, Chakravarty and Grewal focus on how short-term concerns for firm performance and shareholder value drive marketing activities. For example, they argue that a tactic called REAM (real activities management), the practice by which managers deviate from their planned marketing-related expenditures to deliver current period earnings that maintain or increase stock prices, can be a major concern to marketing professionals and academics. They not only discuss different ways in which REAM could destroy firm value but also examine how the incidence of REAM can be reduced.

In the last chapter (Chapter 12), Liu, Chen, Ganesan, and Hess examine the link between product-harm crises and firm value. They start by documenting major trends in product-harm crises across different industries and show how product recalls influence the stock market. In the next part, they discuss the impact of various strategies firms use to manage product-harm crises and how it impacts firm value. In the final section, they document major data sources for research, regulatory processes associated with product recalls, and methodological issues such as endogeneity. This chapter concludes with an excellent discussion of potential areas for research such as the role of media during product-harm crises.

PART I

METRICS AND METHODS

1 Enhancing financial performance: the power of customer metrics
V. Kumar and Nita Umashankar*

INTRODUCTION

The Need For Customer Metrics

One of the greatest challenges marketers face today is the marginalization of the marketing function within the firm (Nath and Mahajan, 2008). Marketing practitioners are under increased pressure to be more accountable and show how marketing expenditures improve firm performance and shareholder value (Doyle, 2000; Kumar and Shah, 2009). In response, academics and practitioners have devised several marketing metrics intended to increase marketing's accountability within the firm and justify spending firm resources on marketing initiatives (Rust et al., 2004a). Alongside this premise, the literature evidences a growing emphasis on firm valuation in terms of customers, instead of products, leading to rich customer-level metrics. The most insightful customer metrics are those that help firms measure marketing productivity, allow managers to develop effective forward-looking marketing strategies, predict a customer's future value to the firm, and predict the firm's future financial performance.

For instance, Progressive Insurance is a good example of a company that has ensured a competitive advantage by utilizing predictive metrics. Using complex customer segmentation and evaluative risk measurement models, Progressive has been able to provide insurance to traditionally 'high-risk drivers' while ensuring profitability from this customer segment. Since many insurance companies will not find the high-risk drivers segment attractive, Progressive's offerings to this segment has provided them with a significant first-mover advantage. Competitors such as Allstate have started to embrace such an approach. Another example of using predictive metrics as a means of gaining competitive advantage is that of Capital One. Backed by superior customer analytics, the credit card company conducts more than 30,000 experimentations a year with different combinations of interest rates and other credit card incentives! The use of such systems increases the likelihood of customers finding a

9

product that matches their credit needs, and ultimately helps in reducing churn (Davenport, 2006).

The practice of pursuing strategies backed by metrics and analytics supplements managerial decision-making and, in some cases, creates fresh business opportunities. Improving data collection techniques has allowed for the development of valuable predictive models, which we will discuss in the following chapter. These tools will continue to be valuable resources for management as they continue to develop and evolve.

In this chapter, we review prominent streams of customer metrics, link these metrics to firm performance and shareholder value, and propose strategies that use these metrics to enhance firm performance (please see Figure 1.1 for the framework). Specifically, we focus on customer metrics pertaining to the following six domains:

1. what your customers are worth: customer value metrics;
2. what your customers think of you: cognitive and affective value metrics;
3. whether your customers' expectations have been exceeded: customer satisfaction metrics;
4. which customers to get hold of and who to keep: acquisition and retention metrics;
5. which customers leave and which ones to get back: churn and winback metrics;
6. the value of customer chatter: referral metrics.

Insights from the customer metrics allow firms to: 1) select the right customers for targeting, (2) understand the behavior and perceptions of their customer base, (3) optimally allocate marketing resources, (4) acquire and retain high-value customers, (5) cultivate customer relationships, (6) invest in building customer-valued brands, and (7) retain customers with valuable social capital. These metrics can be distinguished based on whether they are backward- or forward-looking and whether they are at the individual or aggregate level. Most accounting measures are retrospective in that they examine historical performance. In contrast, the market value of firms hinges largely on growth prospects and sustainability of profits (i.e., how the firm might be expected to perform in the future). Further, while aggregate measures are useful in describing customer segments and average customer behavior, individual metrics allow marketers to follow a targeted approach to improve firm performance.

This chapter is divided into five sections. The first explores the six domains of customer metrics at the individual and aggregate level (see Table 1.1). The second discusses the strategic implications of each metric

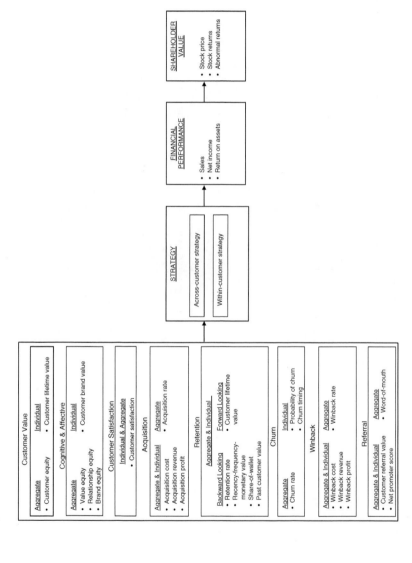

Figure 1.1   Linking customer metrics to financial outcomes

Table 1.1 Customer metric definitions and empirical contexts

Metric Domain	Metric	Definition/Measurement	Context	Reference
Customer value	Customer lifetime value	Sum of cumulated cash flows of a customer over his/her lifetime with the firm. It measures the discounted profit stream of a single customer	High-tech	Venkatesan and Kumar (2004)
	Customer equity	Sum of the lifetime values firm's current and future customers across all the firm's brands. It measures the discounted profit stream from the customers	Airline	Rust et al. (2004a)
Cognitive and affective value	Value equity	Customers' subjective assessment of the utility of a brand based on input and output	Graduate B-school students with knowledge in financial markets	Oliver and DeSarbo (1988)
	Relationship equity	Tendency of a customer to stay in brand relationship. It measures the effects of customer perceptions of key marketing actions on customer attitudes and actual customer behavior as reflected by future sales	European do-it-yourself retailer	Vogel et al. (2008)
	Customer brand value	How a brand is valued or perceived by an individual customer, which includes a customer's brand knowledge, brand attitude, brand behavior intention, and brand behavior	High-tech, Financial services	Kumar (2008a,b)
	Brand equity	The intangible assessment of the brand, beyond its objectively perceived value. It measures the asset value of a brand including awareness, perceived quality, loyalty and associations to a brand, which cannot be easily duplicated by its competitors	Conceptual paper	Keller (1998)

Customer satisfaction	Customer satisfaction	A comparison between customers' expectations and service performance. It measures how customer expectations of product quality interact with the actual experience of product quality to generate satisfaction, and how satisfaction influences the likelihood of subsequent purchases	Airlines, banks, cars, charter travel, clothing retail, department stores, furniture stores, gas stations, insurance, mainframe computers, PCs, railroads and supermarkets	Anderson and Sullivan (1993)
Acquisition	Acquisition rate	The percentage of people targeted by a marketing campaign who actually become customers to a firm	Pharmaceutical, retailing and B2B high-tech manufacturer	Reinartz et al. (2005)
	Acquisition cost	The individual cost of acquiring a customer to a firm. It measures the optimal spending and resource allocation by a firm on each of its individual customers based on the profitability of the customer to the firm	Retailing, pharmaceutical and B2B service	Thomas et al. (2004)
	Acquisition revenue	The individual revenue generated by a customer to a firm. It measures the long-term profitability of each of the individual customers to a firm	Pharmaceutical, retailing and B2B high-tech manufacturer	Reinartz et al. (2005)
Retention	Recency-frequency-monetary	Measures the individual customer's value to a firm. The value of a customer is captured as an index in terms of the time since the last purchase was made by the customer, number of purchases made during a period of time, and the dollar value of purchases	Catalog and mail order	Reinartz and Kumar (2003)

Table 1.1 (continued)

Metric Domain	Metric	Definition/Measurement	Context	Reference
Retention	Share-of-wallet	The degree to which a customer meets his/her needs in a specific category with the firm. It is measured by dividing the customer's dollar amount given in the form of sales to the focal firm by the total dollar amount spent by the customer across all firms in a specific product category	B2B high-tech manufacturer	Venkatesan and Kumar (2004)
	Past customer value	This method extrapolates the results of past customer transactions into the future, to obtain a measure of a customer's future value to the firm. It measures the cumulative contributions until the present period of a customer to the firm	Catalog and mail order	Reinartz and Kumar (2003)
Churn	Churn rate	The percentage of subscribers to a service that discontinue their subscription to that service in a given time period. It is a measure of the rate of customer loss in a given period of time	Mobile phone	Fitchard (2002)
	Probability of churn	It is a measure of probability that a single customer will churn, no longer continuing to contribute revenues to the firm	Telecommunication	Kumar (2008a)

Winback	Winback decision	The process of winning back those passive customers who are at the end of their customer life cycle to a firm or who potentially lose interest in investing with the firm's offerings. Based on their potential future profitability to the firm, the highest potential future profit-generating customers are segmented and won back by the firm	Conceptual paper that has examples from multiple industries including telecom, insurance, restaurants and car dealership	Griffin and Lowenstein (2001)
Referrals	Net promoter's score	The willingness of a customer to promote a firm by recommending it to a friend or a colleague. Does not take into account the cost associated with improving the net promoter's score	Airlines, Internet service providers and car rentals	Reichheld (2003)
	Word-of-mouth	It refers to the spread of message from one individual to another through social network. It is measured by the sum of weighted profits given by all the customers influenced by original sources	Retailer	Kumar and Bhaskaran (2010)
	Customer referral value	It is an individual's expected future referral value with the firm. It is measured by the sum of the referral values for a given customer in all of the time periods during which individuals come to the firm via referrals by the original referring customer	Financial services	Kumar et al. (2010) Kumar et al. (2007)

and guidelines for managers. The third section links customer metrics to firm performance and shareholder value. The fourth discusses metric implementation issues and solutions. Finally, section five concludes the chapter with suggestions for future research.

CUSTOMER METRICS

Customer Value Metrics

In recent years, the academic literature has focused on developing metrics that measure the value of customers, whether at the individual level in the form of customer lifetime value or at the aggregate level in the form of customer equity. Customer lifetime value and customer equity are in widespread use as marketing asset metrics in several industries, most notably in direct marketing and financial services.

Customer lifetime value
Customer lifetime value (CLV) is a forward-looking metric that represents the sum of cumulated cash flows – discounted using the weighted average cost of capital (WACC) – of a customer over her lifetime with the firm. CLV is unique in that it incorporates elements of revenue, expense, and customer behavior to estimate profitability. By knowing the CLV of its customers, firms can decide which customers to provide preferential treatment to, which customers to interact with through inexpensive channels, when to contact customers with an offer, which customers are profitable in the future, and what kind of marketing resources to allocate. The formula to compute CLV is given below:

$$CLV_{it} = \underbrace{\sum_{t=1}^{T_i} \frac{GC_{i,t}}{(1 + d)^{\frac{t}{frequency_i}}}}_{\substack{\text{Present value (PV) of}\\\text{gross contribution}}} - \underbrace{\sum_{l=1}^{n} \frac{\sum_{m} MC_{i,m,l}}{(1 + d)^l}}_{\substack{\text{Present value}\\\text{(PV) of}\\\text{marketing cost}}}$$

where: CLV_{it} = customer lifetime value of customer i at time period t; $GC_{i,t}$ = gross contribution from customer i in purchase occasion t; $MC_{i,m,l}$ refers to marketing cost, for customer i in communication channel m in time period l where, $MC_{i,m,l} = c_{i,m,l}$ (unit marketing cost) * $x_{i,m,l}$ (number of contacts); $frequency_i = 12/expint_i$ (where, $expint_i$ = expected inter purchase time for customer i); d is the discount rate for money; n is the number of years to forecast; and T_i is number of purchases made by distributor i, until the end of the planning period.

In the above CLV model, the term $GC_{i,t}$ predicts the gross contribution margin made by a customer in future purchase instances. The term *frequency$_i$* helps in forecasting the purchase frequency in the future. The term $MC_{i,m,l}$ provides the future marketing cost for each customer. The marketing cost term comprises the cost incurred ($c_{i,m,l}$) and the number of customer contacts ($x_{i,m,l}$) made in a particular channel during a given time period.

It is important to note that earlier versions of CLV models predicted the three parameters (*frequency*, *MC*, and *GC*) independently, giving rise to an endogeneity issue. In other words, the earlier models did not account for whether current MC leads to future GC or whether current GC leads to future MC. This endogeneity issue can be resolved by adopting a system of equations approach wherein all the three parameters are simultaneously obtained. Addressing the endogeneity issue is critical because it provides marketing managers with a way to account for proactive marketing initiatives that will likely change future consumer behavior.

Researchers have studied the drivers and consequences of increasing CLV to uncover optimal customer selection in marketing campaigns and measure marketing effectiveness, post-campaign. For example, Rust et al. (2004a) determine the drivers of customer choice and CLV by projecting the return on marketing expenditures for different types of campaigns and accounting for competitive information using a brand switching matrix. Furthermore, Venkatesan and Kumar (2004) determine an optimal resource allocation strategy using genetic algorithms, resulting in a customer-level resource allocation strategy that maximizes each customer's lifetime value.

Customer equity
Customer equity (CE) is defined as the sum of the lifetime values of all of the firm's current and future customers, where the lifetime value is the discounted profit stream obtained from the customer. The concept of CE brings together customer value management, brand management, and relationship/retention management. In the current competitive marketing environment, CE as a measure of the expected future behavior of a firm's customers is a key strategic asset that must be monitored and nurtured by firms to maximize long-term performance. Firms should work to maximize CE by addressing its three key drivers: value equity, relationship equity, and brand equity (Rust et al., 2004b), metrics that we examine in detail in the following section. The formula to compute CLV is given below:

$$CE = \sum_{i=1}^{N} \sum_{t=1}^{T} CM_{it} \left(\frac{1}{1+r} \right)^{t}$$

where: CE = customer equity of the customer base in \$; CM = average contribution margin in time period t after accounting for the marketing costs; r = discount rate; i = customer index; t = time period; N = number of customers for which the CE is being estimated; T = the number of time periods considered for estimating CE.

While the above CE formula is straightforward, it does not provide a distinction between acquisition and retention of customers. Other approaches have been developed that account for acquisition and retention rates, either individually or collectively, thereby providing a clear distinction between the two rates. A popular approach is to include an average retention rate of a customer segment/cohort in the computation of CLV, and subsequently CE (Berger and Nasr, 1998). Schweidel et al. (2008) recognize the possibility that because customers may choose to discontinue their relationship with the firm, at different points in time, their retention probabilities would vary. To account for this, they provide an approach where customers' varying retention probabilities are factored into the CLV computation, and thereby CE. Another approach is to compute the CE of the firm as the sum of return on acquisition, return on retention, and return on add-on selling (Blattberg et al., 2001). To disentangle retention from acquisition, Gupta and Lehmann (2003) operationalize acquisition cost by dividing the total marketing cost by the number of newly acquired customers for each time period in the computation of CLV, and in extension, CE. Therefore, there are various approaches that distinguish acquisition from retention when computing CE, and managers should use an approach that is applicable to the nature of their business.

Another, albeit related, customer value metric is customer equity share (CES), which is an alternative to market share that takes into account the lifetime value of the customer. Historically, market share, as opposed to CES, has been used as a measure of a firm's overall competitive standing, which can be misleading because it considers only current, and not future, sales. A company that has built the foundation for strong future profits is in better competitive position than a company that is sacrificing future profits for current sales, even if the two firms' current market shares are identical (Rust et al., 2004b).

Cognitive and Affective Value Metrics

Marketing inputs affect customer preferences and customer value, which provide the foundation to determine the CE of the firm. At the individual level, a customer's value equity, relationship equity, and customer brand value tap into his or her attitudes, perceptions, and expectations of the firm's marketing actions, which ultimately influence the firm's CE (Rust et al., 2004a). At the aggregate level, a firm's brand equity addresses the differential effect of brand knowledge on customers' responses to the marketing of the brand (Keller, 1993).

Value equity

Value equity, a driver of loyalty intentions and revenues, can be understood as the perceived ratio of what is received (e.g., a product) to what must be sacrificed (e.g., the price paid for the product). If a customer's outcome–input ratio corresponds to her own reference outcome–input ratio, perceptions of fairness result (Oliver and DeSarbo, 1988). Increasing value equity has been linked to an increase in customer satisfaction and loyalty and a decrease in brand switching propensity (Vogel et al., 2008).

Relationship equity

Relationship equity expresses the tendency of a customer to stay in a relationship with the brand, beyond objective and subjective assessments of the brand. If perceived relationship equity is high, customers believe that they are treated well and handled with particular care. Customers who compare their expectations with their experiences and believe that they are treated better than others are likely to be satisfied with the offering, brand, and store, generating a positive impact on loyalty intentions and future sales (ibid.). Firms can manage customers' expectations by implementing loyalty programs, special recognition and treatment, affinity programs, community-building programs, and knowledge-building programs.

Customer brand value

Customer brand value (CBV) refers to how a brand is valued or perceived by an individual customer. CBV includes a customer's brand knowledge, brand attitude, brand behavior intention, and brand behavior (Kumar, 2008a). CBV can be linked to CLV through a dynamic process in which an individual's brand knowledge affects brand attitude, which then affects brand behavior intention, which in turn affects brand behavior, thus contributing toward her lifetime value (Kumar, 2008b). Customers with higher brand value are more likely to have longer lifetime durations, greater purchase frequency, higher contribution margins, and higher referral value, all contributing to higher CLV (Kumar, 2008a).

Brand equity

Brand equity is an aggregate measure of the incremental discounted cash flows from the sale of a set of products or services, as a result of the brand being associated with those products or services (Keller, 1998). A favorable perception of a brand has a positive impact on affective commitment toward the brand (Bolton et al., 2004), which influences customers' willingness to stay with the brand, repurchase probability, and likelihood to recommend the brand (Rust et al., 2004b). Various financial and non-financial methods have been suggested to measure brand equity. For example, conjoint analysis has been used to provide insight into brand equity by decomposing a product's overall value into value that arises from product attributes and value that arises from brand names (Rangaswamy et al., 1993). Interbrand, a commercial provider of brand equity measures, integrates data on market leadership, stability, internationality, trends of the brand, support, level of protection, and market characteristics of the markets to calculate brand equity (Keller, 1998).

Customer Satisfaction Metrics

Customer satisfaction

The topic of customer satisfaction has been of great interest to marketing and consumer researchers for many years, driven in part by the notion that customer satisfaction can have long-term benefits, including customer loyalty and increased profitability. Prior research has recognized that both cognition and affect significantly predict satisfaction judgments. Satisfaction is a function of a comparison between expectations and performance (Oliver and DeSarbo, 1988) and the affect experienced during the consumption of a service (e.g., joy, happiness, disgust). Customer satisfaction has been empirically linked to a variety of customer repurchase behaviors (e.g., Bolton et al., 2006; Cooil et al., 2007). Oliver (1999) views satisfaction as a necessary step in loyalty formation and argues that for many firms, satisfaction should be the primary goal. In practice, firms commonly emphasize satisfaction, assess their ability to deliver it, and believe it to be the best solution to ensure customer retention. Moreover, researchers in the services area have extensively examined how customer satisfaction is impacted by service failures and service recovery efforts by the firm. For example, when a service failure occurs, the firm's response has the potential either to restore customer satisfaction and reinforce loyalty or to exacerbate the situation and drive the customer to a competing firm (Smith et al., 1999).

Customer satisfaction measures can be obtained from surveys, secondary data, or the American Customer Satisfaction Index (ACSI) reports. The ACSI is an economic indicator that measures customer satisfaction; it is based on modeling customer evaluations of the quality of goods and services purchased in the United States from firms that have a substantial US market share. The ACSI database was developed by the National Quality Research Center at the University of Michigan and the data are collected by interviewing approximately 65 000 customers annually.

Acquisition and Retention Metrics

Acquisition
Firms use various marketing activities to acquire new customers, including mass media, price promotions and advertising, and personalized contacts. For many firms, marketing spending on acquiring customers represents an important expense, and it is widely known that the acquisition process has an important effect on future retention probability (Thomas, 2001). Firms want to optimally allocate their limited acquisition budget to maximize customer equity and, therefore, shareholder value.

Acquisition metrics can be measured at both the individual and aggregate level. Individual acquisition measures include the cost of acquiring a single customer using marketing resources, the revenues generated by the customer, and the profit generated by the customer, all of which contribute to a customer's lifetime value (Kumar, 2008a). Aggregate measures of acquisition include acquisition rate, aggregate acquisition cost, aggregate acquisition revenue, and aggregate acquisition profit. Acquisition rate refers to the percentage of people targeted by a marketing campaign who actually become customers. Managers use this metric because it is simple, easy to understand, easy to track, and can be tied to market share. A downfall of this metric is that there is no clarity as to whether one additional customer adds the same profit as the next customer (Blattberg and Deighton, 1996). Aggregate acquisition cost, the average cost of acquiring a segment of customers, may be misleading because some customers might be very easy to acquire while others may not. By focusing on this metric, firms might overlook the variance in costs across customers and may target the easiest customers to acquire, for example, those with the lowest acquisition costs, as opposed to the most profitable customers. To understand return on acquisition, firms need to not only identify who is likely to be acquired but also how long the customer will stay with the firm and when the purchase activity is likely to occur (Reinartz et al., 2005), as Figure 1.2 illustrates. The formula to compute acquisition rate and cost are provided below:

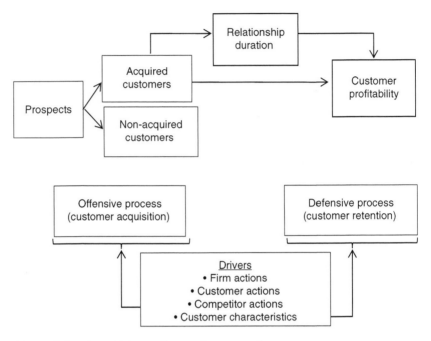

Figure 1.2   Acquisition and retention strategies

$$\text{Acquisition rate (\%)} = \left(\frac{\textit{Number of prospects recovered}}{\textit{Number of prospects targeted}} \right) \times 100$$

$$\text{Acquisition cost (\$)} = \frac{\textit{Acquisition spending}(\$)}{\textit{Number of prospects acquired}}$$

Retention

Customer retention has been a dominant theme among scholars interested in customer relationship management. Affective commitment and loyalty programs that provide economic incentives positively affect both customer retention and customer share development (Verhoef, 2003). Retention rate is defined as the average likelihood that a customer purchases from a focal firm in a period (t), given that the customer has purchased in the last period ($t - 1$). The formula to compute retention rate is provided below:

Retention rate (%) =

$$\left(\frac{\textit{Number of customers in cohort buying in } (t)}{\textit{Number of customers in cohort buying in } (t-1)} \right) \times 100$$

Retention metrics are divided into backward-looking and forward-looking metrics, which differ based on whether customers are going to be active in the future.

Backward-looking metrics   At the aggregate level, firms measure their rate of retention, which refers to the percentage of people who are retained as customers at any given time. At the individual level, traditional metrics used for resource allocation are RFM, SOW, and PCV, which we discuss in detail.

Recency-frequency-monetary (RFM) is a widely used metric in the mail order and catalog industries, and it has been estimated that 71 percent of firms use RFM in their direct marketing efforts (Kumar, 2008a). This technique uses past customer information to evaluate customer value based on: the time elapsed since the customer last placed an order with the company (recency), how often the customer orders from the company in a certain time period (frequency), and the amount that the customer spends on an average transaction (monetary). To compute an RFM score, it is necessary to first determine the value of each of these three elements for each customer, add them together based on the relative weights of the elements, and then rank each customer based on the RFM score (Kumar and Rajan, 2009).

Share-of-wallet (SOW) indicates the degree to which the customer meets her needs in a category with the firm. The SOW metric is widely used in retail businesses to identify whether customers are loyal to a specific store. SOW is computed by dividing the value of sales of the focal firm to a customer in a category by the total amount spent by the customer in that category across all firms (ibid.). The formula to compute SOW is provided below:

$$\text{Individual share-of-wallet} = S_j / \sum_{j=1}^{J} S_j,$$

where: S = sales to the focal customer; j = firm; $\Sigma_{j=1}^{J}$ = sum of the value of sales made by all firms that sell products to a certain buyer.

Past customer value (PCV) is a metric based on the total contribution toward profit made by the customer in the past, adjusted for the time value of money (ibid.). This metric assumes that past profitability of the customer indicates future profitability. PCV is shown formulaically below:

$$\text{Past customer value of a customer} = \sum_{t=1}^{T} GC_{it}*(1 + r)^t$$

where: i = number representing the customer; r = applicable discount rate (for example, 15 percent per annum or 1.25 percent per month); T = number of time periods prior to the current period when the purchase was made; GC_{it} = gross contribution of transaction of the ith customer in time period t.

Forward-looking metrics   At the individual level, firms compute CLV, which serves not only as a customer value metric but also as a retention metric. As previously outlined, CLV represents the sum of cumulated cash flows – discounted using the weighted average cost of capital (WACC) – of a customer over her lifetime with the firm. CLV calculations are used to assess where to allocate marketing resources for retention based on customers' lifetime value to the firm. At the aggregate level, firms compute customer equity as a measure of retention.

Managers are encouraged to refrain from investing in customers with a low CLV and SOW as they add no value to the firm. Firms need to adopt a conversion strategy by upgrading and cross-selling products to high CLV/low SOW customers. Also, managers need to shift resources from low CLV/high SOW customers to high CLV/low SOW customers, with the goal of increasing their SOW. Heavy investments need to be made in high CLV/high SOW customers in order to maintain their loyalty and maximize their profitability to the firm. Firms can also calculate their customers' interpurchase times to impute potential competitive purchase behavior. If a customer tends to follow a general purchasing pattern, it is possible for statistical models to uncover deviations in the purchasing pattern and attribute those deviations to purchases from competitors (Kumar et al., 2008).

Churn and Winback Metrics

Churn
Each year, firms spend vast amounts of money on promotional efforts, much of which are geared toward acquiring new customers. However, few executives appear to recognize the substantially higher cost of losing existing customers. Customer churn, also known as customer attrition or defection, is the loss of customers to the firm, and represents a growing problem for many firms and industries. In particular, customer churn has become a significant problem for firms in the publishing, financial services, insurance, electric utilities, health care, banking, Internet, telecommunications, and

cable service industries. For example, in the cellular phone industry, annual churn rates range from 23.4 percent to 46 percent (Neslin et al., 2006).

Firms can compute churn metrics at the individual level by estimating the probability that a single customer will churn, which consists of two components. The first component involves assessing which customers are likely to defect by identifying the characteristics of customers who have defected in the past and identifying customers who resemble this group. The second component involves knowing when such customers are likely to defect. Both components can be assessed by estimating a propensity-to-quit model either using logistic regression or a hazard model. Churn results in a decrease in a customer's current and future revenue, known as churn revenue. On an aggregate level, churn rate represents the rate of customer loss in a given period. Customer loss can be considered as loss-for-good or always-a-share, with the latter representing customers who might buy other products from competitors but may come back to the firm for another purchase. Churn is explained further below:

$$\text{Churn rate (\%)} = 100 - \text{Retention rate (\%)}$$

Winback
Winback is the process of firms revitalizing relationships with customers who have defected. The importance of winning back customers as a key element of the firm's customer relationship management (CRM) strategy cannot be underestimated. Research shows that a firm has a 60 to 70 percent chance of successfully repeat-selling to an 'active' customer, a 20 to 40 percent chance of successfully repeat-selling to a lost customer, and only a 5 to 20 percent chance of successfully closing the sale on a brand new customer (Griffin and Lowenstein, 2001). Stauss and Friege (1999) find that the net return on investment from a new customer obtained from an external list is 23 percent compared with a 214 percent return on investment from the reinstatement of a customer who has defected.

Individual winback measures include the cost of winning back a single customer using marketing resources (winback cost), the revenues generated by the reinstated customer (winback revenue), and the profit generated by the reinstated customer (winback profit) (Kumar, 2008a). Aggregate measures of winback include winback rate, which refers to the percentage of former customers targeted by a marketing campaign who actually become reinstated.

At the individual level, firms should try to only win back customers with positive CLVs. For these customers, the question then becomes when to intervene and how much to spend on each customer. Subsequently, firms need to decide which products to offer, including whether the intervention should entail additional features in the already adopted product or whether to offer new products. Then, after deciding when to intervene, whether it is worth the cost, and what product to offer, the firm has to decide which contact channel to use to communicate the offer to the customer. At the aggregate level, firms can engage in winback strategies by offering mass promotions and discounts; however, this non-targeted strategy often results in winback of unprofitable customers and considerable marketing costs.

Referral Metrics

Net promoter score
Net promoter score (NPS) refers to the willingness of a customer to promote a firm by recommending it to a friend or a colleague. While this metric focuses on the customer's willingness to promote the firm, it does not measure actual recommending behavior (Reichheld, 2003). Further, there exists a poor correlation between willingness to promote the firm and actual behavior of promoting the firm (Kumar et al., 2010). Also, this metric is simply a correlational measure that ties only to the revenue of the firm, ignoring the costs associated with improving NPS and net profits to the firm.

Word-of-mouth
Word-of-mouth (WOM) pertains to the act of customers spreading the word about a product or service. Marketers are particularly interested in better understanding customers' influence on others because traditional forms of communication appear to be losing effectiveness. For example, past research finds that 40 percent fewer people agree that advertisements are a good way to learn about new products, 59 percent fewer people report that they buy products because of their advertisements, and 49 percent fewer people find that advertisements are entertaining (Trusov et al., 2009). In contrast, referral communication, for example, WOM, can spread with less support from the firm's marketing resources, allowing firms to enjoy larger financial gains from customer acquisition. Currently, WOM marketing is particularly prominent in online social networking sites, which provide numerous venues for customers to share their views, preferences, and experiences with others, as well as opportunities for firms to take advantage of referral marketing. Social networking sites attract more than 90 percent of all teenagers and young adults in the United States and have a market of approximately 80 million members. The bulk of digital content – the driving force of the site's vitality and attractiveness – is produced by its users. Online communities have attracted the atten-

tion of many scholars. For example, Dholakia et al. (2004) study two key group-level determinants of virtual community participation – group norms and social identity – and test the proposed model using a survey-based study across several virtual communities. Kozinets (2002) develops a new approach to collecting and interpreting data obtained from customers' discussions in online forums. Godes and Mayzlin (2004) and Chevalier and Mayzlin (2006) examine the effect of online word-of-mouth communications. Findings show that, on average, approximately one-fifth of a user's friends actually influence his or her activity level on the site (Trusov et al., 2010). Further, customers acquired through WOM add two times the lifetime value of customers acquired through traditional marketing efforts and these customers spread more WOM and bring in twice as many new customers (Wiesel et al., 2008).

Customer referral value
Customer referral value (CRV) refers to an individual customer's expected future referral value with the firm, representing the ability of the customer to generate indirect profit for the firm. The popularity of this metric grew out of work that questioned the NPS, which, as previously discussed, focuses mainly on customers' intent as opposed to their actual referral behavior. CRV is a composite of whether the referred customer would have made a purchase anyway, the predicted future value of the referred customer, the predicted future number of referrals, and the predicted future timing of the referrals. CRV is measured by summing all of the referral values for a given customer in all the time periods during which individuals come to the firm via referrals by the original referring customer. CRV has recently emerged as a topic of interest in the academic literature. For example, Kumar et al. (2008) provide a four-step process for predicting CRV and find that customers with high CLV do not necessarily have high CRV. The formula to compute CRV is provided below:

$$CRV_i = \sum_{t=1}^{T} \sum_{y=1}^{n1} \frac{(A_{ty} - a_{ty} - M_{ty} + ACQ1_{ty})}{(1 + r)^t} + \sum_{t=1}^{T} \sum_{y=n1+1}^{n2} \frac{(ACQ2_{ty})}{(1 + r)^t}$$

Where: T = the number of periods that will be predicted into the future (e.g., years); A_{ty} = the gross margin contributed by customer y who otherwise would not have bought the product; a_{ty} = the cost of the referral for customer y; 1 to $n1$ = the number of customers who would not join w/o the referral; $n2 - n1$ = the number of customers who would have joined anyway; M_{ty} = the marketing costs needed to retain the referred customers; $ACQ1_{ty}$ = the savings in acquisition cost from customers who would not join w/o the referral; $ACQ2_{ty}$ = the savings in acquisition cost from customers who would have joined anyway.

As provided in the above formula, CRV is determined as the summation of values from two components – the value of customers who would not have joined without the referral and, the value of the customers who would have joined anyway at a later time. This formula allows managers to separate those customers who would *not* have joined without the referral from those customers who would have joined even without the referral.

STRATEGIC IMPLICATIONS

Managers use customer metrics to devise marketing strategies, and thus improve firm performance. We next discuss how managers use the customer metric domains outlined in this chapter to create marketing strategies.

Customer Value Strategies

Applications of the CLV and CE framework are consistent with practical management needs. Firms can model the distribution of CLV across its customers, the distribution of CLV share (discounted share-of-wallet) across its customers, and the percentage of the firm's CE provided by the firm's top X percent of its customers to segment their customers on the basis of importance.

Across-customer strategies to maximize CE include efficient customer selection by targeting customers with high profit potential, managing existing sets of customers and rewarding them based on their profit potential, and investing in high-profit customers to prevent attrition and ensure future profitability. Within-customer strategies aim at maximizing profits either by increasing revenues or reducing costs, or by doing both. These strategies include encouraging multichannel shopping (revenue maximization), optimally allocating resources (cost reduction), managing customers' purchase sequence (revenue maximization and cost reduction), and increasing a customer's brand value (revenue maximization).

Cognitive and Affective Value Strategies

Firms can influence customers' value perceptions, their relationship with the firm, and their attitude toward the firm's brands to improve revenues and profitability. This results in increases in value equity, relationship equity, and brand equity. For example, firms can increase value equity by giving customers more of what they want (e.g., expanded offering) or by reducing what customers do not want (e.g., price reduction). A firm can increase its relationship equity by establishing and maintaining sound relationships with customers, which will improve customers' loyalty to the firm. To achieve this, firms can consider setting up initiatives, such as community activities and loyalty programs, which provide 'aspirational value,' and establishing learning relationships with customers (Rust et al., 2001). To improve brand equity, firms are encouraged to understand the dynamics of an evolving customer environment and constantly upgrade the brand to ensure that it maintains its level of relevance to an ever-demanding consumer. Managers must avoid the common practice of employing price promotions and unwise brand extensions with the aim to achieve short-term financial results, causing irreversible deterioration of the value of the brand (Vogel et al., 2008).

Customer Satisfaction Strategies

Firms can use CRM tools to customize offerings and reduce variability in the consumption experience, which enhances perceived quality, and thus, positively affects customer satisfaction. CRM applications also help firms manage customer relationships more effectively across the stages of relationship initiation, maintenance, and termination (Reinartz et al., 2004). In turn, effective management of customer relationships is critical to managing customer satisfaction and customer loyalty (Mithas et al., 2005).

Acquisition and Retention Strategies

Firms can broaden their customer base by allocating marketing resources to acquisition of segments of customers or individual customers, based on their profitability potential. The cost of acquisition per customer should not exceed the expected revenue and referral value of the customer. Firms should integrate their acquisition and retention initiatives to make sure that the right types of customers are being acquired, those that are loyal, profitable, and worth retaining. Specific acquisition strategies include direct marketing, ideally at the optimal level to ensure profitability, offering incentives, price promotions, advertising, and referrals from existing customers. In addition, cross-selling and up-selling strategies offer firms the chance to increase retention profitability, since customers who cross-buy are more profitable than customers who do not (Kumar et al., 2008).

Churn and Winback Strategies

Strategies used to address customer churn include identifying the customers likely to defect, when they are likely to defect, if and when a marketing intervention is advisable, and how much should be spent to avoid the churn of a particular customer. For example, in a non-contractual setting, a firm can intervene to prevent customer attrition by modeling the inter-purchase time (ITP) or purchase amount for its customers and then use the predicted values as a benchmark to predict whether a customer is likely to defect. The firm could then develop an intervention strategy for the customer depending on the customer's lifetime value. Firms have managed to construct useful and informative predictive models to help prevent churn. For example, in order to succeed, communication service providers (CSPs) are forced to aggressively respond to competitive pressures, reduce customer churn, optimize product portfolios, and become more relevant and personalized. CSPs are using business analytic solutions to predict business outcomes, spot trends as they emerge, improve customer service, drive customer value, and reduce churn by building a better understanding of the customer. As a result of implementing such solutions, some CSPs are able to improve their customer satisfaction with customized offers, reduce churn by 20 percent, and increase cross-sell outcomes by 5 to 10 percent over outbound campaigns.[1]

Some firms engage in extensive efforts to win back defected customers or to reactivate lapsed customers. For example, in the telecommunications industry, during the notorious long-distance telephone wars, a particular segment of customers frequently switched providers. These customers switched to benefit from an introductory offer of a competing provider, whereas others simply wanted to solicit a better offer from the original provider (Marple and Zimmerman, 1999). To stimulate purchase activity, Amazon.com offers lapsed customers discounts on their next purchases. Similarly, Honey Baked Ham offers a $10 gift certificate to reactivate customers, and Self Care, a health care products marketer, offers discounts of up to 25 percent to customers who have not ordered from the company in 18 to 24 months. However, 100 percent retention or winback is not always desirable or profitable, particularly when it requires setting a low retention price. It is not worthwhile for firms to try to re-establish relationships with customers who are likely to lapse or to defect rapidly.

Referral Strategies

Firms are now harnessing the power of customer referral behavior and word-of-mouth to disseminate information on current and new products.

For example, BMG Music Service not only spends resources on online ad banners and direct mail but also gives referral incentives (in the form of free CDs) to existing customers to increase the buzz level. Netflix, an online and offline movie rental firm, encourages referrals without any monetary incentive. Gilt, a fashion online retailer, provides monetary incentives and customized offerings for customers who refer another individual. Bank of America has introduced a value-orientated incentive program that gives the referred and referring customers a monetary award. Specifically, they give $25 for a customer referral, $10 for a student referral, and $50 for a business referral, and these incentives appear to be proportional to the typical value brought in by each member in the respective referral groups.

LINKING CUSTOMER METRICS TO PERFORMANCE

We continue with a summary of common financial metrics followed by an exposition of linkages between customer metrics and financial metrics (see Table 1.2).

Financial and Shareholder Value Metrics

Linking marketing actions through customer value to changes in market value is essential to the task of explaining and enhancing market value/capitalization and shareholder value (Srivastava et al., 1998). Similar to customer metrics, financial metrics can be distinguished between backward- and forward-looking measures. Most accounting measures are retrospective in that they examine historical performance. In contrast, the market value of firms hinges largely on growth prospects and sustainability of profits (i.e., how the firm might be expected to perform in the future). This requires tracking off-balance-sheet metrics (e.g., brand equity or customer equity) and focusing on both current and expected performance.

Several measures of firm value rely on measures of stock market performance. For example, market capitalization is the market value of all outstanding shares of a firm, and book value is the difference between a firm's assets and liabilities, according to its balance sheet. The ratio of market capitalization to the book value (the market-to-book ratio) is a useful indicator of the strength of marketing assets. Similarly, Tobin's Q is the ratio of the market value of the firm to the replacement cost of its tangible assets, which include property, equipment, inventory, cash, and investments in stock and bonds. A q value greater than 1 indicates that the firm has intangible assets. Shareholder value is another measure

Table 1.2 Linking customer metrics to performance

Metric	Reference	Findings
Customer lifetime value	Venkatesan and Kumar (2004)	The CLV metric better identifies customers that provide higher future profits than other commonly used customer-based metrics and managers can improve profits by designing marketing communications that maximize CLV
Customer equity	Kumar and Shah (2009); Rust et al. (2004a)	Customer equity increases firms' stock price. Further, a 0.2 point increase in a firm's quality rating results in an increase in customer equity by 1.39% or an ROI of 44.7%
Value equity	Rust et al. (2004a); Vogel et al. (2008)	Value equity has a positive impact on loyalty intentions and future sales. Further, an increase in value equity leads to an increase in customer equity and ROI
Relationship equity	Rust et al. (2004a); Vogel et al. (2008)	Relationship equity is a significant driver of future sales. Further, an increase in relationship equity leads to an increase in customer equity and ROI
Brand equity	Aaker and Jacobson (1994); Barth et al. (1998)	Brand equity has a positive impact on stock returns and market value
Customer satisfaction	Fornell et al. (2006); Gruca and Rego (2005); Ittner and Larcker (1998)	Customer satisfaction increases abnormal returns, cash flows, and excess stock market returns and decreases cash flow variability
Acquisition	Kumar and Shah (2009)	A 1% increase in the acquisition rate of customers could translate into a 1.4% and 1.9% increase in market capitalization for the B2B and B2C firms. However, for the high CLV segment, the increase is 7.9% and 9.2%, respectively
Retention	Gupta et al. (2004); Kumar and Shah (2009)	A 1% improvement in customer retention improves customer, and hence firm, value by about 5%
Churn and winback	Stauss and Friege (1999); Hogan et al. (2003)	The net ROI from a new customer is 23% compared with a 214% ROI from the reinstatement of a customer who has defected. Further, the loss of an early adopter costs the firm much more than the loss of a late adopter
Referral	Schmitt et al. (2011); Villanueva et al. (2008); Kumar et al. (2007, 2010)	Referred customers through word-of-mouth have a higher contribution margin, a higher retention rate, and are more valuable in both the short and the long run. Further, marketing-induced customers add more short-term value, but word-of-mouth customers add nearly twice as much long-term value to the firm

related to economic profit and total shareholder return is the cash flow to shareholders through dividends plus the increase in the share price.

Return on investment (ROI) is a traditional approach to evaluating return relative to the expenditure required to obtain the return. It is calculated as the discounted return (net of the discounted expenditure), expressed as a percentage of the discounted expenditure. The correct usage of ROI measures in marketing requires an analysis of future cash flows (Larréché and Srinivasan, 1981). Other financial impact measures include the internal rate of return, which is the discount rate that would make the discounted return exactly equal to the discounted expenditure; the net present value, which is the discounted return minus the net present value of the expenditure; and the economic value-added, which is the net operating profit minus the cost of capital. In each case, the measures of financial impact weigh the return generated by the marketing action against the expenditure required to produce that return. The financial impact affects the financial position of the firm, as measured by profits, cash flow, and other measures of financial health.

Customer Value Metrics and Performance

Research in marketing is beginning to identify linkages between CLV and CE metrics and firm performance and overall firm value (Gupta, 2009). For example, Lewis (2006) finds that promotionally acquired customers have lower repurchase rates and smaller CLVs. CE and market valuation are intrinsically related because they are two versions of the principle of the present value of a stream of expected future cash flows. This connection helps make marketing more financially relevant and accountable (Srinivasan and Hanssens, 2009). Kumar and Shah (2009) develop a framework linking CE to market capitalization (as determined by the stock price of the firm). Their findings show that marketing strategies directed at increasing CE not only increase the stock price of the firm but also beat market expectations. Furthermore, the relationship between CE and market capitalization is moderated by risk factors in the form of volatility and vulnerability of cash flows from customers. Rust et al. (2004a) provide a unified framework for analyzing the impact of competing marketing expenditures and projecting the ROI that will result from the expenditures. They found that, for example, that a 0.2 point increase in the sample firm's quality rating results in an improvement in customer equity by 1.39 percent ($101.3 million nationally), or an ROI of 44.7 percent. Gupta et al. (2004) use publicly available data from five companies (Amazon, eBay, E*Trade, Ameritrade, and Capital One) to estimate the value of their current and future customers. They find that for three of the five firms (except Amazon and eBay) customer-based valuations provide a good proxy for firm value.

Cognitive and Affective Value Metrics and Performance

Increasing customers' value equity, relationship equity, and brand equity is important for firm sales and profitability. For example, Aaker and Jacobson (1994) examine the influence of brand equity on stock returns by modeling the influence of changes in brand quality perceptions on the market value of 34 corporations. They find that brand equity has a positive impact on stock returns, as does product quality, thus demonstrating the power of brand perceptions. In a related study that explores a wider range of industries, Barth et al. (1998) examine the changes in equity of 1204 brands owned by 183 publicly traded corporations from 1992 to 1997. Their analysis shows that brand equity has a positive statistical association with market value, beyond the effect of two traditional measures, net income and book value of equity. This finding is consistent with other research that suggests that marketing expenditures produce a valuation premium greater than that implied by cash flow (Kirschenheiter, 1997; Srivastava et al., 1998). Superior brands lead to higher levels of customer satisfaction and perceived value of the firm's offering. The consequences of a superior offering are reflected in many aspects of market performance (Srivastava et al., 1998). Focusing on customer brand value, Kumar (2008b) develops a conceptual framework that links an individual's brand value to behavioral outcomes such as purchase frequency and contribution margin, and then links these behavioral outcomes to customer lifetime value and firm value.

Customer Satisfaction Metrics and Performance

Several recent studies have shown a strong link among customer satisfaction, firm profitability, and market value. For example, Fornell et al. (2006) demonstrate that investment in customer satisfaction leads to excess stock market returns. This can be potentially useful to investment managers in building financial portfolios. Moreover, changes in customer satisfaction are associated with increases in abnormal returns (Ittner and Larcker, 1998), increases in cash flows, and decreases in cash flow variability (Gruca and Rego, 2005). Using comprehensive historical data, Luo and Bhattacharya (2006) show that customer satisfaction partially mediates the relationship between corporate social responsibility and firm market value. Further, increases in customer satisfaction lead to lower sales and service costs and greater customer retention, loyalty, and longevity (Hogan et al., 2002; Reichheld, 2003; Kumar et al., 2008) as well as greater market share and profitability (Venkatesan and Kumar, 2004) among the high CLV segment. In summary, when the right set of customers are focused upon, customer satisfaction is significantly related to firm value, though news about changes in customer satisfaction may not result in an immediate change in firm valuation (Srinivasan and Hanssens, 2009).

Acquisition and Retention Metrics and Performance

Firms often trade off between expenditures for acquisition and those for retention; a suboptimal allocation of retention expenditures has a greater impact on long-term customer profitability than does suboptimal acquisition expenditures. For example, Gupta et al. (2004) show that 1 percent improvement in customer retention improves customer, and hence firm, value by about 5 percent. In contrast a similar improvement in margins boosts customer value by only about 1 percent. Improvements in acquisition costs have the smallest impact on value. Kumar and Shah (2009) show that a 1 percent increase in acquisition rate results in a 7.9 percent and 9.2 percent increase in market capitalization among the high CLV segment for a B2B and a B2C firm; while the consequence is a drop in market capitalization of about 3 percent among the negative CLV customer segment. With respect to the retention scenario, Kumar and Shah (2009) demonstrate that by cross-selling one more product, the increase in market capitalization is about 18 percent and 21 percent among the high CLV segment for the B2B and B2C firms while there is a decrease in market capitalization of about 2.1 percent and 1.8 percent among the negative CLV segment for the B2B and B2C firms respectively. However, there appears to be a flat maximum with respect to acquisition and retention expenditures. Specifically, a 10 percent deviation in either acquisition or retention expenditures from their respective optimal levels results in a less than 1 percent change in the long-term profitability of a customer (Tull, 1977; Chintagunta and Dubé, 2005). The customer communications strategy that maximizes long-term customer profitability maximizes neither the acquisition rate nor the relationship duration. Instead, developing a communications strategy to manage long-term customer profitability generally requires a long-term and holistic perspective toward the relationship between acquisition and retention. This perspective tends to give a greater emphasis on interpersonal and interactive communications and less of a focus on acquisition. These conclusions can be used for the strategic advantage of a firm and can have a potentially large impact on the cost and/or revenue aspect of customer profitability (Kumar, 2008a).

Churn and Winback Metrics and Performance

Not every lost customer makes a good winback prospect for the firm. The impact of a lost customer on profitability depends on whether a customer defects to a competing firm or disadopts the product altogether (Hogan et al., 2003). Firms can waste considerable resources on trying to win back all of their lost customers, many of whom turn out to be poor prospects for future profits to the firm (Griffin and Lowenstein, 2001). It becomes important for firms to segment lost customers by winback potential and target lost customers who are likely to offer the highest return on the firms' efforts in contacting them. Thus, a firm's performance increases by segmenting its lost customers based on their potential profitability, evaluating the lost customer's current needs, creating a plan that reinstates trust, and measuring, evaluating, and refining the winback program from time to time.

Referral Metrics and Performance

Firms that can afford to build a customer base organically (i.e., through WOM) face a better long-term profitability outlook and can spend less on customer retention. Positive word-of-mouth, particularly as spread on the Internet, has been shown to be an important indicator of firm performance. For example, chatroom comments are positively linked to TV show ratings (Godes and Mayzlin, 2004), online reviews and ratings have a positive impact on online book sales (Chevalier and Mayzlin, 2006), and blog posts and reviews increase CD sales (Dhar and Chang, 2009). Referred customers (1) have a higher contribution margin, though this difference erodes over time; (2) have a higher retention rate, and this difference persists over time; and (3) are more valuable in both the short and the long run (Schmitt and Van den Bulte, 2011). In addition, marketing-induced customers add more short-term value, but word-of-mouth customers add nearly twice as much long-term value to the firm (Villanueva et al., 2008). Through field experiments, Kumar et al. (2007, 2010) develop and test a new four-step approach that measures CRV. They determine the behavioral drivers of CRV and identify the most effective methods of targeting the most promising customers on the basis of their CLV and CRV scores. The ROI on the specific marketing campaigns whose goal is to increase CLV and CRV is over 10. If the strategies specified in the study can be administered to a base of 1 000 000 customers, the potential for gains reach around $19.4 million in CLV and $20.9 million in CRV. The increases in future profits (through CLV and CRV) have already been shown to increase market capitalization.

Linking Metrics to Customer Value

Firms operating in established markets often rely on financial measures as valuation tools. However, with new business models evolving at an astounding rate, these measures fail to account for the value of a firm's customers. Gupta et al. (2004) examine the validity of customer value metrics in firm valuation in four Internet-based firms and one traditional financial firm in order to juxtapose traditional financial measures with customer value measures. The study finds that while financial valuation works well in firms operating in such traditional markets as banking, firms operating in new spaces (such as dot-com companies) must base a significant proportion (if not all) of their valuation on customer value measures. For example, traditional measures such as price to earnings (P/E) ratio do not present the entire picture when examined at a company such as E*Trade, which, due to its negative earnings, cannot be defined. Instead customer value measures must be utilized to capture the inherent value in the company. However, customer value measures can be misleading if not derived appropriately. The dot-com bubble is a fitting example of misleading customer value. Companies assumed rapid growth and subsequent first-mover advantages outweighed any costs associated with customer acquisition. However, customer acquisition is only a single input of customer value. Customer retention and margins are other important inputs to consider. In other words, a customer who buys and immediately defects will likely have a low customer value when compared to a customer who buys and is inexpensive to retain. Therefore in light of these misleading computations, companies will have to be careful when linking acquisition costs, margins, and retention rates to customer value. In spite of the above constraints, Kumar and Shah (2009) were able to illustrate that accounting for the future profit contributions of retained and newly acquired customers helps predict the shareholder value in B2B and B2C firms.

IMPLEMENTATION OF CUSTOMER METRICS

How do firms implement customer metrics and what challenges are they likely to face? Further, how do firms implement the strategic changes resulting from insights from metric analyses? The answers lie in the ability of the firm to acquire and mine meaningful data, encourage employees to embrace strategic change, and engender an organizational culture that utilizes metrics to propel change.

To begin the process, firms need to have access to behavioral and transactional data reflective of the consumer behavior of their customer base.

Additionally, firms need to have data on customers' perceptions of the firm, the firm's brands, and the firm's service delivery. Ideally, the data should be at the customer level and should reflect transaction history of at least two to three years. Importantly, data on marketing tactics including the use of direct mail, e-mail, customized services, and promotions should be present. Challenges arise when firms do not collect the required data to compute meaningful metrics and their information technology systems are not integrated, precluding disparate data from being consolidated. To overcome data deficiencies, managers can engage in primary data collection to fill in the gaps.

For successful implementation of customer metrics and strategies to improve financial performance, firms need to invest in generating buy-in from one of their most critical internal assets: their employees. Challenges lie in dealing with employees' reluctance to change. To combat internal inertia, firms should generate awareness of the need for change using relevant and effective communication tools. Firms should create a desire from employees to participate and support the change by communicating the initiative's potential benefits and disseminate knowledge about how to change. Most critical is the effort to enable stakeholders to implement the changes on a daily basis. Firms can do this by giving employees the autonomy to interactively respond to customers and providing incentives.

Firms face organizational barriers that restrict them from producing and implementing change initiatives. A primary challenge is changing a firm's focus from product-centric to customer-centric marketing. A product-centric firm focuses on its product portfolio and concentrates on increasing the product line, ignoring customers' specific needs. This can lead to dissatisfaction and defection. A customer-centric approach focuses on serving specific customers and thereby offering customized solutions. Firms are increasingly transitioning from a product-centric to a customer-centric approach and do so by structuring their organization with customer-based segment centers, segment sales teams, and customer relationship managers. In contrast, product-centric firms tend to be internally focused and transaction oriented and are structured with brand managers and product-based profit centers. Firms possessing a customer-centric orientation use customer metrics to identify profitable customers and create relationships with these customers.

AGENDA FOR FUTURE RESEARCH

We make four recommendations on future research directions of customer metrics and firm performance. First, while past research has examined, albeit in depth, each stream of metrics featured in this chapter, future research would benefit from examining the relative effects of each stream in terms of its ability to improve firm performance and shareholder value. Second, improved communications and computational capabilities greatly extend the marketer's ability to target individual customers. Thus, customer metrics increasingly need to be based on individual, rather than aggregate, characteristics, allowing the relative efficiency of using individual-level metrics to maximize firm performance to be evaluated (Petersen et al., 2009). Third, backward-looking metrics, while useful in describing historical purchase behavior, are of limited practical value since the information is available too late to be actionable and often makes the faulty assumption that past behavior translates to future behavior. Future research would benefit from continuing to explore the improvements of emphasizing forward-looking metrics, which are useful for firms to proactively manage their customer base. Fourth, the changing global environment is influencing the market in unprecedented ways. Understanding whether the current repertoire of metrics still apply in emerging markets and whether cross-cultural differences are likely to emerge is a promising direction for future research (Dawar, 2004).

NOTES

*   We thank the editor of this handbook, Shankar Ganesan for giving us the opportunity to contribute. The authors thank Renu for assistance in copy-editing the chapter.
1. See http://www-03.ibm.com/press/us/en/pressrelease/29420.wss; accessed 25 September, 2010.

REFERENCES

Aaker, David A. and Robert Jacobson (1994), 'The Financial Information Content of Perceived Quality,' *Journal of Marketing Research*, **31** (2), 191–201.
Anderson, Eugene W. and Mary W. Sullivan (1993), 'The Antecedents and Consequences of Customer Satisfaction for Firms,' *Marketing Science*, **12** (2), 125–43.
Barth, Mary E., Michael B. Clement, George Foster, and Ron Kasznik (1998), 'Brand Values and Capital Market Valuation,' *Review of Accounting Studies*, **3** (1/2), 41–68.
Berger, P.D. and N.I. Nasr (1998), 'Customer Lifetime Value: Marketing Models and Applications,' *Journal of Interactive Marketing*, **12** (1), 17–30.
Blattberg, Robert C. and John Deighton (1996), 'Manage Marketing by the Customer Equity Test,' *Harvard Business Review*, July-August, 136–44.
Blattberg, R.C., G. Getz, and J.S. Thomas (2001), *Customer Equity: Building and Managing Relationships as Valuable Assets*, Boston: Harvard Business School Press.
Bolton, Ruth N., Katherine N. Lemon, and Matthew D. Bramlett (2006), 'The Effect

of Service Experiences over Time on a Supplier's Retention of Business Customers,' *Management Science*, **52** (12), 1811–23.

Bolton, Ruth N., Katherine N. Lemon, and Peter C. Verhoef (2004), 'The Theoretical Underpinnings of Customer Asset Management: A Framework and Propositions for Future Research,' *Journal of the Academy of Marketing Science*, **32** (3), 271–92.

Chevalier, Judith A. and Dina Mayzlin (2006), 'The Effect of Word of Mouth on Sales: Online Book Reviews,' *Journal of Marketing Research*, **43** (3), 345–54.

Chintagunta, Pradeep K. and Jean-Pierre Dubé (2005), 'Estimating a Stockkeeping-unit-level Brand Choice Model that Combines Household Panel Data and Store Data,' *Journal of Marketing Research*, **42** (3), 368–79.

Cooil, Bruce, Timothy L. Keiningham, Lerzan Aksoy, and Michael Hsu (2007), 'A Longitudinal Analysis of Customer Satisfaction and Share of Wallet: Investigating the Moderating Effect of Customer Characteristics,' *Journal of Marketing*, **71** (1), 67–83.

Davenport, Thomas H. (2006), 'Competing on Analytics,' *Harvard Business Review*, January, 98–107.

Dawar, Niraj (2004), 'What Are Brands Good For?,' *MIT Sloan Management Review*, **46** (1), 31–7.

Dhar, Vasant and Elaine Chang (2009), 'Does Chatter Matter? The Impact of User-generated Content on Music Sales,' *Journal of Interactive Marketing*, **23** (4), 300–307.

Dholakia, Utpal M., Richard P. Bagozzi, and Lisa Klein Pearo (2004), 'A Social Influence Model of Consumer Participation in Network- and Small-group-based Virtual Communities,' *International Journal of Research in Marketing*, **21** (3), 241–63.

Doyle, Peter (2000), 'Value-based Marketing,' *Journal of Strategic Marketing*, **8** (4), 299–311.

Fitchard, Kevin (2002), 'Standing By Your Carrier,' *Telephony*, **242** (11), 36–8.

Fornell, Claes, Sunil Mithas, Forrest Morgeson III, and M.S. Krishnan (2006), 'Customer Satisfaction and Stock Prices: High Returns, Low Risk,' *Journal of Marketing*, **70** (1), 3–14.

Godes, David and Dina Mayzlin (2004), 'Using Online Conversations to Study Word-of-mouth Communication,' *Marketing Science*, **23** (4), 545–60.

Griffin, Jill and Michael W. Lowenstein (2001), 'Winning Back a Lost Customer,' *Direct Marketing*, **64** (3), 49.

Gruca, Thomas S. and Lopo L. Rego (2005), 'Customer Satisfaction, Cash Flow, and Shareholder Value,' *Journal of Marketing*, **69** (3), 115–30.

Gupta, Sunil (2009), 'Customer-based valuation,' *Journal of Interactive Marketing*, **23** (2), 169–78.

Gupta, Sunil and Donald R. Lehmann (2003), 'Customers as Assets,' *Journal of Interactive Marketing*, **17** (1), 9–24.

Gupta, Sunil, Donald R. Lehmann, and Jennifer Ames Stuart (2004), 'Valuing Customers,' *Journal of Marketing Research*, **41** (1), 7–18.

Hogan, John E., Katherine N. Lemon, and Barak Libai (2003), 'What is the True Value of a Lost Customer,' *Journal of Service Research*, **5** (3), 196–208.

Hogan, John E., Katherine N. Lemon, and Roland T. Rust (2002), 'Customer Equity Management: Charting New Directions for the Future of Marketing,' *Journal of Service Research*, **5** (1), 4–12.

Ittner, Christopher and David Larcker (1998), 'Are Non-financial Measures Leading Indicators of Financial Performance? An Analysis of Customer Satisfaction,' *Journal of Accounting Research*, **36** (3, Supplement), 1–35.

Keller, Kevin (1993), 'Conceptualizing, Measuring, Managing Customer-based Brand Equity,' *Journal of Marketing*, **57** (1), 1–22.

Keller, Kevin (1998), *Strategic Brand Management: Building, Measuring, and Managing Brand Equity*, Hemel Hempstead, UK: Prentice-Hall International.

Kirschenheiter, Michael (1997), 'Information Quality and Correlated Signals,' *Journal of Accounting Research*, **35** (1), 43–59.

Kozinets, Robert V. (2002), 'The Field Behind the Screen: Using Netnography for Marketing Research in Online Communities,' *Journal of Marketing Research*, **39** (1), 61–72.

Kumar, V. (2008a), 'Managing Customers for Profit: Strategies to Increase Profits and Build Loyalty,' Upper Saddle River, NJ: Wharton School of Publishing.

Kumar, V. (2008b), 'Customer Lifetime Value – The Path to Profitability,' Delft, the Netherlands: now Publishers.

Kumar, V. and Vikram Bhaskaran (2010), 'How Influential are the Influencers?: Calculating the Word-of-Mouth Value of the Networked Individual,' Working Paper, Georgia State University.

Kumar, V. and Bharath Rajan (2009), 'Profitable Customer Management: Measuring and Maximizing Customer Lifetime Value,' *Management Accounting Quarterly*, **10** (3), 1–19.

Kumar, V. and Denish Shah (2009), 'Expanding the Role of Marketing: From Customer Equity to Market Capitalization,' *Journal of Marketing*, **73** (6), 119–36.

Kumar, V., J. Andrew Petersen, and Robert P. Leone (2007), 'How Valuable is Word of Mouth?,' *Harvard Business Review*, **85** (10), 139.

Kumar, V., J. Andrew Petersen, and Robert P. Leone (2010), 'Driving Profitability by Encouraging Customer Referrals: Who, When, and How,' *Journal of Marketing*, **74** (5), 1–17.

Kumar, V., Rajkumar Venkatesan, and Werner Reinartz (2008), 'Performance Implications of Adopting a Customer-focused Sales Campaign,' *Journal of Marketing*, **72** (5), 50–68.

Larréché, Jean-Claude and V. Srinivasan (1981), 'Stratport: A Decision Support System for Strategic Planning,' *Journal of Marketing*, **45** (4), 39–52.

Lewis, Michael (2006), 'Customer Acquisition Promotions and Customer Asset Value,' *Journal of Marketing Research*, **43** (2), 195–203.

Luo, Xueming and C.B. Bhattacharya (2006), 'Corporate Social Responsibility, Customer Satisfaction, and Market Value,' *Journal of Marketing*, **70** (4), 1–18.

Marple, Mark and Michael Zimmerman (1999), 'A Customer Retention Strategy,' *Mortgage Banking*, **59** (11), 45.

Mithas, Sunil, M.S. Krishnan, and Claes Fornell (2005), 'Why Do Customer Relationship Management Applications Affect Customer Satisfaction?,' *Journal of Marketing*, **69** (4), 201–9.

Nath, Pravin and Vijay Mahajan (2008), 'Chief Marketing Officers: A Study of Their Presence in Firms' Top Management Teams,' *Journal of Marketing*, **72** (1), 65–81.

Neslin, Scott A., Sunil Gupta, Wagner Kamakura, Lu Junxiang, and Charlotte H. Mason (2006), 'Defection Detection: Measuring and Understanding the Predictive Accuracy of Customer Churn Models,' *Journal of Marketing Research*, **43** (2), 204–11.

Oliver, Richard L. (1999), 'Whence Consumer Loyalty?,' *Journal of Marketing*, **63** (Special Issue), 33–44.

Oliver, Richard L. and Wayne S. DeSarbo (1988), 'Response Determinants in Satisfaction Judgments,' *The Journal of Consumer Research*, **14** (4), 495–507.

Petersen J. Andrew, Leigh McAlister, David J. Reibstein, Russell S. Winer, V. Kumar, and Geoff Atkinson (2009), 'Choosing the Right Metrics to Maximize Profitability and Shareholder Value,' *Journal of Retailing*, **85** (1), 95–111.

Rangaswamy, Arvind, Raymond R. Burke, and Terence A. Oliva (1993), 'Brand Equity and the Extendibility of Brand Names,' *International Journal of Research in Marketing*, **10** (1), 61–75.

Reichheld, Frederick F. (2003), 'The One Number You Need to Grow,' *Harvard Business Review*, **81** (12), 46–54.

Reinartz, Werner J. and V. Kumar (2003), 'The Impact of Customer Relationship Characteristics on Profitable Lifetime Duration,' *The Journal of Marketing*, **67** (1), 77–99.

Reinartz, Werner, Manfred Krafft, and Wayne D. Hoyer (2004), 'The Customer Relationship Management Process: Its Measurement and Impact on Performance,' *Journal of Marketing Research*, **41** (3), 293–305.

Reinartz, Werner, Jacquelyn S. Thomas, and V. Kumar (2005), 'Balancing Acquisition and Retention Resources to Maximize Customer Profitability,' *Journal of Marketing*, **69** (1), 63–79.

Rust, Roland T., Katherine N. Lemon, and Valarie A. Zeithaml (2001), *Driving Customer Equity: How Customer Lifetime Value is Reshaping Corporate Strategy*, New York: The Free Press.

Rust, Roland T., Katherine N. Lemon, and Valarie A. Zeithaml (2004a), 'Return on Marketing: Using Customer Equity to Focus Marketing Strategy,' *Journal of Marketing*, **68** (1), 109–27.

Rust, Roland T., Valarie A. Zeithaml, and Katherine N. Lemon (2004b), 'Customer-centered Brand Management,' *Harvard Business Review*, **82** (9), 110–18.

Schmitt, Philipp, Bernd Skiera, and Christophe Van den Bulte (2011), 'Referral Programs and Customer Value,' *Journal of Marketing*, **75** (1), 46–59.

Schweidel, David A., Peter S. Fader, and Eric T. Bradlow (2008), 'Understanding Service Retention Within and Across Cohorts Using Limited Information,' *Journal of Marketing*, **70** (1), 82–94.

Smith, Amy K., Ruth N. Bolton, and Janet Wagner (1999), 'A Model of Customer Satisfaction with Service Encounters Involving Failure and Recovery,' *Journal of Marketing Research*, **36** (3), 356–72.

Srinivasan, Shuba and Dominique M. Hanssens (2009), 'Marketing and Firm Value: Metrics, Methods, Findings, and Future Directions,' *Journal of Marketing Research*, **46** (3), 293–312.

Srivastava, Rajenda K., Tasadduq A. Shervani, and Liam Fahey (1998), 'Market-based Assets and Shareholder Value: A Framework for Analysis,' *Journal of Marketing*, **62** (1), 2–18.

Stauss, Bernd and Christian Friege (1999), 'Regaining Service Customers: Costs and Benefits of Regain Management,' *Journal of Service Research*, **1** (4), 347.

Thomas, Jacquelyn S. (2001), 'A Methodology for Linking Customer Acquisition to Customer Retention,' *Journal of Marketing Research*, **38** (2), 262–8.

Thomas, Jacquelyn S., Werner Reinartz, and V. Kumar (2004), 'Getting the Most Out of All Your Customers,' *Harvard Business Review*, **82** (7/8), 116–23.

Trusov, Michael, Randolph E. Bucklin, and Koen Pauwels (2009), 'Effects of Word-of-mouth Versus Traditional Marketing: Findings from an Internet Social Networking Site,' *Journal of Marketing*, **73** (5), 90–102.

Trusov, Michael, Anand V. Bodapati, and Randolph E. Bucklin (2010), 'Determining Influential Users in Internet Social Networks,' *Journal of Marketing Research*, **47** (4), 643–58.

Tull, Donald S. (1977), '10 Key Factors in Today's Major Trends in Marketing,' *Marketing News*, **11** (10).

Venkatesan, R. and V. Kumar (2004), 'A Customer Lifetime Value Framework for Customer Selection and Resource Allocation Strategy,' *Journal of Marketing*, **68** (4), 106.

Verhoef, Peter C. (2003), 'Understanding the Effect of Customer Relationship Management Efforts on Customer Retention and Customer Share Development,' *The Journal of Marketing*, **67** (4), 30–45.

Villanueva, Julian, Shijin Yoo, and Dominique M. Hanssens (2008), 'The Impact of Marketing-induced Versus Word-of-mouth Customer Acquisition on Customer Equity Growth,' *Journal of Marketing Research*, **45** (1), 48–59.

Vogel, Verena, Heiner Evanschitzky, and B. Ramaseshan (2008), 'Customer Equity Drivers and Future Sales,' *Journal of Marketing*, **72** (6), 98–108.

Wiesel, Thorsten, Bernd Skiera, and Julin Villanueva (2008), 'Customer Equity: An Integral Part of Financial Reporting,' *Journal of Marketing*, **72** (2), 1–14.

2 Time-series models of pricing the impact of marketing on firm value

Xueming Luo, Koen H. Pauwels and Dominique M. Hanssens

INTRODUCTION

Stock prices fluctuate as a result of continuous trading among investors who have different expectations about the firm's future earnings. Thus they represent consensus forecasts of the financial value of the firm. As new value-relevant information about the firm or its environment arrives, these forecasts are updated, either immediately or more gradually over time, and either fully or partially. The extent to which such new information is reflected in stock price adjustments reflects the degree of efficiency in the market.

Time-series methods are well suited to analyze stock price data and quantify their sensitivity to such new information. In particular, methods that focus on equal interval measurements, such as daily, weekly or minute-by-minute data, are adept at sorting out the magnitude of reaction as well as its distribution over time, that is, the time lags. Time-series methods can be employed without having to resort to strong a priori assumptions about investor behavior such as full market efficiency. Thus they can be used to test such assumptions and, where needed, modify them to more accurate representations of investor behavior. Furthermore, time-series methods allow for inferences around the mean and the variance of stock prices, and as such they connect well to the risk/return paradigm in finance. Finally, time-series techniques can be employed with single equations as well as systems of equations. Such systems allow for the possible feedforward and feedback loops between investor behavior and managerial behavior. In conclusion, time-series methods are ideally suited to test and improve our understanding of the relationships between product markets ('Main Street') and financial markets ('Wall Street') (Luo, 2008; Hanssens et al., 2009).

This continuous firm value adjustment process is of major importance to senior executives, and in particular to the stewards of demand generation for the firm, that is, the marketing and sales managers. As argued in Srinivasan and Hanssens (2009), if marketing's contributions were readily visible in quarterly changes in sales and earnings, the task would be simple, because investors are known to react quickly and fully to earnings

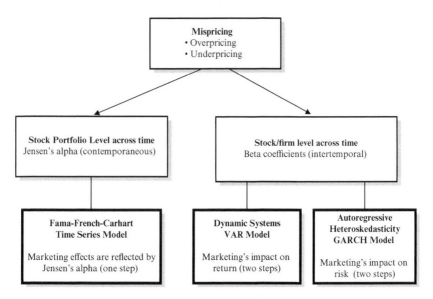

Figure 2.1   Classification of mispricing and matched time-series models

surprises. However, much of good marketing is building intangible assets of the firm, in particular brand equity, customer loyalty, and market-sensing capability. Progress in these areas is not readily visible from quarterly earnings, not only because different non-financial 'intermediate' performance metrics are used (e.g., customer satisfaction measures), but also because the financial outcomes can be substantially delayed.

Taken in combination, the task of evaluating marketing's impact on firm value is strategically important yet empirically challenging. The purpose of this chapter is to describe the most frequently used empirical time-series methods in the context of modeling stock prices. We begin with a discussion of mispricing, that is, departures from full market efficiency. Mispricing is the key obstacle to the smooth coordination between product markets and financial markets. For example, if investors fail to reward firms that invest in long-term brand building with higher and/or less volatile returns, then why would the managers of these firms engage in such investments? Time-series methods allow us to diagnose and measure the degree to which such mispricing occurs.

Figure 2.1 presents the classification of mispricing and how time-series models can be employed to test it empirically. Time-series models can be implemented at the stock portfolio level and at the individual stock/firm level across time periods. They provide insights on the mispricing of both returns and risk due to marketing.

In what follows we will assume that the reader is familiar with standard valuation terminology such as market risk, abnormal stock return, and the like. We refer to Srinivasan and Hanssens (2009) for exact definitions. We also assume a basic familiarity with time-series terminology, such as stationarity, autoregression, and the like, and we refer to Enders (1995) for specifics. An overview of relevant time-series models is provided in Table 2.1. Our discussion will cover, first, the pricing of returns due to marketing.

MISPRICING

This section defines mispricing and how to test mispricing empirically with time-series models. This set of time-series models is quite important for marketing, because ill-specified models may lead to ambiguous and even misleading conclusions. In addition, the task is not trivial because the nascent marketing–finance interface needs solid theoretical and empirical building blocks to recommend appropriate implications, not only for marketers on Main Street but also for investors on Wall Street.

Definition of Mispricing

According to the efficient market hypothesis (EMH), investors are aware of all publicly available information immediately after the news is announced. As such, stock prices reflect all value-relevant information about the firm. The general stock market (through its buying and selling activities) as a whole should always represent a rational assessment of the economy's strength. No investors can beat the general market by earning abnormal returns once the common risk factors are accounted for.

In any given day, some stocks are positively correlated with the market index, while others are negatively correlated. So, classical portfolio theory suggests that, with complete information, one may diversify away the idiosyncratic risk with these two groups of stocks and thus the market would be efficient (i.e., nobody beats the market). Yet, in reality, information is not complete, and is costly to collect and analyze. That is why analysts can make a living on Wall Street. Hence the EMH is a strong assumption and has come under criticism from the behavioral finance and behavioral economics disciplines (Benartzi and Thaler, 1995). So, financial markets may not be fully efficient, as has been demonstrated recently by the global financial crisis. In this context, mispricing may exist theoretically; the challenge is how to test it empirically.

Mispricing can occur in two forms, underpricing and overpricing. At the portfolio level, we illustrate these in the context of investor reactions to new information on customer satisfaction. If a strategy of investing in firms that have higher customer satisfaction results in an abnormal portfolio return that is significant and positive (or outperforms the market), that would be evidence of market underpricing. However, if such an investment portfolio underperforms the market-wide risk-adjusted benchmark portfolio, we would conclude that overpricing has occurred. Thus, at the portfolio level, testing mispricing due to marketing is a one-step process, where researchers construct portfolios and make mispricing inferences based on the abnormal portfolio return. Except for the investment strategy in question (e.g., a strategy focused on customer satisfaction) and the common market-wide risk factors, all other individual firm heterogeneity issues are assumed to be constant and fully diversified away. The abnormal portfolio return itself is a direct test of the stock price impact of the marketing variable in question. No subsequent regression analyses are needed to test possible mispricing effects (Aksoy et al., 2008; Fornell et al., 2009a; Jacobson and Mizik, 2009).

By contrast, testing mispricing due to marketing at the stock or firm level is a two-step process. First, the abnormal stock return of a firm is obtained. Then, the marketing variables in question with time lags (e.g., lags of customer satisfaction or marketing mix actions) are regressed against the abnormal return obtained in step one. The resultant beta coefficients of the lagged marketing variables identify possible marketing mispricing effects.

Marketing Assets and Marketing Actions

Generally speaking, studies of the pricing of marketing assets will use a one-step portfolio approach, because the portfolio return of interest is based on the marketing variable in question. Such assets, including brand equity and customer satisfaction, are not easily observable and tend to move slowly over time, so their financial impact is not readily assessed in short-term stock price movements. Thus it is best to compose hypothetical portfolios of, say, high-asset versus low-asset firms, for the purpose of measuring the importance of the asset.

By contrast, marketing actions such as new product introductions, sales promotions, sponsorships, and advertising campaigns, are immediately visible. Thus they provide an opportunity for investors to update their valuation of the firm if they feel the marketing action is value-relevant. In this case the two-step approach is appropriate, using either a stock return model or an intervention model. Since firm return is observed from the financial market, while the marketing variable in question is observed from the product market, this method enables a direct assessment of the marketing antecedents of a firm's abnormal stock return.

PORTFOLIO-LEVEL TIME-SERIES MODELS FOR TESTING MISPRICING

Marketing Assets

According to the finance literature, one can test mispricing with the portfolio-level asset pricing models by Fama-French-Carhart (Fama and French, 1992, 1993; Carhart, 1997). We will illustrate these principles in the context of the possible mispricing of customer satisfaction, based on data from the American Customer Satisfaction Index (ACSI) (Fornell et al., 2006). This is an important issue in the marketing–finance literature. The marketing literature has long acknowledged the beneficial effects of customer satisfaction on repeat buying and, ultimately, long-run business performance. However, achieving high customer satisfaction may be costly, and thus the question arises whether or not Wall Street appreciates and incorporates such efforts by virtue of higher firm valuation.

In gauging the abnormal ACSI portfolio return for a direct test of mispricing customer satisfaction, this section presents several asset pricing models. The intercept term or Jensen's alpha (a_{p0}) is the exact measurement of the abnormal ACSI portfolio return in the Fama-French-Carhart model:

$$R_{pt} = a_{p0} + b_{p1} RMRF_t + b_{p2}SMB_t + b_{p3}HML_t + b_{p4}UMD_t + \varepsilon_{pt}, \quad (2.1)$$

where the R_{pt} is the month t return on an ACSI portfolio p in excess of risk-free rates, SMB_t is the firm size factor, equal to the average monthly return difference between small and large-cap stocks, and HML_t is the value factor, computed as the average monthly difference in returns between value and growth stocks. UMD_t is the momentum factor that accounts for the tendency for increasing asset prices to increase further, and $RMRF_t$ is the time-series return (in excess of risk-free rates or 30-day treasury bill rates) of the market index (Fama and French, 1993 and Carhart, 1997).[1]

If the abnormal ACSI portfolio return is not statistically significant (or Jensen's alpha $a_{p0} = 0$) in the asset pricing model (2.1), then the observed ACSI portfolio return is the same as that of the market-wide risk-adjusted benchmark portfolio. In this case, customer satisfaction is priced in financial markets, and there is no systematic mispricing of this 'voice of the customer' metric. On the other hand, if Jensen's alpha $a_{p0} > 0$, then customer satisfaction is underpriced. If Jensen's alpha $a_{p0} < 0$, then there is overpricing of customer satisfaction. In other words, the abnormal portfolio return or Jensen's alpha itself is a direct test of the stock price impact of customer satisfaction. No additional regression models are required.

Empirical studies based on the ACSI index (1995–2005) show that, interestingly, the abnormal return for a high ACSI portfolio[2] is statistically significant and positive (a_{p0} = 0.55 percent, $p<0.10$ monthly, or 6.6 percent annualized, for the capital asset pricing model (CAPM); and a_{p0} = 0.45 percent, $p<0.10$ monthly, or 5.4 percent annualized, for the Fama-French three-factor model). This means that portfolios with the highest level of customer satisfaction tend to outperform the market-wide risk-adjusted benchmark portfolio, in support of customer satisfaction under-pricing, as suggested in Fornell et al. (2006, 2009a, 2009b). At the same time, the abnormal ACSI portfolio returns for all other ACSI quintile portfolios (i.e., all but the highest quintile) are statistically insignificant ($p>0.10$). Therefore, these abnormal ACSI portfolio return results suggest that customer satisfaction is right priced in the majority of cases. In conclusion, financial markets may exhibit *some* anomalies in the pricing of customer satisfaction (Fornell et al., 2009a).

Marketing Actions

Our illustrations so far have focused on the pricing of marketing assets such as customer satisfaction and brand equity. An equally interesting question is whether or not investors incorporate marketing actions or events in their valuation. Single equation time-series models such as stock return models (for continuous marketing actions such as advertising campaigns) and event studies (for discrete marketing actions such as new product introductions) may be used to answer such questions. Researchers can also construct portfolios on the basis of spending on the marketing mix such as advertising, R&D, and others, as well as clean, uncontaminated marketing events. Regardless of what marketing variables are used in the investment strategy and stock portfolio construction, the procedures are the same as those illustrated here with the customer satisfaction example.

FIRM-LEVEL TIME-SERIES MODELS FOR TESTING MISPRICING

As discussed previously, at the firm level, testing mispricing due to marketing is a two-step process. In the first step, the abnormal return of a firm is obtained based on the Fama-French-Carhart model as in equation (2.1), but operationalized at the firm level.

In the second step, the marketing variables in question with time lags (e.g., lags of customer satisfaction or marketing mix actions) are regressed against the abnormal return obtained in step one. Consistent with finance theory that the stock market only reacts to unexpected news, researchers typically operationalize marketing actions as an unexpected shock (innovation) to the marketing time-series. The resultant beta coefficients of the marketing variable lags are used to determine mispricing. If any intertemporal coefficients of the marketing variables are significant, then mispricing of that marketing variable is supported. If any contemporaneous coefficients of the marketing variables are significant, then we conclude that the marketing variables are value-relevant, that is, have a same time-period effect on stock prices. Dynamic system models such as vector autoregressive (VAR) can track the time-varying coefficients and thus assess the cumulative effects of all marketing variable lags, while allowing for feedback loops in managerial or consumer behavior.

Dynamic System Models

While stock return models and event studies are appealing when analyzing the immediate stock market reaction to a major event, they are subject to some serious limitations in many marketing applications. First, the immediate reaction within a few days of the event may not equal the total investor reaction. For instance, Pauwels et al. (2004) observe that it takes several weeks for automotive stock prices to adjust to a major new product introduction. In general, the finance literature has observed many such dynamic effects of stock prices, naming them with terms like 'momentum,' 'slip,' and so on (Carhart, 1997). Thus, equating the immediate reaction to the total financial value effect of a major event is only meaningful if one accepts a strong version of the efficient market hypothesis (e.g., Fama and French, 1993; Sorescu and Spanjol, 2008).

This issue is more serious when one accepts the proposition that investors will not always correctly and immediately forecast the firm's future returns. For risky marketing actions such as new product introductions, investors need to correctly assess two major uncertainties: the probability of new product success and the level of profits associated with the new product (Chaney et al., 1991). On the one hand, the stock market may overreact to a product introduction that eventually does not turn out to be a financial success (ibid.). On the other hand, investors may underreact as they focus on current rather than on future revenue streams (Michaely et al., 1995).

Second, many marketing actions do not stand out as a major event, whose announcement day can be pinpointed. Examples are advertising campaigns running over several weeks or even months. While the marketing literature has studied the wear-in and wear-out effects of such actions on consumer and retailer behavior, the stock market dynamics have received little attention (Joshi and Hanssens, 2010). Moreover, the stock

Table 2.1   Methodological building blocks

Methodological Approach	Relevant Literature	Research Questions
1 Unit root tests and cointegration tests		
Augmented Dickey-Fuller test	Dickey and Fuller (1979)	Are performance and marketing variables stationary (mean-reverting) or evolving (unit root)?
Unit root test accounting for endogenous structural breaks	Zivot and Andrews (1992)	
Cointegration test	Johansen and Juselius (1990)	Do evolving variables move together?
2 VAR model		
Vector autoregressive model	Enders (1995) Dekimpe and Hanssens (1995)	How do performance, product introduction, and promotion variables interact, accounting for exogenous factors?
3 Impulse response analysis		
Performance response to a unit marketing shock	Hamilton (1994) Dekimpe and Hanssens (1995) Pauwels et al. (2002)	What is the long-term performance impact of a marketing shock?
Generalized impulse response function	Pesaran and Shin (1998) Pauwels (2004)	What is the long-term performance impact of marketing, without imposing a causal ordering?
4 Variance decomposition analysis		
Forecast error variance decomposition of performance variables	Hamilton (1994) Hanssens (1998)	What fraction of performance variance comes from each marketing action?
Generalized FEVD	Nijs et al. (2007)	Without imposing a causal ordering?

market is only supposed to react to unexpected events. If the consumer and retailer reaction to a new campaign is known after the first week, investors may incorporate the expected future earnings from that reaction into the stock price. Consequently, there should be no further stock price adjustments over the next weeks of the campaign. If such adjustments do occur (i.e., if the lagged effects of the event on stock price changes are significant), the VAR model findings indicate mispricing.

Table 2.2   Dynamic system model studies connecting marketing actions to firm value

Authors	Methodology	Findings
Pauwels et al. (2004)	Vector autoregression Impulse response function Forecast error variance decomposition	New product introductions benefit firm value in the short run and the long run, while rebates hurt firm value in the long run. It takes several weeks for these effects to wear in
Luo (2009)	Vector autoregression Impulse response function	Negative word-of-mouth hurts firm value and increases volatility in the short run and in the long run. It takes four months for these effects to wear in
Joshi and Hanssens (2010)	Vector autoregression Impulse response function Forecast error variance decomposition	Advertising has a direct effect on firm value, beyond its indirect effect through market performance. The advertiser benefits, while competitors of comparable size get hurt

Finally, a dual causality likely exists between marketing actions and stock market performance (Pauwels et al., 2008). While most marketing–finance studies focus on stock market reaction to marketing events, Markovitz et al. (2005) document how managers adjust their marketing actions based on recent stock market performance. Even when managers do not read or use the signals in stock market performance, their future marketing budgets may be affected. For example, successful new products lead to higher revenues and profits that, in turn, can be used to launch additional new products. Likewise, lackluster revenue performance may prompt some companies to engage in aggressive rebate tactics in an effort to boost sales.

Overcoming these three limitations involves modeling a dynamic system of stock market and marketing variables, which (1) provides a flexible treatment of short-term and long-term effects, (2) forecasts an expected baseline for each performance variable, so that we may capture the impact of unexpected events as deviations from this baseline, and (3) allows for dual causality. Dynamic system models provide this capability and take the form of vector autoregressive models (VAR, or VARX if exogenous controls are included) or vector error correction models, depending on model specification tests represented in Table 2.1. Published applications of dynamic system models in marketing–finance are provided in Table 2.2.

Dynamic Model Specification

Depending on the treatment of contemporaneous effects, VAR models can be viewed as either structural or reduced form in nature.

Structural vector autoregressive model
The 'structural' VAR model is represented as:

$$B_0 y_t = c_0 + B_1 y_{t-1} + B_2 y_{t-2} + \ldots + B_p y_{t-p} + \varepsilon_t, \tag{2.2}$$

The $n \times 1$ vector of n endogenous variables y is regressed on constant terms (which may include a deterministic time trend and seasonality terms) and on its own past, with p the number of lags and B the $n \times n$ coefficient matrix of a given lag. p is the maximum order of lags in the model (also known as the order of the system), and is typically based on information criteria such as the Akaike or the Schwartz Bayesian information criterion (SBIC), or on lag exclusion tests (Nijs et al., 2007). Evolving variables are differenced before including them in the model, so that all endogenous variables are stationary.

Note that any contemporaneous effects are captured in the B_0 matrix; as a result the 'structural' errors ε are uncorrelated (orthogonal) across equations. For instance, a bivariate VAR of order 1 (i.e., $n = 2$ and $p = 1$) is displayed in equation (2.3):

$$\begin{bmatrix} 1 & B_{0;1,2} \\ B_{0;2,1} & 1 \end{bmatrix} \begin{bmatrix} y_{1,t} \\ y_{2,t} \end{bmatrix} = \begin{bmatrix} c_{0;1} \\ c_{0;2} \end{bmatrix} + \begin{bmatrix} B_{1;1,1} & B_{1;1,2} \\ B_{1;2,1} & B_{1;2,2} \end{bmatrix} \begin{bmatrix} y_{1,t-1} \\ y_{2,t-2} \end{bmatrix} + \begin{bmatrix} \varepsilon_{1,t} \\ \varepsilon_{2,t} \end{bmatrix} \tag{2.3}$$

This structural form of the VAR model is of direct interest to decision-makers, as it generates predictions of results of various kinds of actions (the orthogonal errors) by calculating their conditional distribution given the action (Sims, 1986). In the context of marketing effects on stock price, the structural VAR can thus pick up contemporaneous effects, as predicted by the efficient market hypothesis. It is also the appropriate form for imposing restrictions, typically on the B_0 matrix. Amisano and Giannini (1997) present an excellent overview of different ways of imposing such restrictions, which may be based on theories of investor behavior. For instance, Keating (1990) uses a rational expectations model to impose a set of nonlinear restrictions on the off-diagonal elements of B_0.

Structural VARs have seen many applications in economics, but few in marketing. One exception is Freo (2005), who studies the response of store performance to sales promotions. The author causally orders the variables by decreasing Granger exogeneity test statistics and deleting coefficients not significantly different from 0.[3] The key finding is that promotions on heavy household items immediately increase store revenues, but promotions in the textile category immediately decrease store revenues. Thus, the structural VAR model may help marketing–finance researchers uncover diametrically opposite firm value effects of marketing actions in different industries or countries. Likewise, structural VAR models have been used in economics to separate temporary from permanent disturbances. Applied to the marketing–finance field, this approach can identify which marketing actions are likely to permanently affect firm value (e.g., advertising) and which produce only a temporary increase (e.g., price promotions to move inventory before the end of quarter).

Structural VAR models are subject to at least two challenges relevant to marketing. First, the high degree of collinearity among the estimated coefficients complicates the exclusion assessment (Freo, 2005). Second, if we follow the test results, the re-estimation of the (appropriately restricted) VAR models may still induce omitted variable bias to the other parameter estimates (Sims, 1980; Faust, 1998). As a general strategy, many econometricians prefer to impose restrictions on the long-run, structural impulse responses (Enders, 1995). Pauwels (2004) and Uhlig (2005) adhere to this strategy of restricted impulse response functions based on a reduced-form vector autoregressive model.

Reduced-form Vector Autoregressive Model

In the absence of imposed restrictions, we can write the structural VAR model (2.2) in reduced form by premultiplying each term by B_0^{-1} to obtain:

$$y_t = B_0^{-1}c_0 + B_0^{-1}B_1y_{t-1} + B_0^{-1}B_2y_{t-2} + \ldots + B_0^{-1}B_py_{t-p} + B_0^{-1}\varepsilon_t, \quad (2.4)$$

which can be written as:

$$y_t = c + A_1y_{t-1} + A_2y_{t-2} + \ldots + A_py_{t-p} + \varepsilon_t \quad (2.5)$$

$$\text{with } \Omega = \mathrm{E}(\varepsilon_t\varepsilon'_t) = \mathrm{E}(B_0^{-1}\varepsilon_t\varepsilon'_t(B_0^{-1})') = B_0^{-1}\sum(B_0^{-1})' \quad (2.6)$$

Note that the residual variance–covariance matrix is no longer diagonal; the reduced form errors are contemporaneously correlated as they now capture the contemporaneous effects among the endogenous variables. Thus, the researcher needs to identify the model, that is, assert a connection between the reduced form and the structure so that estimates of reduced form parameters translate into structural parameters. In the words of Sims (1986, p. 4), 'Identification is the interpretation of historically observed variation in data in a way that allows the variation to be used to predict the consequences of an action not yet undertaken.'

The important advantage of the reduced form model is that all right-hand side (RHS) variables are now predetermined at time t, and the system can be estimated without imposing restrictions or a causal ordering (this identification issue will come back though when calculating impulse response functions in the next section). Moreover, since all RHS variables are the same in each equation, there is no efficiency gain in using seemingly unrelated regression (SUR) estimation. Even if the errors are correlated across equations, ordinary least squares (OLS) estimates are consistent and asymptotically efficient (Srivastava and Giles, 1987, Ch. 2). This feature is especially valuable in marketing–finance applications with many endogenous variables. For example, a five-equation VAR model relating stock price changes, income changes, revenue changes, new product introductions, and price rebates (Pauwels et al., 2004) requires estimation of 5 × 5 = 25 additional parameters for each lag added to the model. In contrast, ordinary least squares (OLS) estimation equation by equation implies that only five additional parameters have to be estimated.

Vector error correction models are appropriate when a long-term equilibrium exists among two or more endogenous variables (i.e., cointegration). In such a situation, knowing the level of one variable will help us predict the level of another variable: any deviation from the long-term equilibrium will tend to be 'corrected' by the system. Therefore, we relate the evolving endogenous variables in first differences but add the error correction term. For example, consider the relation between the (logarithms of) stock price (S) and the price the firm charges its customers in the product market (P):

$$\Delta \ln (S_t) = c + \alpha_0 \Delta \ln (P_t) + \alpha_2 [\ln (S_{t-1}) - \alpha_3 \ln (P_{t-1})] + \varepsilon_t \quad (2.7)$$

where Δ denotes the first differencing operator (defined *as* $\Delta X_t = X_t - X_{t-1}$). Equation (2.7) implies that the growth in stock price depends on the growth in the firm's product price and on the deviation from an equilibrium relation between these two variables (Pauwels et al., 2007).

Long-run Impact of Marketing Actions: Impulse Response Functions

The dynamic system model estimates the baseline of each endogenous variable and forecasts its future values based on the dynamic interactions of all jointly endogenous variables. Based on the dynamic system model coefficients, impulse response functions track the over-time impact of unexpected changes (shocks) to the marketing variables on forecast deviations from baseline for the other endogenous variables. As argued by Mizik and Jacobson (2003), 'when an unanticipated change in strategy occurs, the markets react and the new stock price reflects the long-run implications such change is expected to have on future cash flows' (p. 21).

One potential application of this approach concerns the stock market's reaction to (and possibly mispricing of) customer satisfaction, currently a hotly debated issue. Investors may form expectations of customer satisfaction ratings, for example, based on their own and their friends' experiences with the brand, on company spending in the area, and so on. When actual customer satisfaction differs from this expectation, investors react to the gap with expectations, which may be negative even though the company improved ratings compared to the last period.

To derive the impulse response functions of a marketing action, we compute two forecasts, one based on an information set without the marketing action, and another based on an extended information set that accounts for the marketing action. The difference between these forecasts measures the incremental effect of the marketing action. This model feature is especially attractive for analyses of stock market performance, as investors react to shocks, that is, deviations from their expectations. In finance, these expectations are obtained from econometric forecasting models based on the firm's past financial performance records, and the shocks are obtained as the models forecast errors (e.g., Cheng and Chen, 1997). The dynamic system model is a sophisticated version of such an econometric forecast. In addition, the dynamic effects are not a priori restricted in time, sign or magnitude. Most recent studies have adopted the generalized, simultaneous-shocking approach (Dekimpe and Hanssens, 1999) in which contemporaneous effects are derived from information in the residual covariance matrix, instead of from an imposed causal ordering among the endogenous variables. Applying this approach, Pauwels et al. (2004) find that automobile companies' valuation does improve immediately upon a new product introduction, but also continues to increase for several weeks. However, for rebates, the initial positive reaction turns negative in the long run.

Of academic and practical importance is the magnitude of specific impulse response values and their over-time pattern (Pauwels, 2004). To judge the statistical significance of each impulse response value, a one-standard error band is appropriate (Pesaran et al., 1993; Sims and Zha, 1999). Finally, many marketing applications sum up all significant impulse response values to arrive at the cumulative (or total over-time) impact of marketing on performance (Pauwels et al., 2002).

Special care should be taken when interpreting the impulse response of variables that were differenced before inclusion in the model. The model-based impulse response functions represent the effect of/on the first difference of the variable, and thus need to be translated back to a level effect for interpretation. Three scenarios are possible:

1. The marketing variable is stationary, but the financial performance variable is evolving: in this case, significant effects of marketing on performance change indicate a permanent effect of marketing on performance (hysteresis). Several interesting patterns have been observed, including full hysteresis (a positive impact of marketing on performance change is not followed by any negative readjustment) and partial hysteresis (a subsequent negative impact renders the cumulative effect lower than the initial impact) (Hanssens and Ouyang, 2002).
2. The marketing variable is evolving, but the performance variable is stationary. For instance, in Dekimpe and Hanssens (1999), a permanent change in the price of a consumer product did not create a permanent change in performance. The cumulative response of performance is given directly by the impulse response function; the researcher simply needs to communicate that this is the impact of a *permanent* change in price, as opposed to a temporary price promotion.
3. Both marketing and performance variables are evolving. In this case, significant effects indicate that a permanent change in marketing yields a permanent change to the performance variable.

Relative Importance of Marketing Actions: Forecast Error Variance Decomposition

While impulse response functions trace the effects of a marketing change on performance, forecast error variance decomposition (FEVD) determines the extent to which these performance effects are due to changes in each of the VAR variables. Analogous to a 'dynamic R^2,' the FEVD calculates the percentage of variation in a response variable that can be attributed to both contemporaneous *and* past changes in each of the endogenous variables.

It is often important to compare the short-run and the long-run FEVD. For example, such a comparison could reveal that the initial movements in stock price are attributed mainly to promotion or advertising shocks, but that over time, the contribution of product innovation gradually becomes stronger. Moreover, if one includes product market performance metrics, such as sales and profit, FEVD also addresses whether marketing actions affect firm value *only indirectly* through top-line and bottom-line

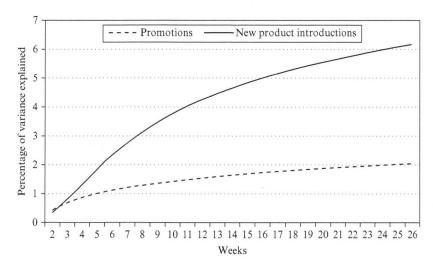

Source: Pauwels et al. (2004).

Figure 2.2   Forecast error variance decomposition of firm value

performance (in which case all firm value forecast deviations are attributed to these performance variables), or have a direct effect above and beyond this performance impact. Hanssens (1998) used FEVD on channel orders and consumer demand data to show that sudden spikes in channel orders have no long-term consequences for the manufacturer, *unless* movements in consumer demand accompany them. Pauwels et al. (2004) show that marketing actions impact automotive stock prices above and beyond their effect on revenues and profits.

Figure 2.2 shows the results of a forecast error variance decomposition of firm value explained by promotions and new product introductions. While sales promotions are initially more important, an increasing percentage of the forecast deviation variance in firm value is attributed to new product introduction. On average, the ability of a new product introduction to explain firm value forecast deviations is eight times higher after two quarters than it is in the week of product launch. This indicates that investors struggle to assess the future firm value impact of an innovation at the time of its introduction.

Forecast error variance decomposition requires the imposition of a causal ordering for model identification purposes. When marketing and finance theory are insufficient to justify such ordering, it is advisable to estimate the generalized forecast error variance decomposition (Pesaran and Shin, 1998), which is linked to the generalized impulse response function using equation (2.8):

$$\theta_{ij}^g(t) = \frac{\sum_{l=0}^{t}\psi_{ij}^g(l)^2}{\sum_{l=0}^{t}\sum_{j=1}^{m}\psi_{ij}^g(l)^2}, i, j = 1, \ldots, m. \tag{2.8}$$

where $\psi_{ij}^g(l)$ is the value of a generalized impulse response function (GIRF) following a one-standard error shock to variable j on variable i at time l.

MISPRICING VOLATILITY: GARCH EXTENSION OF STOCK RESPONSE MODELS

So far we have discussed time-series models for the levels or changes in firm value in terms of return metrics. Equally important is the representation of risk or volatility of these return metrics. Risk is a vitally important stock performance variable because it is directly related to firms' cost of capital, corporate bankruptcy likelihood, and shareholder wealth (Ang et al., 2006). Benchmarking firm risk and relating it to marketing variables may be accomplished by a class of time-series models called generalized autoregressive conditional heteroskedasticity (GARCH) models (Engle, 1982; Bollerslev, 1986).[4]

Note that prior applications in the marketing–finance interface have discussed several approaches to stock volatility (or stock risk). Particularly, total stock risk or volatility of a firm has two parts: systematic and idiosyncratic. The former is the firm's sensitivity to the changes in market returns or to news of broad market changes such as inflation that are common to all stocks. The latter reflects the risk associated with firm-specific strategies such as corporate social performance after the market-wide variation is accounted for (McAlister et al., 2007; Luo and Bhattacharya, 2009; Rego et al., 2009; Tuli and Bharadwaj, 2009; Osinga et al., 2011). However, most of these studies address cross-sectional volatility (systematic or idiosyncratic), rather than time-series volatility (Jacobson and Mizik, 2009; Luo et al., 2010; Bharadwaj et al., 2011).

The GARCH model offers several appealing properties. First, it can simultaneously test the significance of both stock return (first moment) and volatility (second moment) responses to marketing actions. In so doing, GARCH also accommodates the tradeoffs between risk and return: stocks with higher volatility are required to earn higher returns, lest no investors would be interested in them (Luo, 2009). Though an essential part in the intertemporal capital asset pricing models, these tradeoffs, to our knowledge, have not been explicitly accounted for in prior marketing studies (Jacobson and Mizik, 2009).

Second, this method allows for time-varying forecast confidence intervals that can model more precisely the variance of the errors and the confidence intervals. GARCH also generates more efficient estimators because it accounts for heteroskedasticity. Third, it captures autoregressive serial correlation in stock price data by estimating the carry-over effects between historical and future stock returns/volatilities. As such, these advantages suggest that GARCH models can rigorously link marketing actions to firms' stock returns and volatilities over time.

Mathematically, the standard GARCH(1,1) model is specified as:

$$r_t = c + \sum_{l=1}^{L} \rho_l r_{t-l} + \varepsilon_t, \tag{2.9}$$

$$\varepsilon_t | (\varepsilon_{t-1}, \varepsilon_{t-2}, \ldots) \sim N(0, h_t),$$

$$h_t = \alpha_0 + \alpha_1 \varepsilon_{t-1}^2 + \beta_1 h_{t-1},$$

where r_t is stock return, L is the best-fitting autoregressive lag length, ρ is the autoregressive parameter in the conditional mean equation, ε_t is the error term, h_t is the latent conditional variance of error terms, and intercept $\alpha_0 > 0$. If the estimates for α_1 and β_1 are positive and significant statistically, then the latent stock volatility is time-varying and heteroskedastic. Clearly, GARCH can account for and model heteroskedasticity because h_t is allowed to vary over time. In addition, GARCH accommodates autoregressive serial correlation or state dependency because it includes historical lags of both returns and volatilities in the models. According to this GARCH(1,1) model specification, investors update their estimates of stock return and volatility in each period based on the newly revealed surprises only in last period's information (lag = 1).

Higher-order GARCH(p,q) models are developed so as to accommodate the possibility that investors may update their expectations using a series of historical surprises of volatility and forecasted variances (i.e., lags greater than 1). Put differently, it may take some time to fully impound the information content of unexpected news in the financial markets. In higher-order GARCH models, p represents the order of autoregressive ARCH terms, and q is the order of moving-average GARCH terms. The standard GARCH (p,q) model is specified as:

$$r_t = c + \sum_{l=1}^{L} \rho_l r_{t-l} + \varepsilon_t, \tag{2.10}$$

$$\varepsilon_t | (\varepsilon_{t-1}, \varepsilon_{t-2}, \ldots) \sim N(0, h_t),$$

$$h_t = \alpha_0 + \sum_{j=1}^{p} \alpha_j \varepsilon_{t-j}^2 + \sum_{i=1}^{q} \beta_i h_{t-i}.$$

GARCH can also test the tradeoffs between stock return and stock volatility based on Merton's (1973) theory of the intertemporal capital asset pricing model. More specifically, if stock volatility is introduced into the stock return equation, we obtain the GARCH-in-mean (GARCH-m) model as follows:

$$r_t = c + \sum_{l=1}^{L} \rho_l r_{t-l} + v \log(h_t) + \varepsilon_t, \tag{2.11}$$

$$\varepsilon_t | (\varepsilon_{t-1}, \varepsilon_{t-2}, \ldots) \sim N(0, h_t),$$

$$h_t = \alpha_0 + \sum_{j=1}^{p} \alpha_j \varepsilon_{t-j}^2 + \sum_{i=1}^{q} \beta_i h_{t-i},$$

where the parameter (v) captures the risk–return tradeoff. If $v \neq 0$, then there is a significant tradeoff between stock return and stock volatility in GARCH-m models. This means investors would require higher returns for buying stocks associated with higher risks.

In order to test the impact of marketing actions on stock returns and stock volatilities, we introduce shocks in marketing actions as follows:

$$r_t = c + \sum_{l=1}^{L} \rho_l r_{t-l} + v \log(h_t) + \sum_{m=1}^{M} \sum_{n=1}^{N} \varsigma_{m,n} Shock\_MKG_{m,t-n} + \varepsilon_t, \tag{2.12}$$

$$\varepsilon_t | (\varepsilon_{t-1}, \varepsilon_{t-2}, \ldots) \sim GED(0, h_t),$$

$$h_t = \alpha_0 + \sum_{m=1}^{M} \sum_{n=1}^{N} \xi_{m,n} Shock\_MKG_{m,t-n} + \sum_{j=1}^{p} \alpha_j \varepsilon_{t-j}^2 + \sum_{i=1}^{q} \beta_i h_{t-i},$$

where *Shock_MKG*$_{m,t-n}$ is the unexpected shock in the *m*th marketing variable at lagged time period *t−n*. All models in the GARCH system of equations are estimated simultaneously along with bootstrapping methods (Lundblad, 2007). Shocks or unanticipated information of marketing actions can be derived based on VAR models described previously. As such, this GARCH system now provides a direct test of the hypothesis regarding the impact of marketing actions on stock returns and volatilities. The null hypothesis is that $\zeta_{m,n} = 0$, which would suggest that marketing actions have no impact on stock returns. The alternative hypothesis is that $\zeta_{m,n} \neq 0$, which supports the impact of marketing actions on stock returns. In addition, if $\xi_{m,n} = 0$, marketing actions have no impact on stock volatilities. Otherwise $\xi_{m,n} \neq 0$, which would support the stock volatility implications of marketing actions.

On the basis of monthly data of dissatisfaction of consumption experience in the airline industry (1999–2005), Luo (2009) finds that negative consumer word-of-mouth (NWOM) has a significant impact on firm risk. Particularly, GARCH results show that both contemporaneous coefficients and intertemporal coefficients of NWOM are significant. NWOM induces higher stock volatilities of the firm (total impact of the intertemporal coefficients $b = 0.0338$ with multiple lags $t = 10$ past months). This suggests a substantial amount of mispricing of the information of negative word-of-mouth. The market is not able to impound the full information of WOM immediately but rather may take up to ten months to fully reflect the damaging impact of NWOM. These results indicate that NWOM is value-relevant and has mispricing effects (i.e., lasting effects on firm stock prices) with significant underreactions to NWOM information. The harm of NWOM on customer loyalty and brand value may last for a long time, during which the stock market prices the damaging impact *gradually*. Firms with poor ratings in consumer WOM are punished with higher financial risks in a multi-period setting. Thus, firms should communicate in a timely manner the full impact of WOM and disclose marketing information to analysts and investors for improved market efficiency.

CONCLUSIONS AND FUTURE RESEARCH OPPORTUNITIES

If society is to benefit from a smooth market-driven coordination between resource allocation in product markets and financial markets, then investors should place the proper value on what firms and their marketing managers do, that is, creating marketing assets such as brands, and engaging in specific marketing actions such as product launches. This chapter has introduced a range of time-series methods to investigate empirically whether or not such efficient pricing occurs, at the level of stock returns as well as stock volatility.

The application of these methods to various aspects of marketing valuation has revealed that, while investors generally incorporate the value relevance of marketing assets and marketing actions, documented cases exist of overpricing, underpricing and delayed pricing. As a result, there is opportunity for future research to diagnose not only the existence of mispricing, but also its causes, and to recommend remedies to reduce their influence. More specifically, three potential causes merit additional investigation. The first is disclosure, that is, mispricing may occur because investors do not have access to the right metrics. For example, if reported revenue were broken down by revenue from new vs existing customers, separate time-series models on these two revenue sources would likely provide superior projections compared with those generated by combined models. A similar argument can be made for revenue generated at base price vs revenue realized at a discounted price. The second is consumer response dynamics. Time-series models on consumer sales, especially diffusion models for new products, can be used to project more realistic revenue projections for companies that rely on technological innovation for their growth. The third is corporate communications. Since these are expected to represent an optimistic view of the company's future, a time-series analysis on anticipated vs realized stock returns may quantify and adjust for the biasing influence of such communications. Much remains to be discovered in these and related areas by future research on the marketing–finance interface.

NOTES

1. Portfolio-level models in equation (2.1) are time-series models because the estimation is done across time (months). More information on the construction of the four factors may be obtained from the website of Professor Kenneth French (http://mba.tuck.dartmouth.edu/pages/faculty/ken.french/data_library.html).
2. Details on how to define and construct the ACSI portfolios are discussed in Aksoy et al. (2008) and Fornell et al. (2009a).
3. The importance of Granger causality testing and how it is conducted are discussed in Granger (1969) and Luo (2009).
4. Researchers may use other modeling techniques when dealing with lower-frequency firm value measures (e.g., Tobin's Q). Readers are encouraged to consult Fang et al. (2008) and Grewal et al. (2010) for models of Tobin's Q.

REFERENCES

Aksoy, Lerzan, Bruce Cooil, Christopher Groening, Timothy L. Keiningham, and Atakan Yalçın (2008), 'The Long-term Stock Market Valuation of Customer Satisfaction,' *Journal of Marketing*, **72** (4), 105–22.

Amisano, Gianni and Carlo Giannini (1997), *Topics in Structural VAR Econometrics*, New York: Springer.

Ang, Andrew, Robert J. Hodrick, Yuhang Xing, and Xiaoyan Zhang (2006), 'The Cross-section of Volatility and Expected Returns,' *Journal of Finance*, **61** (1), 259–99.

Benartzi, Shlomo and Richard H. Thaler (1995), 'Myopic Loss Aversion and the Equity Premium Puzzle,' *The Quarterly Journal of Economics*, **110** (1), 73–92.

Bharadwaj, Sundar G., Kapil R. Tuli, and Andre Bonfrer (2011), 'The Impact of Brand Quality on Shareholder Wealth,' *Journal of Marketing*, **75** (5), 88–104.

Bollerslev, Tim (1986), 'Generalized Autoregressive Conditional Heteroskedasticity,' *Journal of Econometrics*, **31** (3), 307–27.

Carhart, Mark M. (1997), 'On Persistence in Mutual Fund Performance,' *Journal of Finance*, **52** (1), 57–82.

Chaney, Paul, Timothy Devinney, and Russ Winer (1991), 'The Impact of New-product Introductions on the Market Value of Firms,' *Journal of Business*, **64** (4), 573–610.

Cheng, Agnes C.S. and Charles J.P. Chen (1997), 'Firm Valuation of Advertising Expense: An Investigation of Scaler Effects,' *Managerial Finance*, **23** (10), 41–61.

Dekimpe, Marnik and Dominique M. Hanssens (1995), 'The Persistence of Marketing Effects on Sales,' *Marketing Science*, **14** (1), 1–21.

Dekimpe, Marnik G. and Dominique M. Hanssens (1999), 'Sustained Spending and Persistent Response: A New Look at Long-term Marketing Profitability,' *Journal of Marketing Research*, **36** (4), 397–412.

Dickey, D.A. and W.A. Fuller (1979), 'Distribution of the Estimators for Autoregressive Time Series with a Unit Root,' *Journal of the American Statistical Association*, **74** (366), 427–31.

Enders, W. (1995), *Applied Econometric Time Series*, New York: John Wiley.

Engle, Robert (2002), 'New Frontiers for Arch Models,' *Journal of Applied Econometrics*, **17** (5), 425–46.

Fama, Eugene and Kenneth French (1993), 'Common Risk Factors in the Returns of Stocks and Bonds,' *Journal of Financial Economics*, **33** (1), 3–56.

Fang, Eric, Robert W. Palmatier, and Jan-Benedict E.M Steenkamp (2008), 'Effect of Service Transition Strategies on Firm Value,' *Journal of Marketing*, **72** (5), 1–14.

Faust, Jon (1998), 'The Robustness of Identified VAR Conclusions About Money,' Board of Governors of the Federal Reserve System, International Finance Discussion Paper, No. 610.

Fornell, Claes, Sunil Mithas, and Forrest Morgeson (2009a), 'The Economic and Statistical Significance of Stock Returns on Customer Satisfaction,' *Marketing Science*, **28** (5), 820–25.

Fornell, Claes, Sunil Mithas, and Forrest Morgeson (2009b), 'The Statistical Significance of Portfolio Returns,' *International Journal of Research in Marketing*, **26** (2), 162–3.

Fornell, Claes, Sunil Mithas, Forrest V. Morgeson III, and M.S. Krishnan (2006), 'Customer Satisfaction and Stock Prices: High Returns, Low Risk,' *Journal of Marketing*, **70** (1), 3–14.

Freo, Marzia (2005), 'The Impact of Sales Promotions on Store Performance: A Structural Vector Autoregressive Approach,' *Statistical Methods and Applications*, **14** (2), 271–81.

Granger, C.W. (1969), 'Investigating Causal Relations by Econometric Models and Cross-spectral Methods,' *Econometrica*, **37** (3), 424–38.

Grewal, Rajdeep, Murali Chandrashekaran, and Alka V. Citrin (2010), 'Customer Satisfaction Heterogeneity and Shareholder Value,' *Journal of Marketing Research*, **47** (4), 612–26.

Hamilton, James (1994), *Time Series Analysis*, Princeton, NJ: Princeton University Press.

Hanssens, Dominique M. (1998), 'Order Forecasts, Retail Sales and the Marketing Mix for Consumer Durables,' *Journal of Forecasting*, **17** (3/4), 327–46.

Hanssens, Dominique M. and Ming Ouyang (2002), 'Hysteresis in Marketing Response: When is Marketing Spending an Investment?' *Review of Marketing Science*, No. 419.

Hanssens, Dominique M., Roland Rust, and Rajendra Srivastava (2009), 'Marketing Strategy and Wall Street: Nailing Down Marketing's Impact,' *Journal of Marketing*, **73** (6), 115–18.

Jacobson, Robert and Natalie Mizik (2009), 'The Financial Markets and Customer

Satisfaction: Re-examining the Value Implications of Customer Satisfaction from the Efficient Markets Perspective,' *Marketing Science*, **28** (5), 810–19.

Johansen, Søren and Katarina Juselius (1990), 'Maximum Likelihood Estimation and Inference on Cointegration – with Applications to the Demand for Money,' *Oxford Bulletin of Economics and Statistics*, **52** (2), 169–210.

Joshi, Amit M. and Dominique M. Hanssens (2010), 'The Direct and Indirect Effects of Advertising Spending on Firm Value,' *Journal of Marketing*, **74** (1), 20–33.

Keating John W. (1990), 'Identifying VAR Models under Rational Expectations,' *Journal of Monetary Economics*, **25** (3), 453–76.

Lundblad, Christian (2007), 'The Risk Return Tradeoff in the Long Run: 1836–2003,' *Journal of Financial Economics*, **85** (1), 123–50.

Luo, Xueming (2008), 'When Marketing Strategy First Meets Wall Street: Marketing Spendings and Firms' Initial Public Offerings (IPOs),' *Journal of Marketing*, **72** (5), 98–109.

Luo, Xueming (2009), 'Quantifying the Long-term Impact of Negative Word of Mouth on Cash Flows and Stock Prices,' *Marketing Science*, **28** (1), 148–65.

Luo, Xueming and C.B. Bhattacharya (2009), 'The Debate over Doing Good: Corporate Social Performance, Strategic Marketing Levers, and Firm-idiosyncratic Risk,' *Journal of Marketing*, **73** (6), 198–213.

Luo, Xueming, Christian Homburg, and Jan Wieseke (2010), 'Customer Satisfaction, Analyst Stock Recommendations, and Firm Value,' *Journal of Marketing Research*, **47** (6), 1041–58.

Markovitz, Dmitri G., Joel Steckel, and Bernard Yeung (2005), 'Using Capital Markets as Market Intelligence: Evidence from the Pharmaceutical Industry,' *Management Science*, **51** (10), 1467–80.

McAlister, Leigh, Raji Srinivasan, and MinChung Kim (2007), 'Advertising, Research and Development, and Systematic Risk of the Firm,' *Journal of Marketing*, **71** (1), 35–48.

Merton, R.C. (1973), 'An Intertemporal Asset Pricing Model,' *Econometrica*, **41** (5), 867–87.

Michaely, R., R. Thaler, and K. Womack (1995), 'Price Reactions to Dividend Initiations and Omissions: Overreaction or Drift?,' *Journal of Finance*, **50** (2), 573–608.

Mizik, Natalie and Robert Jacobson (2003), 'Trading Off Between Value Creation and Value Appropriation: The Financial Implications of Shifts in Strategic Emphasis,' *Journal of Marketing*, **67** (1), 63–76.

Nijs, Vincent, Shuba Srinivasan, and Koen Pauwels (2007), 'Retail-price Drivers and Retailer Profits,' *Marketing Science*, **26** (4), 473–87.

Osinga, Ernst C., Peter S.H. Leeflang, Shuba Srinivasan, and Jaap E. Wieringa (2011), 'Why Do Firms Invest in Consumer Advertising with Limited Sales Response? A Shareholder Perspective,' *Journal of Marketing*, **75** (1), 109–24.

Pauwels, Koen (2004), 'How Dynamic Consumer Response, Competitor Response, Company Support and Company Inertia Shape Long-term Marketing Effectiveness,' *Marketing Science*, **23** (4), 596–610.

Pauwels, Koen, Dominique M. Hanssens, and S. Siddarth (2002), 'The Long-term Effects of Price Promotions on Category Incidence, Brand Choice and Purchase Quantity,' *Journal of Marketing Research*, **34** (4), 421–39.

Pauwels, Koen, Shuba Srinivasan, and Philip-Hans Franses (2007), 'When Do Price Thresholds Matter in Retail Categories?,' *Marketing Science*, **26** (1), 83–100.

Pauwels, Koen, Eric Ghysels, Paul Wolfson, and Erwin Danneels (2008), 'Wall Street and New Product Exploration: Vicious or Virtuous Circle?,' Working Paper, Tuck School of Business.

Pauwels, Koen, Jorge M. Silva-Risso, Shuba Srinivasan, and Dominique M. Hanssens (2004), 'New Products, Sales Promotions and Firm Value, with Application to the Automobile Industry,' *Journal of Marketing*, **68** (4), 142–56.

Pesaran, M.H. and Y. Shin (1998), 'Generalised Impulse Response Analysis in Linear Multivariate Models,' *Economics Letters*, **58** (1), 17–29.

Pesaran, Hashem M., Richard G. Pierse, and Kevin C. Lee (1993), 'Persistence, Cointegration and Aggregation: A Disaggregated Analysis of Output Fluctuations in the US Economy,' *Journal of Econometrics*, **56** (1–2), 8.

Rego, L.L., M.T. Billett, and N.A. Morgan (2009), 'Consumer-based Brand Equity and Firm Risk,' *Journal of Marketing*, **73** (6), 47–60.

Sims, Christopher A. (1980), 'Macroeconomics and Reality,' *Econometrica*, **48** (1), 1–48.

Sims, Christopher A. (1986), 'Are Forecasting Models Usable for Policy Analysis?,' Federal Reserve Bank of Minneapolis *Quarterly Review*, **10** (1), 2–15.

Sims, Christopher A. and Tao Zha (1999), 'Error Bands for Impulse Responses,' *Econometrica*, **67** (5), 1113–56.

Sorescu, Alina and Jelena Spanjol (2008), 'Innovation's Effect on Firm Value and Risk: Insights from Consumer Packaged Goods,' *Journal of Marketing*, **72** (2), 114–32.

Srinivasan, S. and D. Hanssens (2009), 'Marketing and Firm Value: Metrics, Methods, Findings and Future Directions,' *Journal of Marketing Research*, **46** (3), 293–312.

Srivastava, Virendra K. and David E.A. Giles (1987), *Seemingly Unrelated Regression Equations Models: Estimation and Inference*, New York: Marcel Dekker.

Tuli, K. and S. Bharadwaj (2009), 'Examining the Relevance of Customer Satisfaction for Wall Street: The Case of Systematic and Idiosyncratic Risk,' *Journal of Marketing*, **73** (6), 184–97.

Uhlig, Harald F.H.V.S. (2005), 'What Are the Effects of Monetary Policy on Output? Results From an Agnostic Identification Procedure,' *Journal of Monetary Economics*, **52** (2), 381–419.

Zivot, Eric and Donald W.K. Andrews (1992), 'Further Evidence on the Great Crash, the Oil-price Shock, and the Unit-root Hypothesis,' *Journal of Business and Economic Statistics*, **10** (3), 251–70.

3 How to better value branded businesses: a conditional multiplier approach
Natalie Mizik

INTRODUCTION

The last few decades have been characterized by high levels of merger and acquisition activity and the growing disparity between the book value of the acquired businesses and their acquisition prices. For example, in June 2005 Procter & Gamble paid $58.6bn for Gillette. This acquisition price was 13 times greater than Gillette's $4.5bn book value ($0.9bn of net working capital and $3.6bn of net property, plant, and equipment). Cadbury plc, a company with a tangible book value of assets of less than $3bn (negative $0.5bn of net working capital and $3bn of net property, plant, and equipment) accepted Kraft's takeover offer of $21.8bn. This offer price was almost a nine-times multiple of Cadbury's book value. Pfizer sold its consumer goods business units to Johnson & Johnson in 2006 and the Swedish government privatized V&S in 2008. The Swedish government considered splitting V&S (best known for its Absolut Vodka brand) and selling each brand individually. All these transactions require estimating the value of the enterprise. For public companies (like Gillette and Cadbury), their stock market valuation serves as a starting reference price in acquisition negotiations, but for most business combinations, which involve private firms or business units, a good estimate of enterprise value is not easily available and needs to be established.

When consumers buy a computer, a pair of sneakers, shaving cream, or a brokerage service, they are paying for more than the physical good or service in question: they are also buying a brand. Dell, Nike, Gillette, and Charles Schwab are businesses whose product market performance and enterprise value are highly dependent on consumer opinions about their brands. For such companies, the brand often defines the very essence of the business and helps its products stand out among the myriad of competitive offerings. For such firms, the brand is just as critical in the product market as it is in the boardroom. Anyone trying to determine the value of a branded business should think carefully about the importance of its brand and the brand's contribution to the enterprise value. Mergers and acquisitions of established businesses, a divesture of a business unit, a sale of a start-up, corporate portfolio management, or expected IPO are just a few situations that require a tool to accurately value branded businesses. It can help entrepreneurs, consultants, and investment bankers to more accurately establish the enterprise value and can help guide negotiations and pricing decisions in divesture, merger, and acquisition transactions.

Traditional valuation approaches work best for valuing mature businesses with low reliance on intangible assets and operating in stable environments. But these approaches become increasingly unreliable for firms and industries where brands are important. Traditional valuation models do not directly account for the impact of intangibles, such as brands, or do so in an ad hoc and highly subjective manner.

This chapter presents an analytically based and data-driven conditional multiplier valuation approach developed by Natalie Mizik and Robert Jacobson for better valuing branded businesses (Mizik and Jacobson, 2009). It enhances traditional multiplier-based valuation methods by explicitly incorporating consumer perceptions of the corporate brand into the valuation model. It significantly improves the predictive accuracy of enterprise valuation: models incorporating information about brand perceptions show a 16 percent average out-of-sample reduction in mean absolute error of enterprise value estimates.

The method described herein has the objective of improving the predictive accuracy of enterprise valuation (i.e., establishing the value of the business entity as a whole). That is, the objective is to build a model that generates better quality forecasts of firm value for branded businesses, rather than to build a model that better explains the impact of brands on firm value, or model that allows the isolation of the value of the brand from the other tangible and intangible assets of the firm, the two primary research objectives academic researchers have been focusing on in marketing literature.[1] As such, the methodological considerations and relevant issues here differ significantly from the issues central to the research focused on building explanatory models.

In contrast to explanatory context, where the consistency of the estimates is of utmost importance, in forecasting context, the external validity of the model is of primary importance: the model must hold and perform well out-of-sample. The quality of forecasting model performance is judged based on the measures of its explanatory power such as mean absolute error (MAE, if the objective is to minimize the average forecast error) or mean square error (if the objective is to minimize average square error in order to minimize the occurrence of extreme forecast errors). In contrast to the explanatory context, where the omitted variable bias is highly undesirable and needs to be avoided, in forecasting context, omitted variable bias is not a problem, and to the extent the information in omitted variables is picked up by the model and helps improve the forecasts, it is in fact desirable. Further, unlike the estimates from the explanatory models, the coefficient estimates from forecasting models cannot be interpreted as structural parameters and cannot be used for guiding policy decision-making. In other words, they are not indicative of causal relationships and should only be viewed as reduced-form estimates and be used exclusively for generating better forecasts, not for explaining the relationships among the constructs included in the model.

TRADITIONAL VALUATION APPROACHES

Most enterprise valuation approaches used by practitioners fall into one of two categories: (1) discounted cash flow (DCF) valuation analysis and (2) multiplier-based valuation analysis. The discounted cash flow analysis seeks to estimate the enterprise value of a business by projecting its future cash flows and discounting them by an appropriate rate to obtain the net present value of future cash flows. This approach is often referred to as a 'direct valuation.' Multiplier-based valuation analysis is based on the premise that similar assets should be similarly priced. It seeks to establish the value of a business by examining the valuation of similar (comparable) businesses. It is known as the 'relative valuation' approach and is often referred to as 'comparable firm valuation' or 'peer group valuation.' While popular with practitioners, relative valuation methods have received very little academic attention.

Both DCF and multiplier-based valuation models have strengths and weaknesses, and they typically produce different results, even when applied to the same case and data. As such, financial analysts usually use them as complements and perform several iterations of each method for a given valuation project, changing their assumptions in DCF analyses and varying the sets of comparable transactions or peer companies included in multiplier-based valuations.

Discounted Cash Flow Analysis

Discounted cash flow analysis relies on the net present value rule, which states that the value of an asset can be measured as a sum of expected discounted future cash flows it will generate. DCF is covered in all accounting and valuation text books and is a basic tool widely used by practitioners. DCF is theoretically appealing, but it is often difficult to implement in practice because of the uncertainty inherent in predicting the future. DCF typically involves much guesswork as it requires making assumptions and projections of future cash flows and discount rates. It is a flexible methodology because it can be tailored to a specific environmental situation and business being valued, and it can easily accommodate the researcher's beliefs about the future. It is also less dependent on publicly available information than multiplier-based valuation.

DCF valuation is, however, very sensitive to the subjective assumptions necessary for forecasting future cash flows and selecting an appropriate discount rate to account for the riskiness of the business venture. Research has shown that DCF valuations are affected by the interests and incentives of the party undertaking the valuation and are subject to 'strategic distortions.' For example, the relative bargaining strength of claim-holders (junior vs senior), the existence of outside bids, management's equity stake, and management turnover introduce systematic errors in DCF valuation (Gilson et al., 2000).

The DCF approach is particularly difficult to implement for young firms, firms operating in changing environments and in industries undergoing technological revolutions, and for firms with significant intangible assets, such as patents or valuable brands. This difficulty is driven by the increased uncertainty about their riskiness and future financial performance. Practitioners compensate for these shortcomings of DCF valuation by running multiple sensitivity analyses and varying their assumptions about the growth and discount rates and by comparing the results of their DCF valuations with the valuations implied by multiplier-based methods.

Multiplier-based Analysis

Multiplier-based valuation does not require making assumptions about the discount rates and making projections of future cash flows. Instead, it relies on the market pricing of similar assets to establish a fair price for the asset that is being valued. It relies on the market pricing mechanism and the assumption that, on average, the market prices assets correctly. In other words, the value of an asset can be ascertained based on the market valuation of similar assets. Multiplier-based valuation boils down the complexity of the discount rates and future cash flows to a simple proportional relation: firm value equals to the level of the selected operating metric (a 'value driver' such as revenue or EBITDA – earnings before interest, taxes, depreciation, and amortization) multiplied by the corresponding multiplier.

The multiplier is determined via the analysis of market prices for similar assets and is often a simple average ratio of market price of these assets to the operating metric used as a value driver in the valuation. The key to successful valuation lies in determining the appropriate multiple. One important decision in the multiplier-based valuation that requires subjective judgment of the analyst pertains to defining the relevant set of comparable companies or precedent transactions for calculating the multiplier ratio. In contrast to DCF valuation, which requires multiple assumptions, the identification of the relevant set of comparables is the only aspect in the multiplier-based valuation where subjective judgment enters the valuation process.

The data on comparables for determining the relative valuation multiplier typically comes from one of two sources: valuation of comparable publicly traded firms or comparable precedent enterprise sales transactions. When public companies are used as comparables, the numerator in the multiplier ratio (i.e., firm enterprise value) is usually computed using the stock price, number of shares outstanding, and debt. When data from precedent transactions is used to compile a set of comparables, the numerator is computed using reported transaction price and net debt for the recently sold comparable businesses.

THE BASIC MULTIPLIER APPROACH TO ENTERPRISE VALUATION

Implementing multiplier-based valuation involves three steps:

1. choosing an operating metric to be used as valuation driver;
2. identifying a set of comparable publicly traded firms or past transactions;
3. computing the average multiplier and applying it to the business being valued.

For most businesses, and particularly for private firms and the individual business units of large public firms, the most readily available operating metric that can be used as a value driver in its valuation is revenue. Revenue data also has the benefit of being less susceptible to accounting distortions, managerial manipulation, and transitory fluctuations. As such, in its simplest form, the enterprise value of a business can be determined by multiplying the sales of that business by the average enterprise value-to-sales ratio of comparable publicly traded firms or recent transactions:

$$Firm\ Value_{it} = \varphi_{it} * Sales_{it}, \tag{3.1}$$

where: *Firm Value*$_{it}$ is a measure of the value of business i at time period t; *Sales*$_{it}$ is a measure of firm i revenues in time period t; and φ_{it} is the sales multiple for firm *i* at time *t*, which can be computed as the average enterprise value-to-sales ratio of firm *i* comparables at time *t*:

$$\hat{\phi}_{it} = \frac{1}{n}\sum\left(\frac{Firm\ Value_{comparable\_i,t}}{Sales_{comparable\_i,t}}\right),$$ (3.2)

where: *n* is the number of comparables in the consideration set for firm *i* valuation.

Because transactional data for recent sales of comparable business is usually very sparse, multiplier-based valuation typically relies on the data from publicly traded companies drawn from the same industrial sector. The use of firms from the same industrial sector controls for the macro-economic effects and ensures that all firms in the analysis are subject to the same general business environment conditions and future growth prospects.

However, even within a given industrial sector, significant variation in the distribution of multipliers can exist. For example, as shown in Figure 3.1, the average enterprise value-to-sales ratio in the high-technology sector is 2.98, but it ranges from 0.16 to 10.68. The average enterprise value-to-sales ratio in the industrial sector is 1.45, with a minimum of 0.28 and a maximum of 5.75. What drives these differences in the enterprise value-to-sales ratio within a given industry?

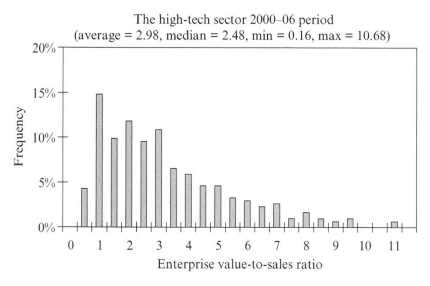

Figure 3.1   Histograms of enterprise value-to-sales ratio

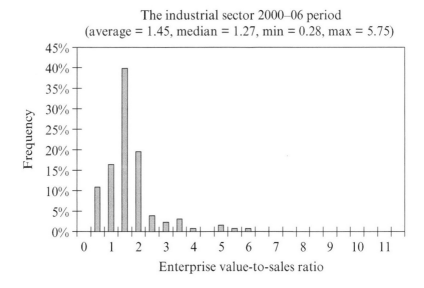

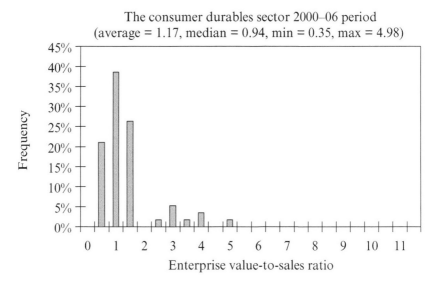

Figure 3.1   (continued)

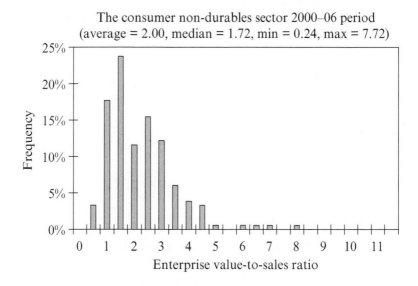

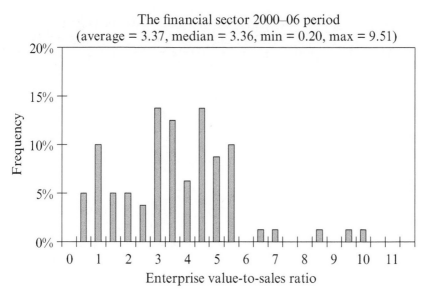

Figure 3.1 (continued)

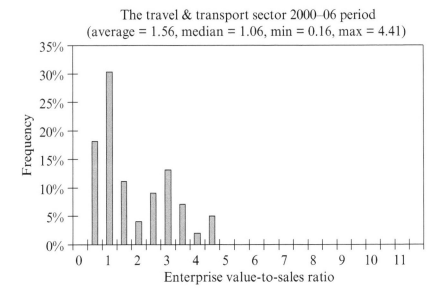

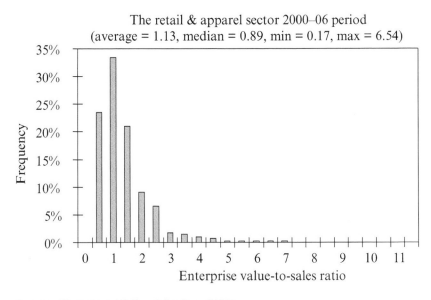

Source: Charts from Mizik and Jacobson (2009).

Figure 3.1   (continued)

THE ROLE OF DIFFERENCES IN PROFITABILITY

One reason this large variation in the enterprise value-to-sales ratio exists for firms operating within a given industrial sector is that, all else being equal, firms with higher profitability tend to have greater value-to-sales multipliers (Barth et al., 1998, 1999; Bajaj et al., 2003). As such, the multiplier φ_{it} in equation (3.1) can be decomposed to allow for the direct effects of firm profitability on its valuation:

$$Firm\ Value_{it} = [\varphi(Baseline)_{it} + \varphi(Current\ Profitability)_{it}]^* Sales_{it}, \quad (3.3)$$

where: $\varphi(Baseline)_{it}$ is the average value-to-sales ratio in the industry in year t; $\varphi(Current\ Profitability)_{it}$ is the incremental sales multiplier due to firm profitability deviating from the industry average profitability in year t, and the other variables are defined as previously.

The multiplier correction for the differences in the firm profitability can be computed by estimating the following regression model on a set of comparable firms:

$$\varphi_{it} = \Sigma\ \varphi_{0,t} ^* Year_t + \varphi_{profitability} ^* Current\ Profitability_{it} + \eta_{it}, \quad (3.4)$$

where: φ_{it} is the enterprise value-to-sales ratio for firm i at time t, $Year_t$ is a set of dummy variables that take on the value of 1 if year $= t$ and zero otherwise, $\varphi_{0,t}$ is the set of regression intercepts for each year and a measure of industry average value-to-sales ratio in year t, $Current\ Profitablity_{it}$ is the measure of profitability margin for firm i in period t, and $\varphi_{profitability}$ is the estimated adjustment coefficient for value multiplier due to firm i accounting profitability deviating from the industry average level of profitability, and η_{it} is the regression error term.

EXTENDING THE BASIC MULTIPLIER-BASED VALUATION APPROACH TO ACCOUNT FOR THE ROLE OF BRAND PERCEPTIONS

Many accounting textbooks contend that the effects of intangible assets are reflected in the differences in current profitability margins of the firms. That is, firms with value-generating intangibles have higher profit margins. Further, they argue that separately accounting for intangibles is not appropriate as it would amount to double-counting their effects (Damodaran, 2002). However, to the extent that brand effects on profitability persist into the future and differ from the effects on current profits, for example, as a result of customer loyalty and attachment, brand impact might not be fully reflected in the differences in contemporaneous profitability metrics (Mizik and Jacobson, 2008). As such, brand assets might have an incremental direct impact on valuation multiples, over and above their effects on current accounting profitability margins.

In order to explicitly account for the direct effects of brand assets on firm valuation, equation (3.3) can be further extended as follows:

$$Firm\ Value_{it} = [\varphi(Baseline)_{it} + \varphi(Current\ Profitability)_{it} + \varphi(Brand)_{it}]^* Sales_{it}, \tag{3.5}$$

where: $\varphi(Brand)_{it}$ is the incremental sales multiplier due to the brand assets of a firm deviating from the industry average value of brand assets (i.e., the portion of brand effect that is not reflected in current profitability margins). The other variables are defined as previously.

Equation (3.5) allows estimating a conditional (profitability and brand perceptions) multiplier for business valuation. It contends that the differences in enterprise value within an industrial sector are driven by differences in contemporaneous profitability and differences in the levels of brand assets the firms possess. The impact of brand assets on enterprise valuation, thus, enters (a) directly through their effect on the level of multiplier $\varphi(Brand)_{it}$ and (b) indirectly through their effect on current profitability margins.

DATA

The following data items are needed for the firm being valued and for its comparable firms in order to undertake relative valuation: Enterprise Value, Operating Income, Sales, and Brand Perceptions. The enterprise value can be computed as $Enterprise\ Value_{it} = Market\ Cap_{it} + Debt_{it} + Minority\ Interest_{it} + Preferred\ Stock_{it} - Cash_{it}$. The data to compute the Enterprise Value and the Operating Income and Sales data can be obtained from the firms' financial statements or Center for Research in Security Prices (CRSP) and Compustat databases. These data can be used to compute enterprise value-to-sales ($\Phi = Enterprise\ Value/Sales$) and return on sales ($ROS = Operating\ Income/Sales$) needed for regression analysis.

The data on brand perceptions are less easily accessible and might need to be collected for each valuation exercise. Alternatively, some commercial vendors undertake systematic surveys of consumer attitudes and perceptions of brands and their data can be used in multiplier-based valuation.

For example, since 2000 the Young and Rubicam's BrandAsset Valuator (Y&R BAV) initiative has undertaken structured large-scale surveys of the US population to assess consumer perceptions of brands. The following perceptual brand measures are collected in the Y&R BAV database and are included in the valuation analysis here:

- Brand Differentiation – perceived distinctiveness of the brand;
- Brand Relevance – perceptions of personal relevance, appropriateness, and the importance of the brand;
- Brand Esteem – the level of regard consumers hold for the brand, which captures the valence of consumer attitude;
- Brand Knowledge – the level of familiarity with the brand and the understanding of the brand identity;
- Brand Energy[2] – perceptions of brand's innovativeness and dynamism, its ability to meet consumers' future needs and respond to changing environmental conditions and consumer tastes.

The Y&R BAV database contains 250 publicly traded mono-brand firms for the 2000–06 time period. These 250 firms are also listed in the Compustat and CRSP databases and have accounting and stock market data available to compute enterprise value-to-sales and earnings-to-sales ratios for a total of 1244 observations. These firms come from seven distinct industrial sectors: Industrial, Consumer Durables, Consumer Nondurables, High-technology, Finance, Travel & Transport, and Retail & Apparel.

REGRESSION ANALYSIS

The following model is derived from the model equation (3.5). It links the log of the enterprise value-to-sales ratio to return on sales, five perceptual brand metrics (Differentiation, Relevance, Esteem, Knowledge, and Energy), and a set of annual dummy variables. Using the logarithms of value-to-sales helps minimize the influence of outliers:

$$\log(\Phi_{it}) = \Sigma \; \varphi_{0,t} * Year_t + \varphi_{ros} * ROS_{it} + \Sigma \; \varphi_{brand\,asset\,b} * Brand$$
$$Asset_{bit} + \eta_{it}, \tag{3.6}$$

where: Φ_{it} is the enterprise value-to-sales ratio for firm i at time t, $Year_t$ is a set of dummy variables that take on the value of 1 if year $= t$ and zero otherwise, $\varphi_{0,t}$ is the set of regression intercepts for each year and a measure of industry average log (value-to-sales ratio) in year t, ROS is the measure of earnings-to-sales ratio for firm *i* in period *t*, and φ_{ros} is the estimated adjustment coefficient due to firm *i* accounting profitability deviating from the industry average profitability, *Brand Asset$_{bit}$* is the measure of perceptual brand measure *b* (e.g., Differentiation, Relevance, Esteem, Knowledge, and Energy) for firm *i* at time *t*, $\varphi_{brand\ asset\ b}$ is the estimated adjustment coefficient due to firm *i* perceptions of brand asset *b* deviating from the industry average value of brand asset *b*, and η_{it} is the regression error term.

Model (3.6) is estimated for the 250 firms as a group and for each of the seven sectors separately.

FINDINGS

Aggregate Analysis

The regression results for a simple valuation model (3.4) that includes the profitability ratio and sector-specific annual dummy variables on the aggregate data (i.e., across all 250 firms and all years) show that return on sales has a highly significant positive association with enterprise value-to-sales ratio. This finding is consistent with prior research: firms with higher profitability have greater value multiples than firms with lower profitability margins. The R-square statistic indicates that a simple model explains about 61 percent of the variation in the data, with return on sales accounting for about 60 percent of its explanatory power and the annual sector dummies accounting for the remaining 40 percent.

Estimating model (3.6), which in addition to ROS and sector-specific dummy variables also incorporates information about brand perceptions on the aggregate data sample, does not substantially improve the predictive power of the valuation model. The incremental explanatory power gained by adding brand variables to the model is very modest. The R-square statistic is only 3.6 percent greater than the R-square statistic derived from the model excluding brand perceptions data. The average absolute value of the in-sample forecast error for the model including brand perceptions is 0.382, which is only a 2.4 percent reduction compared to the 0.391 MAE for the model that does not include brand perceptions data. In sum, in the aggregate analysis, the brand variables provide only a negligible increase in predictive power of the valuation model.

Disaggregate Analysis: Sector-specific Brand Perceptions Effects

The disadvantage of the aggregate analysis is that it does not allow for differential impact of brand perceptions across different industrial groupings. If the brand perceptions have differential value implications across industrial sectors, aggregation might blur the effects and might lead to insignificant findings. Estimating equation (3.6) separately for each industrial sector shows that brand perceptions do indeed have very different impact on enterprise value-to-sales ratios and that incorporating information on brand perceptions significantly improves the accuracy of the value estimates in most sectors.

Results of the in-sample comparison of predictive performance for model (3.4) versus model (3.6) are presented in Table 3.1. For most industrial sectors, the addition of branding data significantly improves the forecast accuracy. Only in the Retail & Apparel sector is the impact of brand information limited. For the other six sectors, gains in valuation accuracy measured by mean absolute error range from 7 percent in Finance to 30 percent in the Consumer Durables sector. The average in-sample improvement in mean absolute error across these six sectors is 10 percent. The improvement in the forecast accuracy as measured by the sum of squared residuals varies between 25 percent in the Industrial sector and 10.8 percent in the Consumer Durables and Consumer Non-durables sectors. R-squared improves from 26 percent in the Consumer Durables and High-technology sectors to 5.6 percent in the Travel & Transport sector. Table 3.1 also highlights the specific perceptual brand metrics that show significant association with enterprise value-to-sales ratio across the industrial sectors and the magnitude of their impact.

It is interesting that no association between the brand perceptions and the enterprise value-to-sales ratio are found for the Retail & Apparel sector. Much of apparel products are highly branded and heavily advertised. Profit margin, however, is the only significant predictor of the value-to-sales ratio in the Retail & Apparel sector. One possible explanation for the apparent lack of significant findings here is that perhaps because tastes and preferences for apparel change very frequently with the seasonal fashions, current perceptions about apparel brands have only contemporaneous effects and little incremental predictive power after profitability margins are considered. In other words, the impact of brand perceptions is fully reflected in current-term profitability margins and does not impact future financial performance of the firms in the Retail & Apparel sector. If so, brand perceptions in this sector are not relevant for enterprise valuation as they do not have a staying power and current profitability margin is a sufficient metric that fully reflects the value implications of brand perceptions. Alternatively, it is possible that brand perceptions do matter, but it is other perceptual dimensions than those included in the present analysis that are relevant for valuation in this sector.

*Table 3.1   Predictive peformance of forecast models with and without
brand perceptions data in-sample*

Sector	% Improvement in the Mean Absolute Forecast Error with the Addition of Brand Metrics	% Improvement in the Sum of Squared Residuals with the Addition of Brand Metrics	% Improvement in the R-square with the Addition of Brand Metrics	Perceptual Brand Metrics Affecting Enterprise Valuation and their Standardized Impact
High-tech	7.0	15.4	25.7	**Differentiation (+0.185)** **Relevance (+0.416)** Esteem (n/s) **Knowledge (−0.287)** Energy (n/s)
Industrial	17.4	24.5	14.3	Differentiation (n/s) Relevance (n/s) Esteem (n/s) Knowledge (n/s) **Energy (+0.148)**
Consumer Durables	30.2	10.8	25.9	**Differentiation (+0.304)** Relevance (n/s) Esteem (n/s) Knowledge (n/s) Energy (n/s)
Consumer Non-durables	9.3	10.8	3.6	Differentiation (n/s) Relevance (n/s) Esteem (n/s) **Knowledge (+0.191)** Energy (n/s)
Finance	7.6	22.1	11.2	**Differentiation (+0.472)** Relevance (n/s) Esteem (n/s) Knowledge (n/s) Energy (n/s)
Travel & Transport	15.7	24.9	5.6	**Differentiation (+0.383)** Relevance (n/s) Esteem (n/s) Knowledge (n/s) Energy (n/s)
Retail & Apparel	2.4	2.3	1.8	Differentiation (n/s) Relevance (n/s) Esteem (n/s) Knowledge (n/s) Energy (n/s)

Note: n/s = not significant.

Model Performance Analysis: Out-of-sample Validation

Y&R BAV data collection surveys were also undertaken prior to 2000 and two waves of that are available for 1997 and 1999. These data were not used in the analyses summarized in Table 3.1 but were set aside for assessing the out-of-sample performance of equation model (3.6). That is, the estimates obtained from the study sample data (2000–06 period) can be used to compute adjustments to the enterprise value-to-sales multipliers for 1997 and 1999 data. Incorporating the estimated brand-related multiplier adjustments to the 1997 and 1999 multipliers significantly improves the valuation accuracy in this hold-out sample. The mean absolute error of the enterprise value forecasts is reduced by an average of 16 percent across the industrial sectors considered in the study.

PRACTICAL APPLICATION OF THE CONDITIONAL MULTIPLIERS: AN ILLUSTRATION FOR HEWLETT-PACKARD VALUATION IN 2005

Illustrating the application and performance of the conditional multiplier model requires an example where the enterprise value-to-sales multiplier is known. This setting allows demonstrating and assessing improvements in the accuracy of enterprise valuation across different valuation models. The case of Hewlett-Packard is presented for this purpose.

The Hewlett-Packard brand was compromised in 2005. Early that year the then CEO Carly Fiorina was ousted due to the popular perception that the company lacked strategic direction and vision and that its acquisitions of Compaq and Bluestone were unsuccessful. Table 3.2 presents the estimates of the enterprise value-to-sales ratio for Hewlett-Packard for 2005 using three alternative valuation models. Model (3.2) is just a simple average enterprise value-to-sales ratio in the high-technology sector in 2005. That is, it ignores the value implications of differences in profitability margins and the value implications of differences in brand perceptions. Model (3.4) is the average high-tech sector multiple in 2005 adjusted for Hewlett-Packard's profitability margins. Model (3.6) is the average high-technology enterprise value-to-sales sector multiple adjusted for both, Hewlett-Packard's profitability margins and its brand perceptions.

In the four quarters of 2005 HP reported a total of $86,696m in revenue. Its enterprise value was $76,298m. As such, the actual enterprise value-to-sales ratio for Hewlett-Packard was 0.88. Valuation models (3.2), (3.4), and (3.6) generate very different estimates of the value multiplier. If the enterprise value-to-sales ratio for HP were not known but needed to be

Table 3.2   Estimating the Hewlett-Packard enterprise value-to-sales ratio for 2005

	Data Inputs[a]		Estimated Model Parameters		Predicted Multiplier		
	2005 high-tech sector average	2005 HP input data	Estimated adjustment coefficient for return on sales	Estimated adjustment coefficients for return on sales and brand effects	Based on sector peer group only	Based on sector peer group and return on sales	Based on sector peer group, return on sales, and brand perceptions
			Model (3.4)	Model (3.6)			
Value-to-sales	2.823				2.823	1.317	0.966
log(value-to-sales)	0.762						
Return on sales	0.214	0.084	3.74	3.98			
Differentiation	−0.315	−0.760		0.185			
Relevance	−0.293	1.072		0.416			
Esteem	−0.466	1.437		−0.207			
Knowledge	−0.635	0.799		−0.287			
Energy	0.318	0.732		0.098			

Note: [a]   All brand variables are z-standardized.

Legend:
In the four calendar quarters of 2005, HP had sales of $86696m and its enterprise value was $76298m. The predicted enterprise value-to-sales multiplier for HP in 2005, which is assumed to be unknown, is, in fact, 0.88.

(i)   Using the high-tech sector mean multiplier value provides an estimate of 2.82.
(ii)   If both the sector mean multiplier and the difference in profitability between HP and the sector are considered, the estimated multiplier is 1.317. This figure is computed based on the exponentiation of the logarithm of the high-tech sector average multiplier of 0.762 plus the estimated coefficient for return on sales in equation (3.4) times the difference in HP return on sales from the sector average $1.317 = \exp(0.762 + (3.74)*[(0.084)-(0.214)])$.
(iii)   If the sector mean multiplier, the difference in HP profitability from the sector, and the differences in HP brand perceptions from the sector mean are considered, the estimated multiplier is 0.9658. This figure is computed based on the exponentiation of the logarithm of the high-tech sector average multiplier of 0.762 plus the estimated coefficient for return on sales in equation (3.6) times the difference in HP return on sales and from the sector average, and the estimated coefficients for the brand assets times the differences in HP brand assets from the sector average; i.e., $0.9658 = \exp(0.762 + (3.98)*[(0.084)-(0.214)] + (0.185)*[(-0.760)-(-0.315)] + (0.416)*[(1.072)-(-0.293)] + (-0.207)*[(1.437)-(-0.466)] + (-0.287)*[(0.799)-(-0.635)] + (0.098)*[(0.732)-(0.318)])$.

Source: This example is drawn from Mizik and Jacobson (2009).

predicted (i.e., the enterprise value data were not available), the simple mean value of the enterprise value-to-sales ratio for the high-technology firms in 2005 could be used. This estimate is 2.82.

A better valuation approach would incorporate Hewlett-Packard's profitability into the analysis. That is, the parameter estimate of the impact profitability margins have on enterprise value-to-sales ratio (model (3.4)) could be used in conjunction with the data on Hewlett-Packard's actual return on sales to generate a better prediction for Hewlett-Packard's value multiplier. This method reflects not just the sector average multiplier but also the difference in Hewlett-Packard's return on sales relative to the sector average return on sales. It generates a better estimate of enterprise value-to-sales multiplier of 1.317.

The conditional valuation multiplier model (3.6) takes into account all three factors, the industry mean value of the multiplier, Hewlett-Packard's current-term profit margins, and the extent to which the perceptions of Hewlett-Packard's brand differ from the average brand perceptions in the high-tech sector. Making use of the estimated parameters from model (3.6), along with the actual Hewlett-Packard's measures of return on sales and brand perceptions, generates a value multiplier of 0.9658, which is much closer to the actual value of Hewlett-Packard's enterprise value-to-sales.

This illustration shows that the 2005 high-tech sector average multiplier (2.83) substantially overstates the actual Hewlett-Packard's enterprise value-to-sales ratio (0.88). Incorporating Hewlett-Packard's data to adjust the average sector ratio significantly enhances its enterprise value forecast. Substantial improvement is achieved by taking into account the extent to which Hewlett-Packard's profitability differs from the average profitability in the high-tech sector. The estimated multiplier decreases to 1.317. Further improvement in accuracy is gained by incorporating consumer perceptions of Hewlett-Packard's brand. The estimated multiplier is 0.9658, which is much closer to the actual value of 0.88.

IMPLICATIONS AND FUTURE RESEARCH DIRECTIONS

Highly branded businesses are different from other businesses. They often derive much of their value from their valuable intangible asset – the brand. Traditional valuation approaches fall short trying to estimate their enterprise value. Directly incorporating measures of brand perceptions into a multiplier-based valuation of branded businesses improves out-of-sample valuation accuracy by an average of 16 percent.

The methodological advances documenting the incremental benefit of directly incorporating information regarding the levels of intangible assets firms possess into the valuation model undoubtedly have important practical value. Conditional multipliers allow for a more accurate valuation of branded businesses.

The analyses presented in this chapter rely on proprietary data of consumer brand perceptions collected by Y&R BAV initiative for mono-brand firms. The valuation method, however, can easily be extended to multi-brand and multi-SBU (strategic business unit) firms by estimating the value of individual SBUs and aggregating their estimated enterprise value. Further, this methodology does not depend on a specific data source and is amenable to other brand perceptions data sources and metrics. In fact, because the multiplier-based valuation is undertaken for a specific business at a specific point in time (only cross-sectional data for the valuation target and its comparable peers is needed), rather than relying on a syndicated data collection service the data collection can be undertaken through a survey for each specific valuation exercise individually, as needed. The costs of such data collection can also be kept to a minimum by focusing on the most predictive perceptual metrics for a given industrial sector.

In addition, the conditional multiplier valuation model also sets up a framework for incorporating the value implications of other perceptual brand metrics and other types of intangible assets. The regression equation used to capture the incremental impact of brand perceptions (model (3.6)) be further extended to capture the value implications of other intangible assets.

For example, in the Hewlett-Packard valuation illustration presented above, the actual enterprise value-to-sales ratio for Hewlett-Packard in the prior year (2004) was 0.68, significantly below its 2005 value of 0.88. The predicted enterprise value-to-sales ratio for 2004 based on model (3.6), however, was 1.07, which is greater than the predicted value for 2005 reported in Table 3.2 (0.966). In other words, the model (3.6) prediction error has a greater negative value in 2004 compared to that of 2005. Although this result could be a mere estimation error, it is consistent with certain events taking place at Hewlett-Packard in 2004 that are not related to consumer perceptions of its brand and are not directly incorporated into the valuation model. Specifically, Carly Fiorina drew heavy criticism in 2004 and was dismissed as the Chairman of the Board and CEO in early 2005. The troubles at the top of the management team could have contributed to increased negative expectations regarding Hewlett-Packard's future performance, which drove down the enterprise value of Hewlett-Packard (and its enterprise value-to-sales ratio) in 2004.

As such, further improvements in forecasting accuracy of enterprise value might be achieved by extending the conditional multiplier valuation methodology to incorporate information about other value-relevant measurable tangible and intangible assets of the firm. Future research can build on the conditional multiplier framework to establish the value implications of management quality, product market strategy, innovation intensity, patents, and product pipelines.

One important lesson that comes from the analyses of conditional multipliers and the role of brand perceptions in enterprise valuation discussed in this chapter is that all such analyses should be sector-specific. The analyses indicate that value implications of tangible and intangible assets and their impact on firm valuation can differ dramatically across different industries.

NOTES

1. In the accounting literature several recent studies have examined the multiplier-based valuation (e.g., Liu et al., 2002, 2007).
2. The construct of Brand Energy was developed in Mizik and Jacobson (2008) and is discussed in detail in Gerzema and Lebar (2008).

REFERENCES

Bajaj, Mukesh, David J. Denis, and Atulya Sarin (2003), 'Mean Reversion in Earnings and the Use of E/P Multiples in Corporate Valuation,' *Journal of Applied Finance*, **14** (1), 4–10.

Barth, Mary E., William H. Beaver, and Wayne R. Landsman (1998), 'Relative Valuation Roles of Equity Book Value and Net Income as a Function of Financial Health,' *Journal of Accounting and Economics*, **25** (1), 1–33.

Barth, Mary E., John A. Elliott, and Mark W. Finn (1999), 'Market Rewards Associated with Patterns of Increasing Earnings,' *Journal of Accounting Research*, **37** (2), 387–413.

Damodaran, Aswath (2002), *Investment Valuation: Tools and Techniques for Determining the Value of Any Asset*, New York: John Wiley and Sons.

Gerzema, John and Ed Lebar (2008), *Brand Bubble*, New York: Wiley.

Gilson, Stuart C., Edith S. Hotchkiss, and Richard S. Ruback (2000), 'Valuation of Bankrupt Firms,' *Review of Financial Studies*, **13** (1), 43–74.

Liu, Jing, Doron Nissim, and Jacob Thomas (2002), 'Equity Valuation Using Multiples,' *Journal of Accounting Research*, **40** (1), 135–62.

Liu, Jing, Doron Nissim, and Jacob Thomas (2007), 'Is Cash Flow King in Valuations?' *Financial Analysts Journal*, **63** (2), 1–13.

Mizik, Natalie and Robert Jacobson (2008), 'The Financial Value Impact of Perceptual Brand Attributes,' *Journal of Marketing Research*, **45** (1), 15–32.

Mizik, Natalie and Robert Jacobson (2009), 'Valuing Branded Businesses,' *Journal of Marketing*, **73** (6), 137–53.

4 Financial portfolio theory and customer management: insights and research directions

Michael D. Hutt, Crina O. Tarasi and Beth A. Walker

For an investor, financial portfolio theory demonstrates that optimal performance, for a given level of risk, can best be achieved by building a diversified mix of investment assets that includes the stocks of both large and small firms, drawn from diverse industry sectors and representing both US and foreign companies. In building a customer portfolio, similar benefits can be realized by diversifying across different customer categories. To illustrate, after the technology bubble, many information technology (IT) companies, like IBM and Microsoft, were surprised to observe that small and medium-sized business (SMBs) fueled the recovery in IT spending (Veverka, 2003). Why? Most of the SMB customers did not overindulge in massive hardware and software upgrades to the same extreme extent during the bubble as their large enterprise counterparts did. So, SMB customers were the first to return and aggressively buy IT products and services. As a result, those IT firms that devoted a meaningful weighting to SMB organizations in the customer portfolio enjoyed an edge over rivals that were less focused on this customer group and were 'caught waiting' for large enterprise customers to return.

Traditional treatments of market segmentation in textbooks and in the broader marketing literature fail to address the issue of risk or to consider the way in which a particular combination of segments might advance or inhibit firm performance during different stages of a business cycle or under different economic scenarios. By highlighting the role that risk management tools can assume in managing the customer assets of the firm, we believe that a financial portfolio perspective presents important implications for the way in which market segmentation and customer portfolio management are conceptualized, practiced, and taught.

In support of a customer portfolio view, Drèze and Bonfrer (2009) demonstrate the performance advantages that a firm can gain by maximizing the value of the overall customer base (customer equity) rather than the customer lifetime value (CLV) of individual customers. 'CLV computes the value of *a customer* to the firm while customer equity (CE) measures the value of *all present and future customers* given a firm's marketing actions (e.g., acquisition policy, marketing mix)' (p. 290; emphasis in original). They find that maximizing CLV is suboptimal from a customer equity (CE) perspective. Firms that optimize CLV generate lower profits and retain fewer customers than those that optimize CE.

Consistent with an emphasis on financial accountability for marketing actions, recent research has often focused on the association between marketing actions and business performance or shareholder value (Srinivasan and Hanssens, 2009). Many studies have focused on the effect of market-based assets (customer equity, customer satisfaction, brand quality) and marketing actions (product innovation and advertising) on company risk. Investments in R&D and advertising result in lower systematic risk, that is, the risk associated with the market (McAlister et al., 2007). However, radical innovation, even though it increases normal and abnormal profits, increases overall company risk due to its higher variability (Sorescu and Spanjol, 2008). Customer satisfaction reduces not only cash flow variability (Gruca and Rego, 2005), but also the systematic and idiosyncratic risk, and also insulates firms in downturns (Tuli and Bharadwaj, 2009). Idiosyncratic risk is the variability in the value of an asset that cannot be explained by variations in the market and systematic risk is the variability that can be explained by variations in the market.

This stream of research focuses on firm-level measures of risk whereas managers also require an understanding of the underlying mechanisms that link the risk–return profiles of individual customers (or market segments) to the risk–return profile of the firm. Recently, Tuli et al. (2010) have shown that, at a customer level, the number of ties a company builds with its best customers ensures not only higher revenue, but also reduces the variability of their purchases. Their study suggests that it may be possible to manage risk through firm actions, but as yet there is little or no evidence that managers consider such risk–return tradeoffs in their marketing decisions. We extend their work by showing that the firm can manage its portfolio of customer relationships to control the overall variability of the firm's cash flow. We show that the risk associated with an individual customer does not arise solely from the probability of defection (which is accounted for in the calculation of customer lifetime value); it also arises from variability in their purchases. Moreover, we show that individual customer risk influences the risk of the entire customer base and (consequently) the company's risk.

The chapter explores how financial portfolio theory can be applied to customer management. First, we review key studies from marketing and regional economics that apply financial portfolio theory, demonstrating the promise of the approach to customer management. Second, we examine how key constructs from financial portfolio theory can be applied in managing customer assets. Customer risk metrics are offered that managers can use to assess the reward-on-risk for customers. Third, we highlight how these measures can be used for customer management and highlight results from a recent study of a B2B firm's customer base (Tarasi et al., 2011a). Finally, guidelines for implementing our portfolio approach along with the associated research implications are detailed.

CUSTOMER PORTFOLIO RESEARCH: EMERGING PERSPECTIVES

Our approach is informed by two literature streams, one in the marketing discipline and a more developed research tradition in regional economics.

Financial Portfolio Applications from Marketing

Marketers have long recognized that the 'customer is a financial asset that companies and organizations should measure, manage and maximize, just like any other asset' (Blattberg et al., 2001, p. 3; see also Rust et al., 2004). To that end, the CLV research tradition offers valuable insights into how profitability can be enhanced by selecting the right customers for targeting and determining the allocation of resources for acquisition, retention, and expansion (e.g., Kumar et al., 2006). For instance, Kumar and his colleagues (2008) demonstrate how the successful implementation of the CLV-based approach at IBM resulted in increased productivity from marketing investments targeted to SMB customers. Other studies seek to guide marketing managers in taking actions that maximize the value of the overall customer portfolio.

Johnson and Selnes (2004) offer a dynamic theory for exploring the nature and evolution of exchange relationships across the customer portfolio of a firm. They assert that the framework 'should open the eyes of the marketing community to focus more on accumulated value creation of a customer portfolio, not on the value created in single relationships' (p. 15). For example, newly acquired customers may become more profitable over time while customers that are highly profitable today may not maintain that status tomorrow. If a firm specializes in creating close relationships with existing customers at the expense of acquiring new ones, profitability decreases dramatically.

Employing dynamic customer portfolio analysis, Homburg et al. (2009) find that static models overestimate the value of top-tier customers and underestimate the value of bottom-tier customers. In line with Johnson and Selnes (2004), they also find that offensive, rather than defensive, strategies have a greater impact on customer value for bottom-tier segments. Customer equity can be increased substantially by sustaining middle segments and by actively promoting the move of bottom-tier customers to middle-tier segments.

Recent research demonstrates the potential value that financial portfolio theory may contribute to customer portfolio management. Dhar and Glazer (2003) demonstrate the critical importance of measuring the riskiness of customers (i.e., customer beta) and illustrate how a firm can maximize returns by acquiring or retaining particular customers or market segments on the basis of how their purchasing patterns contribute to the diversification of the cash flow of the overall customer portfolio. They assert that a portfolio of customers selected on the basis of risk-adjusted CLV will generate higher returns for a given level of risk than one assembled without regard to the risk profile of customers and their effect on the resulting portfolio.

Ryals (2002, 2003) also adopts a financial theory perspective to examine the risk and return characteristics of a customer portfolio and describe how a customer relationship scorecard can be used to assess customer risk. For a particular customer, the relationship scorecard might consider criteria such as probability of defection, payment history, purchasing volatility, and related dimensions. The weighted average cost of capital (WACC) discount rate used to calculate CLV can then be adjusted based on the risk associated with that customer.

Buhl and Heinrich (2008) offer an approach that a firm can use to balance the risk–return profile of its customer portfolio. They argue that CLV research ignores the fact that the risks associated with one customer segment may be balanced by other, less risky segments. Therefore, their quantitative model considers (1) the expected CLV of different customer segments that comprise the portfolio, (2) the risks associated with the estimation of uncertain cash flows, as well as (3) the correlation between the cash flows of different customer segments. Using a case study from the financial services industry, Buhl and Heinrich demonstrate how their model contributes a new optimized customer portfolio that provides higher return and a lower level of risk than the existing portfolio. By identifying target segments that provide better risk diversification and gradually adjusting market segment weightings over time, they suggest that a firm can move toward an optimal portfolio composition.

Kundisch et al. (2008) also apply financial portfolio theory to the issue of customer portfolio optimization. Using a publicly available data set from an online retailer, the researchers examined the purchase histories for over 2300 customers and segmented the customer base into two groups: relationship- and transaction-oriented customers. The average cash flow per purchase provides the foundation for calculating the CLV of each customer segment and risk represents the standard deviation of the CLV within a customer segment. The findings reveal that an optimal portfolio mix includes a representation of both relationship- and transaction-oriented customers. Therefore, while centering strictly on loyal customers might appear to represent the ideal strategy focus, the overall expected utility of the customer portfolio markedly improves by building a balanced portfolio of relationship- and transaction-oriented customers to stabilize cash flows.

Financial Portfolio Applications from Regional Economics

While relatively few studies in marketing have employed financial portfolio theory, the approach has been used to inform economic development strategies at multiple levels of analysis. By applying financial portfolio theory to the analysis of economic diversification, Conroy (1974) launched a major research stream in regional economics (see Dissart, 2003 for a comprehensive review). In this context, a region represents a portfolio and the assets include the industries that make up the local economy whereby each industry yields a return in the form of employment but also a risk in the form of employment variations. A large portfolio variance indicates greater instability in the local economy (greater employment fluctuations around its long-term trends) (Dissart, 2003). Importantly, this approach examines both the internal variability of each industry asset (the employment variance) as well as how each industry's pattern-of-employment fluctuations reinforce or offset those of other industries (the covariances). For example, a negative correlation between two industries indicates countercyclical fluctuations, which tend to stabilize regional employment (Kurre and Weller, 1996).

This portfolio management framework has been used to examine the growth–instability tradeoffs of metropolitan areas (e.g., Conroy, 1974), individual states and the US economy (e.g., Lande, 1994), and international regions, including Western Europe (Chandra, 2003). To illustrate, Lande (ibid.) examines the economic structure of several states, identifying those industry sectors that promote employment growth and stability in an optimal portfolio. Of course, regional policy-makers do not have the same degree of control over their portfolios as do investors and there may be high costs and significant time lags associated with changing the industrial mix of a local economy (Siegel et al., 1995). Moreover, empirical results suffer from the rather unrealistic assumption of easy transferability of workers from one industry to another. However, financial portfolio theory provides a valuable framework that public policy-makers can use to secure special insights into the way in which different industry sectors can compensate for one another when business cycles or external shocks occur. Collectively, studies from the regional economics research tradition lend strong support to our view that financial portfolio theory may provide a valuable framework for evaluating and managing a customer portfolio, particularly for business-to-business firms that serve customers drawn from diverse industry sectors.

CONCEPTUAL FRAMEWORK

This section examines financial portfolio theory and explores the relationship between customer cash flow stability and shareholder value. Special attention is also given to the crucial differences that exist between customer portfolios and financial portfolios.

Financial Portfolio Theory

Financial portfolio theory posits that, even though assets are selected individually, performance is measured on the entire portfolio, where there is a tradeoff between risk and return (Markowitz, 1952). Through diversification, a portfolio of assets enables investors to realize positive returns with lower levels of risk than would be possible by holding any given individual asset. The degree to which a portfolio is diversified depends on: (1) the relative share or proportion that each individual asset represents in a portfolio; (2) the number of different asset classes in the portfolio; and (3) the covariances between returns on the different assets in the portfolio. In a stock portfolio, the lower the correlation of a stock with the total return, the more desirable that particular stock is to the portfolio.

Based on the variability and return of each of the assets, the optimal (efficient) portfolio is considered to be the one that has the least risk for a desired level of return or the highest level of return for a certain level of risk. The set of efficient portfolios form the efficient frontier, which borders the set of all possible portfolios.

The mathematical framework of financial portfolio theory includes two assumptions that spawn criticism. First, asset returns are assumed to be normally distributed. However, recent events demonstrate that market returns are 'fat tailed' rather than following a normal bell-curve distribution process; that is, large changes in asset prices are more likely than presumed in the portfolio construction framework. For example, the S&P 500 stock index has experienced a three-standard deviation monthly return event ten times since 1926, while a normal distribution would predict such extreme returns perhaps one or two times (Kaplan, 2009). Second, financial portfolio theory assumes that the correlations between assets are stable. However, during periods of severe market stress, like the global financial crisis in fall 2008, assets that were previously found to be uncorrelated can suddenly move together (e.g., Hubbard, 2009).

The efficient portfolio concept has also received criticism. To illustrate, DeMiguel et al. (2007) examine 14 different optimal portfolio models that have been advanced in the finance literature, based largely on the capital asset pricing model (CAPM) and find that none is better than a naive approach where an investor allocates a fraction of wealth to each of the available assets. Importantly, however, our approach differs from the CAPM, which assumes that the market portfolio includes all available assets where each asset is weighted by its market capitalization (see Buhl and Heinrich, 2008 for a critique of CAPM in the customer portfolio context). By contrast, as detailed later, we define the market portfolio as the existing customer base of a firm.

Cash Flow Stability and Firm Value

Extending the work of Srivastava et al. (1998), we theorize that the market-based assets of a firm include distinct customer asset classes that are characterized by differing degrees of cash flow variability and vulnerability. Customer asset classes represent the market segments that comprise the existing customer base and embody the outcomes of relationships between the firm and its customers. While investment portfolio decisions involve choices within and among various asset classes of stocks and bonds, customer portfolio decisions involve choices within and among distinct customer asset classes (e.g., governance type, size, industry) that encompass both new and existing customers in the served market and present different risk–return profiles for the firm (Tarasi et al., 2011a).

Table 4.1 contrasts the way in which the asset classes that may comprise an investment portfolio might be aligned with those of a customer portfolio. For example, IBM's customer portfolio features a blend of large enterprise customers, domestic and international, as well as SMB customers, and the firm employs a strategy designed to create long-term relationships that are facilitated by its wide array of services and software offerings. A Wall Street analyst aptly observes: 'Revenue is not the goal at IBM. Its model is about pursuing higher-margin recurring revenue and reducing volatility' (Lohr, 2010). Since the more stable services and software businesses now account for the bulk of IBM's revenue, the firm is less

Table 4.1   Parallel between investment classes and customer segments

Investment Portfolio	Customer Portfolio
Blue chip stocks 　Stock of companies with long 　　operating history, steady earnings 　　and good reputation 　No return is guaranteed, but among 　　stocks, they have the lowest risk 　Little overall growth	Large enterprise customers, long-term relationships 　No return is guaranteed, but trust 　　and commitment have developed 　Predictable 　May not be associated with high 　　growth or high profitability
Medium and small company stocks 　High growth potential 　High risk 　Countercyclical with large company 　　stock	Medium and small business customers 　High growth potential 　High risk 　Often countercyclical with large 　　customers
International stocks 　High growth potential 　High risk (political, exchange rate) 　Report with different accounting 　　systems 　Often countercyclical with other 　　regions/countries	International customers 　Higher growth potential 　Higher risk (political, exchange rate) 　Often countercyclical with other 　　regions/countries
High-quality bonds (AAA) 　High degree of certainty since both 　　the timing and the size of cash flow 　　is known 　Low risk of defaulting 　Presence in the portfolio reduces 　　overall risk	Long-term contracts/close relationships 　Contracts by definition reduce 　　risk and uncertainty in exchange 　　relationships 　The long-term collaboration allows 　　for trust and commitment to 　　develop
Medium-quality bonds (AA to BBB) 　Relatively secure 　Higher return/risk 　Constant rate of return	New contracts 　The short term of the collaboration 　　makes the outcome more 　　uncertain 　Trust and commitment have not yet 　　developed
Treasury securities 　Highly predictable 　Lowest risk (and return)	Rigid contracts 　Highly predictable 　Lowest return

tied to the cyclical swings of the hardware business than many technology companies.

In support of a customer portfolio focus, Gupta et al. (2004, p.9) assert that 'customers are indeed assets, and therefore customer-related expenditures should be treated as investments rather than expenses.'

They demonstrate how the value of the customer base provides a strong guideline for firm value. By representing risky assets, Hogan et al. (2002) argue that valuation methods must consider both the profitability and the associated risks of a customer segment. However, the existing portfolio of most firms reflects incremental and uncoordinated decisions from the past where little attention was given to how newly acquired customers contribute to the profitability and risk of the entire portfolio.

Dhar and Glazer (2003, p. 88) observe that few companies bother to consider 'whether all of their individually desirable customers are, from the standpoint of risk, desirable collectively.' In choosing among customers to add to a portfolio, the less a customer's purchasing behavior promises to be like that of the current portfolio, the stronger its contribution to the stability and predictability of the portfolio; the more the behavior is like that of the existing portfolio, the weaker its contribution.

By developing a risk-adjusted customer portfolio to achieve profit targets, marketing managers can contribute to firm value. Research demonstrates that investors favor stable earnings over volatile earnings (Ang et al., 2006; Srinivasan and Hanssens, 2009) and cash flows that are more stable and predictable reduce working capital needs (Srivastava et al., 1997; Rao and Bharadwaj, 2008). Therefore, managers can enhance shareholder value by reducing the vulnerability and volatility of cash flows from the customer portfolio (Tarasi et al., 2011a).

Financial Versus Customer Portfolios

Although customers, like stocks, represent risky assets and the cost of acquiring them should reflect the cash flow they are expected to generate over time, key differences exist between a financial portfolio and a customer portfolio concerning the nature of the assets, returns, and uncertainty (see Table 4.2).

Assets
Financial assets can be purchased in parcels of any size but customer assets are not infinitely divisible. In turn, a desired financial asset can be identified and readily purchased while there is no assurance that a marketing investment will successfully attract a targeted customer to the portfolio. Moreover, once attracted, continuing investments are required to retain the customer in the portfolio. By contrast, during the holding period, a financial portfolio incurs minimal maintenance expenses.

Compared to customer portfolio managers, investors also readily adjust the portfolio by selling assets at a market price and by changing the weight assigned to particular asset classes. Since there is no liquid market for cus-

Table 4.2 *Financial versus customer portfolios: profiling some key differences*

	Financial Portfolio	Customer Portfolio
Assets	Infinitely divisible	Not infinitely divisible
	Liquid market	Relatively illiquid market
	Portfolio adjustments can be readily made	Portfolio adjustments involve higher transaction and access costs
	Price of a security set by market	Price of a new customer defined by acquisition costs
	Security holdings incur minimal maintenance costs	Existing customers require continuing investments
Return	Capital appreciation (or loss) plus cash yield	Cash flow and profit plus learning, network effects, and referrals
	Return is independent of amount invested	Nonlinear returns from customer asset investments
	Portfolio weight of asset does not impact asset return	Portfolio weight of customer segment impacts returns (e.g., increasing returns to scale)
	Investor cannot influence the return on an asset	Managerial actions influence customer returns
Uncertainty	Variability of expected versus realized return	Variability of expected cash flow and profit versus realized returns plus probability of defection

tomer assets (Kundisch et al., 2008) and customer divestment raises a host of sensitive relationship management issues, corresponding adjustments in the structure of the customer portfolio may be costly and difficult to implement, particularly over a short time horizon.

Return

For the customer portfolio, return is the cash flow and profit (revenue minus cost-to-serve) that accrue to the firm from investments directed to individual customers and market segments (see Table 4.2). However, by potentially providing positive word-of-mouth, learning, or brand-building opportunities, this measure captures but one of the many sources of value customers may provide. Likewise, unlike a financial portfolio where the rate of return is independent of the amount invested, the returns from investing in customers are likely to be nonlinear (Johnson and Selnes, 2004). For example, small marketing investments might be insufficient to attract or retain an individual customer or market segment.

Managerial control represents one of the unique characteristics that distinguish customer investments from financial investments (Devinney and Stewart, 1988). For example, marketing managers can enhance returns by identifying elements of its customer strategy mix that provide the greatest marginal return on additional investments (Bowman and Narayandas, 2004). In adding an asset to a financial portfolio, an investor cannot control the risk and return of that asset. By contrast, the weight a manager assigns to a market segment may affect performance because of increasing or decreasing returns to scale (Johnson and Selnes, 2004).

Uncertainty
Investment uncertainty represents the variability, or risk, in the return of a security or the deviation of the return from expected value during the holding period. For the customer portfolio, the measure of risk is the deviation of customer cash flow and profit from their expected values. Of course, there are other sources of uncertainty that are unique to the customer portfolio, including the risk of defection or a decline in share-of-wallet. Therefore, customer cash flow stability provides a rather narrow measure of the strength or quality of a customer relationship.

Although important differences are evident, a common unifying goal guides the management of customer as well as financial portfolios: to achieve a desired rate of profit (return) over a specified time period without exceeding the firm's (investor's) risk tolerance. Our conceptualization of risk, which captures the risk–return characteristics of the overall customer portfolio, complements and extends past research on customer management that examines other types of risk such as the risk of defection or the probability of achieving customer lifetime value outcomes (e.g., Blattberg et al., 2001; Rust et al., 2004; Bolton et al., 2008).

TOWARD AN EFFICIENT CUSTOMER PORTFOLIO

This section explores customer risk characteristics and the process that managers can follow to build an efficient customer portfolio. A field application of customer portfolio analysis is highlighted.

Customer Lifetime Value and Risk

Prior studies center on customers' contribution to cash flow from the perspective of enhancing expected revenues or margins. Studies of CLV or 'customer equity' (i.e., the value of the customer base) are numerous and they usually measure the discounted value that customers provide to the firm (e.g., Blattberg and Deighton, 1996). Organizations can use forecasts of customer equity, under different scenarios, to determine the amount to invest in acquiring, retaining, and recovering these customers who will maximize return on investment. However, Johnson and Selnes (2005, p. 10) warn that 'when analyzing the forest rather than the trees, weaker customer relationships, judged unprofitable on a CLV basis, may, over time, actually create value as a part of a broader portfolio.' In other words, focusing on the magnitude of cash flow from customers (i.e., expected returns) reveals only half of the story. Managers also need to understand the influence of customers on the volatility and variability of cash flows. Thus, both returns (CLV) and risk (variance) are relevant to customer portfolio decisions.

CLV calculations reflect both risk and return by discounting cash flows using a risk-adjusted rate of return to estimate net present value. Firms often use a single discount rate, the weighted average cost of capital. A second approach, called the certainty equivalent approach, explicitly adjusts cash flow streams for various risk factors – usually the probability of defection – and then discounts them at the risk-free rate (e.g., Hogan et al., 2002). A third approach recognizes risk factors other than defection by calculating CLV using a risk-adjusted discounted rate rather than a weighted average cost of capital. Hogan et al. (ibid.) suggest that this task can be accomplished by either measuring the variance of returns over time for various segments and calculating the appropriate discount rate – analogously to the evaluation of real options – or decomposing customer profitability into additional sources. For example, Ryals (2002) used the capital asset pricing model to assess the risk associated with individual customers and used this information to adjust the worth of each customer. However, prior research has not evaluated the combined risk of customers, the effect of the individual customer risk on the overall risk to the firm, or offered methods for building a customer portfolio. We suggest that the firm can select and invest in customers in a manner that can optimize the customer base and the overall customer cash flow.

Our approach analyzes the combined effect of customers on cash flows (i.e., looking beyond calculations of individual customer CLV) to calculate risk and return implications for the firm. Since cash flow is a highly sensitive measure of financial health, we consider how diversity in the customer base contributes to cash flow magnitude and variability. We also characterize the conditions under which it is better to have a diversified customer base and provide systematic criteria to guide diversification of the customer portfolio (trading off risk and return). Our theoretical approach is based on research from the finance literature, research on market segmentation and customer valuation, and the relationship marketing literature.

Why is it important to understand how the structure of the customer base affects cash flow? Researchers have argued that the market value of a firm is highly dependent on the customer equity accumulated (Gupta et al., 2004; Rust et al., 2004). However, in the financial markets, the value of the firm is also dependent on the risk associated with the firm and its future cash flows. Under these conditions, reducing the risk associated with the customer base will directly enhance shareholder value. In financial markets, investors have no potential effect on the performance of assets, while in the case of the customer portfolio – through its customer strategy – the company can actually affect the level of purchases, giving it one more element of control over the customer risk and purchasing patterns.

Building Efficient Customer Portfolios

Building efficient customer portfolios means identifying optimal portfolios that allow a company to minimize risk for a desired level of return or maximize return for a desired level of risk (Markowitz, 1959). Using the covariance among assets, weights are allocated to each of the assets in order to obtain a portfolio with a minimal level of variability, often resulting in a lower risk than that of any of the assets included in the portfolio.

In the customer context, the problem is more complex than in a financial portfolio context. First, although financial assets are classified relatively easily based on historic risk/return characteristics, the performance history in a customer context exists for current customers but not for potential customers. Therefore, risk-based segmentation should be employed in order to identify customer characteristics that translate into similarities in variability (Tarasi et al., 2011a) and can be used to identify desirable segments to be added to the mix. Investors allocate financial investments by selecting individual assets. By contrast, marketing managers generally allocate resources to segments (asset classes). In turn, returns on investments in a stock portfolio are likely to have a linear relationship relative to the amount invested in each stock. For customer investments, the relationship between investment and return is likely to be nonlinear (Selnes, 2011). A small investment might not elicit a response from a customer or market segment and, beyond a certain amount, the additional investment is likely to result in minimal response. In many cases, however, the relationship between return and revenue is approximated by a linear relationship (Tarasi et al., 2011a).

To reduce variability in a customer portfolio for a desired return, it is possible to identify efficient portfolios and then prioritize customer

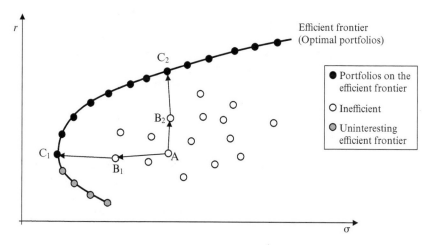

Note: r = return; σ = variability (risk).

Figure 4.1   Toward an efficient customer portfolio

investments in order to move toward the optimal structure. Markowitz (1959) shows that the efficient portfolios border the space of all possible portfolios (see Figure 4.1) and a manager can take steps to reduce risk and move the customer portfolio closer to the efficient frontier. The manager of portfolio A might choose the path A→B₁→C₁ for reaching a portfolio with similar return but lower variability, or A→B₂→C₂ for a portfolio with higher return for a similar level of risk.

Customer Beta

There are several methods for assessing customer variability. Variability per se would not be very informative since it will be highly correlated with the average. Coefficient of variation (standard deviation divided by mean) would provide a more accurate measure of the variability independent of the average level of purchases. However, a more compelling measure is customer beta (Tarasi et al., 2011a), where the variability of a customer's purchases is compared to that of the overall portfolio:

$$\beta_i = \frac{\text{cov}(x_i, x_P)}{V_P},$$

where $\text{cov}(x_i, x_P)$ is the covariance between the individual customer cash flow and the cash flow of the overall customer portfolio, and V_P is the variance of the cash flow for the overall customer portfolio. Beta offers a measure of the contribution of that customer to the overall portfolio. A negative customer beta is likely to reduce the overall variability of the portfolio, while a positive customer beta indicates that by adding that customer to the portfolio, the overall variability of the portfolio is likely to increase.

Customer Reward Ratio

In measuring the rate of return on risk of a customer, or in other words, the reward for assuming variability, Sharpe's pioneering work (1994; see also 1966) provides the foundation for the customer reward ratio (Tarasi et al., 2011a). The reward is measured as the return above the risk-free rate:

$$RR_i = \frac{R_i - R_f}{\sigma_i},$$

where RR_i represents the customer reward ratio, R_i represents the return for customer i and R_f represents the return for the risk-free customer proxy, and σ_i represents the standard deviation of the return. When there is no risk-free asset available, $R_f = 0$ and the equation is simplified to:

$$RR_i = \frac{R_i}{\sigma_i}.$$

Finding a risk-free proxy for the customer portfolio (the equivalent of treasury bills, the benchmark for risk-free investments) is often possible. Some companies, for example, may have a set of low-return customers that they might prefer not to serve, but they choose to do so to fill spare capacity and achieve a modest return. These customers, while not directly targeted, provide a benchmark return. For example, a logistics services company might use transportation managers as a risk-free customer proxy. They are used by logistics service firms to fill at least some capacity for return routes from one-way transports. The customer reward ratio provides a tool for the marketing manager to examine the return-on-variability for segments as well as individual customers.

Customer Portfolio Analysis: An Application

Tarasi et al. (2011a) demonstrate the viability of this customer portfolio approach using purchase history data from a business-to-business logistics company with a diverse customer base. The sponsor company provided monthly sales and profit data (earnings before interest and taxes or EBIT) for all customers for a seven-year period. First, the analysis considers whether customer assets, like financial assets (e.g., blue chip stocks, AAA bonds), share certain risk–return and variability characteristics. To that end, the results show that meaningful differences exist in cash flow variability in existing customer segments (see Table 4.1). Contractual relationships have the smoothest, most predictable cash flows, thereby insulating the firm from troughs (downturns) and peaks (busy times). By serving customers that prefer a contractual relationship, the firm reduces the coefficient of variation for its overall customer portfolio. Likewise, SMB customers demonstrate different patterns of purchasing behavior than customers at large enterprises. The coefficient of variation for customer purchases over time was statistically different for small versus large companies. Moreover, meaningful differences in sales trends were evident for customers from different industries (e.g., Retailing versus Paper & Packaging).

Second, Tarasi et al. (2011a) identify market segments based on purchasing patterns (using standardized monthly purchases over six years) rather than an established segmentation scheme. Using cluster analysis, six customer groups were identified based exclusively on cash flow patterns and the resulting clusters differed in terms of company size, dominant industries, overall variability, and betas. Third, they identify the firm's efficient portfolio and test it against (1) its current portfolio and (2) a hypothetical profit-maximization portfolio. Then, using forward- and back-testing, the authors show that the efficient portfolio has consistently lower variability than the current customer mix or the profit-maximization portfolio. They also demonstrate how managers can use customer beta and the customer reward ratio to evaluate market segments as well as specific individual customers.

To illustrate, Figure 4.2 provides the customer beta, customer reward ratios (with and without the risk-free proxy), and the coefficient of variation. For example, if the firm wishes to reduce overall portfolio risk, the Industrial Transportation segment is the most desirable while the Food & Beverage sector will be the least desirable. However, if the company is satisfied with the level of overall portfolio risk and desires to acquire customers that offer high returns for the level of risk assumed, the Paper & Packaging segment is the best target. If, however, both goals (reducing overall customer portfolio risk *and* acquiring customers with high returns for the level of risk assumed) are sought, the Home Improvement sector may represent the best alternative target for additional marketing resources.

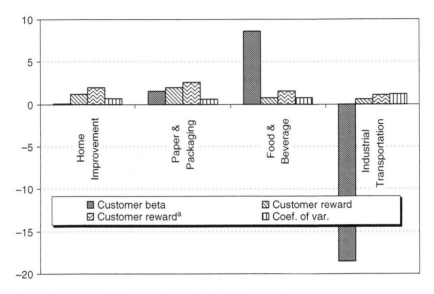

Note: a.   Computed without reference to the risk-free asset.

Figure 4.2   Customer variability indicators

IMPLICATIONS

Table 4.3 integrates the chapter by contrasting the steps involved in managing a customer portfolio versus an investment portfolio. Our portfolio approach, subject to some limitations, raises important implications for practice and research. Concerning limitations, our approach specifically applies to those situations where there are meaningful differences in variability across the market segments that a firm serves. Therefore, our portfolio approach is much better suited for the business market than the consumer market. In particular, it will be less suitable if market segments tend to be highly correlated. Second, the optimal portfolio should be viewed as an ideal customer base that managers can evaluate, revise, and assemble over time. Customer portfolio adjustments entail a host of costs and strategic issues that are beyond the scope of our analysis (Selnes, 2011). Third, the current study is confined to a single firm and industry so further research is needed to test the viability of our approach in different industry contexts and applications.

Table 4.3   Steps in developing a customer portfolio compared with steps in developing an investment portfolio

Investment Portfolio	Customer Portfolio

1 Set investment policy
    Identify client's investment objectives, including those relating to the tradeoff between risk and return
	Set customer acquisition and retention policy
	    Determine objectives for the customer portfolio function of firm's strategy
	    Determine the current structure and risk level of current customers and current customer portfolio

2 Perform financial securities analysis
    Scrutinize individual securities and groups of securities to identify mispriced situations and fast-growing segments
    Based on beta and the amount invested, determine the impact of the proposed securities on the overall portfolio
	Perform customer segment analysis
	    Scrutinize market segments, individual customers, and groups of customers in order to identify underserved needs or markets
	    Estimate the beta of the identified segments relative to the current portfolio
	    Estimate the costs to acquire the identified segments
	    Based on the size of the target segments, estimate the potential impact on the portfolio

3 Construct a portfolio of financial securities
    Identify specific financial securities in which to invest, along with the proportion of investable wealth to be put in each security
	Construct a portfolio of customers
	    Based on the analysis of current and potential customers, determine the efficient frontier portfolios and estimate attainability
	    Identify the most desirable segment(s) to retain and acquire based on return and risk impact, and determine the amount to be invested in each segment
	    Design appropriate acquisition/retention strategies

4 Evaluate portfolio performance
    Determine the actual performance of a portfolio in terms of risk and return, and compare with an appropriate 'benchmark' portfolio
	Evaluate portfolio performance
	    Evaluate cash flow performance in terms of risk and return and compare to previous years or target revenue/risk or other benchmarks
	    Identify events that have an impact on future performance and desirable segments that might alleviate the impact

5 Revise the portfolio
    Assess the current risk and return of the assets in the portfolio and of the overall portfolio
    Determine which financial securities in the current portfolio are to be sold and which securities should be purchased to replace them
	Revise the portfolio
	    Determine the current structure and risk level of current customers and current portfolio
	    Reassess objectives for the customer portfolio function of firm's strategy and objectives
	    Decide allocation of investments in existing customers based on contribution to risk and return
	    Decide whether to pursue new segments (see step 2)

Source: For investment management: Sharpe et al. (1999).

Implications for Practice

We emphasize that a key difference between a customer portfolio and a financial portfolio is that managers can directly influence outcomes. While the CLV research tradition provides valuable insights for advancing firm performance by identifying the right customers and allocating resources accordingly, our approach seeks to increase firm value by identifying the right customer *mix* or portfolio for the firm. First, we demonstrate how customer beta and the customer reward ratio can be used to examine a customer portfolio through a new lens, providing a tool for managers to isolate desirable segments and individual customers. Second, we find support for our belief that financial portfolio theory is relevant in a customer portfolio context. Our analysis of the sponsor firm's portfolio reveals market segments that could be characterized in terms of their risk as well as their return. Third, we present an actionable plan for creating a diversified customer portfolio. We demonstrate that risk management techniques can be applied to stabilize customer cash flow and ensure diversity among existing and potential new customers. Moreover, the data and methods used in our study are readily available to most firms: purchase transactions over time, firmographics, and profitability by cluster.

Implications for Research

The CLV framework provides valuable insights into how profitability can be enhanced by selecting the right customers for targeting and determining the allocation of resources for acquisition, retention, and expansion (Blattberg et al., 2001; Kumar, 2008). By incorporating risk metrics into customer portfolio management, our approach complements, rather than replaces, the CLV framework by providing a measure of reward-on-variability for market segments and individual customers. However, our study merely takes a small first step and further research is needed to more fully integrate the customer portfolio approach into CLV models.

First, because of increasing or decreasing returns to scale, the degree of weight assigned to a market segment within the customer portfolio may affect the profit performance of that segment (Selnes, 2011). Future research might explore methods for isolating those segments that are scalable and those that are not (Billett, 2011). Likewise, future research might investigate how to identify the optimal investment in an individual customer or market segment in order to optimize the customer portfolio. Second, while stock prices are more vulnerable to violent swings than customer purchases, future research is needed to examine the persistence of spending patterns by customer segments. Third, rather than relying on past volatility in financial portfolio analysis, Engle (1982) proposes a weighted moving average model to estimate the future behavior of a financial asset. By analyzing customer purchase histories, future research might consider a similar approach to more accurately predict future customer cash flow variability. Fourth, since some segments in the business market are comprised of few customers, the feasibility of some weighting schemes is limited. We endorse Billett's (2011) call for research that isolates the factors that lead to constraints on feasible portfolio weights for various customer segments and how constrained optimization might lead to more refined weighting schemes (Tarasi et al., 2011b).

Finally, further research might explore if firms with more efficient portfolios are rewarded by investors who display more confidence in the earnings projections of firms with more versus less efficient portfolios. Future research along these lines may lead to further improvements that allow managers to balance the risk and return in the customer portfolio.

REFERENCES

Ang, A., J. Chen, and Y. Xing (2006), 'Downside Risk,' *Review of Financial Studies*, **19** (4), 1191–239.

Billett, M.T. (2011), 'Balancing Risk and Return in a Customer Portfolio: A Comment,' *Journal of Marketing*, **75** (3).

Blattberg, R.C. and J. Deighton (1996), 'Manage Marketing by the Customer Equity Test,' *Harvard Business Review*, **74** (4), 136–44.

Blattberg, R.C., G. Getz, and J. Thomas (2001), *Customer Equity: Building and Managing Relationships as Valuable Assets*, Boston, MA: Harvard Business School Press.

Bolton, R.N., K.N. Lemon, and P.C. Verhoef (2008), 'Expanding Business-to-business Customer Relationships: Modeling the Customer's Upgrade Decision,' *Journal of Marketing*, **72** (1), 46–64.

Bowman, D. and D. Narayandas (2004), 'Linking Customer Management Efforts to Customer Profitability in Business Markets,' *Journal of Marketing Research*, **41** (4), 433–47.

Buhl, H.U. and B. Heinrich (2008), 'Valuing Customer Portfolios under Risk–Return Aspects: A Model-based Approach and its Application in the Financial Services Industry,' *Academy of Marketing Science Review*, **12** (5), 1–32.

Chandra, S. (2003), 'Regional Economy Size and the Growth–Instability Frontier: Evidence from Europe,' *Journal of Regional Science*, **43** (1), 95–122.

Conroy, M.E. (1974), 'Alternative Strategies for Regional Industrial Diversification,' *Journal of Regional Science*, **14** (1), 31–46.

DeMiguel, V., L. Garlappi, and R. Uppal (2007), 'Optimal Versus Naive Diversification: How Inefficient is the 1/N Portfolio Strategy?' *The Review of Financial Studies*, **22** (5), 1916–53.

Devinney, T.M. and D.W. Stewart (1988), 'Rethinking the Product Portfolio: A Generalized Investment Model,' *Management Science*, **34** (September), 1080–95.

Dhar, R. and R. Glazer (2003), 'Hedging Customers,' *Harvard Business Review*, **81** (5), 86–92.

Dissart, J.C. (2003), 'Regional Economic Diversity and Regional Economic Stability: Research Results and Agenda,' *International Regional Science Review*, **26** (4), 423–46.

Drèze, X. and A. Bonfrer (2009), 'Moving from Customer Lifetime Value to Customer Equity,' *QME: Quantitative Marketing and Economics*, **7** (3), 289–320.

Engle, R.F. III (1982), 'Autoregressive Conditional Heteroskedasticity with Estimates of the Variance of U.K. Inflation,' *Econometrica*, **50** (4), 987–1008.

Gruca, T.S. and L.L. Rego (2005), 'Customer Satisfaction, Cash Flow, and Shareholder Value,' *Journal of Marketing*, **69** (3), 115–30.

Gupta, S., D.R. Lehmann, and J.A Stuart (2004), 'Valuing Customers,' *Journal of Marketing Research*, **41** (1), 7–18.

Hogan, J.E., D.R. Lehmann, M. Merino, R.K. Srivastava, J.S. Thomas, and P.C. Verhoef (2002), 'Linking Customer Assets to Financial Performance,' *Journal of Service Research*, **5** (August), 26–38.

Homburg, C., V.V. Steiner, and D. Totzek (2009), 'Managing Dynamics in a Customer Portfolio,' *Journal of Marketing*, **73** (5), 70–89.

Hubbard, D.W. (2009), *The Failure of Risk Management*, Hobokon, NJ: John Wiley & Sons, Inc.

Johnson, M.D. and F. Selnes (2004), 'Customer Portfolio Management: Toward a Dynamic Theory of Exchange Relationships,' *Journal of Marketing*, **68** (2), 1–17.

Johnson, M.D. and F. Selnes (2005), 'Diversifying Your Customer Portfolio,' *MIT Sloan Management Review*, **44** (3), 11–14.

Kaplan, P.D. (2009), 'Déjà Vu All Over Again,' *Morningstar Advisor*, Feb/March, 28–33.

Kumar, V. (2008), *Managing Customers for Profit: Strategies to Increase Profits and Build Loyalty*, Philadelphia, PA: Wharton School Publishing.

Kumar, V., D. Shah, and R. Venkatesan (2006), 'Managing Retailer Profitability – One Customer at a Time!' *Journal of Retailing*, **82** (4), 277–94.

Kumar, V., R. Venkatesan, T. Bohling, and D. Beckmann (2008), 'The Power of CLV: Managing Customer Lifetime Value at IBM,' *Marketing Science*, **27** (4), 585–99.

Kundisch, D., S. Sackmann, and M. Ruch (2008), 'Transferring Portfolio Selection Theory to Customer Portfolio Management – The Case of an e-Tailer,' in D.J. Veit et al. (eds), *Enterprise Applications and Services in the Finance Industry*, Berlin/Heidelberg: Springer, pp. 32–49.

Kurre, J.A. and B.R. Weller (1989), 'Regional Cyclical Instability: An Empirical Examination of Wage, Hours and Employment Adjustments, and an Application of the Portfolio Variance Technique,' *Regional Studies*, **23** (4), 315–29.

Kurre, J.A. and B.R. Weller (1996), 'Interindustry Covariance Patterns: Too Unstable for Portfolio Variance Analysis to be a Useful Tool?' *Economic Development Quarterly*, **10** (1), 91–103.

Lande, P.S. (1994), 'Regional Industrial Structure and Economic Growth and Instability,' *Journal of Regional Science*, **34** (3), 343–60.

Lohr, S. (2010), 'Huge Payoff for IBM After a Shift,' *The New York Times*, 20 January, B1.

Markowitz, H. (1952), 'Portfolio Selection,' *The Journal of Finance*, **7** (1), 77–91.

Markowitz, H. (1959), *Portfolio Selection: Efficient Diversification of Investments*, New York: John Wiley & Sons.

McAlister, L., R. Srinivasan, and M. Kim (2007), 'Advertising, Research and Development and Systematic Risk of the Firm,' *Journal of Marketing*, **71** (1), 35–48.

Rao, R.K.S. and N. Bharadwaj (2008), 'Marketing Initiatives, Expected Cash Flows, and Shareholders' Wealth,' *Journal of Marketing*, **72** (1), 16–26.

Rust, R.T., K.N. Lemon, and V.A. Zeithaml (2004), 'Return on Marketing: Using Customer Equity to Focus Marketing Strategy,' *Journal of Marketing*, **68** (1), 109–27.

Ryals, L. (2002), 'Measuring Risk and Returns in the Customer Portfolio,' *Journal of Database Marketing*, **9** (3), 219–27.

Ryals, L. (2003), 'Making Customers Pay: Measuring and Managing Risk and Returns,' *Journal of Strategic Marketing*, **11** (3), 165–75.

Selnes, F. (2011), 'A Comment on Balancing Risk and Return in a Customer Portfolio,' *Journal of Marketing*, **75** (3).

Sharpe, W.F. (1966), 'Mutual Fund Performance,' *The Journal of Business*, **39** (1), 119–38.

Sharpe, W.F. (1994), 'The Sharpe Ratio,' *Journal of Portfolio Management*, **21** (1), 49–58.

Sharpe, W.F., G.J. Alexander, and J.V. Bailey (1999), *Investments*, Upper Saddle River, NJ: Prentice-Hall.

Siegel, P.B., T.G. Johnson, and J. Alwang (1995), 'Regional Economic Diversity and Diversification,' *Growth and Change*, **26** (2), 261–85.

Sorescu, A. and J. Spanjol (2008), 'Innovation's Effect on Firm Value and Risk: Insights from Consumer Packaged Goods,' *Journal of Marketing*, **72** (2), 114–32.

Srinivasan, S. and D. Hanssens (2009), 'Marketing and Firm Value: Metrics, Methods, Findings and Future Directions,' *Journal of Marketing Research*, **46** (3), 293–312.

Srivastava, R.K., T.A. Shervani, and L. Fahey (1997), 'Driving Shareholder Value: The Role of Marketing in Reducing Vulnerability and Volatility of Cash Flows,' *Journal of Market Focused Management*, **2** (1), 49–64.

Srivastava, R.K., T.A. Shervani, and L. Fahey (1998), 'Market-based Assets and Shareholder Value: A Framework for Analysis,' *Journal of Marketing*, **62** (1), 2–18.

Tarasi, C., R.N. Bolton, M.D. Hutt, and B. Walker (2011a), 'Balancing Risk and Return in a Customer Portfolio,' *Journal of Marketing*, **75** (3), 1–17.

Tarasi, C., R.N. Bolton, M.D. Hutt, and B. Walker (2011b), 'Balancing Risk and Return in a Customer Portfolio: A Reply,' *Journal of Marketing*, **75** (3).

Tuli, K.R. and S.G. Bharadwaj (2009), 'Customer Satisfaction and Stock Returns Risk,' *Journal of Marketing*, **73** (6), 184–97.

Tuli, K.R., S.G. Bharadwaj, and A.K. Kohli (2010), 'Ties that Bind: The Impact of Multiple Types of Ties with a Customer on Sales Growth and Sales Volatility,' *Journal of Marketing Research*, **47** (1), 36–50.

Veverka, M. (2003), 'Little Guys Lead IT Spending Recovery,' *Barron's*, 20 October, 73.

5 Marketing information disclosures: a review and research agenda
*Raji Srinivasan and Debika Sihi**

Corporate information is disseminated through financial reporting required by the SEC (Securities and Exchange Commission) (e.g., 10-K or 10-Q) and through various scheduled (e.g., conference calls) and unscheduled (e.g., press releases) disclosures. A large body of theoretical and empirical work in accounting and finance literature has examined the effects of a firm's information disclosure policies, as well as the costs and benefits of these disclosures (e.g., Leuz and Verrecchia, 2000). In this chapter, we define 'marketing information disclosure' as any information the firm discloses about its marketing activities and programs, marketing assets, and marketing personnel. Accordingly, marketing information disclosures are disclosures about the firm's products, prices, distribution channels, entry into new markets, marketing alliances, and appointments (departures) of marketing executives.

In line with Dierickx and Cool's (1989) concept of 'stock' and 'flows of assets,' marketing activities (e.g., advertising, channel management, branding, customer relationship management) are flows that help firms build value-relevant marketing assets (e.g., brand equity, channel customer equity) (Srivastava et al., 1998). Thus, disclosures of marketing expenditure are of special interest to both senior management and finance executives who are concerned with profitability (Ambler, 2003; Rust et al., 2004) and to analysts following the firms. As Rust et al. (2004, p. 76) note 'the spotlight is not on underlying products, pricing, or customer relationships . . . but on marketing expenditures (e.g., marketing communications, promotions, other activities) and how these expenditures influence marketplace performance.'

Empirically, marketing actions affect stock valuations through various mechanisms, including reduced risk of cash flows (Singh et al., 2005), increased profits (Sorescu and Spanjol, 2008), lower risk (McAlister et al., 2007), lower dispersion in analysts' forecasts (Barron et al., 2002; Tuli and Bharadwaj, 2009), and increased breadth of ownership and liquidity of stocks (Grullon et al., 2004).

Firms may disclose marketing information through their filings with the SEC, including quarterly and annual reports, and in earnings release statements and earnings release calls. A distinctive feature of marketing information is that unlike firms' financial and accounting information (relevant to bankers, regulators, investors, and analysts), marketing information disclosures are relevant to a broader group of audiences, including the firm's customers, channel partners, bankers, regulators, investors, and analysts. An important but unintended consequence of this diverse audience base for marketing information disclosures is that the information released for one audience (e.g., new product updates aimed to customers) can also affect other audiences (e.g., investors, analysts). Therefore, announcements of marketing actions intended for marketing stakeholders, such as customers and even competitors, will also be important information disclosures for the stock market.

We next discuss the mandatory accounting requirements for disclosure of marketing information by publicly listed firms. Statement of Financial Accounting Standards 2 requires publicly listed firms to disclose their research and development (R&D) expenditures for each filing period. In 1994, the SEC passed Financial Reporting Release 44 (FRR 44), which changed the disclosure requirement of advertising expenditures for public firms' annual reports. Before the passage of FRR 44, public firms were required to report advertising spending if it exceeded 1 percent of their total sales. However, after FRR 44, firm managers are only required to report advertising expenses in their annual reports if the spending amount is material. Materiality thresholds are usually set by firm managers with guidance by firm auditors and legal counsel (Heitzman et al., 2010). Thus, managers have considerable discretion in how and what they disclose with respect to their firms' marketing programs and spending. Studying the effects of FRR 44 on firms' disclosure of advertising spending, Simpson (2008) finds that advertising reporting behavior is fairly consistent over time and that firms that tended to continue reporting advertising expenditure after FRR44 were those for which advertising was more effective.

CHALLENGES IN MARKETING DISCLOSURES

We identify three challenges associated with the disclosure of information of firms' marketing programs. First, unlike financial disclosures (e.g., accounting schedules, financing approaches), a firm's marketing programs and strategies (e.g., pricing, new product information) are crucial sources of competitive advantage. Thus, firms may not only lack incentives to disclose this information but also actively strive to keep such information a secret. Second, marketing programs create intangible

Table 5.1   Reported advertising and R&D expenses from Compustat

Fiscal Year	Advertising		R&D	
	Frequency	Percentage	Frequency	Percentage
1998	427	25.34	865	51.34
1999	3096	24.64	5370	42.73
2000	3280	26.56	5157	41.76
2001	3339	28.09	4884	41.09
2002	3338	28.84	4687	40.49
2003	3410	30.00	4569	40.20
2004	3450	30.87	4489	40.16
2005	3373	30.45	4400	39.72
2006	3236	29.51	4236	38.63
2007	3077	28.59	4073	37.85
2008	2933	28.58	3844	37.46
2009	2309	26.85	3071	35.71

assets that are associated with more complex information, have more uncertainty related to their potential value (Kothari et al., 2002), and are characterized by fuzzy property rights (Lev, 2001). Current Generally Accepted Accounting Principles in the United States reflect this view of intangible marketing assets by mandating that expenditures related to the creation of intangible assets (i.e., through advertising and R&D programs) be fully expensed in the fiscal year in which they are incurred. Third, many types of marketing expenditures (e.g., sales promotions, channel-building programs) are not reported separately. Only R&D and advertising spending are reported separately by publicly listed firms and often by only a small percentage of these firms. We discuss recent developments to set up the Marketing Accounting Standards Board (MASB) subsequently in the chapter. Table 5.1 lists the percentage of firms in the Compustat database reporting R&D and advertising data between 1998 and 2009. As Table 5.1 shows, the vast majority of publicly listed firms (between 50 and 75 percent) do not report data on their R&D and advertising expenditures.

As a result, some researchers have used firms' selling, general, and administrative (SG&A) expenditures as proxies. Dutta et al. (1999, p. 556) argue that SG&A is 'a good proxy for the amount the firm spends on its market research, sales effort, trade promotion expenses, and other related activities.' In addition to marketing costs, firms' SG&A expenditures may include rents, salaries, and miscellaneous administration expenditures, which are clearly not related to marketing programs.

Firms are also not required to report separately their expenditures on the different marketing program elements, including, for example, sales promotions. By definition, advertising expenditures disclosed by firms include cost of advertising media (radio, television, newspapers, and periodicals) and promotional expenses. Thus, firms' disclosures of advertising may not measure firms' 'true' advertising. That is, by design, firms' reports of advertising may have proxy errors, the magnitudes of which depend on firms' promotional expenses, which vary across firms and industries and over time (Blattberg and Neslin, 1990).

Therefore, interested stakeholders, including analysts, bankers, and investors, have difficulty examining firms' disclosures of marketing program budgets and understanding their effects on firm performance. This is in contrast with accounting and financial information disclosures, which are subject to strict regulatory restrictions. To compound this problem further, given the inherently creative nature of marketing programs, disclosure of marketing spending is subject to substantive interpretation by recipients. For example, analyst evaluations of advertising dollars likely exhibit greater variance than dollar amounts related to a firm's inventory or accounts receivables. In addition, the benefits of advertising reflect the program's efficacy (Picconi, 1977; Aaker and Carman, 1982), creating further uncertainty about the firm's ability to secure rents from its advertising investments. Likewise, it is difficult to predict whether and when a given R&D program will translate into increased sales and profitability, as the returns to R&D investments are both uncertain and distal (Mansfield, 1981). Accordingly, inputs of marketing spending may at best be noisy indicators of information disclosures.

Information asymmetry characterizes the relationship between the firm and analysts following the firm. Specifically, a firm's executives will have more accurate information about the firm's prospects than its analysts, resulting in an adverse selection problem (Akerlof, 1970). Firms may be able to reduce this problem by undertaking signaling (Spence, 1973). When firms have high advertising and R&D expenditures, which are discretionary, they are signaling to stock market participants that they anticipate their advertising and R&D programs to be effective and that their future performance is likely to be superior. However, because advertising and R&D expenditures are immediately expensed, they can potentially be manipulated by firms to increase earnings. Supporting the earnings manipulation argument, Perry and Grinaker (1994) find a positive relationship between unexpected earnings and unexpected R&D spending.

BENEFITS OF MARKETING INFORMATION DISCLOSURES

To date, the marketing literature has examined the effects of marketing activities and marketing assets on the stock market. As noted previously, the firm's marketing activities and marketing assets are revealed through disclosures in either financial statements or other informational releases, such as press releases. In some situations, information may be made public by a third-party source. For example, the American Customer Satisfaction Index (ACSI) discloses firms' customer satisfaction ratings.

Prior research has examined the financial impact of announcements, including new product introductions (e.g., Chaney et al., 1991; Pauwels et al., 2004; Srinivasan et al., 2004), corporate name changes (Horsky and Swyngedouw, 1987), brand extensions (Lane and Jacobson, 1995), joint ventures (Houston and Johnson, 2000), additions of the Internet channel (Geyskens et al., 2002), product preannouncements (Sorescu et al., 2007), and celebrity endorsements (Agrawal and Kamakura, 1995), using short-term stock market abnormal returns measured around the day of the announcement (Srinivasan and Bharadwaj, 2004). Other studies have investigated the short-term reactions of the stock market in other marketing contexts, including new product introductions (Sorescu et al., 2007), new product delays (Hendricks and Singhal, 1997), brand extensions (Simon and Sullivan, 1993), product recalls (Jarrell and Peltzman, 1985), product quality (Aaker and Jacobson, 1994), and regulations and rulings on false advertising (Peltzman, 1981). Sorescu et al. (2007) provide a comprehensive discussion about the short- and long-term consequences of disclosure of information related to new products, which also apply to firms' disclosures of their marketing programs.

With regard to long-term stock market effects, studies have used various metrics of long-term shareholder value, including market capitalization, stock returns, calendar portfolio, and intangible value. Advertising spending has a positive and long-term impact on firms' market capitalization (Joshi and Hanssens, 2010), and scaled advertising and R&D expenditures lower a firm's systematic risk (McAlister et al., 2007). Prelaunch advertising for a new product both informs consumers about the product and also helps investors form expectations about the firm's profit performance (Joshi and Hanssens, 2009), and new product announcements increase calendar portfolio returns (Sorescu et al., 2007). Marketing information disclosures also affect firm intangible value. A firm's choice of branding strategy, whether corporate branding, mixed branding, or house-of-brands strategy (Rao et al., 2004), affects its intangible value. A firm's channel strategy, specifically whether operations are vertically integrated or franchised (Srinivasan, 2006), also affects its intangible value.

Finally, disclosure of marketing performance metrics also affects firms' shareholder value. Focusing on brand quality, Bharadwaj et al. (2011) find a contingent effect of brand quality, specifically that an unanticipated increase (decrease) in current period earnings enhances (depletes) the positive impact of unanticipated changes in brand quality on stock returns but mitigates (enhances) their deleterious effects on changes in systematic risk. Customer satisfaction ratings, compiled by the ACSI, can affect the firm's stock value gap (Luo and Homburg, 2008) and long-term abnormal returns (Aksoy et al., 2008). In addition, customer satisfaction increases cash flow growth and reduces cash flow volatility (Gruca and Rego, 2005). Recently, work in marketing has begun to focus on the implications of marketing information disclosure on analysts' perceptions of firm value. Positive changes in customer satisfaction, reported by ACSI, not only improve analyst recommendations but also lower dispersion in those recommendations (Tuli and Bharadwaj, 2009; Luo et al., 2010).

COSTS OF MARKETING INFORMATION DISCLOSURES

Marketing information disclosures, as with other corporate information disclosures, are costly for firms. Volatility of returns may rise with R&D spending, imposing real costs on investors and possibly affecting the cost of capital for R&D-intensive firms (Chan et al., 2001). For example, this volatility may be due to investor uncertainty about firms' R&D activities, which may be remedied with greater or more specific disclosure regarding such endeavors (Chan et al., 2001).

Firms with greater marketing disclosure may also have higher variance among analyst forecasts. Analysts perceive 'high intangible firms' as having a higher amount of non-recurring or mismatched revenues. Thus, analyst forecasts of these firms are more likely to be influenced by their idiosyncratic adjustments for non-recurring or mismatched revenue. Thus, higher forecast dispersion exists among analysts' forecasting earnings for high intangible firms than for low intangible firms (Barron et al., 2002). High analyst forecast dispersion has been linked to lower returns on equity (Diether et al., 2002). Dispersion is also negatively correlated with accounting return on equity (Han and Manry, 2000) but strongly correlated with future volatility of stock returns (Abarbanell et al., 1995).

Research in accounting and finance has examined other effects of marketing information disclosures, especially the release of R&D and advertising information. Analyst coverage is significantly greater for firms with larger advertising (Barth et al., 2001) and R&D (Barth et al., 2001; Barron et al., 2002) expenditures. Frieder and Subrahmanyam (2005) report that a firm's increased brand perceptions, a direct outcome of its increased advertising, increase individual investors' ownership of the firm's stock, compared with institutional investors, because of their preferences for stocks with higher quality information (advertising provides information to a firm's stockholders). Reinforcing this finding, Grullon et al. (2004) report that increased advertising increases both the liquidity and the breadth of ownership of a firm's stock.

In addition, R&D intensity is positively associated with return volatility (Kothari et al., 2002). Analysts exhibit greater disagreement about year-ahead earnings for R&D-intensive firms than for other firms (Barth et al., 2001), and post-investment earnings are more highly variable for firms with high R&D levels than for firms with low R&D levels (Chambers et al., 2002).

Thus, our review of the literature indicates a wealth of insights into the benefits, costs, and effects of marketing information disclosures for firms. However, we note that unlike scholars in accounting and finance, marketing scholars, for the most part, have primarily focused on the benefits of marketing information disclosures. Thus, the cost of marketing information disclosures emerges as an opportunity to extend marketing literature.

A CONCEPTUAL FRAMEWORK AND RESEARCH AGENDA FOR MARKETING INFORMATION DISCLOSURES

We propose an organizing conceptual framework that relates marketing information disclosures to capital market consequences (Figure 5.1). We discuss the proposed conceptual framework and identify research questions in the area of marketing information disclosures emerging from this framework.

Antecedents of Marketing Information Disclosures

We propose that firms' characteristics more generally and their marketing strategies more specifically influence the extent and type of marketing information disclosures. In addition, we anticipate that marketing information disclosure activities vary across industries. For example, firms with lower managerial ownership and significant government ownership are associated with increased disclosure, while an increase in outside directors

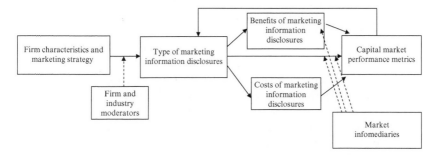

Figure 5.1   Antecedents and consequences of marketing information disclosures

reduces corporate disclosure (Eng and Mak, 2003). Previous work also finds that firms with higher levels of advertising and R&D expenses tend to obtain significantly higher ratings from investor relations programs or voluntary publications. This suggests that firms with high levels of intangible marketing assets rely on voluntary disclosures as a mechanism for information dissemination (Gelb, 2002).

We propose that following the release of certain types of marketing information disclosures by a few firms in an industry, other firms in the industry will also be constrained to disclose marketing information. We also propose that the effects of firms' characteristics on their marketing information disclosures will be influenced by other firm characteristics (e.g., their financial leverage, extent of institutional shareholdings).

The following research questions pertain to the antecedents of marketing information disclosures:

- Which marketing strategies encourage/discourage information disclosure practices? For example, is Wal-Mart, a price leader, more likely to provide greater disclosure than Target, a quality leader, or Nordstorm, a niche market player? Similarly, are firms with a history of innovation (e.g., Hewlett-Packard, IBM, Apple) likely to provide more disclosure than cost leaders, such as Dell? What are the implications of marketing information disclosures by these different types of firms?
- Which firm characteristics (e.g., firm performance, size, financial leverage, institutional shareholding) influence the disclosure of different types of marketing information?
- Which marketing characteristics (e.g., branding strategy, advertising and R&D intensity, marketing intensity of the top management, presence of a chief marketing officer) influence the disclosure of

different types of marketing information? Are any of these characteristics contingent on the firm's marketing information disclosures?

- How do marketing information disclosures (e.g., extent, type) vary across industries? Across different firms within an industry? Over time in a given industry? Are marketing information disclosures different for firms across economic cycles? For example, do they vary between market recessions and expansions?
- Given that disclosures often serve a signaling function, how do the characteristics of the firm's customer base affect its propensity to voluntarily disclose marketing information? Do practices vary between business-to-business and business-to-consumer industries? Does information disclosure by one firm affect the information disclosure by other firms?

These questions can be studied with respect to different types of marketing information disclosures (which we discuss next).

Characteristics of Marketing Information Disclosures

Firms' marketing information disclosures can vary in terms of their quality, quantity, temporal focus, and mode. Some marketing information disclosures may be of very high quality. For example, a firm may provide specific information on its marketing performance metrics, such as an expected increase in market share. Other disclosures may not be of high quality, such as vague and non-specific information on a firm's future marketing programs. The marketing information disclosed can also be numerical (e.g., specific numbers pertaining to the firm's marketing programs) or descriptive (e.g., description of the creative strategy of the firm's proposed advertising campaign) in nature. The sentiment of the marketing information disclosed can also vary substantially, with some disclosures having positive, neutral, or negative sentiment, as presented by the firm. Tetlock (2007) finds that negative media sentiment predicts downward pressure on stock market prices and may significantly affect trading volume. Marketing researchers can extend this work by understanding the implications of marketing disclosure sentiment on the stock market.

In addition, firms can decide to release a little (e.g., number of new stores opening the next quarter) or a lot of (e.g., information on products, distribution, and advertising campaigns for the next three quarters) marketing information. Marketing information can also be disclosed over a very short period (e.g., during an earnings conference call) or an extended period (e.g., several press releases over a six-month period). Moreover, firms can release only marketing information or release marketing and other accounting information. Some marketing information disclosures may also be periodic (e.g., quarterly, annual), while other information disclosures may be more irregular (e.g., disclosure related to entry into an emerging market, disclosure regarding product recalls).

Variation also may occur in whether firms disclose information related to past or completed marketing initiatives, ongoing activities, or future marketing endeavors. A firm's choice of temporal focus may be construed as a litmus test from which to gauge whether the firm is forward-looking in its marketing initiatives or tied to past ideas.

Finally, firms may disclose marketing information through multiple modes of communication (e.g., conference calls, annual reports, press releases, analysts' meetings) and by different executives (e.g., chief executive officer, chief financial officer, investor relations). In some cases, the marketing information disclosures may be targeted to the investment community (e.g., conference calls), and in other cases, they may be diffused to other stakeholders, including customers, employees, vendors, and regulatory authorities. In addition, a new and important mechanism for the release of marketing information is Internet-related media – including the World Wide Web in general but also social networking sites, such as Twitter and Facebook, and various investors' and consumers' blogs.

Against this general background of marketing information disclosures, marketing scholars have recently called for disclosure of specific metrics, such as customer equity (Wiesel et al., 2008). Wiesel et al. (2008) note that firms that aim to increase the value of their customer base should report forward-looking customer metrics because such reports align customer management with corporate goals and investors' perspectives. Furthermore, they develop a specific model for Netflix and apply it to quarterly data from September 2001 to September 2006.

The following research questions pertain to the characteristics of marketing information disclosures:

- Which types of marketing information disclosures (in terms of content, quality, quantity, and mode) are more prevalent, and why? Are information disclosures of the firm's marketing performance metrics more or less common than disclosures of their marketing assets? Are the effects of different types of disclosures on capital market outcomes different?
- Are certain types of marketing information disclosures more likely from certain sources (e.g., chief executive officers, chief financial officers)? What are the costs and benefits of the different types of marketing information disclosures? Do they vary across firms?

- Are the costs, benefits, and effects of targeted marketing information disclosure toward the investment community (e.g., conference
  calls) different from those of diffused marketing information disclosures (e.g., aimed at customers)? Does the release of pure marketing
  information versus marketing information combined with accounting information have different costs or benefits? For example, how
  do analysts process marketing information? Do they process such
  information in conjunction with financial ratios, or do they make
  an estimate based on financial information first and then adjust the
  estimate slightly depending on marketing efforts?
- What is the prevalence of different modes of marketing information
  disclosures (e.g., press releases, conference calls) more generally and
  the Internet-based model of marketing information disclosures (e.g.,
  Twitter, Facebook, user blogs)?
- What are some of the implications or perceptions related to the use
  of different modes? How do firm characteristics affect the incidence
  of these different modes of marketing information disclosures?
  What are the interaction effects of the different modes of marketing
  information disclosures? When do they co-occur?

Costs and Benefits of Marketing Information Disclosures

Information disclosures are simultaneously costly and beneficial for firms.
Specifically, there may be costs related to production and dissemination of
marketing information. In addition, the costs of marketing information
disclosures may include a loss of competitive advantage. The benefits of
marketing information disclosure for firms, as with other types of corporate information disclosures, may include liquidity of the firm's stock and
lower cost of capital.

The following research questions pertain to the characteristics of
marketing information disclosures:

- What are the costs of marketing information disclosures for firms?
  For example, is there a loss of competitive advantage? Do these
  costs vary for different firms? Do the costs outweigh the benefits of
  information disclosures? Or vice versa?
- Are certain types of disclosures more costly to the firm than others?
  For example, description of a firm's new advertising campaign may
  result in a greater loss of competitive advantage than disclosure only
  of advertising expenditure amounts.
- What are the benefits of marketing information disclosures for
  firms? Do these benefits vary for different firms? Do they vary by

industries? What are the industries in which marketing disclosures result in the greatest financial gains (e.g., abnormal returns, Tobin's Q)?

- Are the benefits and costs of marketing information disclosures different across economic cycles?
- Are the costs and benefits of marketing information disclosures different from the costs and benefits of accounting information disclosures for firms? Do these costs and benefits change when firms release both marketing and accounting information simultaneously?

Methodological Issues Related to Marketing Information Disclosures

Prior research in finance and accounting, in the domain of disclosures, has relied heavily on AIMR's (Association for Investment Management and Research) disclosure rankings. The AIMR rankings are analysts' assessments and cover the period from 1979 to 1996. Overall rankings are a weighted average of the following three categories: ranking on annual reports, ranking on quarterly reports, and ranking on investor relations programs. The AIMR discontinued these rankings in 1996. After AIMR became the CFA Institute, this ranking process was not reinstated.

Prior work in the domain of disclosures has used multivariate regression to model the impact of disclosures on various response factors, such as the cost of equity capital (Botosan and Plumlee, 2002), institutional investment holding (Bushee and Noe, 2000), and analyst following (Lang and Lundholm, 1996). Multivariate techniques have also been used to capture the impact of firm characteristics on a firm's disclosure practices. Eng and Mak (2003) use ordinary least squares regression to examine the impact of ownership structure and board composition on voluntary disclosure. These studies identify control measures that may be required when examining relationships between disclosures and various dependent measures (e.g., standard deviation of return on equity relevant for analyst following), and they provide insight into the impact of disclosures on firm operations and the stock market. However, a large avenue for research remains open for marketing scholars.

None of the past work focuses specifically on marketing disclosures. In addition, there are new sources of data related to corporate disclosure. Standard & Poor's (S&P) launched a corporate disclosure ranking in 2002.[1] Currently, these disclosure rankings are a part of an overall corporate governance ranking for emerging markets within an S&P product called GAMMA. The criteria for these disclosure rankings focus on financial, accounting, and legal disclosures; however, understanding the impact of such disclosures may provide an initial step for analyses of marketing disclosures in emerging markets. The advancement of textual analysis software (e.g., Harvard's General Inquirer, ATLAS.ti) has also made obtaining quantity, content, and sentiment of disclosures more feasible. Researchers can create their own disclosure rankings based on analyses of firm filings or call transcripts. Finally, other estimation processes and modeling approaches can be used to examine disclosures. The following questions and topics are geared toward methodological issues related to marketing disclosures:

- What are effective criteria for identifying and separating marketing disclosures? For example, should researchers examine the combined impact of marketing disclosures in annual reports or separately analyze disclosures related to channels from disclosures related to advertising?
- Similar to AIMR's ranking system, can the American Marketing Association or other marketing organizations create a marketing disclosure ranking system, with rankings provided by customer, channel, and analyst constituencies? Data of this nature would be useful to marketing academics and practitioners.
- Do past findings on disclosures remain consistent when empirically tested with marketing disclosures rather than overall disclosure rankings?
- Do past findings on disclosures remain consistent when analyzing emerging markets' disclosures with new sources of data, such as GAMMA?
- Can stochastic frontier estimation be used to gauge efficiency in marketing disclosures at the industry level?
- Duration analysis may be applied to model the impact of a firm's marketing disclosure on events, such as mergers and acquisitions. Do marketing disclosures significantly affect the time of a firm's merger or acquisition?

Market Infomediaries

Firms' marketing information disclosures are aimed at different market infomediaries, such as investors, analysts, and financial institutions. Each of these infomediaries may have different information needs and may also interpret the disclosure of marketing information differently. Most infomediaries interpret the marketing information disclosed by firms as reflected in costs, benefits, and capital market outcomes.

The following research questions pertain to the release of marketing information to market infomediaries:

- Do the effects of different types of marketing information disclosures vary across different types of market infomediaries? If so, how do they vary? For example, do they vary by type, quantity, quality, or mode of marketing information disclosures?
- Do infomediaries place greater importance on certain marketing disclosures when making investment decisions or recommendations?
- Are there specific market infomediaries (e.g., analysts, institutional investors) for whom marketing information disclosures affect capital market performance metrics? Are there interdependencies in the effects of marketing information disclosures among various market infomediaries on capital market performance metrics?
- Given the globalization of investors, are there any differences in the effects of marketing information disclosures across domestic and global infomediaries?

Effects of Marketing Information Disclosures

The final link in the conceptual framework relates the disclosure of marketing information to its effects on capital market outcomes, an area in which a large body of empirical work exists (see the review by Srinivasan and Hanssens, 2009). These outcomes include stock returns, abnormal stock returns, market capitalization, and intangible value.

The following research questions pertain to the capital market effects of marketing information disclosures:

- What are the effects of the different types of marketing information disclosures (see previous discussion) on various capital market performance metrics (e.g., stock returns, systematic risk, idiosyncratic risk, calendar portfolio)? Are the effects different across the different metrics?
- What are the effects of the medium of marketing information disclosures (e.g., who releases the information, where the information is released, over what period the information is released) on capital market performance metrics?
- Are the effects of costs and benefits of marketing information disclosures on capital market outcomes different across firms? Do the characteristics of the firm's market infomediaries moderate these effects?

Standards for Marketing Information Disclosures

In 2004, responding to mounting pressure from corporate boardrooms for accountability in the marketing function, a cross-industry, cross-disciplinary body of marketing scientists initiated The Boardroom Project. Members recognized that measurement standards (tied to financial performance) were essential for the efficient and effective functioning of a marketing-driven business because decisions about the allocation of resources and assessment of results rely heavily on credible, valid, transparent, and understandable information. After comprehensive review of current practices, needs, and accountability initiatives sponsored by industry organizations, the group determined that while marketing was not ignoring the issues surrounding metrics and accountability, the practices and initiatives underway were narrow in focus, lacking integration, and generally not tied to financial performance.

The group then drafted Objectives of Marketing Standards and defined the Marketing Measurement Audit Protocol (MMAP) for connecting marketing activities to the financial performance of the firm. This process includes the conceptual linking of marketing activities to intermediate marketing outcome metrics, such as cash flow drivers of the business, as well as the validation and causality characteristics of a sound metric. Finally, members concluded that marketing will move from discretionary business expense to board-level strategic investment only through an independent standards-setting 'authority' for measuring (forecasting and improving) the financial return from marketing activities.

The establishment of the American National Standards Institute and International Organization for Standardization for manufacturing and product quality and the Financial Accounting Standards Board and International Accounting Standards Board for accounting and financial reporting, significantly improved reporting and business practices in the related areas. Likewise, marketing academics and practitioners viewed establishment of the MASB as an important opportunity to approach the metrics foundation of accountability and continuous improvement at the highest level: across industries, disciplines, and domains, with common language, purpose, and financial denominators and with collaboration and coordinated efforts over time. Thus, in the fall of 2007, The Boardroom Project launched the MASB of the Marketing Accountability Foundation with ten charter members, a long-term plan, and a dozen initial standards projects. The goal of the MASB is to set the standards and processes necessary for evaluating marketing measurement in a manner that ensures credibility, validity, transparency, and understanding. We perceive an important role of MASB for marketing practitioners and academics alike. For practitioners, we anticipate that uniform and more extensive reporting of marketing information will help elevate the role of marketing information and, therefore, marketing activities and investments in the eyes of crucial stakeholders (e.g., investors, financial institutions, finance executives). For marketing academics, we anticipate that the extensive release of marketing information disclosure will provide empirical research opportunities to explore questions (some of which we identify in this chapter) that have been hitherto unexamined because of a lack of availability of data.

CONCLUSION

Many research opportunities exist to generate insights into the disclosure of marketing information and extend the marketing metrics literature. We have identified several research questions that we hope will spur marketing scholars to work in this area. The research questions cover many facets of marketing information disclosures and highlight the need for multiple methods of data collection (e.g., text analyses, data collection from websites, conference calls, and annual reports) and analytical methods (e.g., duration models, stochastic frontier analyses, regression models). In doing so, marketing scholars will not only extend the marketing literature but also make important contributions to the influential finance and accounting literature on corporate information disclosures. We hope that marketing scholars will rise to this challenge.

NOTES

* We thank the two anonymous reviewers for their useful feedback on a previous version of the chapter.
1. For the disclosure ranking, see http://www.businessweek.com/investor/oct2002/pi20021015_6208.htm; accessed 1 March, 2011.

REFERENCES

Aaker, D.A. and J.M. Carman (1982), 'Are You Overadvertising?,' *Journal of Advertising Research*, **22** (4), 57–70.
Aaker, D.A. and R. Jacobson (1994), 'The Financial Information Content of Perceived Quality,' *Journal of Marketing Research*, **31** (2), 191–201.
Abarbanell, J.S., W.N. Lanen, and R.E. Verrecchia (1995), 'Analysts' Forecasts as Proxies for Investor Beliefs in Empirical Research,' *Journal of Accounting and Economics*, **20** (1), 31–60.
Agrawal, J. and W. Kamakura (1995), 'The Economic Worth of Celebrity Endorsers: An Event Study Analysis,' *Journal of Marketing*, **59** (3), 56–62.
Akerlof, G. (1970), 'The Market for Lemons: Quality Uncertainty and Market Mechanism,' *Quarterly Journal of Economics*, **84** (3), 488–500.
Aksoy, L., B. Cooil, C. Groening, T.L. Keiningham, and A. Yalcin (2008), 'The Long-term Stock Market Valuation of Customer Satisfaction,' *Journal of Marketing*, **72** (4) 105–22.
Ambler, T. (2003), *Marketing and the Bottom Line*, London: Financial Times/Prentice Hall.

Barron, O.E., D. Byard, C. Kile, and E.J. Riedl (2002), 'High-technology Intangibles and Analysts' Forecasts,' *Journal of Accounting Research*, **40** (2), 289–312.

Barth, M., R. Kasznik, and M. McNichols (2001), 'Analyst Coverage and Intangible Assets,' *Journal of Accounting Research*, **39** (1), 1–34.

Bharadwaj, S.G., K.R. Tuli, and A. Bonfrer (2011), 'The Impact of Brand Quality on Shareholder Value,' *Journal of Marketing*, **75** (5), 88–104.

Blattberg, R.C. and S.A. Neslin (1990), *Sales Promotion: Concepts, Methods, and Strategies*, Englewood Cliffs, NJ: Prentice Hall.

Botosan, C.A. and M.A. Plumlee (2002), 'A Re-Examination of Disclosure Level and the Expected Cost of Equity Capital,' *Journal of Accounting Research*, **40** (1), 21–40.

Bushee, B.J. and C.F. Noe (2000), 'Corporate Disclosure Practices, Institutional Investors, and Stock Return Volatility,' *Journal of Accounting Research*, **38** (3), 171–201.

Chambers, D., R. Jennings, and R.B. Thompson (2002), 'Excess Returns to R&D-intensive Firms,' *Review of Accounting Studies*, **7** (2–3), 133–58.

Chan, L.K.C., J. Lakonishok, and T. Sougiannis (2001), 'The Stock Market Valuation of Research and Development Expenditures,' *Journal of Finance*, **56** (6), 2431–56.

Chaney, P., T. Devinney, and R. Winer (1991), 'The Impact of New Product Introductions on the Market Valuation of Firms,' *Journal of Business*, **64** (4), 573–610.

Dierickx, I. and K. Cool (1989), 'Asset Stock Accumulation and Sustainability of Competitive Advantage,' *Management Science*, **35** (12), 1504–11.

Diether, K., C. Malloy, and A. Scherbina (2002), 'Differences of Opinion and the Cross Section of Stock Returns,' *Journal of Finance*, **57** (5), 2113–41.

Dutta, S., O. Narasimhan, and S. Rajiv (1999), 'Success in High-technology Markets: Is Marketing Capability Critical?,' *Marketing Science*, **18** (4), 547–68.

Eng, L.L. and Y.T. Mak (2003), 'Corporate Governance and Voluntary Disclosure,' *Journal of Accounting and Public Policy*, **22** (4), 325–45.

Frieder, L. and A. Subrahmanyam (2005), 'Brand Perceptions and the Market for Common Stock,' *Journal of Financial & Quantitative Analysis*, **40** (1), 57–85.

Gelb, D.S. (2002), 'Intangible Assets and Firms' Disclosures: An Empirical Investigation,' *Journal of Business Finance and Accounting*, **29** (3/4), 457–76.

Geyskens, I., K. Gielens, and M. Dekimpe (2002), 'The Market Valuation of Internet Channel Additions,' *Journal of Marketing*, **66** (2), 102–19.

Gruca, T.S. and L.L. Rego (2005), 'Customer Satisfaction, Cash Flow, and Shareholder Value,' *Journal of Marketing*, **69** (3), 115–30.

Grullon, G., G. Kanatas, and J.P. Weston (2004), 'Advertising, Breadth of Ownership and Liquidity,' *The Review of Financial Studies*, **17** (2), 439–61.

Han, B. and D. Manry (2000), 'The Implications of Dispersion in Analysts' Earnings Forecasts for Future ROE and Future Returns,' *Journal of Business Finance & Accounting*, **27** (1/2), 99–125.

Heitzman, S., C. Wasley, and J. Zimmerman (2010), 'The Joint Effects of Materiality Thresholds and Voluntary Disclosure Incentives on Firms' Disclosure Decisions,' *Journal of Accounting and Economics*, **49** (1–2), 109–32.

Hendricks, K.B. and V.R. Singhal (1997), 'Delays in New Product Introductions and the Market Value of the Firm: The Consequences of Being Late to the Market,' *Management Science*, **43** (4), 422–36.

Horsky, D. and P. Swyngedouw (1987), 'Does It Pay to Change Your Company's Name? A Stock Market Perspective,' *Marketing Science*, **6** (4), 320–35.

Houston, M.B. and S.A. Johnson (2000), 'Buyer–Supplier Contracts versus Joint Ventures: Determinants and Consequences of Transaction Structure,' *Journal of Marketing Research*, **37** (1), 1–15.

Jarrell, G. and S. Peltzman (1985), 'The Impact of Product Recalls on the Wealth of Sellers,' *Journal of Political Economy*, **93** (3), 512–36.

Joshi, A.M. and D.M. Hanssens (2009), 'Movie Advertising and the Stock Market Valuation of Studios: A Case of "Great Expectations?",' *Marketing Science*, **28** (2), 239–50.

Joshi, A.M. and D.M. Hanssens (2010), 'Direct and Indirect Advertising Spending on Firm Value,' *Journal of Marketing*, **74** (1), 20–33.

Kothari, S.P., T. Laguerre, and A. Leone (2002), 'Capitalization Versus Expensing: Evidence on the Uncertainty of Future Earnings from Capital Expenditures versus R&D Outlays,' *Review of Accounting Studies*, **7** (4), 355–82.

Lane, V. and R. Jacobson (1995), 'Stock Market Reactions to Brand Extension Announcements: The Effects of Brand Attitude and Familiarity,' *Journal of Marketing*, **59** (1), 63–77.

Lang, M. and R. Lundholm (1996), 'Corporate Disclosure Policy and Analyst Behavior,' *The Accounting Review*, **71** (4), 467–92.

Leuz, C. and R.E. Verrecchia (2000), 'The Economic Consequences of Increased Disclosure,' *Journal of Accounting Research*, **38** (3), 91–124.

Lev, B. (2001), *Intangibles: Management, Measurement, and Reporting*, Washington, DC: Brookings Institution.

Luo, X. and C. Homburg (2008), 'Satisfaction, Complaint, and the Stock Value Gap,' *Journal of Marketing*, **72** (4), 29–43.

Luo, X., C. Homburg, and J. Wieseke (2010), 'Customer Satisfaction, Analyst Stock Recommendations, and Firm Value,' *Journal of Marketing Research*, **47** (6), 1041–58.

Mansfield, E. (1981), 'Composition of R&D Expenditures: Relationship to Size of Firm, Concentration and Innovative Output,' *Review of Economics and Statistics*, **63** (4), 610–14.

McAlister, L., R. Srinivasan, and M. Kim (2007), 'Advertising, Research and Development, and Systematic Risk of the Firm,' *Journal of Marketing*, **71** (1), 35–48.

Pauwels, K., J. Silva-Risso, S. Srinivasan, and D.M. Hanssens (2004), 'New Products, Sales Promotions, and Firm Value: The Case of the Automobile Industry,' *Journal of Marketing*, **68** (4), 142–56.

Peltzman, S. (1981), 'The Effects of FTC Advertising Regulation,' *Journal of Law and Economics*, **24** (3), 403–48.

Perry, S. and R. Grinaker (1994), 'Earnings Expectations and Discretionary Research and Development Spending,' *Accounting Horizons*, **8** (4), 43–51.

Picconi, M.J. (1977), 'A Reconsideration of the Recognition of Advertising Assets on Financial Statements,' *Journal of Accounting Research*, **15** (2), 317–26.

Rao, V.R., M. Agarwal, and D. Dahloff (2004), 'How is Manifested Branding Strategy Related to the Intangible Value of a Corporation?,' *Journal of Marketing*, **68** (4), 126–41.

Rust, R.T., T. Ambler, G.S. Carpenter, V. Kumar, and R.K. Srivastava (2004), 'Measuring Marketing Productivity: Current Knowledge and Future Directions,' *Journal of Marketing*, **68** (4), 76–89.

Simon, C.J. and M. Sullivan (1993), 'The Measurement and Determinants of Brand Equity: A Financial Approach,' *Marketing Science*, **12** (1), 28–52.

Simpson, Ana (2008), 'Voluntary Disclosure of Advertising Expenditure,' *Journal of Accounting, Auditing and Finance*, **23** (3), 403–36.

Singh, M., S. Faircloth, and A. Nejadmalayeri (2005), 'Capital Market Impact of Product Marketing Strategy: Evidence from the Relationship Between Advertising Expenses and Cost of Capital,' *Journal of the Academy of Marketing Science*, **33** (4), 432–44.

Sorescu, A. and J. Spanjol (2008), 'Innovation's Effect on Firm Value and Risk: Insights from Consumer Packaged Goods,' *Journal of Marketing*, **72** (2), 114–32.

Sorescu, A., V. Shankar, and T. Kushwaha (2007), 'New Product Preannouncements and Shareholder Value: Don't Make Promises You Can't Keep,' *Journal of Marketing Research*, **44** (3), 468–89.

Spence, M. (1973), 'Job Market Signaling,' *Quarterly Journal of Economics*, **87** (3), 355–74.

Srinivasan, R. (2006), 'Dual Distribution and Intangible Firm Value: Franchising in Restaurant Chains,' *Journal of Marketing*, **70** (3), 120–35.

Srinivasan, R. and S. Bharadwaj (2004), 'Event Studies in Marketing Strategy Research,' in C. Moorman and D.R. Lehmann (eds), *Assessing Marketing Strategy Performance*, Cambridge, MA: Marketing Science Institute.

Srinivasan, S. and D. Hanssens (2009), 'Marketing and Firm Value: Metrics, Methods, Findings, and Future Directions,' *Journal of Marketing Research*, **46** (3), 293–312.

Srinivasan, S., K. Pauwels, D.M. Hanssens, and M.G. Dekimpe (2004), 'Do Promotions Benefit Manufacturers, Retailers, or Both,' *Marketing Science*, **50** (5), 617–29.

Srivastava, R., T. Shervani, and L. Fahey (1998), 'Market-based Assets and Shareholder Value: A Framework for Analysis,' *Journal of Marketing*, **62** (1), 2–18.

Tetlock, P.C. (2007), 'Giving Content to Investor Sentiment: The Role of Media in the Stock Market,' *Journal of Finance*, **62** (3), 1139–68.

Tuli, K.R. and S.G. Bharadwaj (2009), 'Customer Satisfaction and Stock Returns Risk,' *Journal of Marketing*, **73** (6), 184–97.

Wiesel, T., B. Skiera, and J. Villanueva (2008), 'Customer Equity: An Integral Part of Financial Reporting,' *Journal of Marketing*, **72** (2), 1–14.

PART II

CREATING, COMMUNICATING, DELIVERING, AND SUSTAINING VALUE AND FIRM PERFORMANCE

6   Innovation and the market value of firms
Alina Sorescu

INNOVATION AS A DRIVER OF SHAREHOLDER VALUE

A generally accepted tenet of strategy is that innovation is a critical strategic goal, a main source of competitive advantage, and a primary driver of shareholder value for firms. For decades, researchers have sought to understand the magnitude of this value and its determinants. Yet we still lack a set of clear guidelines on what type of innovation maximizes shareholder wealth, and how to organize for it. In practice, the rate of new product introductions seems ever increasing, but the rate of new product failure is also excessive, with some estimates as high as 75 percent (Cooper et al., 2004). At the same time, there is no shortage of successful innovations and we frequently encounter products, process, and business model innovations that are changing consumer behavior, rendering industry paradigms obsolete, and significantly increasing the wealth of their parent firms. For instance, Amazon.com is now selling more eBooks than hardcover editions: in June 2010 it sold 180 Kindle editions for every hardcover (Kennedy, 2010). As a result, and in spite of the recessionary period, the 2010 revenues of Amazon.com are expected to pass the $30 billion mark, up from $25.5 billion in 2009 (Alva, 2010). Zara's implementation of the innovative 'fast fashion' business model has led to significant merchandising and distribution changes in the apparel industry, and has turned Zara into the world's largest apparel retailer (Bjork, 2010). Self-service DVD rental kiosks (e.g., Redbox), or the ability to stream video rentals over the Internet (e.g., Netflix) have changed the manner in which people rent and view videos. While incumbent Blockbuster filed for bankruptcy, Redbox's 2009 revenue exceeded $1 billion (Coinstar Earnings Report, 2010) and Netflix's revenue is steadily increasing over 2009 levels (*Investors' Business Daily*, 2010).

The examples above highlight the breadth of innovation in today's marketplace as well as the many challenges that researchers and managers alike face in assessing its financial consequences. First, innovation[1] can take many forms, come from many sources, and its success may depend just as much on how it is marketed as it does on its intrinsic characteristics. Second, new product development (NPD) processes and the drivers of innovation success differ significantly across industries, but many insights in academic research are obtained using specialized, industry-specific datasets, and thus cannot be easily generalized to other industries. Third, there is no clear consensus on which metrics best capture the short- and long-term success of innovations, making it difficult to draw empirical generalizations from prior research. Moreover, shortening product life cycles and a highly dynamic, competitive, and global environment may call into question current benchmarks for the effectiveness and efficiency of NPD processes. Thus, many questions remain unanswered and much extant knowledge needs to be re-examined and updated.

To best understand the value of innovation, we need to distinguish between three types of innovation: product, process, and business model innovation. The majority of extant research focuses on the most salient (and arguably most prevalent) type: product innovation. Less attention has been dedicated to process and business model innovation, perhaps because details in these cases are more closely guarded by firms seeking to build and protect their competitive advantage.

Process innovation combines 'the adoption of a process view of the business with the application of innovation to key processes' (Davenport, 1993, p. 1). While process innovation has been the subject of two excellent books (Davenport, 1993; Pisano, 1997), it has not been widely studied in the academic literature (see Hatch and Mowery, 1998; Adner and Levinthal, 2001 and Kirner et al., 2009 for exceptions), and to my knowledge no paper has explicitly studied its relation with market value. Process innovation has, however, occasionally been combined with product innovation in empirical research focused on the valuation of innovation. For instance, the UK's Science Policy Research Unit (SPRU) database from which Blundell et al. (1999) draw their sample defines innovation as 'the successful commercial introduction of new or improved products, processes or materials' (Blundell et al., 1999, p. 551).

Business model innovation is another topic that has only recently gained momentum in academic research, perhaps spearheaded by the increase of this type of innovation in practice. Shortening product cycles have raised the relevance of business model innovations as drivers of competitive advantage, since they are more complex, less visible, and thus harder to replicate. Further, a firm's business model impacts both its NPD process and the manner in which it commercializes products. The same product commercialized in two different ways may have markedly different contributions to shareholder value (Chesbrough, 2010). We would expect, therefore, that investors recognize the importance of the business model – the mechanism that outlines how a firm creates and appropriates value (Zott and Amit, 2010) – and that stock prices positively react to innovations that improve the effectiveness or efficiency of a firm's business model. However, no academic research, to my knowledge, examines the returns to business model innovation. Only one industry study offers some insights: a Boston Consulting Group study in 2010 reports that, on average, firms pursuing business model innovation earned 2.7 percent excess stock returns over a ten-year period, compared to 1.7 percent excess stock returns for firms pursuing product and process innovation (Lindgardt et al., 2009).

While research on the value-added by process and business model innovation is still in its infancy, new product innovation has been extensively studied. Successful new products can increase shareholder value directly, by driving firm revenues, and also indirectly, by strengthening firms' brand equity and – if they are hard to imitate – by erecting barriers of entry. Two main research streams have examined the relation between product innovation and market value. First, a large body of work has set out to assess whether this relation is, on average, positive. Second, an equally large stream of research focuses on what types of innovation are more valuable, or under which conditions innovation is more valuable.

It is the second question that is perhaps of most interest to both managers and academics. This chapter is structured around it. First, I examine the determinants of a successful innovation. I explain that returns to innovation are different when innovation is measured using patents versus new products, or when the innovation is radical versus incremental. Also important is whether the innovation is generated by the firm alone, as a result of an alliance, or simply outsourced from another firm or from an open community of inventors. Second, I analyze the various metrics of shareholder value that have been used in the literature with the goal of identifying those measures that are best suited to measure the value of innovation, given the statistical challenges related to measuring equity returns. I conclude with a forward-looking research agenda related to the relation between innovation and shareholder value.

CHARACTERISTICS OF INNOVATION AND THEIR CONSEQUENCES ON MARKET VALUATION

Stages of the Innovation Process

The NPD process has multiple stages, from idea to commercialization. As a result, firm-level innovation has been operationalized in many ways across studies, ranging from innovation in its earliest stages, such as R&D expenditures and patents, to actual new products. Not surprisingly, the returns to innovation vary significantly depending on what innovation stage is being evaluated. Intuitively, the earlier the stage, the more uncertain the innovation outcome, the smaller the incremental returns attributed to innovation, ceteris paribus. However, Sood and Tellis (2009) measured stock market returns across a set of events that trace the progress of an innovation project and found that returns to a new product launch are the lowest among all events tracked. Further, they found that the total stock market returns to innovation, or the sum of returns across all significant events in an innovation project, from securing funding, to establishing NPD alliances, to submitting patents, to launch, are 13 times higher than the returns to an individual innovation event. Sood and Tellis's findings suggest that it is important to construe innovation as a process, and that all stages of this process contribute to the overall stock market valuation of innovation (also see Kelm et al., 1995).

Researchers who focus on the early stages of the innovation process have examined the valuation of R&D expenditures, patent output, and product preannouncements. While R&D is technically an input into the innovation process, rather than an actual measure of innovation, many authors implicitly assume a direct link between R&D expenditures and innovation output and use the latter to build the conceptual arguments and the former to empirically test these arguments (e.g., Kelm et al., 1995 and Yang and Chen, 2004). R&D expenditures have generally been found to positively impact the firm values. Positive relations between R&D expenditures and, respectively, market value (Chauvin and Hirschey, 1993; Greenhalgh and Rogers, 2006), Tobin's Q (Hall and Oriani, 2006; Ceccagnoli, 2009) and stock returns (Pakes, 1985; Lev and Sougiannis, 1996) have been documented, but the variance in the magnitude of results indicates the presence of contingencies that may require further study.

There is less clarity in the literature on the stock market value of patents. Some authors have questioned their economic value. For instance, in a much cited article, Ariel Pakes states: 'most of the variance in the stock market rate of return has little to do with the firm's inventive endeavors, at least as measured by its R&D input and its patent output' (Pakes, 1985, p. 407). Others found that the value of patents depends upon firm and patent characteristics: for instance, the stock of patents is a significant determinant of Tobin's Q only for the firms in the top Tobin's Q quantiles (Coad and Rao, 2006). Alternatively, patenting activities are valued by the stock market only when they are highly visible: for instance, Greenhalgh and Rogers (2006) found that firms that receive only UK patents have no significant market premium; rather, they have to be obtained through the European Patent Office for a premium to materialize. Other authors argue that the *relative* number of patents to R&D expenditures and patent citations to patent counts are actual drivers of stock market value (Hall et al., 2005). Yet others report a robust relation between patents and market value (e.g., Connolly and Hirschey, 1988; Austin, 1993).

Further ahead in the NPD process are the products that have been developed but are not quite ready for launch. Some firms choose to release pre-launch information about them. A small stream of literature documents positive stock market returns to preannouncements of new products (Mishra and Bhabra, 2002; Sorescu et al., 2007b; Sood and Tellis, 2009). This finding suggests that firms have the appealing option of incorporating the expected cash flows from a new product in its market value prior to the product's market introduction. However, preannouncing is not without peril: delaying a previously preannounced product decreases the market value of the firm by 5.25 percent (Hendricks and Singhal, 1997) and reduces any potential gains from future preannouncements (Bayus et al., 2001).

Finally, a sizeable research stream has examined the stock market response to new products that have already been launched. Findings in this area include a positive relation between the stock of innovation and the market value of the parent firm (e.g., Blundell et al., 1999), Tobin's Q (e.g., Sorescu and Spanjol, 2008) and long-term abnormal returns (ibid.). Others document a positive relation between announcements of new product introductions and short-term cumulative abnormal returns (e.g., Chaney et al., 1991) or long-term abnormal returns (e.g., Pauwels et al., 2004). Findings in all of these studies vary considerably as to the determinants of relation between innovation and value, as well as the metrics used to measure the value of innovation. I return to this later in the chapter with a detailed discussion of the determinants of innovation as well as an analysis of the metrics used for measuring shareholder value.

Degree of Innovativeness: Radical Versus Incremental Innovation

Many papers that examine the shareholder value created by innovation share a common limitation: though authors refer to innovation in general terms, their empirical analysis often relies on samples of radical or otherwise highly salient innovations. For instance, Blundell et al. (1999, p. 539) use a sample of 'technologically significant and commercially important' innovations from SPRU. Several authors conduct their empirical analysis on samples of new product announcements that are reported in the *Wall Street Journal*, which typically does not herald mere incremental innovations (e.g., Chaney et al., 1991; Kelm et al., 1995; Lee and Chen, 2009). This, of course, raises the issue of whether innovation in general can create shareholder wealth, or whether most effects found in prior research are caused by *radical* innovation.

There is strong evidence that breakthrough or radical products, when explicitly identified as such, have an unequivocal positive effect on stock prices and this effect is apparent even in cross-country studies (Tellis et al., 2009). For instance, Srinivasan et al. (2009) find that among a set of determinants of stock returns, new-to-the-market innovations are associated with the largest stock returns, and that 'the advent of pioneering innovations dominates all other explanatory variables in the models' (Srinivasan et al., 2009, p. 36). Sorescu and Spanjol (2008) show that breakthrough innovations in the Consumer Packaged Goods (CPG) industry have a positive effect on both Tobin's Q and long-term abnormal returns, but also increase firm risk. In contrast, incremental innovations positively impact Tobin's Q only, suggesting that they are necessary for firms to achieve normal profits, but they are not a source of economic rents. Indeed, while managers may be tempted to mitigate financial risk by exploiting existing platforms, an imitative approach has never been associated with a superior financial performance. Case in point, 88 percent of participants from a recent study of senior managers from CPG firms believe that new products fail because they lack differentiation (Curewitz, 2009).

Where is Innovation Generated?

Not all innovations are the products of firms' own R&D labs. While many innovations are developed in-house, others are developed through technological alliances, obtained from acquired firms, or even developed with the help of customers, suppliers or individuals who are otherwise unrelated to the firm. Most prior research assumes that innovations are developed in-house, but a significant stream of research examines performance outcomes of technological alliances, a frequent mode of innovation in the high-tech sector. For instance, Das et al. (1998) find that stock market responses to announcements of technological alliances are more favorable than responses to marketing alliances, presumably because of the innovation outcomes that investors expect from technological alliances. Kalaignanam et al. (2007) examine the stock returns to R&D alliance announcements and find higher gains for innovative alliance partners. Thus, the stock market appears to value attempts to create innovation through cooperation, which contributes pooled resources and complementary knowledge to the NPD process.

An alternative – and increasingly popular – way to generate innovation is to rely on the community of inventors at large, which includes customers, suppliers, channel partners or individuals otherwise unaffiliated with the company but who are engaged in knowledge creation. Termed either 'open innovation' (Chesbrough, 2003) or 'consumer co-creation' (Hoyer et al., 2010), this is an exciting revolution in the innovation domain. Firms are no longer bound to their R&D labs and now have a seemingly infinite creative base to tap upon for new product ideas. Intuitively, a significantly larger pool of projects that could be developed for commercialization should increase the likelihood that more successful projects will be selected. Thus, the performance of innovation and its contribution to shareholder value should also increase.

While direct evidence on the relation between open innovation and shareholder value is not yet available, several recent papers suggest that the relation between the quantity of open innovation and firm revenues is inverted U-shaped (Laursen and Salter, 2006; Stam, 2009). It may actually be inefficient to search too widely and deeply for innovation outside the firm. Alternatively, a much focused effort might result in a too narrow pool of ideas that may not include projects with high potential. The tradeoffs between the resources dedicated to open innovation and how much this type of innovation can contribute to shareholder value are important topics for future research.

DETERMINANTS OF THE SHAREHOLDER VALUE CREATED BY INNOVATION

Firm Resources and Capabilities as Determinants of the Market Value of Innovation

One of the most frequently studied determinants of the relation of innovation to market value is firm size. At first sight, it seems to be a controversial one, with some authors arguing that large firms earn more from innovation than small firms do (e.g., Blundell et al., 1999; Sorescu et al., 2003) while others claim that small firms benefit the most (e.g., Lee and Chen, 2009; Sood and Tellis, 2009). These seemingly contradictory results are due to the metrics used in each paper: cumulative abnormal stock returns (CARs), a relative measure of increase in shareholder value, tend to favor small firms while net present value (NPV), an absolute dollar value, tends to favor large firms. Austin (1993) explains this tradeoff in the context of stock market reaction to patent announcements and suggests that it would be misleading to conclude that patents from large firms are worth less than the ones from a small firm simply on the basis of CARs. He finds that larger firms have smaller abnormal returns to patent announcements but larger dollar abnormal returns. Nevertheless, he concludes that it is hard to disentangle the value of innovation from the resources of the firm that markets it.

While small firms may not be able to increase their market value in an absolute dollar sense as much as large firms do, there are other determinants of the relation between innovation and market value that they can leverage. One such factor is legitimacy: having previously introduced a successful new product, or having a reputed executive or scientist work for the firm has been shown to increase the returns to innovation (Rao et al., 2008). Another is R&D intensity, which is positively related to Tobin's Q, and this relation is stronger for firms with high effectiveness of patent protection (Ceccagnoli, 2009). Greater R&D intensity also strengthens the performance of open innovation (Stam, 2009). The manner in which parent firms leverage extant knowledge also impacts the market value of innovations. Heeley and Jacobson (2008) find that the firms whose new patents utilize medial-aged technological inputs experience higher returns than firms whose patents either draw from the technological input frontier or rely on old patents. Finally, Tellis et al. (2009) find that internal corporate culture is an important driver of radical innovation, which in turn increases the market value of firms across nations.

A critical determinant of market success, and consequently of the value created by innovation, is the marketing support allocated to the innovation. This support has to be provided ex ante, in the form of marketing research meant to clarify current needs and trends. It also has to be provided ex post, in order to build brand equity and product differentiation. Further, if these forms of support are misaligned, the innovation is likely to fail. Case in point is the Souper-Combo, launched in the late 1980s by Campbell, which combined a frozen bowl of soup and a sandwich. The results of pre-launch marketing predicted a blockbuster, but insufficient post-launch support turned it into yet another entry in the cemetery of brand failures (Curewitz, 2009). While there is evidence that variables proxying post-launch marketing support, such as firm advertising expenditures (Srinivasan et al., 2009) or selling and general administrative expenditures (Lee and Chen, 2009), increase the returns to innovation, more research is needed to understand how pre-launch marketing efforts contribute to the shareholder value of innovation.

Innovation Valuation and Firm Ownership

The stock market value of innovation may depend on firm ownership. Prior research suggests that firm ownership impacts the choice of corporate innovation strategies. For instance, Hoskisson et al. (2002) found that managers of public pension funds prefer that the firms whose stock they own pursue internal innovation, while managers of professional investment funds prefer that firms focus on acquiring external innovation. This stream of research has also fostered a debate on whether institutional investors are myopic, focused on short-term gains or look for long-term benefits from their investments in firm equity. Kochhar and David (1996) review this literature, empirically test the effects of institutional ownership on innovation, and conclude that the presence of institutional investors does not foster short-term behavior on the part of firm managers. Indeed, institutional investors may be better equipped to handle risk, given their diversified portfolios, than private investors. Consequently, the managers of firms whose ownership is primarily institutional may be more likely to encourage radical innovation and may gain more from innovation in the long term. A fruitful avenue for future research is to clarify how managerial incentives and firm ownership structure impacts the choice of NPD projects and the horizon over which stock market value accrues to these projects.

While the focus of this chapter is the impact of innovation on stock market value, it is worth noting that we cannot have a complete understanding of the value of innovation without taking into consideration innovation generated by private firms. Forbes's latest ranking of America's largest private companies contains 223 companies that account for $1.3 trillion in revenues (Forbes, 2010). Among these are companies such as Mars, Chrysler or Cargill, which are just as likely to generate innovation as their publicly owned competitors. But performance data from these companies is scarce, and – in the absence of stock prices – forward-looking measures of innovation performance cannot be computed. A few insights on the value of innovation by private firms can be gleaned from the value of such firms' IPOs (e.g., Heeley et al., 2007) or from the acquisition premiums paid when such companies are acquired (e.g., Capron and Shen, 2007), but more research is needed to provide clear insights on the value of innovation from private firms.

Environmental Factors that Impact the Market Value of Innovation

Competitive pressure does not only affect the level of innovation, but also the financial rewards associated with it. In general, the weight of evidence supports the Schumpeterian hypothesis, that is, returns to innovations are higher in less than fully competitive markets (e.g., Greenhalgh and Rogers, 2006). Competitors' resources have also been found to impact the shareholder value created by innovation. For instance, returns to patents depend on the R&D intensity of firms' direct competitors: firms whose research overlaps an area actively researched by other firms have more patents and enjoy higher returns on their R&D expenditures. This finding, however, does not hold for firms with very low R&D expenditures (Jaffe,

1986). Further, the returns to patents and R&D increase as the level of appropriability within an industry increases (Cockburn and Griliches, 1988). Finally, recent evidence also suggests that R&D valuation varies by country, and each country may have unique drivers of innovation value, such as the ownership structure of firms (e.g., Hall and Oriani, 2006; Tellis et al., 2009).

The current recessionary environment is also impacting the types of innovations being introduced and their ability to generate rents. There is an increase in *frugal* innovation in the marketplace, and the United States is not leading the way. Firms in emerging markets, having served low-income customers for decades, are best positioned to produce it (*Economist*, 2010). When value for money becomes the primary metric used by consumers to evaluate new products, companies have to reconsider their value propositions and strategic innovation objectives, and should identify and map out the new drivers of innovation value.

METRICS FOR ASSESSING THE SHAREHOLDER VALUE OF INNOVATION

Value Creation Process

What is the best way to measure the value that innovation creates for the shareholder? A successful innovation generates high earnings, as well as high consumer satisfaction and favorable attitudes toward the product. Yet, it is difficult to fully measure the value of innovation using these metrics alone. Consumer-based measures, which often rely on discrete measurement scales, do not typically allow for a range of variance in responses that would appropriately reflect the true variance in the market potential of innovations. Net earnings are more appropriate, but it is often difficult to isolate the fraction of earnings that corresponds directly to a specific innovation. Another major limitation is that earnings should be measured over the entire lifetime of the product to effectively assess the value of innovation. Stock prices provide an alternative that remedies this limitation. Fundamentally, the value of a stock is the present value of future cash flows, discounted at the risk-adjusted cost of equity (Fama and Miller, 1972). The announcement of an innovation causes investors to change their expectations about the parent firm's future cash flows, which, in turn, results in a change in stock prices. That change, if correctly measured, corresponds to investors' estimate of the NPV of all future cash flows associated with the innovation in question. It also reflects the effect that the innovation has on all other metrics, such as earnings and consumer attitudes. While this argument rests upon the often questioned assumption of perfectly efficient stock markets, I will shortly discuss why this assumption is not critical with improved methods that measure stock returns over the *long term*.

Firms create shareholder value by earning economic rents. To do so, they must sell their products and services at a premium – a price higher than the cost of production and capital. More generally, to earn rents, firms must identify – and execute – projects with positive NPV. With few exceptions, economic rents are passed on to the firms' shareholders, so the shares of a successful innovator will earn a rate of return higher than that required by investors as compensation for risk and time value of money. These excess returns – known as abnormal returns – can be measured through pricing models such as the capital asset pricing model (CAPM) or the Fama-French model. Depending on how quickly investors can understand the value created by innovation, abnormal returns can become apparent in the short term, over a few days or weeks, or in the long term over several months or years. In addition to producing excess returns, the expectation of future economic rents also inflates the market value of the firm's assets in relation to its book value – a concept known as Tobin's Q. In simple terms, the market value of the firm's assets can be viewed as the book value of assets plus the net present value of the firm's future innovations and other investment projects. The higher the firm's future expected rents from innovation, the higher its market value of assets, the higher the Tobin's Q.

Comparing abnormal returns with Tobin's Q, we see that the abnormal returns are a flow variable because they capture the present value of economic rents earned during a specific time period. By contrast, Tobin's Q is a stock variable and can be best thought of as a picture in time of the market's estimate of all future economic rents the firm expects to earn. In the following sections I review – in the context of the innovations literature – the main methods used for measuring the creation of shareholder value. I note that these are not the only metrics of financial performance used in strategy research, but the most prevalent ones used in assessing the stock market value of innovation.

Tobin's Q Measure

Conceptually, Tobin's Q is the ratio of the market value of the firm's assets (itself the discounted value of the firm's future cash flows) to the replacement value of assets. Because Tobin's Q is a stock variable, it is particularly useful in cross-sectional or panel data studies where the stock of shareholder wealth is compared to the stock of innovation or to the stock of another variable related to the firm's strategy. Indeed, this metric has been used to assess the value created by R&D expenditures (Ceccagnoli, 2009), patents (Hall et al., 2005), and new products (Sorescu and Spanjol, 2008).

However, Tobin's Q is not without limitations. Results obtained using the Q are difficult to interpret because cross-sectional differences in Q values do not necessarily reflect differences in economic rents. Q values can differ across firms due to differing accounting choices in reporting total assets. Moreover, Q levels vary significantly across industries due to differences in growth rates and discount rates, making it a poor metric for cross-industry studies. Q values are also not directly comparable for the same firm across time, so changes in Q should not be used to capture the effect of innovations occurring during a given time period. This is because the value of Q can change significantly due to depreciation, mergers, acquisitions, or changes in accounting reporting conventions. Instead, abnormal return measures – to be discussed shortly – should be used if the objective is to capture changes in shareholder value over a finite time period. Finally, Tobin's Q assumes that the stock market is perfectly efficient, in the sense that stock prices correctly and completely incorporate all future effects of innovation. This assumption, challenged by recent research in behavioral finance, is perhaps the biggest limitation of the Tobin's Q measure. To overcome most of these limitations one has to turn to a new class of shareholder wealth measures, abnormal returns.

Abnormal Return Measures

Unlike Tobin's Q, which is a static measure of shareholder value, abnormal returns are dynamic, and measure firm-specific *changes* in shareholder value due to economic rents. Depending upon the assumptions one is willing to make about the efficiency of the stock market, abnormal returns can be measured in the short term, typically during the few days surrounding an event or announcement, or over the longer term, typically over one to three years. Regardless of the time horizon, all abnormal return measures consist of comparing the realized stock return with the rate of return investors require as compensation for risk and time value of money. The most challenging task with abnormal returns is to choose an appropriate benchmark, which ensures that the econometric tests are well specified. This is particularly true for long-term abnormal returns, where an incorrect benchmark could lead to erroneous inferences about the economic relation between two variables.

Short-term cumulative abnormal returns (CARs)
The most established measure of abnormal returns are the cumulative abnormal returns (CARs) measured over a short time horizon (Brown and

Warner, 1985). To compute CARs, firm-specific stock returns are added together over a three- to seven-day window surrounding a corporate event such as an innovation announcement. From this total, we subtract the cumulative rate of return of a benchmark that captures investors' required rate of return during that same period. Given the relatively short event windows used for measuring CARs, the choice of a benchmark is not critical and most researchers simply use a 'market adjusted' model, in which the benchmark is simply the average return of the stock market. Brown and Warner (1985) show that results using this 'market adjusted' model are just as well specified as those obtained using a 'market model' where the benchmark specifically adjusts for systematic risk. Event studies using CARs have been used extensively in the innovation literature (e.g., Chaney et al., 1991; Sood and Tellis, 2009). Some researchers have multiplied the CARs with the market value of equity, thus providing a dollar value of the NPV of the project featured in the respective corporate announcement (e.g., Austin, 1993; Sorescu et al., 2003).

A considerable advantage of the CARs metric is that it is forward-looking: it measures the innovation's economic rents earned not only during the time period when the CARs are measured, but also during the future useful economic life of the innovation. But the ability of CARs to provide useful information about the creation of shareholder value is limited by the somewhat restrictive assumptions that are inherent in that methodology – that stock markets are efficient and investors are able to accurately estimate and discount the firm's future cash flows associated with a particular project or innovation. These assumptions, as I discuss below, have recently been challenged by behavioral finance researchers. Their criticism has opened the way to a new generation of abnormal return measures, those based on long-term event windows.

Long-term abnormal returns
The efficient market hypothesis (EMH) is based on two major assumptions. The first is that investors' decision-making process follows the rational expectations model. The second is that investors have complete structural knowledge of the laws of economics and are able to correctly estimate the incremental cash flows resulting from innovation. These two assumptions have come under increased research scrutiny, and it is now generally accepted that, at least in some instances, investors could make use of heuristics in evaluating stock prices, or simply require additional information to correctly understand the true value created by innovation. In response to these challenges, researchers have developed methods of measuring stock returns over longer time periods, typically ranging from one to five years.

Like CARs, long-term abnormal return measures still capture the discounted value of *all* future cash flows resulting from innovation, not only the cash flows generated during the measurement period. The major difference with CAR methods is that information is no longer presumed to be immediately incorporated into stock prices, but over a period of time. I discuss here the two most common methods for measuring long-term abnormal returns: buy-and-hold abnormal returns (BHARs), and calendar time portfolio abnormal returns (CTARs).

Buy-and-hold abnormal returns   (BHARs) The most intuitive measure of long-term abnormal returns is one that captures the actual experience of a hypothetical investor who buys – and holds – the stock for a predetermined period of time. The BHARS are computed by taking the cumulative returns of a firm's stock over a window of one year or longer, and subtracting the cumulative performance of a benchmark comprised of stocks whose risk profile closely matches that of the firm over the same period. Daniel et al. (1997) propose, as benchmark, a portfolio of stocks with similar size, book-to-market, and momentum.

However, due to high cross-sectional correlation, the BHARs tend to produce inflated *t*-statistics. BHARs are most useful in cross-sectional analysis because they preserve rank ordering, and, indeed, several studies in marketing have used BHARs as dependent variables in cross-sectional and panel models (e.g., Sorescu et al., 2007a). One should note, however, that BHARs tend to produce significant outliers, especially on the positive side, and the use of methods such as winsorizing is recommended to diminish the effects of these outliers.

Calendar time portfolio abnormal returns (CTARs)   The calendar time measure was developed in response to BHARs' mis-specification problem. When correctly measured, CTARs are well specified, and have become the method of choice among finance researchers for measuring long-term abnormal returns. CTARs are computed by first grouping into a portfolio all firms that share a common characteristic such as a common event or corporate strategy. An example would be firms that had at least one radical innovation in the past year. To compute CTARs, we would form a single portfolio that invests in the stocks of radical innovators for exactly one year. The monthly returns of the resulting portfolio are then regressed on factors that are known to predict stock returns, such as size, book-to-market, and momentum. The resulting intercept – or 'alpha' – provides an estimate of the portfolio's abnormal return during that period. In the innovation domain the CTARs have been used to assess the stock market valuation of R&D expenditures (Chan et al., 2001) and new product preannouncements (Sorescu et al., 2007b).

CTARs' main limitation, however, is that they can only be computed at a portfolio level, not at an individual firm level, making them a poor fit for longitudinal studies or cross-sectional analysis. Researchers interested in using CTARs to study cross-sectional differences among firms with different strategies must group firms into several portfolios according to the values of the independent variable of interest, and then measure a separate 'alpha' for each portfolio. Inferences about the cross-sectional effects of the independent variable can be drawn by comparing the 'alphas' across portfolios.

Another limitation of CTARs is their notoriously low power (Loughran and Ritter, 2000). For abnormal returns of the order of 5 to 10 percent per year, the power of the test rarely exceeds 50 percent. This means that researchers should be cautious in interpreting tests with insignificant t-statistics as 'proof' that abnormal returns are zero. Given their low power, CTARs should be used primarily for rejecting the null; otherwise, the test result is inconclusive, except if magnitude of the point estimate of alpha is very small, or if its sign is the opposite of what was conjectured.

Table 6.1 provides a list of selected articles that have examined the effect of various forms of innovation on shareholder value, and highlights the metrics used to assess this value, as well as the type of innovation and the sources of data used in the empirical analysis.

RESEARCH AGENDA FOR THE VALUATION OF INNOVATION

Macroeconomic Implications of Innovation

Aggregate market returns

As mentioned previously, the NPV of innovation accrues to the firms' shareholders, and manifests in the form of abnormal returns. When the abnormal returns of all innovating firms are aggregated at the national level, that nation's stock market delivers a rate of return higher than expected, because the stock market is the mechanism by which rents from innovation are distributed back to the society. This could perhaps explain the extraordinary growth in US stock prices over the past century. With an inflation-adjusted growth rate of 8.06 percent, stocks overperformed bonds by 6.92 percent per year during the period from 1889 to 2000. The difference between the returns of stocks and bonds, or the equity premium, is much higher than what economists estimate would be a fair compensation for risk (Mehra and Prescott, 1985, 2003). Did the level of aggregate

Table 6.1 Selected list of papers that have examined the shareholder value created by innovation

Authors	Title	Year	Journal	Metric	Stage of the Innovation Process	Innovation Data Source	Industry
Blundell et al.	Market Share, Market Value and Innovation in a Panel of British Manufacturing Firms	1999	*Review of Economic Studies*	Market value	New products (innovation stock)	Panel of British firms	Multi-industry
Ceccagnoli	Appropriability, Preemption, and Firm Performance	2009	*Strategic Management Journal*	Tobin's Q	R&D (stock of expenditures)	Compustat	Multi-industry
Chan et al.	The Stock Market Valuation of Research and Development Expenditures	2001	*Journal of Finance*	CTAR	R&D expenditures (stock)	Compustat	Multi-industry
Chaney et al.	The Impact of New Product Introductions on the Market Value of Firms	1991	*Journal of Business*	ST (short-term) CARs	New products	WSJ announcements	Multi-industry
Chauvin and Hirschey	Advertising, R&D Expenditures and the Market Value of the Firm	1993	*Financial Management*	Market value	R&D expenditures	Compustat	Multi-industry
Coad and Rao	Innovation and Market Value: A Quantile Regression Analysis	2006	*Economics Bulletin*	Tobin's Q	Patents	NBER patent database	Multi-industry
Cockburn and Griliches	Industry Effects and Appropriability Measures in the Stock Market's Valuation of R&D and Patents	1988	*American Economic Review*	Market value	Patents and R&D expenditures	NBER patent database	Multi-industry
Connolly and Hirschey	Market Value and Patents: A Bayesian Approach	1988	*Economics Letters*	Excess market value	Patents	Not specified	Multi-industry

Author	Title	Year	Journal	Market value	Patents and R&D expenditures	Data source	Industry
Greenhalgh and Rogers	The Value of Innovation: The Interaction of Competition, R&D and IP	2006	*Research Policy*		Patents and R&D expenditures (industry level)	FAME and databases of European Patent Offices	Multi-industry
Hall and Oriani	Does the Market Value R&D Investment by European Firms? Evidence from a Panel of Manufacturing Firms in France, Germany, and Italy	2006	*International Journal of Industrial Organization*	Tobin's Q	R&D expenditures	Financial statements of European firms	Multi-industry
Hall et al.	Market Value and Patent Citations	2005	*RAND Journal of Economics*	Tobin's Q	Patents and R&D expenditures	USPTO data	Multi-industry
Heeley and Jacobson	The Recency of Technological Inputs and Financial Performance	2008	*Strategic Management Journal*	Stock returns	Patents	USPTO data	Multi-industry
Hendricks and Singhal	Delays in New Product Introductions and the Market Value of Firms; the Consequences of Being Late to the Market	1997	*Management Science*	ST CARs	Preannouncements (announcement of delay to the market)	Archival searches in news databases	Multi-industry
Jaffe	Technological Opportunity and Spillovers of R&D: Evidence from Firms' Patents, Profits, and Market Value	1986	*The American Economic Review*	Tobin's Q	Patents and R&D expenditures	USPTO data	Multi-industry
Kelm et al.	Shareholder Value Creation during R&D Innovation and Commercialization Stages	1995	*The Academy of Management Journal*	ST CARs	Multiple forms of innovation across stages	WSJ announcements	Multi-industry
Lee and Chen	The Immediate Impact of New Product Introductions on Stock Price: The Role of Firm Resources and Size	2009	*Journal of Product Innovation Management*	ST CARs	Products	WSJ announcements	Multi-industry

Table 6.1 (continued)

Authors	Title	Year	Journal	Metric	Stage of the Innovation Process	Innovation Data Source	Industry
Lev and Sougiannis	The Capitalization, Amortization, and Value-relevance of R&D	1996	*Journal of Accounting and Economics*	Monthly stock returns	R&D expenditures (levels and stock)	Compustat	Multi-industry
Pakes	On Patents, R&D, and the Stock Market Rate of Return	1985	*Journal of Political Economy*	Annual stock returns	Patents and R&D expenditures	USPTO data	Multi-industry
Rao et al.	The Fruits of Legitimacy: Why Some New Ventures Gain More from Innovation Than Others	2008	*Journal of Marketing*	ST CARs	Products	FDA	Biotech
Sharma and Lacey	Linking Product Development Outcomes to Market Valuation of the Firm: The Case of the U.S. Pharmaceutical Industry	2004	*Journal of Product Innovation Management*	ST CARs	Product (both successes and failures)	Recombinant	Pharma-ceutical
Sood and Tellis	Do Innovations Really Pay Off? Total Stock Market Returns to Innovation	2009	*Marketing Science*	ST CARs	Multiple forms of innovation across stages	Archival searches in news databases	Multi-industry

Sorescu and Spanjol	Innovation's Effect on Firm Value and Risk: Insights from Consumer Packaged Goods	2008	*Journal of Marketing*	BHARs, Tobin's Q	Products	Productscan	CPG
Sorescu et al.	Sources and Financial Consequences of Radical Innovation: Insights from Pharmaceuticals	2003	*Journal of Marketing*	ST CARs	Products	FDA	Pharmaceutical
Sorescu et al.	New Product Preannouncements and Shareholder Value: Don't Make Promises You Can't Keep	2007	*Journal of Marketing Research*	ST CARs and CTAR	Preannouncements	Archival searches in news databases	Computer hardware and software
Srinivasan et al.	Product Innovations, Advertising, and Stock Returns	2009	*Journal of Marketing*	Weekly stock returns	Products	J.D. Power and Associates	Automobile
Tellis et al.	Radical Innovation Across Nations: The Preeminence of Corporate Culture	2009	*Journal of Marketing*	Market-to-book ratio	Products	Archival searches	Multi-industry

Note: WSJ = *Wall Street Journal*; USPTO = United States Patent and Trademark Office; FDA = Food and Drug Administration; CPG = Consumer Packaged Goods.

innovation in the United States play a role in this remarkable perform-ance? And is there a relation between a country's level of aggregate inno-vation and the returns to its stock market? How do returns to innovation differ across countries? Future research is needed to understand how inno-vation contributes to the aggregate stock market returns and GDP growth around the world.

General welfare implications

Not all members of a society seem to benefit equally from innovation. When an innovating firm earns economic rents, it does so by exerting some monopoly power over its new product. This monopoly power – which can take several forms from patent protection to branding to loyalty programs – ultimately results in a level of consumer prices that is higher than what would be obtained in a perfectly competitive environment. It has been gen-erally accepted since Schumpeter (1934) that this type of ex post monopoly protection is actually necessary to provide ex ante incentives to innovate. Thus shareholders and consumers perceive the benefits of innovation very differently. What then, is the net impact that innovation has on the society? Future research should attempt to understand an optimal tradeoff that would maximize the value that different economic stakeholders derive from innovation.

Industry-specific Studies

A disproportionate part of innovation research focuses on technologi-cal innovation. One has to wonder to what extent studies that measure innovation with patents or R&D expenditures provide any useful insights in industries where technological innovation is rare, or appears only as process innovation. A prime example is the services industry, a pillar of the US economy; retail is another example. In services, innovation does not take a product form; rather it ranges from core or supplementary service innovation, to service delivery innovation (Bettencourt, 2010). Further, the determinants of the relation between innovation and shareholder value may be fundamentally different from the ones in manufacturing. Firm size and R&D expenditures may well be replaced by scalability, the quality of the employee training program or other more relevant industry-specific factors. The dearth of research on the drivers of innovation, and of innovation value, in these important industries will be remedied only if we acknowledge that when it comes to innovation, it is best to recog-nize industry-specific idiosyncrasies rather than attempt futile empirical generalizations.

Perhaps the least explored area of the innovation literature relates to innovations in financial products and services. The advent of derivative securities has made it possible for banks to introduce new financial products designed to allow consumers and businesses to insure against new sources of risk. In the past two decades we have seen a phenomenal wave of new financial products launched on the market with varying degrees of success. For example, Enron pioneered 'weather derivatives' to allow consumers to insure against adverse weather effects. The recent explosion in exchange traded funds (ETFs) now allows ordinary consumers to purchase, at low costs, investments in macroeconomic assets such as gold, oil, foreign exchange, or interest rates, investments that were previously accessible only to the wealthy and to professional investors. Nevertheless, recent problems experienced with the asset-backed securities sector (such as securities backed by subprime mortgage loans) illustrate some of the potential pitfalls of financial innovation. As these types of products become more widespread, more research is needed to study their net benefit to the innovator and to the society.

Understudied, But More Prevalent Types of Innovation

As argued earlier, process and business model innovations are increasingly frequent. While the number of patent applications is higher than ever, so is the ability to reverse engineer and imitate a product. Even the most innovative companies acknowledge that they have to supplement product innovation with strong brand support and a flexible business model that can continuously adapt to market conditions. Process and business model innovation hold much promise, because they tend to be multifaceted and difficult to imitate. Empirical studies on how to succeed at these types of innovation would fill an important literature gap.

The same can be said about open innovation. The interest in this type of innovation is high, but structured knowledge that would offer insights on how to navigate through a large, and fairly noisy, pool of ideas, is still lacking. Knowing how to extract the highest NPV projects from this pool, how to set boundaries, how to best leverage internal R&D to increase the efficiency of the external search, and how to protect this type of innovation from imitation are all questions that deserve a well-documented answer.

Qualitative Determinants of the Shareholder Value Created by Innovation

The innovativeness of a new product is not the only characteristic that determines its value. Some of the most successful new products in the marketplace have yielded impressive cash flows not because they were technological wonders, but because they provided unmatched consumer benefits. Apple's iPod was not the first MP3 player on store shelves, but it was the most streamlined, elegant, and easiest to use. Go-Gurt, the first yogurt in a tube, earned $100 million in sales in its first year on the market not because it brought a new technology to the market, but rather because it completely transformed yogurt consumption (Reyes, 2000). Qualitative characteristics such as ease of use or the ability to save consumers time can tremendously increase the value of an innovation, but are yet to be systematically studied.

Likewise, we know that advertising is a significant moderator of the relation between innovation and market value. We should now turn our attention to other qualitative, perhaps user-generated measures of post-launch support (or lack of thereof), such as positive or negative word-of-mouth. In an environment where consumers contribute insights that become part of a new product's image, the impact of their voices on the extent of shareholder value generated by innovation should be examined and quantified.

Measurement and Sample Selection Issues

A concern with research showing a positive effect of innovation on shareholder value is selection bias. Studies showing null effects have little chance of being published (for an exception see Eddy and Saunders, 1980). It is highly probable, however, that under certain conditions innovation may not be valuable. For managers, understanding what factors negatively impact the rents from innovation or what characteristics of innovation make it more likely to be a failure, would be just as valuable as understanding the determinants of innovation success.

Indeed, there is a significant asymmetry in the attention dedicated to product failures versus product successes. While many practitioners lament the virtual absence of systematic post-mortem practices meant to analyze failures, researchers are just as likely to ignore them. Yet the scarce evidence on failures suggests that they have dire consequences, with the magnitude of the negative stock response to failure being disproportionately higher than the positive response to success. Sharma and Lacey (2004) found 1.56 percent CARs to FDA drug approvals and −21.03 percent CARs to FDA drug rejections. Their results could be in part explained by the fact that much of the effect had already been incorporated, and the response to failure includes the downward adjustment of a stock price that could have been increased in anticipation of the drug's approval. Nevertheless, more research on the valuation of failures is needed.

High failure rates highlight another understudied characteristic of innovations: risk. A few studies document a positive relation between innovation and risk. Specifically, R&D intensity is positively associated with return volatility (Chan et al., 2001). In addition, new product announcements increase financial risk (Devinney, 1992), and firms with a higher stock of breakthrough innovations have higher risk as well (Sorescu and Spanjol, 2008). While investors may mitigate risk through a diversified portfolio, other stakeholders, such as employees and debt-holders would prefer a stable stream of cash flows to a volatile one. If innovation increases shareholder value but also firm risk, it may have an adverse impact on stakeholders other than shareholders, particularly in firms with severe agency conflicts. Future research is needed to better understand the link between innovation, risk, agency conflicts, and corporate governance.

NOTE

1. This chapter focuses on innovation construed as a firm output, rather than on the innovativeness of firms construed as a capability. Prior studies have also documented a positive relation between innovativeness as a firm capability and shareholder value (e.g., Cho and Pucik, 2005).

REFERENCES

Adner, R. and Daniel L. (2001), 'Demand Heterogeneity and Technology Evolution: Implications for Product and Process Innovation,' *Management Science*, **47** (5), 611–28.

Alva, M. (2010), 'Amazon's New Kindle Off to Fast Start,' *Investors Business Daily*, 27 August, A01.

Austin, D.H. (1993), 'An Event-study Approach to Measuring Innovative Output: The Case of Biotechnology,' *American Economic Review*, **83** (2), 253–8.

Bayus, B.L., J. Sanjay, and A. Rao (2001), 'Truth or Consequences: An Analysis of Vaporware and New Product Announcements,' *Journal of Marketing Research*, **38** (1), 3–13.

Bettencourt, L. (2010), *Service Innovation: How to Go from Customer Needs to Breakthrough Services*, New York: McGraw-Hill.

Bjork, C. (2010), 'Inditex Profit Jumps On Zara Chain's Sales,' *The Wall Street Journal*, Eastern Edition, 10 June, B6.

Blundell, R., R. Griffith, and J. Van Reenen (1999), 'Market Share, Market Value and Innovation in a Panel of British Manufacturing Firms,' *Review of Economic Studies*, **66** (3), 529–54.

Brown, S.J. and J.B. Warner (1985), 'Using Daily Stock Returns: The Case of Event Studies,' *Journal of Financial Economics*, **14** (1), 3–31.

Capron, Laurence and Jung-Chin Shen (2007), 'Acquisitions of Private vs. Public Firms: Private Information, Target Selection, and Acquirer Returns,' *Strategic Management Journal*, **28** (9), 891–911.

Ceccagnoli, M. (2009), 'Appropriability, Preemption, and Firm Performance,' *Strategic Management Journal*, **30** (1), 81–98.

Chan, L.K., J. Lakonishok, T. Sougiannis (2001), 'The Stock Market Valuation of Research and Development Expenditures,' *Journal of Finance*, **56** (6), 2431–56.

Chaney, P.K., T.M. Devinney, and R.S. Winer (1991), 'The Impact of New Product Introductions on the Market Value of Firms,' *Journal of Business*, **64** (4), 573–610.

Chauvin, K.W. and M. Hirschey (1993), 'Advertising, R&D Expenditures and the Market Value of the Firm,' *Financial Management*, **22** (4), 128–40.

Chesbrough, H. (2003), *Open Innovation: The New Imperative for Creating and Profiting from Technology*, Boston, MA: Harvard Business Press.

Chesbrough, H. (2010), 'Business Model Innovation: Opportunities and Barriers,' *Long Range Planning*, **43** (2/3), 354–63.

Cho, H. and V. Pucik (2005), 'Relation Between Innovativeness, Quality, Growth, Profitability, and Market Value,' *Strategic Management Journal*, **26** (6), 555–75.

Coad, A. and R. Rao (2006), 'Innovation and Market Value: A Quantile Regression Analysis,' *Economics Bulletin*, **15** (13), 1–10.

Cockburn, I. and Z. Griliches (1988), 'Industry Effects and Appropriability Measures in the Stock Market's Valuation of R&D and Patents,' *American Economic Review*, **78** (2), 419–23.

Coinstar, Inc. at Morgan Stanley Technology, Media & Telecom Conference (2010), transcript from Fair Disclosure Wire (Quarterly Earnings Reports), 3 March, 2010.

Connolly, R.A. and M. Hirschey (1988), 'Market Value and Patents: A Bayesian Approach,' *Economics Letters*, **27** (1), 83–7.

Cooper, R.G., S.J. Edgett, and E.J. Kleinschmidt (2004), 'Benchmarking Best NPD Practices – I,' *Research Technology Management*, **47** (1), 31–43.

Curewitz, B. (2009), 'Innovate with Balance,' *Marketing Management*, **18** (3), 18–23.

Daniel, K., M. Grinblatt, S. Titman, and R. Wermers (1997), 'Measuring Mutual Fund Performance With Characteristic-based Benchmarks,' *Journal of Finance*, **52** (3), 1035–58.

Davenport, T.H. (1993), *Process Innovation: Reengineering Work Through Information Technology*, Boston, MA: Harvard Business School Press.

Devinney, T.M. (1992), 'New Products and Financial Risk Changes,' *Journal of Product Innovation Management*, **9** (3), 222–31.

Economist (2010), 'The Power to Disrupt,' **395** (8678), 16–18.

Eddy, A.R. and G. Saunders (1980), 'New Product Announcements and Stock Prices,' *Decision Sciences*, **11** (1), 90–97.

Fama, Eugene F. and Merton H. Miller (1972), *The Theory of Finance*, New York: Holt, Rinehart and Winston.

Forbes (2010), 'America's Largest Private Companies,' available at: http://www.forbes.com/lists/2010/21/private-companies-10_land.html; accessed 23 December 2010.

Greenhalgh, C. and M. Rogers (2006), 'The Value of Innovation: The Interaction of Competition, R&D and IP,' *Research Policy*, **35** (4), 562–80.

Hall, B.H., A. Jaffe, and M. Trajtenberg (2005), 'Market Value and Patent Citations,' *RAND Journal of Economics*, **36** (1), 16–38.

Hall, B.H. and R. Oriani (2006), 'Does the Market Value R&D Investment by European Firms? Evidence from a Panel of Manufacturing Firms in France, Germany, and Italy,' *International Journal of Industrial Organization*, **24** (5), 971–93.

Hatch, N.W. and D.C. Mowery (1998), 'Process Innovation and Learning by Doing in Semiconductor Manufacturing,' *Management Science*, **44** (11), 1461–77.

Heeley, Michael B. and R. Jacobson (2008), 'The Recency of Technological Inputs and Financial Performance,' *Strategic Management Journal*, **29** (7), 723–44.

Heeley, Michael B., Sharon Matusik, and Neelam Jain (2007), 'Innovation, Appropriability, and the Underpricing of Initial Public Offerings,' *Academy of Management Journal*, **50** (1), 209–25.

Hendricks, K.B. and V.R. Singhal (1997), 'Delays in New Product Introductions and the Market Value of the Firm: The Consequences of Being Late to the Market,' *Management Science*, **43** (4), 422–36.

Hoskisson, Robert E., Michael A. Hitt, Richard A. Johnson, and Wayne Grossman (2002), 'Conflicting Voices: The Effects of Institutional Ownership Heterogeneity and Internal Governance on Corporate Innovation Strategies,' *Academy of Management Journal*, **45** (4), 697–716.

Hoyer, W.D., R. Chandy, M. Dorotic, M. Krafft, and S.S. Singh (2010), 'Consumer Cocreation in New Product Development,' *Journal of Service Research*, **13** (3), 283–96.

Investor's Business Daily (2010), 'Netflix Misses, but Shares Jump,' 21 October, A01.

Jaffe, A.B. (1986), 'Technological Opportunity and Spillovers of R&D: Evidence from Firms' Patents, Profits, and Market Value,' *American Economic Review*, **76** (5), 984–1001.

Kalaignnanam, K., V. Shankar, and R. Varadarajan (2007), 'Asymmetric New Product Development Alliances: Win–Win or Win–Lose Partnerships?' *Management Science*, **5** (3), 357–74.

Kelm, K.M., V.K. Narayanan, and G.E. Pinches (1995), 'Shareholder Value Creation during R&D Innovation and Commercialization Stages,' *The Academy of Management Journal*, **38** (3), 770–86.

Kennedy, S. (2010), 'Internet Waves, Ebooks by the Numbers,' *Information Today*, **27** (9), 15–17.

Kirner, E., S. Kinkel, and A. Jaeger (2009), 'Innovation Paths and the Innovation Performance of Low-technology Firms – An Empirical Analysis of German Industry,' *Research Policy*, **38** (3), 447–58.

Kochhar, Rahul and Parthiban David (1996), 'Institutional Investors and Firm Innovation: A Test of Competing Hypotheses,' *Strategic Management Journal*, **17** (1), 73–84.

Laursen, K. and A. Salter (2006), 'Open for Innovation: The Role of Openness in Explaining Innovation Performance Among U.K. Manufacturing Firms,' *Strategic Management Journal*, **27** (2), 131–50.

Lee, R.P. and Q. Chen (2009), 'The Immediate Impact of New Product Introductions on Stock Price: The Role of Firm Resources and Size,' *Journal of Product Innovation Management*, **26** (1), 97–107.

Lev, B. and T. Sougiannis (1996), 'The Capitalization, Amortization, and Value-relevance of R&D,' *Journal of Accounting and Economics*, **21** (1), 107–38.

Lindgardt, C., Martin Reeves, George Stalk, and Michael S. Deimler (2009), 'Business Model Innovation,' *Boston Consulting Group Report* (December).

Loughran, T. and J. Ritter (2000), 'Uniformly Least Powerful Tests of Market Efficiency,' *Journal of Financial Economics*, **55** (3), 361–89.

Mehra, R. and E.C. Prescott (1985), 'The Equity Premium: A Puzzle,' *Journal of Monetary Economics*, **15** (2), 145–61.

Mehra, R. and E.C. Prescott (2003), 'The Equity Premium in Retrospect,' in G.M. Constantinides, M. Harris, and R. Stulz (eds), *Handbook of Economics and Finance*, Amsterdam: North Holland.

Mishra, D.P. and H.S. Bhabra (2002), 'Assessing the Economic Worth of New Product Pre-Announcement Signals: Theory and Empirical Evidence,' *Journal of Product and Brand Management*, **10** (2), 75–93.

Pakes, A. (1985), 'On Patents, R&D, and the Stock Market Rate of Return,' *Journal of Political Economy*, **93** (2), 390–409.

Pauwels, K., J. Silva-Risso, S. Srinivasan, and D.M. Hanssens (2004), 'New Products, Sales Promotion, and Firm Value: The Case of the Automobile Industry,' *Journal of Marketing*, **68** (4), 142–56.

Pisano, G.P. (1997), *The Development Factory: Unlocking the Potential of Process Innovation*, Boston, MA: Harvard Business School Press.

Rao, R., R.K. Chandy, and J.C. Prabhu (2008), 'The Fruits of Legitimacy: Why Some New Ventures Gain More from Innovation than Others,' *Journal of Marketing*, **72** (4), 58–75.

Reyes, S. (2000), 'Groove Tube,' *Brandweek*, **41** (40), M110–M114.

Schumpeter, J. (1934), *The Theory of Economic Development*, Boston, MA: Harvard University Press.

Sharma, A. and N. Lacey (2004), 'Linking Product Development Outcomes to Market Valuation of the Firm: The Case of the U.S. Pharmaceutical Industry,' *Journal of Product Innovation Management*, **21** (5), 297–308.

Sood, A. and G.J. Tellis (2009), 'Do Innovations Really Pay Off? Total Stock Market Returns to Innovation,' *Marketing Science*, **28** (3), 442–56.

Sorescu, A. and J. Spanjol (2008), 'Innovation's Effect on Firm Value and Risk: Insights from Consumer Packaged Goods,' *Journal of Marketing*, **72** (2), 114–32.

Sorescu, A., R. Chandy, and J.C. Prabhu (2003), 'Sources and Financial Consequences of Radical Innovation: Insights from Pharmaceuticals,' *Journal of Marketing*, **67** (4), 82–101.

Sorescu, A., R. Chandy, and J.C. Prabhu (2007a), 'Why Some Acquisitions Do Better Than Others: Product Capital as a Driver of Long-term Stock Returns,' *Journal of Marketing Research*, **44** (1), 57–72.

Sorescu, A., V. Shankar, and T. Kushwaha (2007b), 'New Product Preannouncements and Shareholder Value: Don't Make Promises You Can't Keep,' *Journal of Marketing Research*, **44** (2), 468–89.

Stam, W. (2009), 'When Does Community Participation Enhance the Performance of Open Source Software Companies?' *Research Policy*, **38** (8), 1288–99.

Tellis, Gerard, Jaideep Prabhu, and Rajesh Chandy (2009), 'Radical Innovation Across Nations: The Preeminence of Corporate Culture,' *Journal of Marketing*, **73** (1), 3–23.

Yang, C. and J. Chen (2004), 'Innovation and Market Value in Newly-industrialized Countries: The Case of Taiwanese Electronics Firms,' *Asian Economic Journal*, **17** (2), 205–20.

Zott, C. and R. Amit (2010), 'Business Model Design: An Activity System Perspective,' *Long Range Planning*, **43** (2/3), 216–26.

7 Branding and firm value
Shuba Srinivasan, Liwu Hsu and Susan Fournier

INTRODUCTION

Although branding is widely recognized as an important marketing activity, marketing executives are increasingly challenged to prove the value of branding in clear financial terms (Ambler, 2003). In response to this call, there has been growing academic research on branding impact on shareholder value and firm risks (Lehmann and Reibstein, 2006; Marketing Science Institute, 2008). Several major conferences focus on linking marketing strategy to Wall Street, including Marketing Science Institute events in 2002 (Dallas) and 2009 (Emory Marketing Institute, Atlanta), as well as a third conference in 2011 (Boston University). Dedicated publications address the topic, including two special issues in the *Journal of the Academy of Marketing Science* (2003) and the *Journal of Marketing* (2009) and two books (Ambler, 2003; Rutherford and Knowles, 2007). More than ten years ago, Kerin and Sethuraman (1998, p. 260) stated that:

> it is generally claimed that brand names are a corporate asset with an economic value that creates wealth for a firm's shareholder. However, the scholarly literature has neither provided a comprehensive theoretical basis for this claim nor documented an empirical relationship between brand value and shareholder value.

The marketing field has since come a long way in demonstrating that branding influences the shareholder value, with chief executive officers, chief financial officers, and boards now truly paying attention to building, developing, and maintaining their brands.

The objective of this chapter is to integrate emerging insights from the literature on branding and shareholder value into a process framework that helps enumerate and explain the brand–finance link. Figure 7.1 provides the conceptual framework for investigating the effects of branding on shareholder value and provides a road map for the organization of the chapter. This figure builds from Lehmann's (2004) marketing productivity chain linking marketing actions to firm value by incorporating a decompositional model of brand equity (Feldwick, 1996a; Keller and Lehmann, 2006).

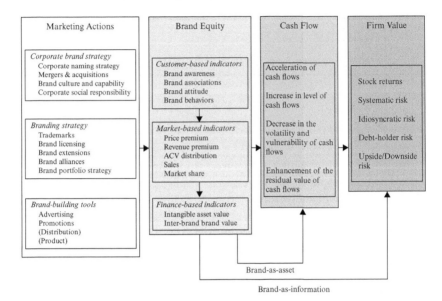

Note: ACV = all commodity volume.

Figure 7.1   Conceptual framework: how branding affects firm value

This chapter proceeds as follows. First, we discuss the reasons why shareholder value (i.e., stock returns and risks) is an appropriate metric to assess brand performance and brand value. In the context of discussing the firm value approach, we introduce common measures of the core dependent variable: shareholder value, exploring such concepts as Tobin's Q, abnormal returns, and idiosyncratic and systematic risk. As brand equity is a complex concept, we focus on three principle and distinct perspectives on brand equity (i.e., customer-based, product market-based, and finance-based indicators) in explaining the branding–shareholder value link. Second, the chapter delineates two mechanisms that govern the branding–finance interface to address whether and how branding affects shareholders: the brand-as-information and the brand-as-asset routes. Key findings from the extant literature on branding and shareholder value are summarized to support these process routes. Third, the chapter considers two strategy-level antecedents of brand equity creation, again reviewing extant literature to qualify effects on firm value and cash flow: organization-level strategy (e.g., corporate name strategy, mergers & acquisitions) and brand strategy (e.g., brand extensions and brand portfolio strategy). Fourth, we discuss brand management tools such as advertising and promotions for building brand equity and influencing shareholder value.[1] The chapter concludes with an agenda for future studies that addresses gaps and challenges in this important and growing area of research.

BRANDING AND FIRM VALUE

In assessing the value impact of branding, most prior research has focused on intermediary market outcome metrics such as price (Chaudhuri and Holbrook, 2001) and market share (Smith and Park, 1992). Aaker and Jacobson (2001, p.485) proposed that current-term accounting measures, such as return on investment (ROI) and earnings, cannot appropriately reflect firm value, because 'they fail to capture the benefits of investing in intangible assets such as brands.' In reality, developing a successful brand requires significant investments of effort and resources. In addition, a defining characteristic of brand assets (e.g., brand equity) is that they are inherently slow-moving and not immediately visible (Srinivasan and Hanssens, 2009); changes in a well-managed brand's equity are usually slow to manifest on a firm's bottom-line measures (Ambler, 2003). As such, long-term brand value is less likely to be captured by backward-looking accounting measures such as profit and return on assets. Furthermore, non-financial market measures of brand valuation can suffer from shortcomings such as inherent subjectivity, lack of theoretical underpinnings, and inadequacy through representation in a single brand equity measure. Given these realities and challenges, the gold standard metric for assessing branding's impact on the firm is shareholder value, which is determined by levels of stock returns and the volatility associated with those returns (Srinivasan and Hanssens, 2009). According to the shareholder value perspective, the main objective of companies is to maximize shareholders' return on their equity (Rappaport, 1997). Rappaport (1987, p.57) also notes that '[b]y closely reading the stock market, managers can find out whether proposed strategies will be effective.' Commonly used metrics of shareholder value include stock returns, market capitalization, and Tobin's Q; systematic risk and idiosyncratic risk also serve as key metrics for publicly traded companies (Tuli and Bharadwaj, 2009) (see the last column titled 'Firm Value' in Figure 7.1). Table 7.1 provides an overview of common financial metrics, including their definitions and operationalizations.

Branding can be viewed as a strategic tool for managing a firm's risk exposure. A strong brand, for example, can encourage broader stock ownership, insulate a company from market downturns, grant protection from equity dilution in the case of product failures, and reduce variability in future cash flows (Frieder and Subrahmanyam, 2005; Rego et al., 2009). Still, with some exception (Madden et al., 2006; Luo and Bhattacharya,

Table 7.1 Relevant financial metrics for assessing brand equity

Financial Metrics	Definition	Measure	Characteristics	Illustrative Papers
Returns/levels metrics				
Stock returns	Change in the total value of a stock over some period of initial investment	$\dfrac{Price_t + Dividend_t - Price_{t-1}}{Price_{t-1}}$	A stationary time-series of stock returns is obtained as a dependent variable	Mizik and Jacobson (2003) Srinivasan et al. (2009)
Tobin's Q (*q*-values)	Ratio of market value of the firm to the replacement cost of the firm's assets	$\dfrac{Market\ price}{Replacement\ cost\ of\ asset}$	Tobin's Q estimates have smaller average errors and greater correlation with true measures as compared with accounting rates of return	Simon and Sullivan (1993) Rao et al. (2004)
Market-to-book ratio (M/B)	Ratio of current share price to the book value per share	$\dfrac{Market\ value}{Book\ equity}$	M/B > 1 signals firm creating value for its shareholders	Kerin and Sethuraman (1998) Pauwels et al. (2004)
Market capitalization	Share price multiplied by the number of outstanding shares	$Stock\ price$ $\times Number\ of\ shares\ outstanding$	Forward-looking measure, providing investor expectations of the firm's future profit	Fornell et al. (2006)

Risk/volatility metrics

Cash flow volatility	Ratio of firm's cash flow coefficient of variation (CV) to the market's cash flow coefficient of variation (CV)	$$\frac{\textit{Firm's cash flow CV}}{\textit{Market's cash flow CV}}$$	Can explain as much as 80% of the variation in systematic market risk	Gruca and Rego (2005) Fischer et al. (2009)
Abnormal returns (α_i)	Difference between the expected return of a stock and the actual return	*Carhart four-factor model:* $$R_{it} - R_{rf,t} = \alpha_i + \beta_i(R_{mt} - R_{rf,t})$$ $$+ s_t SMB_t + h_t HML_t + u_t UMD_t + \varepsilon_{it}$$ where $\varepsilon_{it} \sim N(0, \sigma_{\varepsilon_{it}})$	Positive abnormal returns indicates outperformance	Joshi and Hanssens (2009) Hsu et al. (2010)
Systematic risk (β_i)	The part of stock volatility that is explained by changes in average market portfolio returns		Cannot be mitigated through diversification	Fornell et al. (2006) Madden et al. (2006) McAlister et al. (2007)
Idiosyncratic risk ($\sigma_{\varepsilon_{it}}$)	The variability that is not explained by changes in average market portfolio return but instead by firm-specific events		Accounts for approximately 80% of total risk on average	Luo (2007) Luo and Bhattacharya (2009)
Downside (Upside) risk	The observed variability in a firm's stock returns accounted for by equity market movements when the stock market declines (rises)	$$\frac{\mathrm{cov}(r_i, r_m | r_m < \mu_m)}{\mathrm{var}(r_m | r_m < \mu_m)}$$ where $r_i (r_m)$ is security i's (the market's) excess return, and μ_m is the average market excess return[a]	Only assets that magnify the market's downward swings are viewed as risky	Bawa and Lindenberg (1977) Rego et al. (2009) Tuli and Bharadwaj (2009)

Note: a. Here, we provide the measure of downside risk. For details on the measure of upside risk, please see Chen (1982).

159

2009; Rego et al., 2009), few studies examine branding effects on firm risk. Given that managers and investors are inherently risk-averse (Swedroe and Grogan, 2009) and seek to maximize returns while minimizing risk exposure, it is crucial for management to consider risks. Without considering stock price volatility, managers are not able to assess 'whether expected returns offer adequate compensation for the inherent level of risk' (Anderson, 2006, p. 587).

Total risk has two components: systematic risk and idiosyncratic or firm-specific risk. Systematic risk stems from exogenous macroeconomic factors that affect the overall stock market or particular industries (e.g., interest rate shifts, exchange rates, macroeconomic developments, industry concentration). Systematic risk reflects sensitivity to overall market changes and is a function of the extent to which a firm's stock returns change when the overall market changes. Idiosyncratic risk is the risk associated with micro, firm-specific circumstances, characteristics, or activities (e.g., research and development pipeline, marketing mix decisions, brand portfolio strategy), after general market variation is accounted for; it concerns the proportion of returns that move independently of market-wide returns. Although idiosyncratic risk accounts for upwards of 80 percent of total risk (Goyal and Santa-Clara, 2003), there is robust evidence supporting the importance among managers and investors of examining systematic risk as well as idiosyncratic risk as both have been shown to be related to firm value (Bansal and Clelland, 2004; Ang et al., 2006; Brown and Kapadia, 2007; Ferreira and Laux, 2007).

Different stakeholders have different perspectives on firm risks. Rego et al. (2009) view risk from both debt-holder and equity-holder perspectives. Per finance theory, the former deals with the vulnerability of the firm's future cash flows because it determines the ability of the firm to deal with existing debt (Merton, 1974). The latter focuses on the total equity risk as the variability of a firm's stock returns, which is driven by the capital asset pricing model (Sharpe, 1964). Recently, researchers have started to distinguish between upside risk, the firm's stock risk when stock returns are increasing overall (Rego et al., 2009; Tuli and Bharadwaj, 2009), and downside risk, the firm's stock risk when stock returns are decreasing overall (Harlow, 1991; Miller and Leiblein, 1996; Ang et al., 2006).[2] We highlight the important characteristics of each financial metric as shown in Table 7.1.

Metrics of Brand Equity

To assess the impact of branding on firm performance, marketers need a clear understanding of brand equity and the associated metrics whereby it can be gauged. Brand equity is a complex concept with many different applications and meanings among academics, marketing managers, and marketing research professionals. A useful way of organizing these varied conceptions is provided in the brand value chain, which posits three distinct components of brand equity: brand meaning, brand strength, and brand value (Feldwick, 1996b). As interpreted by Keller and Lehmann (2006), these components vary in terms of whether the perspective of the consumer (customer-based brand equity or CBBE), product market (market-based brand equity or MBBE) or financial market (financial-based brand equity or FBBE) is adopted. From the customers' perspective, brand equity reflects how customers perceive and react differentially to a branded offering versus an unbranded commodity offering. From the product market perspective, brand equity is the value-added performance of a branded offering compared to an equivalent unbranded one. From the financial market perspective, brand equity represents the value of an asset that can be traded and can be thought of as the net present value of anticipated future purchases of the brand. As seen in the column titled 'Brand Equity' in Figure 7.1, the brand equity chain can be viewed as a hierarchy-of-effects model wherein CBBE is a precursor of MBBE, which, in turn, is a precursor of FBBE. Research supports that all three components of brand equity have direct links to cash flows but can also drive firm value directly (Barth et al., 1998; Srivastava et al., 1998; Madden et al., 2006). This framework is sufficiently general in that it allows for both simultaneous effects as well as complex patterns of temporal causality concerning the effects of marketing actions on shareholder value. In what follows, we summarize the measurement and valuation of brand equity at these three different levels of operationalization and set the stage for a review of research on branding–firm value effects.

Customer-based brand equity (CBBE)
Customer-based brand equity, defined as 'the differential effect of brand knowledge on consumer response to the marketing of the brand' (Keller, 1993), is the most commonly used equity measure among both researchers and practitioners (Agarwal and Rao, 1996). The differential consumer response to the brand has been operationalized by a range of market research suppliers, each supporting different metrics. Some of the more popular CBBE indicators are EquiTrend's perceived quality measure, Millward Brown's BrandZ indicator, and Ipsos's Equity*Builder, which measure the consumers' emotional attachment to a brand. Young & Rubicam's BrandAsset Valuator (BAV) model proposes two dimensions of brand equity, each with two sub-components: brand strength includes brand differentiation and the relevance of the brand to the consumer,

whereas brand stature considers the brand's esteem and consumer's knowledge (awareness and understanding) of the brand (Agres and Dubitsky, 1996). A recent addition is brand energy, which captures the degree to which a brand is perceived as innovative and dynamic (Mizik and Jacobson, 2008).

Researchers have also considered the classical hierarchy of perceptual and behavioral metrics of CBBE namely, brand awareness (aided and unaided), brand associations, brand attitude, and brand behaviors, notably brand loyalty. Brands associations comprise the network of cognitive linkages that consumers hold in their memory regarding the brand (Keller, 1993). Brand attitude is defined as consumers' integrated evaluations of a brand (Wilkie, 1986; Keller, 1993); customer satisfaction as measured by the American Customer Satisfaction Index (ACSI) serves as a popular attitudinal brand equity metric (Anderson et al., 1994). Perceived brand quality, defined as the consumer's perception about a product's overall satisfaction with reference to the available alternatives (Zeithaml, 1988), is also notable as are measures of corporate reputation such as Fortune's most admired brands (Roberts and Dowling, 2002) and Kinder, Lydenberg, and Domini's measure of corporate social performance (KLD) (Kinder, Lydenberg, Domini & Co. Inc., 1999). In terms of behavioral indicators, commonly used metrics include the net promoter score (Reichheld, 2003) and brand loyalty. Oliver (1999, p. 34) defines brand loyalty as 'a deep-held commitment to rebuy or repatronize a preferred product/service consistently in the future, thereby causing repetitive same-brand or same-brand-set purchasing, despite situational influences and marketing efforts having the potential to cause switching behavior.' Overall, while CBBE measures comprehensively reflect customer assessments of brand equity, a legitimate criticism is the absence of indicators of both the brand's product market and financial performance in such metrics (Taylor et al., 2007).

Market-based brand equity (MBBE)

A second perspective on brand equity is based on market-level manifestations. Some researchers claim that no matter how brand equity is measured or for what purposes measurement serves, the value of the brand 'must ultimately be derived in the marketplace' (Hoeffler and Keller, 2003, p. 421). Metrics that reflect marketplace performance of the brand include price premium, revenue premium, increased advertising elasticity, and the ability to obtain distribution channel and shelf space, in addition to traditional market performance measures such as sales, profit, and market share (Boulding et al., 1994). Amongst these, the most commonly used metric is the price premium measuring the premium consumers are willing to pay for a national brand over a private label brand (Aaker, 1992, 1996; Chaudhuri and Holbrook, 2001). The price premium commanded by a strong brand can increase the firm's profit and provide resources to reinvest in the brand (Aaker, 1992). Ailawadi et al. (2003) propose revenue premium as another market-level measure of brand equity. Similar to price premium, revenue premium is the difference in revenue (i.e., price × volume) for a branded good versus a private label good. Although many managers consider MBBE, which measures brand performance on a product market level, a crucial measure of success for branding efforts, at publicly traded companies, the board of directors is typically more concerned with whether a linkage between branding and shareholder value exists at the financial market level. Still, MBBE measures are relatively easy to calculate and fully reflect the top-line performance measures that serve as standing goals for a majority of marketing managers. As for customer-based metrics, MBBEs also fall short since they do not link branding with the ultimate firm performance metric of shareholder value.

Financial-based brand equity (FBBE)

A third approach to measuring brand equity is based on financial market performance (Amir and Lev, 1996). Here, brand equity is estimated from the residual in the model of the value of a firm's assets (Simon and Sullivan, 1993). Such approaches typically decompose firm value into tangible assets such as plant and equipment or net receivables, and intangible components reflecting goodwill and brand investments and other forms of intellectual property. From an accounting perspective, brand equity is an accumulated intangible asset enhanced by marketing expenditures and brand management tools (Ambler, 2003) that generates future cash flows or reduces the volatility of future cash flows. Investors appear to consider brand value in their stock evaluations (Barth et al., 1998).

Increasingly, researchers have used a composite of customer-based and market-based brand equity metrics to derive estimates of finance-based brand equity. An example of this 'price–earnings multiple' approach is Interbrand's brand equity valuation (Kerin and Sethuraman, 1998), which considers branded earnings (i.e., economic profits attributable to brand) times brand strength (as an indication of the discount rate for future brand revenue streams). The Interbrand valuation metric thus combines the subjective consumer mindset of brand equity with objective brand performance in the product market. FBBE is growing in appeal and in use as a metric of brand equity that goes well beyond short-term sales, profits, and market share. Still, FBBEs are subject to criticisms of subjectivity and lack strong theoretical underpinnings.

HOW DOES BRANDING AFFECT FIRM VALUE?

In this section we turn to the question of how exactly branding affects firm value. In Figure 7.1, we posit two process mechanisms that make explicit the contribution of branding to firm value creation. First is a direct route wherein the brand-as-asset enhances firm value directly through its effects on cash flows. Second is an indirect route that considers the brand not as an asset but as information. In this route, the brand acts as a visible signal of the financial well-being of the firm.

Cash Flow Framework: Brands-as-assets

Research suggests that investors perceive incremental information on branding activities as contributing to expectations of future cash flows (Srinivasan and Hanssens, 2009). Arguing from a resource-based view of the firm, Doyle (2001) proposes that brands are intangible assets that increase the level of cash flows and reduce the vulnerability of these flows. Srivastava et al. (1998) propose that market-based assets such as brands can increase shareholder value through (1) an acceleration of cash flows, (2) an increase in the level of cash flows, (3) a decrease in the volatility and vulnerability of cash flows, and (4) an enhancement on the residual value of cash flows. Under the efficient markets model (Fama, 1970), stock prices at any point in time fully reflect available information and provide an expectation of discounted future cash flows. For example, when a brand extension announcement occurs, investors will decide to buy or sell company stock based on expectations of how the brand extension will affect future cash flows (Lane and Jacobson, 1995). If investors value such brand extensions, this will result in increases in stock price. Apple's announcement of successive generations of the iPhone (3G, 3GS, 4G) resulted in acceleration of cash flows as well as increases in the levels of cash flows for Apple. The enhanced cash flows that investors value favorably derive from marketing advantages of strong brands such as greater customer loyalty, increased marketing communication effectiveness, and elevated perceptions of product market performance, resulting in improved top-line and bottom-line performance. Successful co-branding alliances, such as, for example, General Mills's partnership with Hershey to provide Betty Crocker brownie mix co-branded with Hershey's chocolate, enables both firms to enhance their cash flows (Bucklin and Sengupta, 1993; Leuthesser et al., 2003). The leverage of strong brands through extensions or alliances allows brands to increase revenues by exploring new markets and extending the customer base.

Strong brands can also reduce volatility of cash flows because they are perceived as higher-quality offerings (Aaker and Jacobson, 1994) that can lower price sensitivity among consumers and in turn, protect cash flows (Sivakumar and Raj, 1997). As an example, Kellogg's profits in 3Q 2009 rose 6 percent despite an economic downturn as a result of strong loyalty to its brands (Skidmore, 2009). The vulnerability of cash flows is also reduced since strong brands are less susceptible to the harmful effects of marketing crises and competitive marketing actions (Aaker, 1996). For example, consider the 2009 safety scandal involving Toyota's Prius hybrid. Although Toyota's market share in the US dropped from 16.6 percent to 15.2 percent through the first three quarters of 2010, their total sales increased by 16.8 percent in September 2010 as compared to September 2009, indicative of a healthy rebound in market performance (The Wall Street Journal Market Data Center, 2010).

The residual of value of cash flows reflects the expected value of market-based brand assets beyond the market forecast (Rappaport, 1997). Cash flow residuals are positively influenced by successful brand extensions or the size and loyalty of the customer base, which accounts for a significant proportion of the net present value of a business. For example, Apple Inc. shares traded above $300 for the first time on 13 October, 2010, primarily due to the release of iPad tablet, which sold more than 3 million units in its first quarter of availability (Sherr, 2010).

Each of these four drivers inherently involve supply-side/demand-side advantages and disadvantages, which, in turn, influence the future levels and riskiness of cash flows (Rao et al., 2004).

Signaling Framework: Brands-as-information

Research suggests that stock markets reflect an environment of information asymmetry between firms and investors (Myers and Majluf, 1984). The signaling framework (Spence, 1973) contends that economic information that is uniquely known by management (e.g., competitive viability) will be conveyed to shareholders through various signals, one of which is the brand. The socio-cultural view of branding (McCracken, 1988; Holt, 2004) also emphasizes the role of brand as a meaning-laden signaling device. Specifically, Keller (2007) defines brand as a collection of associations that convey information to consumers. Brand positioning is the strategic discipline through which brand information is summarized, but all brand actions and programs send signals of brand meaning and equity to consumers and investors of the firm.

Consistent with this view of brands-as-information, several studies in marketing (Agrawal and Kamakura, 1995; Lane and Jacobson, 1995; Mathur and Mathur, 1995, 1996) use a signaling perspective to explain the effects of branding on firm stock prices. Research suggests that firms with high brand equity as gained through increased advertising expenditures have a larger breadth of ownership of the firms' stock because investors perceive greater and more accurate information flows about such companies (Grullon et al., 2004). Similarly, firms with strong brands are well-known and this reputation effect signals lower risks of the firm's stock to the investors (McAlister et al., 2007; Rego et al., 2009). There is evidence that investors prefer to seek and hold the stocks of well-known firms because investors are cognitively unable to apply the same level of expertise across an entire universe of stocks (Shiller, 2002; Frieder and Subrahmanyam, 2005). In this context, advertising can help attract a disproportionate number of investors who, at least in part, make their investments based on brand familiarity rather than fundamental information (Grullon et al., 2004; Singh et al., 2005). Furthermore, investors are particularly sensitive to signals of a firm's action beyond publicly available information such as corporate news releases and third-party business publications (Ross, 1977). Investors favor firms with more reliable information (Klein and Bawa, 1977) and greater information flows (Merton, 1987).

FINDINGS ON BRANDING AND FIRM VALUE

The questions of whether and how branding affects firm performance have been addressed in many recent studies on branding and firm value. In the three sections to follow, we summarize key findings concerning our conceptual framework (see Figure 7.1) and organize our discussion as follows. First, we discuss whether branding even matters and, if so, how branding affects shareholder value by considering branding's impact at the three levels of customer-, market- and financial-based brand equity. We then turn to the antecedents or drivers of strong brands to discuss findings concerning corporate strategy and brand strategy on firm value. We then discuss the relationship between brand management tools (e.g., advertising) and shareholder value.

FINDINGS ON BRAND EQUITY AND FIRM VALUE

Customer-based Brand Equity

Table 7.2 details each dimension of brand equity and its effects on financial metrics.

Table 7.2 Summary of key findings on the impact of brand equity metrics on firm value[a]

	Definition	Empirical Findings	Data Sources	Illustrative Papers
1. Customer-based brand equity				
Brand strength				
Brand differentiation	The ability of the brand to stand apart from its competitors	Brand distinctiveness has positive influence on overall financial performance Brand differentiation has lagged effect The positive relationship between brand equity and shareholder value is most pronounced when using the market-to-book value as an indicator of shareholder value	Y&R BAV model DataStream CRSP Compustat	Aaker (2003) Mizik and Jacobson (2008) Pahud de Mortanges and Van Riel (2003) Wong and Merrilees (2008)
Brand relevance	Personal relevance and appropriateness and perceived importance of the brand	Brand relevance provides incremental information and has the potential to generate higher future profit		
Brand energy	The ability of a brand to meet customers' needs and adapt to changing tastes in the future	Brand energy provides incremental information in explaining stock performance		
Brand stature				
Brand esteem	The extent to which consumers like a brand and hold it in high regard	There is no direct effect of esteem on stock return The investors perceive incremental effect of esteem in the future only when the increase in brand esteem enhances the profits	Y&R BAV model Survey CRSP Compustat	Baldauf et al. (2003) Frieder and Subrahmanyam (2005)

Table 7.2 (continued)

	Definition	Empirical Findings	Data Sources	Illustrative Papers
Brand knowledge	Brand awareness and consumers' understanding of the brand identity	There is no significant direct effect of brand knowledge on stock return. Brand knowledge indirectly affects the firm value through its influence on sales growth		Mizik and Jacobson (2008) Pahud de Mortanges and Van Riel (2003)
Brand behavior				
Brand attitude	Consumers' overall evaluations of a brand	Brand attitude is associated with stock return and provides incremental information contained in accounting measures. Improvement in the predictive power of firm value by 16% in models that take into account brand metrics	Techtel Corporation Landor Image Power Survey Y&R BAV model	Aaker and Jacobson (2001) Lane and Jacobson (1995) Mizik and Jacobson (2009)
Brand/customer loyalty	A deep-held commitment to rebuy or repatronize a preferred product/ service consistently in the future, thereby causing repetitive same-brand or same brand-set purchasing, *despite* situational influences and marketing efforts having the potential to cause switching behavior	1% improvement in retention increases firm value by 5%	Annual reports 10-K statement 10-Q statement	Gupta et al. (2004)

Construct	Definition	Findings	Data source	References
Perceived quality	Consumer's judgment about a brand's overall excellence or superiority	Improved perceived quality has a positive impact on stock prices; Perceived quality significantly increases brand profitability, market share, and customer perceived value	EquiTrend	Aaker and Jacobson (1994); Baldauf et al. (2003)
2. Market-based brand equity				
Revenue premium	The difference in revenue between a branded good and a private label good	Revenue premium as the measure of brand equity reflects the change of brand value over time; There is a strong link between consumer-based brand equity and market performance	Dominick's database; Marketing FactBook	Ailawadi et al. (2003); Kartono and Rao (2007)
Sales/Revenue	Top-line performance	New product introductions have strong effects on sales and firm value. Sales promotion has an immediate positive effect on sales but a negative effect on firm value	J.D. Power I/B/E/S database	Pauwels et al. (2004)
3. Market-based brand equity				
Intangible asset	Residual market value after other tangible sources of firm value are accounted for	Brand equity accounts for both the revenue-enhancing and the cost-reducing capabilities; Marketing factors such as brand assets are valued by the financial community	CRSP; Compustat; National Bureau of Economic Research (NBER)	Simon and Sullivan (1993); Barth et al. (1998)

169

Table 7.2 (continued)

	Definition	Empirical Findings	Data Sources	Illustrative Papers
Brand value	Branded earnings, which are based on the brand strength, are discounted to a net present value and aggregated to arrive at a brand value	Strong brand delivers greater stock returns and do so with less risk Financial brand values have a positive relationship to market-to-book ratios Firms can suffer a significant firm value decline due to depreciation of its brand-name capital Markets initially overreact negatively to recall news, providing further support for the depreciation of brand-name capital effect	Interbrand Press releases and articles Dow Jones Interactive database	Kerin and Sethuraman (1998) Madden et al. (2006) Mitchell (1989) Govindaraj et al. (2004)

Note: [a.] Data sources and illustrative papers for brand equity metrics are common across all sub-categories of these metrics and hence are mentioned only once. We follow a similar reporting format in Tables 7.3, 7.4, and 7.5.

170

Research supports that the CBBE metrics of brand strength and brand stature, all measured by Y&R's BrandAsset Valuator model, are positively related to shareholder value (Pahud de Mortanges and Van Riel, 2003). Brand distinctiveness, which enables a firm to communicate with the stakeholders more efficiently and effectively (Aaker, 2003), has a positive influence on overall financial performance through growth rates in sales, market share, and profitability (Wong and Merrilees, 2008). Mizik and Jacobson (2008) assess the five 'pillars' that form the updated Young & Rubicam BrandAsset Valuator model (i.e., differentiation, relevance, esteem, knowledge, and energy) and find that the brand asset metrics of perceived brand relevance and energy provide incremental information to accounting measures in explaining stock returns. In contrast, the stock return effects of esteem and knowledge are reflected in current-term accounting measures and in brand relevance and energy. In addition, their findings suggest that firms increasing brand differentiation might not receive abnormal returns contemporaneously but do so in subsequent periods.

Brand attitude and brand name familiarity jointly influence the stock market in the context of brand extension announcements (Lane and Jacobson, 1995). Aaker and Jacobson (2001) estimate a model that assesses brand attitude in high-technology markets (e.g., Apple, Compaq, and IBM) to provide incremental value relevance to stock market performance. Their study finds that a change in brand attitude has a significant influence on stock return comparable to that of unanticipated returns on equity. In other words, the financial markets perceive that brand attitude affects expectations of future-term performance beyond those reflected in current-term earnings.

Turning to the CBBE metric of loyalty, Gupta et al. (2004) find that a 1 percent improvement in customer retention increases firm value by 5 percent whereas 1 percent improvement in margin or acquisition cost generates improvements of only 1 percent and 0.1 percent in firm value, respectively. This result is consistent with suggestions of customer retention as the dominant theme in customer relationship management (Baldauf et al., 2003; Thomas et al., 2004).

The CBBE metric of perceived quality has a positive impact on brand profitability, market share, customer perceived value, and stock prices (Aaker and Jacobson, 1994; Baldauf et al., 2003). Frieder and Subrahmanyam (2005), using brand perceptions data (i.e., brand familiarity and brand perceived quality) of 300 strong brands find that investors prefer to invest in firms with high information flows and are more influenced by brand visibility than by perceptions of brand quality. The greater the familiarity with firms, the more information investors can have; hence, investors exhibit a propensity toward companies with highly well-recognized brands. More recently, Bharadwaj et al. (2011) examine the impact of changes in brand quality as measured by EquiTrend and find that such changes enhance shareholder wealth by improving stock returns and reducing idiosyncratic risk. However, unanticipated changes can also erode shareholder wealth as they have a positive association with systematic risk.

As for the impact of CBBE on firm risks, research suggests that CBBE is negatively associated with both firms' debt-holder and equity-holder risks (Rego et al., 2009). In particular, CBBE plays a more important role in reducing idiosyncratic risk than systematic risk. Furthermore, high CBBE can reduce down-side risk more efficiently than upside risk because high CBBE firms have more loyal and committed consumers, which lowers the vulnerability of cash flows, especially during times of economic uncertainty. Results from this stream of research are summarized in Table 7.2. Our conclusion is that CBBE is positively related to firm value and negatively related to both idiosyncratic and systematic risk.

Market-based Brand Equity

Recently, a few studies have examined the link between CBBE and MBBE models to demonstrate that customer mindset measures affect the brand's performance in the market (e.g., Srinivasan et al., 2010). Ailawadi et al. (2003) show that revenue premium as a measure of brand equity is not only stable but reflects changes in brand value over time; they do not, however, consider stock performance impact. Kim et al. (2003) find that brands' perceived quality, image, and loyalty are positively associated with firm revenues within the hotel industry. While a few studies examine the market valuation impact of MBBE, focusing mostly on top-line per-formance (e.g., Pauwels et al., 2004), more research is needed in this area including, notably, an assessment of the impact of MBBEs on risk. Our overall conclusion is that the MBBE is, on average, positively related to firm value.

Financial-based Brand Equity

Barth et al. (1998) find that brand value estimates are significantly posi-tively associated with advertising expense, brand operating margin, and brand market share. Importantly, brand value estimates are significantly positively related to share prices after controlling for recognized brand assets and analysts' earnings forecasts. Barth et al. provide compelling evidence relating to the reliability of estimates of brand values based on the methodology developed by Interbrand. Also using Interbrand's esti-mation of brand equity, Kerin and Sethuraman (1998) find that there is a positive relationship between financial brand value and market-to-book (M/B) ratio.

Madden et al. (2006) compare an ex ante portfolio of 111 companies' brands that appeared on the Interbrand list of World's Most Valuable Brands at least once between 1994 and 2001 to a benchmark to explore firm value creation through brands. They show that by investing in brand-ing and cultivating strong brand assets, a company can create greater shareholder value and do so with less risk. Mizik and Jacobson (2009) show that by taking into account brand metrics that reflect accounting variables (e.g., sales), the predictive power of firm value is improved by a significant 16 percent reduction in prediction error. Although there exists ongoing and intense discussion about the admission of brands into financial statements in the accounting community (Lev and Sougiannis, 1996; Barth et al., 1998), there is little disagreement that brands operate as intangible assets of a firm.

Just as marketing resources can be deployed to build customer- and market-based brand equity, so too can crisis events subject financial-based brand equity to deterioration and decay. Crises such as product recalls, ethical breaches, firm misconduct, and unfortunate events that threaten product or brand reputation can precipitate considerable drops in firm market value through reductions in financial- and market-based brand equity indicators. Theory suggests that when the product quality of a brand falls below the expected level, the value of the firm's brand-name capital declines, and the price premium that consumers were willing to pay for the brand is lost (Klein and Leffler, 1981).

The Tylenol poisonings provide perhaps the most well-known brand crisis example, in which seven people were killed as a result of ingesting cyanide-laced capsules of the over-the-counter pain-killer drug. Mitchell (1989) examines the Tylenol crisis to estimate the financial losses caused by brand-name capital depreciation, and to understand the degree to which a firm's brand name suffers a loss of value even when the firm is clearly not at fault. Mitchell concludes that Johnson & Johnson suffered a significant $1.24 billion wealth decline (14 percent of the forecasted value of the company) due to deprecation of its brand-name capital, thereby supporting the link between firm value and financial indicators of equity in the brand.

The Ford Explorer-Firestone tire product recall provides a second test of the link between financial-based brand equity metrics and firm value, as exposed through crisis events. Govindaraj et al. (2004) examine the stock price effects of events related to the Ford-Firestone product recall and confirm that losses in market value far exceed tangible and direct costs associated with the recall. They conclude that markets initially overreact negatively to recall news, providing further support for the depreciation of brand-name capital effect.

Finally, Simon and Sullivan (1993) develop a technique for estimating a firm's financial-based brand equity and demonstrate that their measure responds appropriately to marketing events that enhance customer- and market-based brand equity (i.e., the introduction of Diet Coke and FDA approval of aspartame for use in soft drinks) or shift demand to competitors overall (i.e., the introduction of New Coke). This study demonstrates that investors do not ignore brand equity factors; financial-based brand equity indicators are reflected in the stock prices of firms.

In summary, improvements (deterioration) in FBBE have a significant and positive (negative) impact on firm valuation and, although less studied, improvements in FBBE can also serve to reduce firm risk. While these results are well-documented, research has yet to investigate the mechanisms driving these effects.

CORPORATE BRAND STRATEGY

Branding can create value not just for products and services, but also for corporations, and organization-level brand strategies are important to the financial performance of the firm. We consider research on the effects of four classes of corporate brand strategy, as shown in Figure 7.1, and summarize key findings in Table 7.3. First, is the link between corporate naming strategies and firm value, whereby the signals conveyed in a name change can increase brand awareness and preference and drive value creation for the firm. Second, we explore how corporate mergers and acquisitions can enhance firm value by positively influencing the diversity of the brand portfolio (discussed in more detail below) and by creating synergistic effects of the acquirer's marketing capabilities in building brand equity. Third, we examine research on how the internal organizational culture can drive brand equity and hence increase firm value, paying attention to the branding mindset and branding capabilities of the firm. Finally, investments in corporate social responsibility, which have been shown to be related to firm value, can build strong brands by positively influencing brand evaluations, brand choice, and brand recommendations (Klein and Dawar, 2004), thereby enhancing firm value overall.

Table 7.3 Summary of key findings on the impact of corporate brand strategy on firm value

Classes of Corporate Brand Strategy	Illustrative Metrics	Empirical Findings	Data Sources	Illustrative Papers
1. Corporate naming strategy	Announcement of corporate name change	*Findings from the literature are mixed:* No statistically significant stock price reactions associated with corporate name change events A positive impact of name change on stock price only when the name change signals a change in corporate image The positive effect of name change announcements on abnormal stock returns is heightened when the change is accompanied by strategic investment support The positive overall effect of corporate name changes on stock prices is stronger for industrial versus consumer firms, risky versus low-risk firms, and poorly performing versus well-performing firms Companies that change their name to a 'dotcom' name earn significant cumulative abnormal returns from 1998 to 1999. After the burst of the Internet bubble (mid-2000), companies that deleted '.com' from their corporate names produce cumulative abnormal returns	Press releases and articles SEC filing Hoover Datastream International	Horsky and Swyngedouw (1987) Cooper et al. (2001) Cooper et al. (2005) Howe (1982) Karpoff and Rankine (1994) Bosch and Hirschey (1989) DeFanti (2006) Lee (2001)
2. Mergers & acquisitions (M&A)	Announcement of M&A	Acquirer and target characteristics (i.e., marketing capability and brand portfolio diversity) affect a target's brand value positively The positive impact of an acquirer's brand portfolio diversity and the positive effect of a target's marketing capability on a target's brand value are lower when the acquisition is synergistic	SEC filing SDC Platinum Advertising Age NBER USPTO	Bahadir et al. (2008)

Table 7.3 (continued)

Classes of Corporate Brand Strategy	Illustrative Metrics	Empirical Findings	Data Sources	Illustrative Papers
3. Brand orientation and brand management capability	Employee mindset Brand thrust Brand management effectiveness Brand management efficiency	Brand orientation positively affects brand performance, and in turn, leads to high financial performance Brand orientation has an indirect influence on brand performance through brand distinctiveness and innovation Companies with a strong brand thrust, compared to competitors, generate up to a 3% higher shareholder return Brand management capabilities are related to shareholder value performance, from both an accounting cash flow and stock market perspective	Questionnaire design Thomson Financial Extel	Wong and Merrilees (2008) Ohnemus and Jenster (2007) Morgan et al. (2009)
4. Corporate social responsibility (CSR)	Corporate social performance (CSP)	Firms that are viewed more favorably for CSR initiatives enjoy higher market value CSP helps reduce firm idiosyncratic risk. Advertising and R&D play a moderating role in the impact of CSP on firm idiosyncratic risk The simultaneous pursuit of CSP, advertising, and R&D is harmful with increased idiosyncratic risk	Fortune's MAC (Most Admired Companies)	Luo and Bhattacharya (2006) Luo and Bhattacharya (2009)

Corporate Naming Strategy and Firm Value

A common approach to understanding how corporate naming strategy affects firm value is to examine announcements of corporate name
changes, and apply the event study methodology from modern finance
theory to quantify stock price effects. These studies use a market signaling perspective that recognizes that a firm's name is infused with meaning
and reputation, thereby providing information that drives brand image
and equity perceptions among investors. Horsky and Swyngedouw (1987)
provide general support for the signaling theory approach as applied to
name changes. While the financial popular press has long argued that
corporate name changes result in permanent value creation for firms
(Emshwiller, 1999; Wingfield, 1999), empirical results on the effects of
corporate name change on firm value have been mixed.

Several researchers provide evidence that changes in corporate naming
have an immediate and significantly positive impact on the firm's stock
price. Horsky and Swyngedouw (1987) report a statistically positive overall
effect of corporate name changes on stock prices, with effects stronger for
industrial versus consumer firms, risky versus low-risk firms, and poorly
performing versus well-performing firms. Several researchers examine one
particular form of corporate name change: companies that add or delete
'.com' or the word 'Internet' to and from their names. Cooper et al. (2001)
document what they call 'a strikingly positive dotcom effect' (p. 2371) for
dot.com name changes, with cumulative abnormal returns on the order
of 74 percent for the ten days surrounding the announcement and no evidence of post-announcement negative drift. Cooper et al. (2005) explore
corporate naming decisions after the burst of the Internet bubble and
support that the stock prices for companies that deleted '.com' from their
corporate names after mid-2000 experienced statistically significant positive abnormal stock returns as high as 12.6 percent. Lee (2001) examines
dot.com name changes that are purely cosmetic versus those that signal
deeper strategic investments. Positive effects on abnormal stock returns
and trading volume are found for name change announcements, the effect
heightened when the change is accompanied by investment support.

Using various samples and announcement windows, others find no statistically significant stock price reactions associated with corporate name
change events (e.g., Howe, 1982; Karpoff and Rankine, 1994). Bosch and
Hirschey (1989) expose a positive pre-announcement effect, but this is followed by negative post-announcement drift that cancels out the effect. To
negotiate these mixed findings, DeFanti and Busch (2009) explore brand
equity moderators of the name change effect. Two types of name changes
are considered, each sending different brand signals: (1) name changes

that reflect a repositioning or substantive change in corporate image, and (2) name changes that provide news of a change in the corporate entity (e.g., acquisitions, changes in ownership). The magnitude of change in the name was also considered: in major changes (e.g., Anderson Consulting to Accenture), the new corporate name is not immediately recognizable as related to the previous corporate name whereas with a minor change (e.g., US Airways to US Air), the new corporate name is highly similar to the previous one. Findings show a positive impact of name change on stock price only when the name change is major and signals a change in corporate image. These findings contrast with Horsky and Swyngedouw (1987) who found statistically insignificant differences for major versus minor name changes. Kashmiri and Mahajan (2009) similarly explore moderators of the shareholder value impact of corporate name changes. They find positive effects when the name change signals a meaningful future change in marketing strategy rather than a retroactive re-alignment, and when the firm has a CMO on the management team.

Overall, findings suggest a contingency view of the effects of corporate brand naming strategies on firm value, with strong positive impact only when the change is supported with sufficient brand investments and backed by management capabilities, and when the name signals a relevant future shift in market strategy or repositioning of the brand.

Mergers, Acquisitions, and Firm Value

Brands are critical assets in mergers and acquisitions (M&As) and their cash flow expectations can drive significant price premiums from acquiring firms. The M&A setting is also useful for understanding brand equity effects on firm value: as of 2001, the Securities & Exchange Commission (SEC) requires the reporting of intangible brand assets in M&A transactions, thus granting a finance-based indicator of brand equity value to the firm.

Research by Bahadir et al. (2008) explores the factors that drive brand value (as measured by estimates of the dollar value the acquirer attached to the target firms' brands in the M&A transaction) and hence shareholder value in the context of M&A. Studying 133 M&A transactions among US-based public firms from 2001 to 2005, and considering both the characteristics of the target brand and the less-considered acquirer's perspective on brand value, the authors find that the brand marketing capabilities of both the acquirer and target companies (i.e., the ability to combine efficiently several marketing resources to engage in productive activity and attain marketing objectives) have positive effects on the target firm's brand value. Marketing-competent acquirers leverage the target's brands more effectively by spending more efficiently to achieve revenue objectives, extending the target's brands more effectively to new markets, and by better withstanding competitive pressures from other brands, thereby improving cash flows. Further, the brand portfolio diversity of the acquirer (i.e., the degree to which a firm chooses to serve different markets with different brands) has positive effects on the target firm's brand value: an acquirer firm with high diversity can keep more of the target's brands active after the acquisition, whereas new brands are likely divested in low diversity firms. Observed positive effects are attenuated in situations where the M&A creates redundancies among acquirer and target brand portfolios and marketing capabilities, thereby dampening cash flow expectations and cannibalizing cash flows.

Overall, M&As create shareholder value only when they enhance the diversity of acquirer brand portfolios and strengthen the target's marketing capabilities through non-redundant capabilities and skills.

Brand Orientation, Brand Management Capability, and Firm Value

The organization's branding environment can affect management's ability to develop and leverage brand assets, thereby increasing firm value by enhancing cash flows, encouraging greater levels of growth in cash flows, or reducing the volatility of cash flows. Aspects of this relationship have been investigated using two different organization-level constructs: (1) a brand-supportive organizational culture and (2) the capabilities of managers in their brand stewardship roles.

Wong and Merrilees (2008) investigate this issue by exploring whether being 'brand-oriented' affects brand strength (measured by brand differentiation), brand performance (indicated by brand awareness and loyalty), and financial performance (indicated in market share and the growth rate of sales). Brand orientation is 'a mindset that recognizes that the brand will be recognized, featured, and favored in strategy' (ibid., p. 374); it guarantees the brand as a corporate focus starting point in the formulation of corporate strategy (Mosmans and van der Vorst, 1998). Using survey methodology and structural equation modeling to test hypothesized effects, Wong and Merrilees find that brand orientation positively affects brand performance, which, in turn, leads to high financial performance. Brand orientation also exerts an indirect influence on brand performance through brand differentiation effects.

Ohnemus and Jenster (2007) also examine a firm's orientation to branding, but use a resource-based financial indicator of this commitment rather than measures of management attitudes and beliefs. The study posits a positive relationship between 'brand thrust,' the amount of financial resources a company allocates over time to build and maintain its brand (as measured in terms of staff overheads, distribution expenditures, and marketing/advertising expenditures) and the company's financial perform-ance (as measured by return on assets). Based on a sample of 2158 compa-nies within 113 different industries, companies with a strong brand thrust, compared to competitors, generate up to a 3 percent higher shareholder return.

Morgan et al. (2009) add to our understanding of how brands enhance financial performance by exploring the capabilities of managers in build-ing and leveraging brand assets. Drawing on dynamic capabilities theory and the resource-based view, the authors consider two aspects of brand management capability: (1) brand management effectiveness, the firm's ability to create desired brand equity outputs and (2) brand management efficiency, the firm's resources consumed in achieving realizing brand equity outputs. Using a sample of 1000 brands for the years 2000 through 2009, findings indicate that brand management capabilities are related to shareholder value performance, from both an accounting cash flow and stock market perspective, as measured by Tobin's Q.

In summary, a high-performing, brand-supportive culture drives firm value through effective and efficient management of brands.

Corporate Social Responsibility (CSR) and Firm Value

CSR has been positively linked to multiple indicators of brand equity. Recent research supports a positive relationship between a company's CSR actions and consumers' attitudes toward that company and its prod-ucts (Brown and Dacin, 1997; Creyer and Ross, 1997; Ellen et al., 2006), enhancing the customer-based measure of brand equity. Similarly, CSR efforts enhance market-based brand equity since consumers are more willing to consume from a company after exposure to information about its CSR efforts (Brown and Dacin, 1997; Murray and Vogel, 1997). Based on comprehensive historical data, Luo and Bhattacharya (2006) show that firms that are viewed more favorably for their CSR initiatives enjoy higher market value. Furthermore, the firm's customer satisfaction level at least partially mediates the influence of CSR on market value. An explanation is that the positive 'moral capital' that results from CSR could directly affect market value by improving employee morale and productivity. In addition, by creating public goodwill, CSR provides an 'insurance-like' protection for shareholder wealth. Luo and Bhattacharya (ibid.) also find that CSR helps reduce the firm's idiosyncratic risk. In addition, the simul-taneous pursuit of corporate social performance, advertising, and R&D leads to increased firm idiosyncratic risk.

Overall, investments in CSR are positively related to brand equity and to firm value, and to firm idiosyncratic risk.

BRANDING STRATEGY

Brand strategy provides the long-term plan for the systematic development of brand equity to enable the attainment of brand objectives and thereby increase shareholder value. In this section, we consider five 'big picture' strategic mechanisms designed to enhance brand performance and drive firm value, as identified in Figure 7.1: trademark and licensing strategy, brand extension strategy, brand alliances, brand portfolio strategy, and brand crisis management. Results from this collection of research papers are summarized in Table 7.4.

Trademarks and Firm Value

Trademarks are important intellectual property assets that play a significant role in company valuation (Berman, 2002). A trademark is 'any word, name, symbol, device or combination thereof that is adopted and used by a manufacturer or merchant to identify goods and distinguish them from those manufactured or sold by others' (Lanham Act, 15 U.S.C. 1127 1982). Trademark strategy provides the unique identifying iconography and symbol system that will be used on the public face of the brand. Through trademarking, a company obtains legally supported brand protection and demonstrates that an offering is uniquely theirs. Trademarks help create equity by establishing brand differentiation and helping consumers avoid confusion in the marketplace, by making it easier for a firm to create and build reputational capital, and by providing a basis for brand extensions. Trademarks are fiercely policed and managed in light of their value-creating roles. Research has shown that brand equity is diluted through counterfeiting and trademark infringement, thus supporting the value-creating functions that trademarks serve (Morrin et al., 2006).

Krasnikov et al. (2009) consider two types of trademarks and their effects on shareholder value. First are brand-identifying trademarks in the form of the brand's name (McDonald's), logo, and symbols (the Golden Arches). Identifying trademarks create value by enabling brand awareness and recognition (Henderson and Cote, 1998) and by serving as signals of likely product performance (Erdem and Swait, 1998). A second category of trademarks seeks to establish meaning-laden associations rather than simply facilitate brand identification, as, for example, with brand slogans (e.g., 'Staples: That was Easy') and brand characters or icons (e.g., the

Table 7.4 Summary of key findings on the impact of branding strategy on firm value

Classes of Branding Strategy	Illustrative Metrics	Empirical Findings	Data Sources	Illustrative Papers
1. Trademarks	Brand-identification trademarks Brand-association trademarks	Brand association trademarks create value by affecting brand attitudes Brand's protected names and symbols drive firm value through both the awareness-enhancing brand identification and meaning-laden brand association routes The brand association trademarks available to a firm enhance cash flow, Tobin's Q, ROA, and stock returns while reducing cash flow variability	USPTO's Trademark Electronic Search System (TESS) Firm's annual reports	Krasnikov et al. (2009) Henderson and Cote (1998) Keller (1993)
2. Brand extensions	Brand extension announcement	Stock market reactions are most positive when extensions are of brands that either rate high on familiarity and attitude or rate low on both familiarity and attitude Prestige niche brands that are high on esteem attitudes but low on familiarity experience negative excess returns through extension	Landor Image Power Survey	Lane and Jacobson (1995)
3. Brand licensing	Brand license agreements	Strong brands emphasizing brand protection over revenue generation in establishing license contracts have a negative association with royalty rates and hence financial performance Licensing generates higher stock return to investors only when licensed brands have a better fit with the brand concept	RoyaltyStat SEC filing	Jayachandran et al. (2009)
4. Brand alliances	Announcement of celebrity endorsement contracts Celebrity endorser event	Market quickly reacts positively to announcements of celebrity endorsement contracts in advertising In the short term, a brand's alliance with an athlete endorser leads to positive effects on sales and firm value. On average, firms announcing contracts with celebrities experienced a gain of 0.44% in excess returns	Press releases and articles Press releases and articles LexisNexis	Barbulescu et al. (2008) Agrawal and Kamakura (1995) Elberse and Verleun (2010)

Topic	Constructs	Findings	Data sources	References
		Brand alliances with athlete endorser leads to the positive effects on brand ally's equity, which in turn leads to further gains in sales and stock returns		Louie et al. (2001)
		In the long run, reputation-enhancing performances by the allied brand lead to further gains in sales and stock returns, albeit at a decreasing rate		Knittel and Stango (2010)
		A firm's stock market performance is negatively related to celebrity endorsers' blameworthiness when they are involved in undesirable events		
		Celebrity scandals send negative market-wide signals about the reputation risk associated with a celebrity brand		
5. Brand portfolio strategy	Portfolio characteristics (number of brands the firm owns and markets; number of segments; intraportfolio competition) Continuum of brand portfolio strategy Brand acquisition and disposal announcement	A firm's portfolio strategy explains 2–21% of the variance in financial performance and 8–16% of the variance in the marketing effectiveness and efficiency	American Customer Satisfaction Index (ACSI)	Morgan and Rego (2009)
		Owning a large number of brands reduces cash flow variability and has higher Tobin's Q	Hoover	Rao et al. (2004)
		Scope of market coverage is associated with greater cash flow variability and lower levels of Tobin's Q	Firm's website	Hsu et al. (2010)
		Inter-brand competition within the portfolio is unrelated to the firm's cash flow performance but drives lower Tobin's Q	Firm's annual reports	Wiles et al. (2009)
		A branded house strategy delivers the greatest shareholder returns. Sub-branding outperforms all other strategies in terms of returns, but at the highest levels of risk. Endorsed branding strategies are effective risk control mechanisms	Datamonitor Nielsen LexisNexis	
		The hybrid strategy is a poor performer with the lowest returns at moderate risk	Press releases and articles	
		There is a positive response to the pruning of portfolio brands		
		Investors reward brand acquisitions when the buying firm has strong marketing capabilities and gains synergy		

Energizer Bunny). Brand association trademarks create value by affecting brand attitudes and shaping brand knowledge (Keller, 1993). By examining 22 060 trademark registrations among 108 firms, Krasnikov et al. (2009) demonstrate that the brand's protected names and symbols drive firm value through both the awareness-enhancing brand identification and meaning-laden brand association routes. The stock of brand association trademarks available to a firm enhances cash flow, Tobin's Q, return on assets (ROA), and stock returns while reducing cash flow variability. Brand identification trademarks exert indirect effects by increasing awareness and enhancing the cash flows generated by brand association trademarks. However, increasing consumer awareness through brand identification trademarks diminishes the positive effects of brand association trademarks on Tobin's Q and stock returns. The authors speculate that this effect is due to the attraction of less-informed individuals versus institutional investors, which is known to reduce stock returns.

Overall, trademarks can create firm value by driving customer-based brand equity metrics and enhancing cash flow effects.

Brand Extensions and Firm Value

The asset-based view of branding emphasizes that incremental firm value can be generated by developing a strong brand that can be extended into new product categories, new markets, or across geographic lines. In brand leveraging, an established brand name is attached to a new product in an attempt to tap into consumers' favorable brand associations and thereby create incremental value at lower risk and cost. Extensions offer a number of advantages that not only facilitate market acceptance of the new offering in a competitive environment, but also enhance customer-based brand equity by generating positive feedback effects to the company and the brand. In terms of consumer reception, brand extensions can benefit from high awareness of the parent brand, transfer of positive affect from the parent, improved brand image halos from the parent brand, and reduced risk perceptions from the transfer of parent brand quality judgments, all of which drive trial and increase brand sales (Boush et al., 1987; Aaker and Keller, 1990; Sullivan, 1990; Bottomley and Holden, 2001). Brand extensions can also improve the image of the parent brand through reverse feedback effects and clarify or augment brand meaning (Keller and Aaker, 1992), thus supporting a virtuous value creation cycle. Brand extensions can also gain market-based equity advantages in the form of increased probability of distribution, sales, and share among new customers through increased market coverage, and improved cash flows from reduced costs of advertising and marketing programs and increased efficiencies in marketing spend (Smith and Park, 1992; Aaker, 1996). Still, brand leverage effects are not systematically positive: extensions with poor fit or poor quality can lead to image dilution and cannibalization (Aaker and Keller, 1990; Sullivan, 1990; Loken and John, 1993) and the inferences generated by certain parent brand associations can create negative brand extension attitudes overall (Bridges et al., 2000). Further, extensions may restrict financial equity by precluding opportunities provided only through a new and unconnected branded offering, thereby constraining value creation in the firm (Aaker, 1990). Research suggests that brands can benefit or suffer from extensions depending on the conditions and tradeoffs they engage.

Lane and Jacobson (1995) apply event study methodology to explore the financial impact of 89 brand extension announcements and, specifically, whether stock market responses depend upon customer-based brand equity indicators of familiarity with and attitude towards the extension brand. Empirical results indicate that investors sometimes expect the negative consequences of leverage decisions to offset expected gains, thereby justifying concerns about potential negative long-run repercussions from extensions (Sullivan, 1990; Loken and John, 1993). Stock market returns depend interactively and non-monotonically on brand attitude (as measured by Y&R's esteem construct) and familiarity (as indicated by share of mind). Stock market reactions are most positive when extensions are of brands that either rate high on familiarity and attitude (e.g., Coca-Cola) or rate low on both familiarity and attitude (e.g., Yuban), the latter class comprising brands that have everything to gain but nothing to lose. Prestige niche brands high on esteem attitudes but low on familiarity experience negative excess returns through extension. These brands have significant restrictions on expansion potential that derives from an aura of exclusivity that extensions threaten to dilute.

Overall, the effects of brand extensions on firm value are complex, with effects contingent on qualities of the extensions and their parent brands.

Licensing and Firm Value

As brands become widely recognized, they can also create firm value through the generation of licensing revenue. In licensing, a trademark holder (the licensor) grants permission to a third party (the licensee) to use the firm's trademarks in association with the licensee's products/services for specified purposes and for a defined period of time in exchange for a royalty or licensing fee (Raugust, 2008). The legally binding license agreement not only generates incremental revenue streams but also protects the brand from misappropriation, thereby reducing risk. Srivastava et al. (1999) suggest that strong brands should generate higher royalty rates and hence firm value because they allow licensees to build stronger businesses. Jayachandran (2009) find, interestingly, that strong brands emphasize brand protection over revenue generation in establishing license contracts, such that brand strength has a negative association with royalty rates and hence financial performance.

Agency theory also suggests that licensing may reduce firm performance through the mechanism of increased brand dilution risks. License agreements are agency relationships wherein goals and risks preferences of licensees and licensors may not be aligned. Whereas the licensor is interested in protecting the equity of a strong brand, the licensee may enter the agreement to generate short-term revenues through brand exploitation (Quelch, 1985). In the license setting, the management, production, and marketing of the licensed extension are outside the firm's direct stewardship and control, which can adversely affect consumers' brand attitudes and diminish brand equity and negatively affect sales of all products carrying the brand name.

Using an event study method, Barbulescu et al. (2008) investigate the effects of brand license announcements on the licensor's abnormal stock returns and find that although licensing generates a significant stock return to investors, a notable proportion of announcements have negative effects on returns. In line with theories explaining successes in brand extensions, stock returns are higher only when licensed brands have a better fit with the brand concept, are leveraged across a large number of product categories at the brand benefit level (i.e., brand breadth), and create synergies in market spend, thereby lowering brand advertising investments.

Overall, results support a license–shareholder value linkage, with effects determined by the quality and fit of the licensed brand.

Brand Alliances and Firm Value

A brand alliance is a short- or long-term association between two or more individual brands that is engaged in the hope that the brand equity of the linked entity is increased by virtue of the affiliation, wherein the whole is greater than the sum of the parts (Rao and Ruekert, 1994). Brand alliances can strengthen brand equity by two central routes: (1) they create meaningful 'secondary brand associations' (Keller, 1993) that are transferred between partner brands and enhance brand attitudes (Kamins et al., 1989), brand preferences (Kahle and Homer, 1985; Kamins et al., 1989; Ohanian, 1991; Heath et al., 1994) and brand associations (Rao and Ruekert, 1994; Park et al., 1996; Washburn et al., 2004) directly, and (2) they enhance the value of advertising expenditures and marketing investments by positively influencing brand awareness (Petty et al., 1983) and hence the firm's working capital needs (Srivastava et al., 1998). The use of alliances constitutes a significant investment in intangible brand assets (Agrawal and Kamakura, 1995). Thus, brand alliances have potential to influence brand equity through the three routes outlined in Figure 7.1.

The shareholder payoff of investments in one form of brand alliance – those involving celebrity endorsers – has received particular research attention. Using an event study methodology to examine 110 celebrity endorsement contracts, Agrawal and Kamakura (1995) demonstrate that a firm's stock market valuation increases when it signs celebrity endorsers, suggesting that investors view celebrity endorsement contracts as worthwhile advertising investments. Elberse and Verleun (2010) focus on alliances between professional sports athletes and consumer goods companies and probe deeper to explore intermediate market-based effects on firm sales. They find that in the short term, a brand's alliance with an athlete endorser leads to positive effects on sales and firm value, as measured in terms of stock returns. In the long run, reputation-enhancing performances by the allied brand maximize the likelihood of further positive news regarding the brand ally's equity, which leads to further gains in sales and stock returns, albeit at a decreasing rate. Alliances with strong athlete brands generate the largest gains in revenues and stock returns, further supporting the mediating role of customer-based indicators of brand equity on performance results.

Some studies expressly recognize that the awareness and association effects generated by celebrity affiliation are not uniformly positive, and that celebrities can become involved in reputation-damaging scandals as well as performance-enhancing events (Janiszewski and Van Osselaer, 2000; Washburn et al., 2004). Louie et al. (2001) demonstrate how negative events involving endorsers of high-quality products can negatively impact firm valuation. Knittel and Stango (2010) analyze the Tiger Woods scandal to link celebrity endorsements not just to stock market effects but also firm risk. They find that firms with products endorsed by Woods suffered significant declines in stock market value, relative to both the entire stock market and to a set of competitor firms. Some sponsors' losses were competitors' gains, suggesting that celebrity endorsement deals are at least partially a business-stealing strategy. Results also show that negative effects are particularly strong among firms who are endorsement intensive. Overall, scandals send negative market-wide signals about the reputation risk associated with celebrity brands.

In summary, the research supports that while brand alliances and celebrity endorsements can positively drive brand equity in the short run and firm value in the long run, scandals and other negative-quality signals can have negative effects.

Brand Portfolio Strategy and Firm Value

Most large firms go to market with not one brand but many, and brand portfolio strategies help organize and guide resource allocation for the company's collection of products and brands (Aaker, 2004). The brand portfolio strategy specifies the structure of the brand portfolio and the scope, roles, and interrelationships among portfolio brands. Brand portfolios differ in terms of their design and complexity: breadth concerns the number and nature of different products and brands linked to a firm's offerings; depth concerns how short or long the product line is for a given offering (Keller, 2007). Portfolios also differ in the degree to which branded offerings are unified through a linkage with common brand names, logos, or symbols. In the branded house, an umbrella corporate brand applies for all brands and products, while in a house of brands, a collection of stand-alone, independent brands is in play. Brand portfolio strategy fundamentally affects a firm's financial performance by influencing the ability to compete and garner sales, distribution, and market share; by allowing manufacturing and distribution scale economies; and by affording efficiencies in marketing and advertising spend. Portfolio strategy affects the brand positioning and marketing investment for each branded offering, thereby driving customer-based brand equity metrics such as awareness, associations, attitudes and behaviors. As companies grow, portfolio management becomes yet more critical as expanded portfolios are streamlined through brand deletion and product line pruning plays a critical role (Kumar, 2003). Despite the criticality of brand portfolio strategy to firm performance, different theories-in-use guide management decisions (Hill et al., 2005) and the effectiveness of different design characteristics remains unclear.

To address this gap, Morgan and Rego (2009) analyze firm value creation as a function of three central portfolio characteristics: the number of brands the firm owns and markets, the scope of market coverage or number of segments in which brands are marketed, and the degree to which the brands in the portfolio compete with each other by being similarly positioned or directed to the same consumer targets. They find that a firm's portfolio strategy is a significant predictor of financial and marketing performance, with strategy explaining 2–21 percent of the variance in financial performance and 8–16 percent of the variance in the marketing effectiveness and efficiency. Exactly how portfolio characteristics affect returns is complex, however, with different characteristics driving directionally different effects through different intermediary routes. Findings suggest that owning a large number of brands is positively associated with customer-based loyalty, reduced cash flow variability, and higher Tobin's

Q, but also higher sales, general, and administrative (SG&A) expenditures and lower market share. Scope of market coverage is associated with lower advertising and SG&A expenditures and higher market share, but greater cash flow variability, and lower levels of Tobin's Q, cash flow, and loyalty. Competition within the portfolio lowers relative SG&A and advertising expenses, is unrelated to the firm's cash flow performance, and drives lower loyalty and Tobin's Q. From a marketing performance standpoint, the research suggests that a greater number of brands marketed across a smaller number of segments, with a low level of inter-brand competition drives loyalty; the opposite pattern drives increased market share. The research supports that the ideal portfolio structure depends on the market or financial result desired by the firm.

Rao and colleagues (2004) examine three different brand portfolio strategies that differ in their supply- and demand-side advantages/disadvantages and find differential effects on Tobin's Q. A branded house strategy in which all offerings share a common corporate brand designation delivers the greatest shareholder returns. This strategy benefits from significant supply-side advantages in terms of economies of scale in marketing, lower costs of advertising/promotion, lower costs of creating brand equity, and lower costs of new product introductions that accelerate and enhance cash flows; demand-side advantages from easier brand extensions also accrue. Findings regarding underperformance among house of brands strategists lead these researchers to speculate that the markets 'do not value the house of brands strategy appropriately' and might 'underestimate the potential benefits of a differentiated brand approach for diverse target segments and products.' Further, they hypothesize, markets 'under-appreciate that a house-of-brands strategy distributes risk over more brands, thereby improving the firm's financial profile overall' (p. 139).

Hsu et al. (2010) extend Rao et al.'s (2004) analysis by considering a continuum of five portfolio strategies (branded house, sub-branding, hybrid, endorsed branding, and house of brands) and including effects on risk as well as returns. They find that sub-branding (e.g., Apple iPod, BMW 7-series) outperforms all other strategies in terms of returns, but generates the highest levels of risk. Strategies that create distance from the corporate entity (endorsed branding) are effective risk control mechanisms, while strategies that create separation (house of brands) lower systematic but not idiosyncratic risk. In contrast to the logic of financial portfolio theory that seeks risk management through diversification, the hybrid strategy is a poor performer with the lowest returns at moderate risk.

Wiles et al. (2009) examine how the acquisition or deletion of brands in the portfolio affects a firm's stock performance. Their event study of stock market reactions to 232 brand acquisition and 163 disposal announcements in the consumer packaged goods industry suggests a positive response to the pruning of portfolio brands, but no evidence of abnormal returns for brand acquisitions. Stock performance is affected by several characteristics of the disposed brands: non-core business brands, larger brands, and brands for which the sale price is greater than anticipated generate firm value rewards. The authors find some evidence that investors may reward brand acquisitions under certain conditions, such as when the buying firm has strong marketing capabilities, when the brand acquisition is in a market segment adjacent to the firm's current business, or when the acquired brand brings new distribution resources to the firm.

This research collectively supports that strategic decisions regarding a firm's brand portfolio affect a firm's marketing and financial performance in complex ways.

BRAND-BUILDING TOOLS: DRIVERS OF STRONG BRANDS AND FIRM VALUE

Arguably the most important issue facing managers is how to build and maintain strong brands. Managers can build strong brands by investing in marketing programs targeting current or potential customers. We consider links between investments in advertising and promotions to brand equity and to firm value, as shown in Figure 7.1, and summarize key findings in Table 7.5.

Advertising, Brand Equity, and Firm Value

Advertising can influence brand equity through the three routes outlined in Figure 7.1. First, it enhances the customer-based indicators of brand equity, essentially moving the consumer forward through a hierarchical sequence of events, including cognition (e.g., awareness, knowledge), affect (e.g., liking, desire) and, ultimately, behavior (purchase and loyalty) as argued by Vakratsas and Ambler (1999). Second, advertising can boost market-based indicators of brand equity by differentiating brands, which can then be leveraged to extract superior product market performance. Finally, advertising can serve to build financial-based indicators of brand equity by building intangible asset value (Joshi and Hanssens, 2009).

Research has shown that a firm's advertising directly affects stock

Table 7.5 Summary of key findings on the impact of the drivers of strong brands on firm value

Drivers of Strong Brands	Illustrative Metrics	Empirical Findings	Data Sources	Illustrative Papers
1. Advertising	Advertising dollars (e.g., Compustat) Advertising dollars (e.g., TNS Media)	Advertising directly affects stock returns over and above the indirect effect of advertising through lifting sales revenues and profits. Advertising will have a direct effect on firm value through two mechanisms: spillover and signaling Investors, cognizant of the benefits of increased advertising through enhanced brand equity, may look beyond a firm's current cash flows and translate the long-term effects of advertising into firm valuation Advertising may act as a signal of the firm's financial well-being or competitive viability Firms that raise significant amounts of equity capital increase their advertising significantly more than firms with higher financial leverage (i.e., higher levels of debt relative to equity capital)	Compustat TNS Media IMS	Frieder and Subrahmanyam (2005) Grullon et al. (2004) Joshi and Hanssens (2009) Barth et al. (1998) Luo and Donthu (2006) Mathur et al. (1997) Gifford (1997) Grullon et al. (2006) McAlister et al. (2007) Osinga et al. (2011) Srinivasan et al. (2009)

Table 7.5 (continued)

Drivers of Strong Brands	Illustrative Metrics	Empirical Findings	Data Sources	Illustrative Papers
		Advertising lowers systematic market risk while increasing idiosyncratic risk		
		Communicating the differentiated added value created by product innovation yields higher firm-value effects of these innovations, especially for pioneering innovations		
		Firms that are more productive in converting advertising and promotion resources into marketing outputs may create greater shareholder value over time		
2. Price promotions	Promotional expenditures	Price promotions diminish long-term firm value, even though they have positive effects on revenues and, in the short run, on profits	J.D. Power and Associates Scott-Levin & PERQ/HCI (Pharma)	Pauwels et al. (2004) Srinivasan et al. (2009) Osinga et al. (2011)
		A policy of aggressive new product introductions acts as an antidote for excessive reliance on consumer incentives		
		Price promotions in the pharmaceutical industry have a positive effect on idiosyncratic risk		

returns over and above the indirect effect of advertising by enhancing top- and bottom-line performance (Grullon et al., 2004; Joshi and Hanssens, 2009). A recent meta-analysis shows that advertising and promotional spending have positive effects on the market value of a firm (Conchar et al., 2005). Specifically, a firm's advertising affects its visibility with the investors, resulting in a direct effect on the firm's market capitalization (Joshi and Hanssens, 2009). In addition, advertising acts as a signal of the firm's financial well-being (Gifford, 1997; Mathur et al., 1997; Mathur and Mathur, 2000). Investors, aware of the benefits of increased advertising through enhanced brand equity (Barth et al., 1998; Rao et al., 2004), may also look beyond a firm's current cash flows and translate the long-term effects of advertising into firm valuation.

Recent studies confirm that advertising expenditures create intangible brand assets (Grullon et al., 2004), one that is not readily transferable in the event of bankruptcy. Using a sample of firms that raise significant amounts of equity capital, this study finds that such firms increase their advertising significantly more than firms with higher financial leverage (i.e., higher levels of debt relative to equity capital). Srinivasan et al. (2009) find that communicating the differentiated added-value created by product innovation or advertising to consumers yields higher firm value effects of these innovations, with results even stronger for pioneering innovations. Further, advertising enhances market penetration, makes it easier to launch product extensions, and increases customer loyalty. Through these mechanisms, advertising reduces cash flow volatility (Fischer et al., 2009) and hence firm risk overall. Advertising also can influence investor portfolio choices. Individual investors, unlike institutional ones, prefer holding stocks of well-known firms (Frieder and Subrahmanyam, 2005). Firms that engage in higher levels of advertising tend to have a relatively large number of individual stockholders whose buy and sell decisions would be less coordinated (Xu and Malkiel, 2003). This scenario could reduce systematic risk. Consistent with this, recent research indicates that advertising and R&D indeed lower a firm's systematic risk (McAlister et al., 2007; Osinga et al., 2011). As for idiosyncratic risk, recent research has found that direct-to-consumer advertising (DTCA) in the pharmaceutical industry increases idiosyncratic risk even though this increase does not affect investors who maintain a well-diversified portfolio. Osinga et al. (2011) argue that the increase in idiosyncratic risk likely occurs because investors perceive DTCA as a risky investment given its limited sales impact.

In summary, advertising – a key driver of strong brands – positively influences intangible firm value, decreases the systematic risk, and increases the idiosyncratic risk of the firm.

Promotions, Brand Equity, and Firm Value

Sales promotions are generally seen as detrimental to brand equity, even though they produce positive short-term impacts on sales and revenue (Winer, 1986; Mela et al., 1997). The effect of promotions on brand equity occurs primarily through market-based brand equity indicators in lowering the price premium; when the per-unit margin of the promoted brand is affected, there may be increased switching from higher- to lower-margin brands (or vice versa). While many studies examine the impact of price promotions on revenues, their impact on firm valuation is relatively under-researched. Recent research finds that investor reactions to price promotions are negative (Pauwels et al., 2004; Srinivasan et al., 2009). Osinga et al. (2011) find that direct-to-physician (DTP) price promotions in the pharmaceutical industry have a positive effect on idiosyncratic risk, which is in line with the negative stock return impact. These negative impacts on returns and volatility likely occur for two reasons: price promotions may signal desperation and forecast decreased firm earnings. Managerial inertia explains why the short-run success of promotions makes it attractive for managers to continue using them (Nijs et al., 2007). This results in a vicious cycle of competitive promotion escalation, eventually eroding brand equity, profit margins, and firm value.

In summary, price promotions are negatively related to brand equity and to firm value in the long run.

CONCLUSIONS AND DIRECTIONS FOR FUTURE RESEARCH

This chapter has assembled research that emphasizes and demonstrates the importance of branding activities in building shareholder value. A key contribution of this chapter is the development of an integrative conceptual framework that links branding strategies and tactics to the creation of brand equity and identifies two mechanisms by which brands drive the components of shareholder value. Specifically, the cash flow perspective views brands-as-assets with investments in brands enhancing firm value directly through their effects on cash flows, while the signaling perspective views brands-as-information with brands serving as visible signals of financial well-being of a firm. A second contribution is the provision of a framework for organizing and relating metrics of brand equity to those of shareholder value creation, an activity that advances the marketing metrics imperative overall (Lehmann and Reibstein, 2006).

This chapter has reviewed 56 research articles seeking to establish the link between branding and shareholder value. While much has been learned about the value-creating effects of brands, significant gaps in our understanding remain:

- Is there a hierarchy governing the effects of consumer-, market- and financial-based brand equity and their links to shareholder value generation? More importantly, are some of these metrics of brand equity leading indicators of shareholder value losses and gains?
- What is the best approach to quantifying the value of brands and assessing their impact on cash flows, growth, and risk?
- Are the signaling and information routes equally effective in driving shareholder value? When does the brand-as-asset dominate over the brand-as-information route?
- How does a brand's participation in social media drive shareholder value, if at all?
- How can firms mitigate the value-destroying consequences of brand crisis events?
- What is the theory of risk as it pertains to brands and brand equity?
- Does the notion of risk diversification apply to brand strategy and firm value effects?
- What are the mechanisms whereby brands create shareholder value?
- How do internal organizational factors such as employees' engagement with the brand or internal branding programs drive shareholder value?

From a conceptual and empirical perspective, much remains to be learned about the nature and role of risk in the brand–firm value relationship. Specifically, a stronger conceptualization of the risk constructs and mechanisms is needed, with attention to the particulars of the branding environment at hand. Very few marketing papers even consider risk within the brand–shareholder value environment, and those studies that do view brands merely as an insurance-like protection mechanism that helps firms weather difficult times or equity challenges. But, the finance literature suggests other mechanisms through which branding may affect the firm's risk profile; for example, risks can be managed through information flows. We need to understand how and whether the risk frameworks and mechanisms from finance apply to brands.

Further, our conceptualizations of risk are arguably underdeveloped for exposing desired brand effects. We have considered systematic and idiosyncratic risk, but our theorizing needs sharpening on the differential effects of branding on these components of risk. We should perhaps consider whether a different conceptualization of risk is appropriate in branding situations. For example, much consumer behavior literature highlights the risks of brand dilution and reputation; future research needs to consider these potentially different forms of brand-related risk and how they relate to the components of firm risk. It may be that to advance our understanding of the link between branding and shareholder value, we need to develop unique theories of branding and risk with new constructs and mechanisms that are tailored to the branding situation at hand.

Lastly, conclusive research on the branding–shareholder value linkage hinges on brand valuation metrics that are relevant, predictive, calibrated, reliable, sensitive, transparent, and objective. The marketing discipline is not even in general agreement that brands are assets that need to be represented as such on the balance sheet (Marketing Accountability Standards Board Conference, 2010). Further, there exist significant complications from the accounting perspective that prohibit advancement on this front. Sufficiently broad-based investor support is lacking and other critical aspects of financial reporting are being prioritized (Bielstein, 2010). It is therefore imperative for multiple stakeholders including marketers, accountants, and the investor community, to work together to advance this goal.

NOTES

1. We do not discuss the findings on distribution and new product decisions even though these are part of the 4Ps that clearly influence brand equity and firm value, since their influences on firm value are reviewed in other chapters in the book.
2. The detailed review of upside and downside risk can be found in Nawrocki (1999).

REFERENCES

Aaker, D.A. (1990), 'Brand Extensions: The Good, the Bad, and the Ugly,' *Sloan Management Review*, **31** (4), 47–56.
Aaker, D.A. (1992), 'The Value of Brand Equity,' *Journal of Business Strategy*, **13** (4), 27–32.
Aaker, D.A. (1996), 'Measuring Brand Equity across Products and Markets,' *California Management Review*, **38** (3), 102–20.
Aaker, D.A. (2003), 'The Power of the Branded Differentiator,' *MIT Sloan Management Review*, **45** (1), 83–7.
Aaker, D.A. (2004), *Brand Portfolio Strategy: Creating Relevance, Differentiation, Energy, Leverage, and Clarity*, New York: Free Press.
Aaker, D.A. and R. Jacobson (1994), 'The Financial Information Content of Perceived Quality,' *Journal of Marketing Research*, **31** (2), 191–201.
Aaker, D.A. and R. Jacobson (2001), 'The Value Relevance of Brand Attitude in High-technology Markets,' *Journal of Marketing Research*, **38** (4), 485–93.
Aaker, D.A. and K.L. Keller (1990), 'Consumer Evaluations of Brand Extensions,' *Journal of Marketing*, **54** (1), 27–41.

Agarwal, M.K. and V.R. Rao (1996), 'An Empirical Comparison of Consumer-based Measures of Brand Equity,' *Marketing Letters*, **7** (3), 237–47.

Agrawal, J. and W.A. Kamakura (1995), 'The Economic Worth of Celebrity Endorsers: Event Study Analysis,' *Journal of Marketing*, **59** (3), 56–62.

Agres, S.J. and T.M. Dubitsky (1996), 'Changing Needs for Brands,' *Journal of Advertising Research*, **36** (1), 21–30.

Ailawadi, K.L., D.R. Lehmann, and S.A. Neslin (2003), 'Revenue Premium as an Outcome Measure of Brand Equity,' *Journal of Marketing*, **67** (4), 1–17.

Ambler, T. (2003), *Marketing and the Bottom Line*, London: FT Press.

Amir, E. and B. Lev (1996), 'Value-relevance of Nonfinancial Information: The Wireless Communications Industry,' *Journal of Accounting and Economics*, **22** (1–3), 3–30.

Anderson, E.W. (2006), 'Invited Commentary – Linking Service and Finance,' *Marketing Science*, **25** (6), 587–9.

Anderson, E.W., C. Fornell, and D.R. Lehmann (1994), 'Customer Satisfaction, Market Share, and Profitability: Findings from Sweden,' *Journal of Marketing*, **58** (3), 53–66.

Ang, A., J. Chen, and Y. Xing (2006), 'Downside Risk,' *Review of Financial Studies*, **19** (4), 1191–239.

Ang, A., R.J. Hodrick, Y. Xing, and X. Zhang (2006), 'The Cross-section of Volatility and Expected Returns,' *Journal of Finance*, **61** (1), 259–99.

Bahadir, S.C., S.G. Bharadwaj, and R.K. Srivastava (2008), 'Financial Value of Brands in Mergers and Acquisitions: Is Value in the Eye of the Beholder?,' *Journal of Marketing*, **72** (6), 49–64.

Baldauf, A., K.S. Cravens, and G. Binder (2003), 'Performance Consequences of Brand Equity Management: Evidence from Organizations in the Value Chain,' *Journal of Product and Brand Management*, **12** (4/5), 220–34.

Bansal, P. and L. Clelland (2004), 'Talking Trash: Legitimacy, Impression Management, and Unsystematic Risk in the Context of the Natural Environment,' *Academy of Management Journal*, **47** (1), 93–103.

Barbulescu, A., K.R. Tuli, and A.K. Kohli (2008), 'Investor Response to Brand Licensing Announcements: The Role of Brand Characteristics,' Working Paper.

Barth, M.E., M.B. Clement, G. Foster, and R. Kasznik (1998), 'Brand Values and Capital Market Valuation,' *Review of Accounting Studies*, **3** (1/2), 41–68.

Bawa, V.S. and E.B. Lindenberg (1977), 'Capital Market Equilibrium in a Mean–Lower Partial Moment Framework,' *Journal of Financial Economics*, **5** (2), 189–200.

Berman, B. (2002), *From Ideas to Assets: Investing Wisely in Intellectual Property*, Hoboken: John Wiley & Sons.

Bharadwaj, S.G., K.R. Tuli, and A. Bonfrer (2011), 'The Impact of Brand Quality on Shareholder Wealth,' *Journal of Marketing*, **75** (5), 88–104.

Bielstein, S. (2010), 'The FASB and Accounting Standards-setting,' Annual Marketing Accountability Standards Board Conference, Boston.

Bosch, J.-C. and M. Hirschey (1989), 'The Valuation Effects of Corporate Name Changes,' *Financial Management*, **18** (4), 64–73.

Bottomley, P.A. and S.J.S. Holden (2001), 'Do We Really Know How Consumers Evaluate Brand Extensions? Empirical Generalizations Based on Secondary Analysis of Eight Studies,' *Journal of Marketing Research*, **38** (4), 494–500.

Boulding, W., E. Lee, and R. Staelin (1994), 'Mastering the Mix: Do Advertising, Promotion, and Sales Force Activities Lead to Differentiation?,' *Journal of Marketing Research*, **31** (2), 159–72.

Boush, D., S. Shipp, B. Loken, E. Gencturk, S. Crockett, E. Kennedy, B. Minshall, D. Misurell, L. Rochford, and J. Strobel (1987), 'Affect Generalization to Similar and Dissimilar Brand Extensions,' *Psychology & Marketing*, **4** (3), 225–37.

Bridges, S., K.L. Keller, and S. Sood (2000), 'Communication Strategies for Brand Extensions: Enhancing Perceived Fit by Establishing Explanatory Links,' *Journal of Advertising*, **29** (4), 1–11.

Brown, G. and N. Kapadia (2007), 'Firm-specific Risk and Equity Market Development,' *Journal of Financial Economics*, **84** (2), 358–88.

Brown, T.J. and P.A. Dacin (1997), 'The Company and the Product: Corporate Associations and Consumer Product Responses,' *Journal of Marketing*, **61** (1), 68–84.

Bucklin, L.P. and S. Sengupta (1993), 'Organizing Successful Co-Marketing Alliances,' *Journal of Marketing*, **57** (2), 32–46.

Chaudhuri, A. and M.B. Holbrook (2001), 'The Chain of Effects from Brand Trust and Brand Affect to Brand Performance: The Role of Brand Loyalty,' *Journal of Marketing*, **65** (2), 81–93.

Chen, S.N. (1982), 'An Examination of Risk–Return Relationship in Bull and Bear Markets Using Time-varying Betas,' *Journal of Financial and Quantitative Analysis*, **17** (2), 265–86.

Conchar, M., M. Crask, and G. Zinkhan (2005), 'Market Valuation Models of the Effect of Advertising and Promotional Spending: A Review and Meta-analysis,' *Journal of the Academy of Marketing Science*, **33** (4), 445–60.

Cooper, M.J., O. Dimitrov, and P.R. Rau (2001), 'A Rose.Com by Any Other Name,' *Journal of Finance*, **56** (6), 2371–88.

Cooper, M.J., A. Khorana, I. Osobov, A. Patel, and P.R. Rau (2005), 'Managerial Actions in Response to a Market Downturn: Valuation Effects of Name Changes in the Dot.Com Decline,' *Journal of Corporate Finance*, **11** (1–2), 319–35.

Creyer, E.H. and W.T. Ross (1997), 'The Influence of Firm Behavior on Purchase Intention: Do Consumers Really Care About Business Ethics?,' *Journal of Consumer Marketing*, **14** (6), 421–32.

DeFanti, M.P. (2006), 'The Effect of a Corporate Name Change Related to a Change in Corporate Image Upon a Firm's Stock Price,' dissertation, Texas A&M University.

DeFanti, M.P. and P.S. Busch (2009), 'The Effect of a Corporate Name Change Related to a Change in Corporate Image Upon a Firm's Stock Price,' Marketing Strategy Meets Wall Street Conference. Emory University.

Doyle, P. (2001), 'Shareholder-value-based Brand Strategies,' *Journal of Brand Management*, **9** (1), 20–30.

Elberse, A. and J. Verleun (2010), 'Brand Alliances and the Value of Reflected Glory: The Case of Athlete Endorsements,' Working Paper.

Ellen, P., D. Webb, and L. Mohr (2006), 'Building Corporate Associations: Consumer Attributions for Corporate Socially Responsible Programs,' *Journal of the Academy of Marketing Science*, **34** (2), 147–57.

Emshwiller, J.R. (1999), 'Follow the Dotted Line: First Up – Then Down,' *Wall Street Journal*, 3 March.

Erdem, T. and J. Swait (1998), 'Brand Equity as a Signaling Phenomenon,' *Journal of Consumer Psychology*, **7** (2), 131–57.

Fama, E.F. (1970), 'Efficient Capital Markets: A Review of Theory and Empirical Work,' *Journal of Finance*, **25** (2), 383–417.

Feldwick, P. (1996a), 'Do We Really Need "Brand Equity?",' *Journal of Brand Management*, **4** (1), 9–28.

Feldwick, P. (1996b), 'What Is Brand Equity Anyway, and How Do You Measure It?,' *Journal of the Market Research Society*, **38** (2), 85–104.

Ferreira, M.A. and P.A. Laux (2007), 'Corporate Governance, Idiosyncratic Risk, and Information Flow,' *Journal of Finance*, **62** (2), 951–89.

Fischer, M., H. Shin, and D.M. Hanssens (2009), 'Marketing Spending and the Volatility of Revenues and Cash Flows,' *UCLA Working Paper Series*.

Fornell, C., S. Mithas, F.V. Morgeson III, and M.S. Krishnan (2006), 'Customer Satisfaction and Stock Prices: High Returns, Low Risk,' *Journal of Marketing*, **70** (1), 3–14.

Frieder, L. and A. Subrahmanyam (2005), 'Brand Perceptions and the Market for Common Stock,' *Journal of Financial and Quantitative Analysis*, **40** (01), 57–85.

Gifford, D.J. (1997), 'The Value of Going Green,' *Harvard Business Review*, **75** (5), 11–12.

Govindaraj, S., B. Jaggi, and B. Lin (2004), 'Market Overreaction to Product Recall

Revisited – the Case of Firestone Tires and the Ford Explorer,' *Review of Quantitative Finance and Accounting*, **23** (1), 31–54.

Goyal, A. and P. Santa-Clara (2003), 'Idiosyncratic Risk Matters!,' *Journal of Finance*, **58** (3), 975–1007.

Gruca, T.S. and L.L. Rego (2005), 'Customer Satisfaction, Cash Flow, and Shareholder Value,' *Journal of Marketing*, **69** (3), 115–30.

Grullon, Gustavo, George Kanatas, and Piyush Kumar (2006), 'The Impact of Capital Structure on Advertising Competition: An Empirical Study,' *Journal of Business*, **79** (6), 3101–24.

Grullon, G., G. Kanatas, and J.P. Weston (2004), 'Advertising, Breadth of Ownership, and Liquidity,' *Review of Financial Studies*, **17** (2), 439–61.

Gupta, S., D.R. Lehmann, and J.A. Stuart (2004), 'Valuing Customers,' *Journal of Marketing Research*, **41** (1), 7–18.

Harlow, W.V. (1991), 'Asset Allocation in a Downside-risk Framework,' *Financial Analysts Journal*, **47** (5), 28–40.

Heath, T.B., M.S. McCarthy, and D.L. Mothersbaugh (1994), 'Spokesperson Fame and Vividness Effects in the Context of Issue-relevant Thinking: The Moderating Role of Competitive Setting,' *Journal of Consumer Research*, **20** (4), 520–34.

Henderson, P.W. and J.A. Cote (1998), 'Guidelines for Selecting or Modifying Logos,' *Journal of Marketing*, **62** (2), 14–30.

Hill, S., R. Ettenson, and D. Tyson (2005), 'Achieving the Ideal Brand Portfolio,' *MIT Sloan Management Review*, **46** (2), 85–90.

Hoeffler, S. and K.L. Keller (2003), 'The Marketing Advantages of Strong Brands,' *Journal of Brand Management*, **10** (6), 421–45.

Holt, D.B. (2004), *How Brands Become Icons: The Principles of Cultural Branding*, Cambridge, MA: Harvard Business Press.

Horsky, D. and P. Swyngedouw (1987), 'Does It Pay to Change Your Company's Name? A Stock Market Perspective,' *Marketing Science*, **6** (4), 320–35.

Howe, J.S. (1982), 'A Rose by Any Other Name? A Note on Corporate Name Changes,' *Financial Review*, **17** (4), 271–8.

Hsu, L., S. Fournier, and S. Srinivasan (2010), 'Brand Portfolio Strategy Effects on Firm Value and Risks,' Working Paper, Boston University.

Janiszewski, C. and S.M.J. Van Osselaer (2000), 'A Connectionist Model of Brand-quality Associations,' *Journal of Marketing Research*, **37** (3), 331–50.

Jayachandran, S., K. Hewett, and P. Kaufman (2009), 'Intellectual Property Rights and Brand Licensing: The Importance of Brand Protection,' *MSI Working Paper Series*, No. 09-209.

Joshi, A.M. and D.M. Hanssens (2009), 'Movie Advertising and the Stock Market Valuation of Studios: A Case Of "Great Expectations?",' *Marketing Science*, **28** (2), 239–50.

Kahle, L.R. and P.M. Homer (1985), 'Physical Attractiveness of the Celebrity Endorser: A Social Adaptation Perspective,' *Journal of Consumer Research*, **11** (4), 954–61.

Kamins, M.A., M.J. Brand, S.A. Hoeke, and J.C. Moe (1989), 'Two-sided Versus One-sided Celebrity Endorsements: The Impact on Advertising Effectiveness and Credibility,' *Journal of Advertising*, **18** (2), 4–10.

Karpoff, J.M. and G. Rankine (1994), 'In Search of a Signaling Effect: The Wealth Effects of Corporate Name Changes,' *Journal of Banking & Finance*, **18** (6), 1027–45.

Kartono, Benjamin and Vithala R. Rao (2007), 'Linking Consumer-based Brand Equity to Market Performance: An Integrated Approach to Brand Equity Management,' Working Paper, Cornell University, Ithaca, NY.

Kashmiri, S. and V. Mahajan (2009), 'The Name's the Game: Exploring the Link between Corporate Name Changes and Firm Value,' *MSI Working Paper Series*, No. 09-212.

Keller, K.L. (1993), 'Conceptualizing, Measuring, and Managing Customer-based Brand Equity,' *Journal of Marketing*, **57** (1), 1–22.

Keller, K.L. (2007), *Strategic Brand Management*, Upper Saddle River, NJ: Prentice Hall.

Keller, K.L. and D.A. Aaker (1992), 'The Effects of Sequential Introduction of Brand Extensions,' *Journal of Marketing Research*, **29** (1), 35–50.

Keller, K.L. and D.R. Lehmann (2006), 'Brands and Branding: Research Findings and Future Priorities,' *Marketing Science*, **25** (6), 740–59.

Kerin, R. and R. Sethuraman (1998), 'Exploring the Brand Value–Shareholder Value Nexus for Consumer Goods Companies,' *Journal of the Academy of Marketing Science*, **26** (4), 260–73.

Kim, H.B., W.G. Kim, and J.A. An (2003), 'The Effect of Consumer-based Brand Equity on Firms' Financial Performance,' *Journal of Consumer Marketing*, **20** (4), 335–51.

Kinder, Lydenberg, Domini & Co. Inc. (1999), *Socrates: The Corporate Social Ratings Monitor*, Cambridge, MA: Kinder, Lydenberg, Domini & Co. Inc.

Klein, B. and K.B. Leffler (1981), 'The Role of Market Forces in Assuring Contractual Performance,' *Journal of Political Economy*, **89** (4), 615–41.

Klein, J. and N. Dawar (2004), 'Corporate Social Responsibility and Consumers' Attributions and Brand Evaluations in a Product-harm Crisis,' *International Journal of Research in Marketing*, **21** (3), 203–17.

Klein, R.W. and V.S. Bawa (1977), 'The Effect of Limited Information and Estimation Risk on Optimal Portfolio Diversification,' *Journal of Financial Economics*, **5** (1), 89–111.

Knittel, C.R. and V. Stango (2010), 'Celebrity Endorsements, Firm Value and Reputation Risk: Evidence from the Tiger Woods Scandal,' Working Paper.

Krasnikov, A., S. Mishra, and D. Orozco (2009), 'Evaluating the Financial Impact of Branding Using Trademarks: A Framework and Empirical Evidence,' *Journal of Marketing*, **73** (6), 154–66.

Kumar, N. (2003), 'Kill a Brand, Keep a Customer,' *Harvard Business Review*, **81** (12), 86–95.

Lane, V. and R. Jacobson (1995), 'Stock Market Reactions to Brand Extension Announcements: The Effects of Brand Attitude and Familiarity,' *Journal of Marketing*, **59** (1), 63–77.

Lee, P.M. (2001), 'What's in a Name.Com?: The Effects of ".Com" Name Changes on Stock Prices and Trading Activity,' *Strategic Management Journal*, **22** (8), 793–804.

Lehmann, D.R. (2004), 'Metrics for Making Marketing Matter,' *Journal of Marketing*, **68** (4), 73–5.

Lehmann, D.R. and D.J. Reibstein (2006), *Marketing Metrics and Financial Performance*, Cambridge, MA: Marketing Science Institute.

Leuthesser, L., C. Kohli, and R. Suri (2003), '2 + 2 = 5? A Framework for Using Co-branding to Leverage a Brand,' *Journal of Brand Management*, **11** (1), 35–47.

Lev, B. and T. Sougiannis (1996), 'The Capitalization, Amortization, and Value-relevance of R&D,' *Journal of Accounting and Economics*, **21** (1), 107–38.

Loken, B. and D.R. John (1993), 'Diluting Brand Beliefs: When Do Brand Extensions Have a Negative Impact?,' *Journal of Marketing*, **57** (3), 71–84.

Louie, T.A., R.L. Kulik, and R. Jacobson (2001), 'When Bad Things Happen to the Endorsers of Good Products,' *Marketing Letters*, **12** (1), 13–23.

Luo, X. (2007), 'Consumer Negative Voice and Firm-idiosyncratic Stock Returns,' *Journal of Marketing*, **71** (3), 75–88.

Luo, X. and C.B. Bhattacharya (2006), 'Corporate Social Responsibility, Customer Satisfaction, and Market Value,' *Journal of Marketing*, **70** (4), 1–18.

Luo, X. and C.B. Bhattacharya (2009), 'The Debate over Doing Good: Corporate Social Performance, Strategic Marketing Levers, and Firm-idiosyncratic Risk,' *Journal of Marketing*, **73** (6), 198–213.

Luo, Xueming and Naveen Donthu (2006), 'Marketing's Credibility: A Longitudinal Investigation of Marketing Communication Productivity and Shareholder Value,' *Journal of Marketing*, **70** (4), 70–91.

Madden, J.T., F. Fehle, and S. Fournier (2006), 'Brands Matter: An Empirical Demonstration of the Creation of Shareholder Value through Branding,' *Journal of the Academy of Marketing Science*, **34** (2), 224–35.

Marketing Accountability Standards Board Conference (2010), available at: http://www.themasb.org/articles-Presentations; accessed 8 December 2011.

Marketing Science Institute (2008), *Marketing Science Institute Research Priorities 2008–2010*, Boston, MA: Marketing Science Institute.

Mathur, L.K. and I. Mathur (1995), 'The Effect of Advertising Slogan Changes on the Market Values of Firms,' *Journal of Advertising Research*, **35** (1), 59–65.

Mathur, L.K. and I. Mathur (1996), 'Is Value Associated with Initiating New Advertising Agency–Client Relations?,' *Journal of Advertising*, **25** (3), 1–12.

Mathur, L.K. and I. Mathur (2000), 'An Analysis of the Wealth Effects of Green Marketing Strategies,' *Journal of Business Research*, **50** (2), 193–200.

Mathur, L.K., I. Mathur, and N. Rangan (1997), 'The Wealth Effects Associated with a Celebrity Endorser: The Michael Jordan Phenomenon,' *Journal of Advertising Research*, **37** (3), 67–73.

McAlister, L., R. Srinivasan, and M. Kim (2007), 'Advertising, Research and Development, and Systematic Risk of the Firm,' *Journal of Marketing*, **71** (1), 35–48.

McCracken, G. (1988), *Culture and Consumption*, Bloomington, IN: Indiana University Press.

Mela, C.F., S. Gupta, and D.R. Lehmann (1997), 'The Long-term Impact of Promotion and Advertising on Consumer Brand Choice,' *Journal of Marketing Research*, **34** (2), 248–61.

Merton, R.C. (1974), 'On the Pricing of Corporate Debt: The Risk Structure of Interest Rates,' *Journal of Finance*, **29** (2), 449–70.

Merton, R.C. (1987), 'A Simple Model of Capital Market Equilibrium with Incomplete Information,' *Journal of Finance*, **42** (3), 483–510.

Miller, K.D. and M.J. Leiblein (1996), 'Corporate Risk–Return Relations: Returns Variability Versus Downside Risk,' *Academy of Management Journal*, **39** (1), 91–122.

Mitchell, M.L. (1989), 'The Impact of External Parities on Brand-name Capital: The 1982 Tylenol Poisonings and Subsequent Cases,' *Economic Inquiry*, **27** (4), 601.

Mizik, Natalie and Robert Jacobson (2003), 'Trading Off Between Value Creation and Value Appropriation: The Financial Implications of Shifts in Strategic Emphasis,' *Journal of Marketing*, **67** (1), 63–76.

Mizik, N. and R. Jacobson (2008), 'The Financial Value Impact of Perceptual Brand Attributes,' *Journal of Marketing Research*, **45** (1), 15–32.

Mizik, N. and R. Jacobson (2009), 'Valuing Branded Businesses,' *Journal of Marketing*, **73** (6), 137–53.

Morgan, N.A. and L.L. Rego (2009), 'Brand Portfolio Strategy and Firm Performance,' *Journal of Marketing*, **73** (1), 59–74.

Morgan, N.A., D.W. Vorhies, and C.H. Mason (2009), 'Market Orientation, Marketing Capabilities, and Firm Performance,' *Strategic Management Journal*, **30** (8), 909–20.

Morrin, M., J. Lee, and G.M. Allenby (2006), 'Determinants of Trademark Dilution,' *Journal of Consumer Research*, **33** (2), 248–57.

Mosmans, A. and R. van der Vorst (1998), 'Brand Based Strategic Management,' *Journal of Brand Management*, **6** (2), 99–110.

Murray, K.B. and C.M. Vogel (1997), 'Using a Hierarchy-of-effects Approach to Gauge the Effectiveness of Corporate Social Responsibility to Generate Goodwill Toward the Firm: Financial Versus Nonfinancial Impacts,' *Journal of Business Research*, **38** (2), 141–59.

Myers, S.C. and N.S. Majluf (1984), 'Corporate Financing and Investment Decisions When Firms Have Information That Investors Do Not Have,' *Journal of Financial Economics*, **13** (2), 187–221.

Nawrocki, D.N. (1999), 'A Brief History of Downside Risk Measures,' *Journal of Investing*, **8** (3), 9–25.

Nijs, V.R., S. Srinivasan, and K. Pauwels (2007), 'Retail-price Drivers and Retailer Profits,' *Marketing Science*, **26** (4), 473–87.

Ohanian, R. (1991), 'The Impact of Celebrity Spokespersons' Perceived Image on Consumers' Intention to Purchase,' *Journal of Advertising Research*, **31** (1), 46–54.

Ohnemus, L. and P.V. Jenster (2007), 'Corporate Brand Thrust and Financial Performance,' *International Studies of Management & Organization*, **37** (4), 84–107.

Oliver, R.L. (1999), 'Whence Consumer Loyalty?,' *Journal of Marketing*, **63** (Special Issue), 33–44.

Osinga, C.E., P.S.H. Leeflang, S. Srinivasan, and J.E. Wieringa (2011), 'Why Do Firms Invest in Consumer Advertising with Limited Sales Response? A Shareholder Perspective,' *Journal of Marketing*, **75** (1).

Pahud de Mortanges, C. and A. Van Riel (2003), 'Brand Equity and Shareholder Value,' *European Management Journal*, **21** (4), 521–7.

Park, C.W., S.Y. Jun, and A.D. Shocker (1996), 'Composite Branding Alliances: An Investigation of Extension and Feedback Effects,' *Journal of Marketing Research*, **33** (4), 453–66.

Pauwels, K., J. Silva-Risso, S. Srinivasan, and D.M. Hanssens (2004), 'New Products, Sales Promotions, and Firm Value: The Case of the Automobile Industry,' *Journal of Marketing*, **68** (4), 142–56.

Petty, R.E., J.T. Cacioppo, and D. Schumann (1983), 'Central and Peripheral Routes to Advertising Effectiveness: The Moderating Role of Involvement,' *Journal of Consumer Research*, **10** (2), 135–46.

Quelch, J.A. (1985), 'How to Build a Product Licensing Program,' *Harvard Business Review*, **63** (3), 186–97.

Rao, A.R. and R.W. Ruekert (1994), 'Brand Alliances as Signals of Product Quality,' *Sloan Management Review*, **36** (1), 87–97.

Rao, V.R., M.K. Agarwal, and D. Dahlhoff (2004), 'How Is Manifest Branding Strategy Related to the Intangible Value of a Corporation?,' *Journal of Marketing*, **68** (4), 126–41.

Rappaport, A. (1987), 'Stock Market Signals to Managers,' *Harvard Business Review*, **65** (6), 57–62.

Rappaport, A. (1997), *Creating Shareholder Value: A Guide for Managers and Investors*, New York: Free Press.

Raugust, K. (2008), *The Licensing Business Handbook*, New York: EPM Communications, Inc.

Rego, L.L., M.T. Billett, and N.A. Morgan (2009), 'Consumer-based Brand Equity and Firm Risk,' *Journal of Marketing*, **73** (6), 47–60.

Reichheld, F.F. (2003), 'The One Number You Need to Grow,' *Harvard Business Review*, **81** (12), 46–54.

Roberts, P.W. and G.R. Dowling (2002), 'Corporate Reputation and Sustained Superior Financial Performance,' *Strategic Management Journal*, **23** (12), 1077–93.

Ross, S.A. (1977), 'The Determination of Financial Structure: The Incentive-Signalling Approach,' *Bell Journal of Economics*, **8** (1), 23–40.

Rutherford, D. and J. Knowles (2007), *Vulcans, Earthlings and Marketing ROI: Getting Finance, Marketing and Advertising onto the Same Planet*, Waterloo, Ontario: Wilfrid Laurier University Press.

Sharpe, W.F. (1964), 'Capital Asset Prices: A Theory of Market Equilibrium under Conditions of Risk,' *Journal of Finance*, **19** (3), 425–42.

Sherr, I. (2010), 'Apple's Stock Tops $300 Ahead of Earnings, Event,' available at: http://online.wsj.com/article/SB10001424052748703673604575550083011562338.html; accessed 8 December 2011.

Shiller, R.J. (2002), 'Bubbles, Human Judgment, and Expert Opinion,' *Financial Analysts Journal*, **58** (3), 18–26.

Simon, C.J. and M.W. Sullivan (1993), 'The Measurement and Determinants of Brand Equity: A Financial Approach,' *Marketing Science*, **12** (1), 28–52.

Singh, M., S. Faircloth, and A. Nejadmalayeri (2005), 'Capital Market Impact of Product Marketing Strategy: Evidence from the Relationship between Advertising Expenses and Cost of Capital,' *Journal of the Academy of Marketing Science*, **33** (4), 432–44.

Sivakumar, K. and S.P. Raj (1997), 'Quality Tier Competition: How Price Change Influences Brand Choice and Category Choice,' *Journal of Marketing*, **61** (3), 71–84.

Skidmore, S. (2009), 'Kellogg 3Q Profit Rises on Strong Brand Loyalty,' available at: http://seattletimes.nwsource.com/html/businesstechnology/2010161163_apusearnskellogg.html; accessed 8 December 2011.

Smith, D.C. and C.W. Park (1992), 'The Effects of Brand Extensions on Market Share and Advertising Efficiency,' *Journal of Marketing Research*, **29** (3), 296–313.

Spence, M. (1973), 'Job Market Signaling,' *Quarterly Journal of Economics*, **87** (3), 355–74.

Srinivasan, S. and D.M. Hanssens (2009), 'Marketing and Firm Value: Metrics, Methods, Findings, and Future Directions,' *Journal of Marketing Research*, **46** (3), 293–312.

Srivastava, R.K., T.A. Shervani, and L. Fahey (1998), 'Market-based Assets and Shareholder Value: A Framework for Analysis,' *Journal of Marketing*, **62** (1), 2–18.

Srivastava, R.K., T.A. Shervani, and L. Fahey (1999), 'Marketing, Business Processes, and Shareholder Value: An Organizationally Embedded View of Marketing Activities and the Discipline of Marketing,' *Journal of Marketing*, **63** (Special Issue), 168–79.

Srinivasan, S., M. Vanhuele, and K. Pauwels (2010), 'Mind-set Metrics in Market Response Models: An Integrative Approach,' *Journal of Marketing Research*, **47** (4), 672–84.

Srinivasan, S., K. Pauwels, J. Silva-Risso, and D.M. Hanssens (2009), 'Product Innovations, Advertising, and Stock Returns,' *Journal of Marketing*, **73** (1), 24–43.

Sullivan, M. (1990), 'Measuring Image Spillovers in Umbrella-branded Products,' *Journal of Business*, **63** (3), 309–29.

Swedroe, L. and K. Grogan (2009), 'The Maturity of Fixed-income Assets and Portfolio Risk,' *Journal of Investing*, **18** (4), 107–10.

Taylor, S.A., G.L. Hunter, and D.L. Lindberg (2007), 'Understanding (Customer-based) Brand Equity in Financial Services,' *Journal of Services Marketing*, **21** (4), 241–52.

The Wall Street Journal Market Data Center (2010), 'What's Moving: U.S. Auto Sales,' available at: http://online.wsj.com/mdc/public/page/2_3022-autosales.html; accessed 8 December 2011.

Thomas, J.S., R.C. Blattberg, and E.J. Fox (2004), 'Recapturing Lost Customers,' *Journal of Marketing Research*, **41** (1), 31–45.

Tuli, K.R. and S.G. Bharadwaj (2009), 'Customer Satisfaction and Stock Returns Risk,' *Journal of Marketing*, **73** (6), 184–97.

Vakratsas, D. and T. Ambler (1999), 'How Advertising Works: What Do We Really Know?,' *Journal of Marketing*, **63** (1), 26–43.

Washburn, J.H., B.D. Till, and R. Priluck (2004), 'Brand Alliance and Customer-based Brand-equity Effects,' *Psychology and Marketing*, **21** (7), 487–508.

Wiles, M.A., N.A. Morgan, and L.L. Rego (2009), 'The Effect of Brand Acquisition and Disposal on Stock Returns,' *MSI Working Paper Series*, No. 09-103.

Wilkie, W. (1986), *Consumer Behavior*, New York: John Wiley & Sons, Inc.

Winer, R.S. (1986), 'A Reference Price Model of Brand Choice for Frequently Purchased Products,' *Journal of Consumer Research*, **13** (2), 250–56.

Wingfield, N. (1999), 'It Can Become a Pain to Shift Your Name, Even to Fatbrain.Com,' *Wall Street Journal*, 29 March.

Wong, H.Y. and B. Merrilees (2008), 'The Performance Benefits of Being Brand-orientated,' *Journal of Product and Brand Management*, **17** (6), 372–83.

Xu, Y. and B.G. Malkiel (2003), 'Investigating the Behavior of Idiosyncratic Volatility,' *Journal of Business*, **76** (4), 613–44.

Zeithaml, V.A. (1988), 'Consumer Perceptions of Price, Quality, and Value: A Means–End Model and Synthesis of Evidence,' *Journal of Marketing*, **52** (3), 2–22.

8 The marketing–finance interface in channels of distribution research: a roadmap for future research
Katrijn Gielens and Inge Geyskens

INTRODUCTION

For each product and service, manufacturers have to set up distribution channels to reach their end-users, be they final consumers or business buyers. The design of these distribution channels can differ considerably and involves three major decisions: (1) a channel length decision, (2) a channel intensity decision, and (3) a multichannel decision. First, manufacturers have to decide on the length of the channel. In some instances, it can be beneficial to cater to the end-user directly, whereas in other circumstances manufacturers will use a set of (independent) intermediaries or resellers to make their products or services available to end-users. When such indirect channels are used, the manufacturer has to decide on the number of layers of different types of intermediaries that are built in between the manufacturer and the end-user. For example, is a wholesale and a retail level necessary or does a retail level suffice? Manufacturers also have to make a channel intensity decision by deciding on the number of intermediaries at each level of the channel. Will the product be offered exclusively through one intermediary per trading area, selectively through just a couple of intermediaries per trading area, or intensively through many intermediaries per trading area? Beyond the channel length and channel intensity decisions within a given channel, manufacturers need to decide on the number of different distribution channels they will be using to reach their end-users. This is the multichannel decision.

Once a good channel design is in place, manufactures may find that their interests are not always aligned with their channel intermediaries' objectives. As such, the manufacturer has to make decisions on how to manage or coordinate its distribution channel. Should they integrate the intermediary so as to avoid all potential conflict, work through close partnerships, or use arm's-length contracts? Needless to say, all these design and management decisions have vast implications for the success of the channel and the manufacturer's performance.

Because of the high cost of poor decision-making in this area, distribution channel research has long emphasized the importance of recognizing the performance implications of channel decisions. This has fueled a significant multifaceted literature. An important stream of literature, starting with Jeuland and Shugan (1983) and McGuire and Staelin (1983), and including the more recent contributions of Raut and colleagues (2008) and Wang et al. (2009), has extensively analyzed the performance implications of a wide variety of channel decisions (e.g., use of exclusive resellers, coordination of channel efforts) game theoretically.

In addition to the extensive game theoretical literature, many studies have tested the performance implications of channel decisions empirically. A number of empirical studies have used factual or 'objective' performance measures, such as sales, return on assets or investments, profits, or market share (e.g., Buchanan, 1992; Ambler et al., 1999). Although it would seem that factual measures are the ideal way to measure channel performance, their use can be questioned for conceptual as well as operational reasons.

Conceptually, performance is a multifaceted construct and examining any single performance facet in isolation is not likely to produce an adequate overall assessment (Kumar et al., 1992; Richard et al., 2010). This is particularly important in a distribution channel context, since the performance effects of distribution decisions can be wide-ranging. On the demand side, distribution decisions may affect sales in several ways, such as through market expansion (when new segments of customers are reached), through brand switching (by winning customers from or losing customers to competitors), and/or through relationship deepening (by selling more to existing customers). Distribution channel decisions may also affect a firm's prices. For example, when a distribution decision affects customers' brand loyalty positively, this may translate into higher prices (because loyal customers are less price sensitive). On the supply side, distribution channel decisions may have an effect on physical distribution costs, such as transaction processing, transportation, or inventory costs, and/or transaction costs, such as monitoring costs to ensure that the firm's distributors live up to their agreements. Most studies on the performance implications of distribution decisions have dealt with one specific performance outcome, but have not considered the overall performance effect of the channel decision. Indeed, it would be difficult for any single factual measure to capture all these facets. Although some studies have tried to address this by using combinations of factual measures to assess performance, 'the theoretical rationale for the selection of the criteria is typically absent or underdeveloped,' and these (ad hoc) combinations still leave a number of performance dimensions unaddressed (Kumar et al., p. 238). Studying a single performance dimension is particularly problematic when managers need to trade off multiple countervailing performance measures against one another in making strategic distribution decisions. For example, in a recent study by Mooi and Ghosh (2010), the authors convincingly argue and demonstrate that farsighted managers need to be cognizant of tradeoffs between ex ante design costs and ex post transaction costs in deciding about the appropriate level of contract specificity.

Operationally, commonly used factual performance measures such as return on sales or return on assets may be less appropriate indicators of channel decisions' value because they have a historical orientation as opposed to a forward-looking focus – they are not well suited to capturing anticipated future revenue streams (Kalyanaram et al., 1995). Yet, the financial outcomes of many distribution channel decisions can be substantially delayed although the costs of the investments made are incurred and recognized (i.e., put on the books) immediately, in the periods they materialize (Srinivasan and Hanssens, 2009). When firms have a mixture of short-term and long-term goals with their channels, using a traditional factual performance metric such as return on sales may thus cause firms to underinvest in channels with primarily long-term advantages (cf. Sa Vinhas et al., 2010). In addition, the temporal aggregation level of factual performance measures sometimes makes the link to specific distribution channel events or decisions difficult. End of the year accounting numbers may be influenced by many marketing and strategic decisions that took place during the year, of which the distribution channel decision is just one.

Since, for both conceptual and operational reasons, performance appraisal of channel decisions using factual performance data can be quite difficult, numerous empirical studies have used perceptual as opposed to factual performance measures (e.g., Kumar et al., 1992; Jap, 1999). Indeed, perceptual measures (1) can be designed to encompass multiple facets of performance that may not be reflected in commonly used factual measures of performance (see e.g., Kumar et al., 1992 who include, among others, reseller competence, loyalty, and compliance in addition to reseller contribution to sales and profits in their measure of reseller performance), (2) can be designed to have a forward-looking focus (see e.g., Jap, 1999 who measures not only profit performance but also more long-term competitive advantages), and (3) can be designed to relate to specific events (see e.g., Grewal et al., 2010 who measure the performance of an electronic market).

Perceptual measures come along with their own set of problems, however. First, research has shown that managers are not very accurate in their performance judgments (Mezias and Starbuck, 2003). Through psychological processes such as positive illusion, ego enhancement or ego protection, and cognitive consistency, managers' perceptions of performance may not correspond to true performance. In addition, Ailawadi et al. (2004) show that resellers are not able to correctly incorporate market potential into their perceptions of their relative performance, and to calibrate their performance relative to others and relative to the resources they invest. Second, longitudinal performance measurement through surveys is typically impractical given the often prohibitive expenses in terms of time and money for academic researchers faced with limited budgets and marketing practitioners faced with limited time (Rindfleisch et al., 2008). Finally, perceptual performance measures may create common method bias in case perceptual data on both performance and its potential drivers are obtained from the same respondents.

Finance scholars have long argued that shareholder value is an important metric for studying company performance in a competitive marketplace (Srivastava et al., 1998). Interestingly, shareholder value combines the advantages of factual and perceptual measures. Like perceptual measures, shareholder value integrates multiple dimensions of performance into a single 'net effect' measure. Since investors are cognizant of accounting deficiencies (such as distribution investments being fully expensed), they also rely on non-financial information that may be captured by perceptual measures (Amir and Lev, 1996). From an operational point of view, the market value of firms hinges largely on growth prospects and sustainability of profits (i.e., how the firm is expected to perform in the future), in contrast to most accounting measures that are retrospective in examining historical performance. All shareholder value-related methods (e.g., event studies, stock return response models; see Srinivasan and Hanssens, 2009 for an overview) share this advantage of impounding into current stock price the effects of strategic distribution decisions whose financial impact will be felt in many years to come. One particular type of method, namely the event study methodology, has the additional advantage that it allows for measuring the impact of a specific, discrete event on daily (i.e., temporally disaggregated) stock returns, and thus can be thought of as a controlled experiment (Mizik and Jacobson, 2004).

Finally, from a more practical point of view, respondents are often unwilling to share factual performance data or they provide it in a way that is difficult to compare with that provided by other firms, for example, in an international context (Siguaw et al., 1998; Deshpandé and Farley, 2004). Similarly, business-to-business respondents (manufacturers, resellers) are often unwilling or too time-constrained to take part in surveys. In contrast, shareholder value measures are publicly available and less easily manipulated by managers (Geyskens et al., 2002; Srinivasan and Bharadwaj, 2004).

The purpose of this chapter is to integrate the extant knowledge and to push the envelope on the impact of distribution channel decisions on shareholder value. We first summarize the empirical findings to date on how distribution channel decisions affect shareholder value. We then frame a number of important questions for future research on channel design and coordination issues that are particularly amenable to shareholder value analysis.

OVERVIEW OF EXTANT LITERATURE

Despite the logical fit between distribution channel decisions and shareholder value, there are few insights into the relationship between distribution strategy and shareholder value to date. A literature review of the *International Journal of Research in Marketing*, *Journal of Marketing*, *Journal of Marketing Research*, and *Marketing Science* identified only four empirical studies on the shareholder value implications of distribution channel decisions.

Geyskens et al. (2002) investigate the impact of adding a new Internet channel to a firm's existing channel portfolio on shareholder value. They argue that an Internet channel addition can be performance enhancing as readily as it can be performance destroying. Making use of event study methodology, the authors assess the impact of adding an Internet channel on a firm's stock market return, a measure of the change in expected future cash flows. They find that, on average, Internet channel investments are positive net present value investments. On average, firms establishing an Internet channel experienced a cumulative average abnormal return (CAAR) of 0.71 percent, which corresponds to an increase in market value of €16.38 million in two days for a median-sized firm in their sample. Still, in 30 percent of the cases, negative stock returns were found. The authors then identify firm, introduction strategy, and marketplace characteristics that influence the direction and magnitude of the stock market reaction. The results indicate that powerful firms with a few direct channels are expected to achieve greater gains in financial performance than are less powerful firms with a broader direct channel offering. In terms of order of entry, early followers have a competitive advantage over both innovators and later followers. The authors also find that Internet channel additions that are supported by more publicity are perceived as having a higher performance potential.

The authors motivate their use of the event study methodology on the basis of both conceptual and operational reasons. Conceptually, they argue that it is first and foremost important to understand the overall net performance impact of establishing an Internet channel. Operationally, they argue that the event study enables them to measure the impact of the specific event on temporally disaggregated (daily) stock returns. They further indicate that Internet channels operate in a setting in which current accounting results are almost bound to suggest poor performance, which is undesirable, since Internet investments are known to take several years before they fully translate into bottom-line performance effects. The stock market reaction, in contrast, compares investment costs with the expected revenues. Geyskens et al. (2002) point out that, whereas researchers can obviously investigate the long-term consequences of Internet channel additions using factual data by waiting until realized cash flow data will eventually become available, this precludes a timely assessment of the potential of this distribution channel decision. Since shareholder value guides the decisions of top management (Lehmann, 2004), waiting several years until more factual data become available may not be a wise strategy.

Also Lee and Grewal (2004) study the impact of the adoption of the Internet by traditional store-based retailers on the market valuation of the firm. Their results show that the adoption of the Internet as a communications channel and an e-alliance formation positively influences firm performance. The adoption of the Internet as a sales channel, however, affects performance only for firms that have pre-existing catalog operations. Lee and Grewal (ibid.) operationalize the market valuation of the firm as Tobin's Q, a forward-looking stock-market-based measure. The advantage of using Tobin's Q over accounting measures is that it incorporates multiple dimensions of a firm's financial viability within one stable measure that is relatively insulated from management manipulation. Tobin's Q 'captures the relationship between the replacement cost of a firm's tangible assets and the market value of the firm' (ibid., p. 162). Thus, it has the forward-looking benefits of stock price, while also incorporating the value of the firm's assets. Finally, Lee and Grewal also point to the fact that Tobin's Q can be used to compare across industries because it is not affected by accounting conventions.

Also Gielens et al. (2008) study the impact of channel additions, albeit in an entirely different context and not on the focal firm but on its competitors. They examine the value-destroying and value-enhancing effects of Wal-Mart's entry into the United Kingdom (through its acquisition of Asda) on incumbent European retailers. Their measure of performance impact is the change in shareholder value around the announcement date, which, they argue, is an important metric for studying company performance in a competitive marketplace (Srivastava et al., 1998). The strategic moves by a company may affect its own as well as its competitors' shareholder value through changes in cash flows and discount rates.

The advantages of using shareholder value as a performance metric in this case are not only that it is forward-looking and integrating multiple dimensions of performance, but also that it is less easily manipulated by managers than other measures (Srinivasan and Bharadwaj, 2004).[1] This makes upfront comparisons of the effect of a single event across a number of competitors easier and more reliable. The authors find that the shareholder value of incumbent retailers is negatively affected by the degree of overlap with Wal-Mart in assortment, positioning, and country of entry. Indeed, incumbent retailers overlapping highly with Wal-Mart were worst off, their CAAR being −4.9 percent. Yet, if these seriously threatened retailers had built a capacity to withstand threats by accumulating substantial experience in competing with Wal-Mart and operating in highly competitive markets, their CAAR increased from −4.9 percent to −1.3 percent. Retailers positioned differently from Wal-Mart can even benefit from the positive changes Wal-Mart brings to European distribution systems (CAAR of 1.3 percent up to 3.8 percent, depending on whether those retailers' capacity to withstand the threat was low versus high).

Srinivasan (2006) investigates the impact of a firm's dual distribution systems – systems in which firms use vertical integration and market governance simultaneously – on intangible firm value in the setting of franchising in restaurant chains. Using panel data on 55 publicly listed US restaurant chains, she tests the effect of the proportion of a chain's franchised units to the total number of its units in its distribution system on the chain's intangible value, measured by Tobin's Q. She finds that a firm's dual distribution strategy significantly affects its intangible value, but there is firm heterogeneity in the value relevance of dual distribution; dual distribution does not offer the same benefits to all firms. Instead, it is contingent on firm characteristics, including marketing and financial strategies. For example, a firm with high financial liquidity can decrease its emphasis on dual distribution to increase its shareholder value. Srinivasan (ibid.) argues that her study is important for marketing practice because of the increasing scrutiny of the financial accountability of marketing investments – which create intangible assets that are not reflected on balance sheets – from various stakeholders.

Based on this limited set of studies, some first conclusions can be drawn. First, very little research has related distribution channel decisions to shareholder value. This is surprising given that, of all the marketing decisions made by a firm, distribution channel decisions are arguably the most long term in nature, for example by serving as entry barriers for other firms or by serving as launching pads for new products. Second, all four studies focus on channel design issues, whereas channel coordination issues have so far been ignored in the finance–marketing interface tradition. This may be explained by the fact that channel design decisions, being discrete in nature, lend themselves particularly well to the event study method, arguably the most widespread shareholder value method in marketing. In contrast, channel coordination is 'not a one-time achievement, but an ongoing process' (Coughlan et al., 2001, p. 38). This does not imply that shareholder value methods cannot offer added-value to study channel coordination issues. Alternative stock price analysis approaches exist for assessing activities that are more continuous in nature – such as the use of stock return response models (see Mizik and Jacobson, 2004 for more information on these models) or the use of Tobin's Q-based methods (see e.g., Anderson et al., 2004 for an example on customer satisfaction) – but these are yet to be applied to channel coordination problems.

FUTURE RESEARCH AGENDA

The presence of only four studies demonstrates the room for more research in this area. We will first discuss research related to the shareholder value implications of channel design decisions before elaborating on potential research avenues related to channel coordination.

Channel Design

We will discuss areas for future research pertaining to two major channel design decisions: (1) the channel intensity decision, that is, the number of distributors in each channel distributing a manufacturer's product, and (2) the multichannel decision, that is, the number of different channel types used. Channel design issues are excellent candidates to be addressed by event study methods. These decisions are typically discrete in nature and their event dates can easily be traced.

Channel intensity decisions

Exclusivity arrangements are rapidly gaining way in grocery retailing. Industry observers (PricewaterhouseCoopers/TNS Retail Forward, 2007) expect this practice to increase dramatically in the coming years. In a 2007 GfK survey for the UK Competition Commission among over 450 grocery product suppliers, 35 percent reported that they had been asked to enter into an exclusivity agreement for their branded products with one of their retail customers. Two-thirds of those requests came from one of the four largest supermarkets. Overall, 19 percent of all suppliers signed at least one such exclusivity agreement.

Interestingly, this practice goes against conventional wisdom that convenience goods 'should be distributed as *intensively as possible*,' as buyers will not expend much effort to purchase them (Coughlan et al., 2001, p. 288, italics added; see also Bucklin et al., 2008). Exclusivity, by definition, limits the brand's exposure to one retailer. Unlike private labels, however, the exclusively available brand remains owned, branded, and marketed by the manufacturer, as is also clearly communicated to the consumer (Shugan, 1989).

Manufacturers and retailers vary in their perception and evaluation of the phenomenon. Retailers tend to favor exclusivity, since it can drive up their sales and create differentiation in highly competitive markets. Still, it is hard for them to quantify (in revenue and/or profit terms) how much they really gain from an exclusivity right. Ideally, the exclusive brand will attract new customers to the store, who may buy not only the brand itself, but also other products in the same and/or other categories. Manufacturers, in contrast, generally prefer intensive distribution for convenience goods. Indeed, exclusivity may be detrimental to the brand's overall performance if many potential buyers are not willing to make the effort to visit (switch to) that retailer. One of the reasons for them to accept (or even actively look for) an exclusivity agreement is to facilitate access to the limited shelf space of a leading retailer, or to improve retailer support for their other products carried in the same or other categories (ibid.). Also, manufacturers may believe that a differentiated channel offering helps them to better cater to the needs of an increasingly differentiated market. Still, they are likely to forego sales opportunities by limiting the distribution intensity of their products (Frazier and Lassar, 1996). Moreover, they run the risk of alienating their other retailers. For the latter, it is important to know how much sales they lose because of the exclusivity granted to their competitor, which will be crucial information when negotiating with that manufacturer for some form of compensation. To minimize foregone sales, manufacturers may be inclined to always favor the largest retailer as partner in the exclusive arrangement. While this makes sense from a revenue point of view, and while it reduces the importance of negative reactions from excluded retailers, it is not necessarily the best strategy from a profit perspective. The profitability of the exclusive deal hinges on the associated margin negotiations, the size of which depends on the power balance between the manufacturer and the focal retailer.

Even though exclusive agreements in grocery retailing are becoming more prevalent, little is known about the net overall effect of the large variety of performance effects that may result. One of the most crucial performance components to assess the overall profitability of exclusivity decisions is (gross and net) margin information. Unfortunately, this information is rarely made publicly available or shared for research purposes due to its sensitivity (for notable exceptions, see Ailawadi and Harlam, 2004, 2009 and Ailawadi et al., 2006). In the absence of such data, shareholder value analysis (in particular, event studies, given the discrete nature of the event) may be a sensible and pragmatic first step to understanding the overall performance impact of exclusive distribution decisions.

Multichannel decisions

Geyskens et al. (2002) have studied the performance implications for a manufacturer of adding an Internet channel to an indirect distribution channel system. Lee and Grewal (2004) have explored the adoption of the Internet as an additional sales channel by retailers. In a similar vein, future research could look at the addition of any new format to a retailer's format portfolio. To cater to a broader (and perhaps more heterogeneous) mix of consumer groups, shopping trips, and cultures, retailers are increasingly diversifying their store portfolio and venturing into new formats. For many retailers, the next growth phase will be about segmentation and localization through operating multiple formats and multiple concepts, targeted to specific customer segments, in specific local markets, for specific needs and occasions (Planet Retail, 2010). Whereas, on the positive side, retailers may increase their market coverage by adding formats, they also face a number of challenges. For example, adding a discount-oriented concept to a retailer's format portfolio may increase price competition in the market, which may result in a downward pressure on retailer margins. In addition, the question remains to what extent a retailer can add a new discount format to its high-service portfolio, or vice versa, without jeopardizing its original image and positioning, and its credibility.

Shareholder value analysis may help in quantifying the net performance impact of all these effects that come into play. In addition, since a channel format addition may represent a fundamental shift in a retailer's strategy, it may affect the retailer's future performance in years to come. A lag between the actual format addition and single-year accounting measures may therefore manifest itself, and make the latter less appropriate. As explained before, forward-looking shareholder value-based metrics overcome this hurdle. In addition, a study looking into format additions of major retailers is likely to be international in scope. In contrast to accounting measures, which are sensitive to different national accounting conventions and tax laws, shareholder value measures have the advantage of greater comparability across firms from different countries.

Channel Coordination

Considerable academic marketing research has focused on the need to coordinate activities within the distribution channel (Coughlan et al., 2001). Coordinating channel activities is challenging because manufacturers and distributors may have different and potentially conflicting goals. Three major ways in which manufacturers can coordinate a channel of distribution are through (1) vertically integrating the distribution channel, (2) building partnerships with distributors, and (3) the use of power. We will discuss areas for future research using shareholder value analysis pertaining to all three coordination mechanisms.

Vertical integration revisited

Throughout the marketing and business literature, a large body of research has touched upon the performance implications of vertical integration decisions (see Geyskens et al., 2006 for a meta-analysis of this research). Vertical integration is often described as the ultimate tool to keep all parties involved in the distribution channel aligned as total control can be asserted. This gain in control comes, however, at a price. Not only are vertical integration decisions expensive, they involve commitments that are difficult to reverse. Consequently, over the last decades, vertical integration has lost its appeal; the overwhelming sentiment was to favor disintegration rather than integration.

Yet, trends in organizational structures keep changing and vertical integration is back in vogue (*Wall Street Journal*, 2009). The current wish to control outlets (and supplies) is making vertical integration popular again. Recent examples include Pepsi and Coca-Cola who acquired their bottlers to increase control over beverage distribution, and Apple who vertically integrated the distribution for its iPad – the iPad itself is sold only in Apple stores. This 'new style vertical integration' involves not only integrating distributors but also suppliers. Returning to the iPad example, Apple has also vertically integrated backward to increase control over the quality of its components, and has designed its own processor and its own operating system software to power the iPad. This is a major strategy change since until then Apple had used chips made by others, like Intel (for the iMac) and Samsung (for the iPhone) (*Newsweek*, 2010). The predominant focus in extant research has been on vertical integration decisions for *either* the downstream (distribution) level *or* the upstream (supply) level. From a theoretical standpoint, it would be interesting to study whether the performance implications from a firm's vertical integration decision at the distribution level depend on its vertical integration decisions at the supplier level.

Why can shareholder value analysis help in addressing this question? First, this new integration trend begs for more insight into the *net* impact of obtaining complete control over one's supply chain. As has been documented in many studies, vertical integration may lead to various efficiency gains, but also brings along a number of costs (e.g., the fixed costs of retaining one's own distribution channel, a decreased flexibility to strike out in innovative directions). The picture becomes more complex for fully integrated supply chains, as the costs and benefits of vertical integration at different levels may not simply add up. For example, whereas vertical integration at a given level (upstream or downstream) has been shown to reduce flexibility, where system-wide flexibility is required, vertical integration of *both* upstream and downstream levels may allow for the speed and coordination in achieving simultaneous adjustment throughout the entire vertical chain. Shareholder value analysis may help to arrive at a holistic performance evaluation that incorporates the various tradeoffs involved in deciding whether to fully integrate one's supply chain. In addition, the performance implications of vertical integration decisions are hard to evaluate using historical accounting measures since several outcomes of these decisions are substantially delayed. Consequently, traditional metrics do not capture the full – short-term *and* long-term – extent of these decisions. Finally, vertical integration studies are often carried out across industries. Because of industry differences in accounting practices, a comparison of accounting measures across industries may be problematic, a drawback that is overcome by analyzing shareholder value.

Partnerships revisited
Also, partnerships can be used to coordinate manufacturer–distributor relationships. Most research to date has investigated how partnerships can be created, which has led to a number of generalizable insights (Geyskens et al., 1999). In contrast, empirical evidence on the performance implications of partnerships is scarce and inconsistent. Kalwani and Narayandas (1995) were the first study to study the performance consequences of partnerships. Specifically, they assessed the impact of long-term supplier–customer relationships on supplier performance using a cross-sectional time-series database compiled from Compustat. They found that maintaining long-term relationships with select customers does not come at the expense of the rate of sales growth. Suppliers in long-term relationships are able to achieve the same level of growth as firms that employ a transactional approach to servicing their customers. These suppliers are able to reduce costs over time through better inventory utilization; however, this reduction in cost seems to be bargained away by their customers through

lower prices over time. Finally, supplier firms in long-term relationships achieve higher profitability by differentially reducing their discretionary expenses such as selling, general, and administrative overhead costs to a greater extent than their counterparts who use a transactional approach to servicing their customers.

The research that has been undertaken since this seminal paper provides inconsistent evidence for the performance impact of partnerships. Palmatier et al. (2007) examine the effects of relationship marketing on a buyer's concurrent person-to-firm relationship with the selling firm and his or her interpersonal relationship with the salesperson. They find that relationship marketing programs indeed build buyer relationship quality, but whether those relationship-building effects reside with the salesperson or the selling firm depends on buyer perceptions regarding salesperson versus selling firm control of those programs. Buyer relationship quality with both salesperson and selling firm positively affects seller financial outcomes, but the effect of this relationship quality is enhanced as perceived selling firm consistency increases.

Corsten and Kumar (2005) studied the performance impact of collaborative manufacturer–retailer relationships based on efficient consumer response (ECR). More specifically, the authors empirically investigate whether the extent to which suppliers of a major retailer adopt ECR has a beneficial impact on their outcomes. The results demonstrate that, whereas ECR adoption has a positive impact on supplier economic performance and capability development, it also generates greater perceptions of negative inequity on the part of the supplier.

Whereas these studies have led to important insights into the potential benefits and pitfalls of long-term distribution relationships, the results are hard to compare since different studies have looked at different facets of performance. To reconcile these insights, a study may be called for that 'integrates' several of the above used performance metrics. Shareholder value-based performance metrics allow for such integration. For example, event study methods can be used to study the announcement of partnerships, such as the announcement of ECR adoption. Stock return response models, on the other hand, are suited to studying the performance outcomes of more process-based evolutions. For example, following the suit of the customer relationship literature, stock return response models may be used to link temporal changes in publicly reported dealer satisfaction indices (as, for example, annually reported by the Canadian Automobile Dealers Association for a period of 20 years) to stock returns or to Tobin Q measures. Shareholder value analysis may thereby provide important empirical evidence as to the net effect of investing in dealer satisfaction on manufacturer performance.

Power revisited

An ongoing debate in the field of distribution channels deals with the question whether the rise of global retailers such as Wal-Mart, Best Buy, and Amazon has led to a power shift from brand manufacturers to retailers. Historically, power in distribution channels has rested upstream with brand marketers such as Philip Morris, manufacturers like Ford, or franchisers such as McDonald's and PepsiCo. In contrast to these multinational suppliers, most retailers, dealers, and franchisees were local and fragmented. Retailing, and more generally distribution, had an image of being a simple, unsophisticated business. Nowadays, retailers are increasingly trying to dictate pricing, assortment, and branding strategies, often resulting in severe conflicts between brand manufacturers and retailers and ultimately impacting the profitability of all parties involved.

The impact of retailer–manufacturer power shifts on profitability was first studied about 20 years ago by Farris and Ailawadi (1992). Studying accounting metrics such as return on sales and return on assets, Farris and Ailawadi (ibid.) questioned the conventional wisdom that the balance of power in interactions between packaged goods manufacturers and retailers has shifted towards the latter. Their analysis of trends in retailer and manufacturer profits did not support the purported power shift. They found that, if anything, manufacturer profitability had improved relative to retailers. Subsequently, other researchers studied different measures of performance and came to the same conclusion (e.g., Ailawadi et al., 1995; Messinger and Narasimhan, 1995). In summary, the extant literature does not provide evidence that higher retailer power has translated into higher retailer performance. The question remains to what extent these 15-year-old insights (during the early phases of retail internationalization) remain valid in today's retailscape in which retailers have turned into even more powerful entities that insist on change at the manufacturers' side. Have retailers become able to translate power into shareholder value as their power has further grown? Stock return response models can be specified to establish whether changes in retailers' and manufacturers' power contribute to a change in these firms' valuations.

One specific power-related area that would benefit from more research is the effectiveness of retail buying groups. A buying group is an organization that seeks to combine the buying power of several independent retailers in order to acquire goods or services at a rate that is better than might be achieved through individual negotiation. In addition, buying groups may be formed in order to obtain goods and services that might otherwise be unavailable, such as private labels or products that cannot be produced cost-effectively on a smaller scale. Buying groups are now amongst the most powerful participants in the European grocery market (IGD, 2006). For example, of the ten largest grocery buyers in Europe, five are buying groups rather than 'standalone' businesses. How does the bundling of purchase power through buying groups – particularly those spanning several national markets – impact retailers' and manufacturers' performance? One of the best ways to gauge insight into the net effect of these operations may be to relate the entry and exit of retailers to buying groups to forward-looking shareholder value-related metrics.

In order to do business with major retail customers, suppliers must increasingly adhere to a set of criteria and uphold a series of values that they might otherwise not adhere to. Studying to what extent this coercive power use by retailers affects manufacturers' performance may constitute another interesting area for future research. For example, Wal-Mart demanded that its top suppliers put RFID (radio frequency identification) tags on their products. To meet these requirements, suppliers invested heavily in costly technology (Ganesan et al., 2009). Whereas these investments will negatively impact short-term profits, cost and sales benefits may only manifest themselves in the longer run. Not only will investments in IT technology help to smooth out suppliers' supply chains (thereby reducing costs of operation), the newly available information will allow suppliers to learn more about consumers' behavior inside the store environment, allowing them to fine-tune and even customize their offerings to these consumers (thereby positively impacting future sales). Especially when investigating notoriously secretive retailers who refuse to share scanner data information with outside data providers (such as Wal-Mart), shareholder value analysis can be extremely valuable.

Taking it one step further, retailers increasingly use their coercive power to encourage suppliers to accept socially responsible practices and integrate externalities into their operations. For example, Wal-Mart has recently committed to sell products that are sustainable. Consumers are becoming increasingly aware of the consequences of their choices, not only for their own well-being, but also for other people in society. In response, manufacturers and distributors are increasingly focusing on sustainability. This is particularly visible in the retailing sector. Sustainability concerns in retailing reach further than the supply of green products. Many retailers have been pursuing an environmental agenda seeking to minimize both inputs and outputs in order to reduce the overall impact of their operations. Retailers are making progress in areas such as store design refrigeration, heating ventilation and cooling packaging use and recycling, sourcing, and supply chain logistics. The question that arises is to what extent the 'green burden' is shifted upstream by powerful retailers and carried by manufacturers. Shareholder value analysis is an ideal first step to shed light on how sustainability initiatives by retailers affect manufacturers' shareholder value.

TO CONCLUDE

Very little research has related distribution channel decisions to shareholder value. This is surprising given that, compared to other marketing mix decisions made by a firm, distribution channel decisions are arguably the most long term in nature. In this chapter, we outlined a couple of avenues that allow distribution channel researchers to further embrace stock return methods.

A literature review revealed surprisingly few studies in the distribution channel area using shareholder value analysis. The hesitance and even fear for shareholder value-based methods in distribution channel research can be tracked town to the efficient market assumption, which lies at the heart of stock market analyses. The efficient market hypothesis assumes that the stock price is an *unbiased* reflection of *all* publicly available information. This has given rise to two frequently aired concerns: (1) can investors integrate all relevant performance components into one holistic evaluation, and (2) do stock prices reflect investors' rational, unbiased expectations of future cash flows?

Can investors integrate the relevant information on the underlying performance?

This first concern is more general in nature, and applies to most economic (and other) models. Milton Friedman (1953) argues that even though people may not be able to make the calculations captured in the economic model (in our case, in the conceptual model), they still act *as if* they could do so. Using the analogy of an expert billiards player, Thaler (1992) argues in this respect that the expert player may not know the underlying, governing laws of physics, but could still make shots as if he or she had that knowledge. Similarly, one can question whether time-pressured consumers solve a mental optimization problem during every supermarket purchase, but in the often-used logit analyses, we still assume consumers acted as if they indeed did so.

Admittedly, *individuals* make mistakes and may occasionally act irrational, but this is not a problem in explaining *aggregate* behavior as long as these mistakes tend to cancel out. Trading of irrational investors, provided this is not expressed in a systematic or consistent manner cross-sectionally, tends to be self-canceling, leaving the determination of prices and price changes in the hands of the more rational investors (Rubinstein, 2000). Large investors, as well as stock analysts, tend to be well-informed, and indeed use valuation methods based on discounted cash flows (see e.g., Bodie et al., 1993, p. 533; Fabozzi, 1995, p. 197). To that end, such investors have been found to 'closely scrutinize . . . companies' ability to . . . generate revenues while managing costs' (James, 2000, p. 13).

Even then, one could question whether *each* of these more informed players has *complete* information on all relevant issues. Markets, however, tend to exert an 'information aggregation function', rendering the market more rational in viewing and interpreting information than the individual investors that comprise them (see in this respect Ball, 1995; Rubinstein, 2001; and especially Hayek, 1945).

Do stock prices reflect investors' rational expectations of future cash flows?
The above argumentation relied on the assumption of non-systematic irrational behavior, and no longer holds when errors tend to systematically go in the same direction (e.g., in case of herd behavior). Even though current financial markets are thought to be among the most efficient ones (because of the rapid speed of information dissemination and the higher incentives in those markets to act optimally/rationally – Thaler, 1992), empirical anomalies have indeed been observed in those markets (see e.g., Ball, 1995). For example, the stock market may be characterized by periods of frenzied buying (bubbles) or selling (crashes), driven by emotion and collective irrationality of investors.

In this respect, one could argue that the positive stock market evaluation one observes reflects a general hype instead of rational expectations of future cash flows. Careful research should therefore perform several tests of this alternative herding explanation. For example, results can be shown to be robust across up and down markets. Similarly, findings should be similar across periods with a lot of events (if firms would attempt to take advantage of a hype effect, events would be clustered in certain 'hot' market periods) and periods with very few events. Thus, it is up to the researcher to provide empirical evidence that his or her results are not driven by sometimes encountered stock market anomalies.

In sum, when carried out carefully, we believe shareholder value analysis may be very useful to extend our knowledge in the domain of distribution channel research. While shareholder value analyses may be valuable in their own right – given that shareholders are an important stakeholder of the firm – we deem them to be particularly useful as one of the first steps in the development of a scientific domain to study recent and less documented trends. Stock price data are good present estimates of future returns, given the information available at that time, but at some later date, actually realized cash flow data may become available that are almost certainly better than any expectation at the time of the event (Bromiley et al., 1988). Still, for all practical purposes, working with these expectations may be the best option available to an applied researcher who wants to assess the impact of a relatively recent phenomenon for which the number of post-event data points on temporally aggregated accounting variables is limited, precluding in most instances the use of time-series-based intervention analyses. The latter problem is particularly pertinent in distribution channel contexts, where the number of post-event data points needed would be considerable, given that highly strategic distribution channel decisions may take several years to fully translate into bottom-line performance effects.

We hope this chapter will provide a background for thinking about the ways in which future research can examine whether and how distribution channel decisions affect shareholder value.

NOTE

1. Mizik and Jacobson (2007) show how myopic firms may still be able to temporarily inflate their stock market valuation. Such practices, however, are not easy and come at a high cost.

REFERENCES

Ailawadi, K.L. and B.A. Harlam (2004), 'An Empirical Analysis of the Determinants of Retail Margins: The Role of Store Brand Share,' *Journal of Marketing*, **68** (1), 147–66.

Ailawadi, K.L. and B.A. Harlam (2009), 'Retailer Promotion Pass-through: A Measure, Its Magnitude, and Its Determinants,' *Marketing Science*, **28** (4), 782–91.

Ailawadi, K.L., N. Borin, and P.W. Farris (1995), 'Market Power and Performance: A Cross-industry Analysis of Manufacturers and Retailers,' *Journal of Retailing*, **71** (3), 211–48.

Ailawadi, K.L., B.A. Harlan, J. César, and D. Trounce (2006), 'Promotion Profitability for a Retailer: The Role of Promotion, Brand, Category, and Store Characteristics,' *Journal of Marketing Research*, **43** (4), 518–35.

Ailawadi, K.L., R.P. Dant, and D. Grewal (2004), 'The Difference Between Perceptual and Objective Performance Measures: An Empirical Analysis,' Marketing Science Institute Working Paper No. 04-001.

Ambler, T., C. Styles, and W. Xiucun (1999), 'The Effect of Channel Relationships and Guanxi on the Performance of Inter-province Export Ventures in the People's Republic of China,' *International Journal of Research in Marketing*, **16** (1), 75–87.

Amir, E. and B. Lev (1996), 'Value-relevance of Nonfinancial Information: The Wireless Communications Industry,' *Journal of Accounting and Economics*, **22** (1–3), 3–30.

Anderson, E.W., C. Fornell, and S.K. Mazvancheryl (2004), 'Customer Satisfaction and Shareholder Value,' *Journal of Marketing*, **68** (4), 172–85.

Ball, R. (1995), 'The Theory of Stock Market Efficiency: Accomplishments and Limitations,' *Journal of Applied Corporate Finance*, **8** (1), 4–17.

Bodie, Zvi, Alex Kane, and Alan J. Marcus (1993), *Investments*, Homewood, IL: Richard D. Irwin.

Buchanan, L. (1992), 'Vertical Trade Relationships: The Role of Dependence and Symmetry in Attaining Organizational Goals,' *Journal of Marketing Research*, **29** (1), 65–75.

Bromiley, P., M. Govekar, and A. Marcus (1988), 'On Using Event Study Methodology in Strategic Management Research,' *Technovation*, **8** (1–3), 25–42.

Bucklin, R.E, S. Siddarth, J.M. Silva-Risso (2008), 'Distribution Intensity and New Car Choice,' *Journal of Marketing Research*, **45** (4), 473–86.

Corsten, D. and N. Kumar (2005), 'Do Suppliers Benefit from Collaborative Relationships with Large Retailers? An Empirical Investigation of Efficient Consumer Response Adoption,' *Journal of Marketing*, **69** (3), 80–94.

Coughlan, A.T., E. Anderson, L.W. Stern, and A.I. El-Ansary (2001), *Marketing Channels*, Upper Saddle River, NJ: Pearson.

Deshpandé, R. and J.U. Farley (2004), 'Organizational Culture, Market Orientation, Innovativeness, and Firm Performance: An International Research Odyssey,' *International Journal of Research in Marketing*, **21** (1), 3–22.

Fabozzi, Frank J. (1995), *Investment Management*, Englewood Cliffs, NJ: Prentice Hall.

Farris, P. and K. Ailawadi (1992), 'Retail Power: Monster or Mouse?' *Journal of Retailing*, **68** (4), 351–69.

Frazier, G.L. and W.M. Lassar (1996), 'Determinants of Distribution Intensity,' *Journal of Marketing*, **60** (4), 39–51.

Friedman, M. (1953), 'The Case of Flexible Exchange Rates,' in *Essays in Positive Economics*, Chicago, IL: University of Chicago Press, pp. 157–203.

Ganesan, S., M. George, S. Jap, R.W. Palmatier, and B. Weitz (2009), 'Supply Chain Management and Retailer Performance: Emerging Trends, Issues, and Implications for Research and Practice,' *Journal of Retailing*, **85** (1), 84–94.

Geyskens, I., K. Gielens, and M.G. Dekimpe (2002), 'The Market Valuation of Internet Channel Additions,' *Journal of Marketing*, **66** (2), 102–19.

Geyskens, I., J.B.E.M. Steenkamp, and N. Kumar (1999), 'A Meta-analysis of Satisfaction in Marketing Channel Relationships,' *Journal of Marketing Research*, **36** (2), 223–38.

Geyskens, I., J.B.E.M. Steenkamp, and N. Kumar (2006), 'Make, Buy, or Ally: A Transaction Cost Theory Meta-analysis,' *Academy of Management Journal*, **49** (3), 519–43.

Gielens, K., L.M. Van de Gucht, J.B.E.M. Steenkamp, and M.G. Dekimpe (2008), 'Dancing With a Giant: The Effect of Wal-Mart's Entry into the United Kingdom on the Performance of European Retailers,' *Journal of Marketing Research*, **45** (5), 519–34.

Grewal, R., A. Chakravary, and A. Saini (2010), 'Governance Mechanisms in Business-to-business Electronic Markets,' *Journal of Marketing*, **74** (4), 45–62.

Hayek, F.A. (1945), 'The Use of Knowledge in Society,' *American Economic Review*, **35** (4), 519–30.

IGD (2006), 'European Grocery Buying Groups', fact sheet, available at: http://www.igd.com.

James, D. (2000), 'Don't Wait – Reciprocate. Online Deals Demand Creativity, Accountability,' *Marketing News*, 20 November.

Jap, S. (1999), 'Pie Expansion Efforts: Collaboration Processes in Buyer–Supplier Relationships,' *Journal of Marketing Research*, **36** (4), 461–75.

Jeuland, A.P. and S.M. Shugan (1983), 'Managing Channel Profits,' *Marketing Science*, **2** (3), 239–72.

Kalwani, M.U. and N. Narayandas (1995), 'Long-term Manufacturer–Supplier Relationships: Do They Pay Off for Supplier Firms?' *Journal of Marketing*, **59** (1), 1–16.

Kalyanaram, G., W.T. Robinson, and G.L. Urban (1995), 'Order of Market Entry:

Established Empirical Generalizations, Emerging Empirical Generalizations, and Future Research,' *Marketing Science*, **14** (3), G212–G221.

Kumar, N., L.W. Stern, and R.S. Achrol (1992), 'Assessing Reseller Performance From the Perspective of the Supplier,' *Journal of Marketing Research*, **29** (2), 238–53.

Lee, R.P. and R. Grewal (2004), 'Strategic Responses to New Technologies and Their Impact on Firm Performance,' *Journal of Marketing*, **68** (4), 157–71.

Lehmann, D. (2004), 'Metrics for Making Marketing Matter,' *Journal of Marketing*, **68** (4), 73–5.

McGuire, T.W. and R. Staelin (1983), 'An Industry Equilibrium Analysis of Downstream Vertical Integration,' *Marketing Science*, **2** (2), 161–91.

Messinger, P. and C. Narasimhan (1995), 'Has Power Shifted in the Grocery Channel?' *Marketing Science*, **14** (2) 189–223.

Mezias, J.M. and W.H. Starbuck (2003), 'Studying the Accuracy of Managers' Perceptions: A Research Odyssey,' *British Journal of Management*, **14** (1), 3–17.

Mizik, N. and R. Jacobson (2004), 'Stock Return Response Modeling,' in C. Moorman and D.R. Lehmann (eds), *Assessing Marketing Strategy Performance*, Cambridge, MA: Marketing Science Institute.

Mizik, N. and R. Jacobson (2007), 'Myopic Marketing Management: Evidence of the Phenomenon and its Long-term Performance Consequences in the SEO Context,' *Marketing Science*, **26** (3), 361–79.

Mooi, E.A and M. Ghosh (2010), 'Contract Specificity and Its Performance Implications,' *Journal of Marketing*, **74** (2), 105–20.

Newsweek (2010), 'Going Vertical,' 29 January, available at: http://www.newsweek.com/2010/01/29/going-vertical.html#; accessed 6 December 2011.

Palmatier, R.W., L.K. Scheer, and J.B.E.M. Steenkamp (2007), 'Customer Loyalty to Whom? Managing the Benefits and Risks of Salesperson-owned Loyalty,' *Journal of Marketing Research*, **44** (2), 185–99.

Planet Retail (2010), *Discounters, Rapid Growth or Gross Myth*, Trend Report.

PricewaterhouseCoopers/TNS Retail Forward (2007), *Retailing 2015: New Frontiers.*

Raut, S., S. Swami, E. Lee, and C.B. Weinberg (2008), 'How Complex Do Movie Channel Contracts Need to Be?' *Marketing Science*, **27** (4), 627–41.

Richard, P.J., T.M. Devinney, G.S. Yip, and G. Johnson (2010), 'Measuring Organizational Performance: Towards Methodological Best Practice,' *Journal of Management*, **35** (3), 718–804.

Rindfleisch, A., A.J. Malter, S. Ganesan, and C. Moorman (2008), 'Cross-sectional Versus Longitudinal Survey Research: Concepts, Findings, and Guidelines,' *Journal of Marketing Research*, **45** (3), 261–79.

Rubinstein, M. (2001), 'Rational Markets: Yes or No? The Affirmative Case,' *Financial Analysts Journal*, **57** (3), 15–29.

Sa Vinhas, A., S. Chatterjee, S. Dutta, A. Fein, J. Lajos, S. Neslin, L. Scheer, W. Ross, and Q. Wang (2010), 'Channel Design, Coordination, and Performance: Future Research Directions,' *Marketing Letters*, **21** (3), 223–37.

Shugan, S.M. (1989), 'Branded variants,' *Research in Marketing. AMA Educators' Proceedings*, 33–8.

Siguaw, J.A., P.M. Simpson, and T.L. Baker (1998), 'Effects of Supplier Market Orientation on Distributor Market Orientation and the Channel Relationship: The Distributor Perspective,' *Journal of Marketing*, **62** (3), 99–111.

Srinivasan, R. (2006), 'Dual Distribution and Intangible Firm Value: Franchising in Restaurant Chains,' *Journal of Marketing*, **70** (3), 120–35.

Srinivasan, R. and S. Bharadwaj (2004), 'Event Studies in Marketing Strategy Research,' in C. Moorman and D. Lehmann (eds), *Assessing Marketing Strategy Performance*, Marketing Science Institute.

Srinivasan, S. and D.M. Hanssens (2009), 'Marketing and Firm Value: Methods, Findings, and Future Directions,' *Journal of Marketing Research*, **46** (3), 293–312.

Srivastava, R.K., T.A. Shervani, and L. Fahey (1998), 'Market-based Assets and Shareholder Value: A Framework for Analysis,' *Journal of Marketing*, **62** (1), 2–18.

Thaler, R.H. (1992), *The Winner's Curse: Paradoxes and Anomalies of Economic Life*, Princeton, NJ: Princeton University Press.
Wall Street Journal (2009), 'Companies More Prone to Go "Vertical",' November.
Wang T., E. Gal-Or, and R. Chatterjee (2009), 'The Name Your Own Price Channel in the Travel Industry: An Analytical Exploration,' *Management Science*, **55** (6), 968–79.

9 The marketing–finance interface: an organizational perspective

Peter C. Verhoef and Joost M.E. Pennings

INTRODUCTION

Within the marketing literature there is an increasing debate on the declining role of marketing. Webster et al. (2005) specifically discuss the decline and also dispersion of marketing, where dispersion means that nowadays everyone is responsible for marketing. Nath and Mahajan (2008, p. 65) maintain 'that over the past three decades marketing academics have raised their concern with marketing's decreasing influence at the level of corporate strategy.' They also state that the roles of the general managers, chief financial officers (CFOs) and 'other penny pinchers and number crunchers' have become more important than the role of chief marketing officers (CMOs). Recently, Verhoef and Leeflang (2009) investigated this declining role and showed that marketing has become mainly responsible for advertising, promotions, relationship marketing initiatives, and customer satisfaction measurement. Distribution and pricing have become the responsibility of other departments, such as sales and finance. Their findings seem to confirm that marketing is now mainly involved with tactical decisions (Sheth and Sisodia, 2005), where in fact they are only responsible for a limited set of these decisions, mainly focusing on advertising and customer relationship building.

One of the crucial problems mentioned in these discussions is the assumed weak link between marketing and finance and the lack of contribution of marketing to firm performance. In this respect some statements are rather blunt. For example, McGovern and colleagues (2004, p. 70) argue that 'misguided marketing strategies have destroyed more shareholder value, and probably more careers, than shoddy fiscal accounting.' Schultz (2003) specifically blames marketing for not being accountable. A study by Cranfield Business School of top UK companies suggests that top management views marketing directors as unaccountable, untouchable, slippery, and expensive (Baker and Holt, 2004).

Jointly the above statements suggest that marketing has a bad reputation within the firm and specifically top management and finance are concerned about marketing's financial reputation. As a consequence the link between marketing and finance within firms has become of crucial

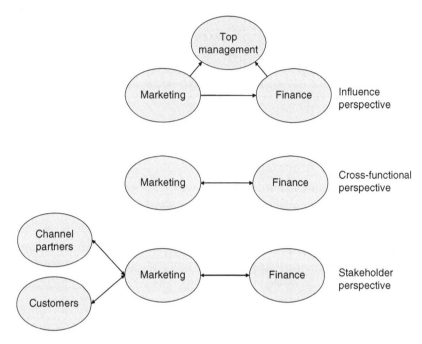

Figure 9.1   Conceptual perspectives on marketing–finance interface

importance for marketing in order to remain influential or to regain influence within firms. In this chapter, we will discuss the extant literature on the marketing–finance interface and potential strategies for marketing to improve this. In doing so, we take three perspectives, as shown in Figure 9.1. The first perspective is the influence or power perspective, in which we focus on the power of marketing vs finance within firms and perspectives within finance on marketing. In the second perspective we take a cross-functional view and focus on the marketing–finance interface as such. In the third perspective, we focus on how the marketing–finance interface affects relationships between marketing and its key stakeholders, such as customers and channel partners.

INFLUENCE PERSPECTIVE

Marketing Department Influence

There is wide acknowledgement within the literature that marketing as a function is declining. However, there are also case-wise examples that marketing is actually gaining more influence in specifically technically oriented firms. For example, Comstock et al. (2010) describe how marketing became an important and dominant function within General Electric. Generally three broad explanations for the decline of marketing influence are provided (e.g., Webster et al., 2005). First, firms are said to focus more on short-term earnings, resulting in a stronger focus on sales instead of on marketing. Second, external developments, such as increased channel power and increased market fragmentation are blamed for inducing a lower influence. Third, marketing has become a victim of its own success. Due to an increasing adoption of the marketing concept within the total organization, resulting in strong market-oriented firms, marketing is today everyone's responsibility. As a consequence marketing is dispersed within the organization.

Within the academic marketing literature there has been a continuing but scarce attention to the role of marketing within firms and specifically the influence of the marketing department. Important studies at the end of the 1990s are those by Homburg et al. (1999) and Moorman and Rust (1999). Homburg et al. (1999) suggest that marketing and sales are the dominant functions within firms. Moorman and Rust (1999) measure perceived influence of the marketing function and show a positive relationship between this influence and business performance. Beyond that they propose that marketing should have a strong influence within firms, as it plays a key role in connecting customers with key processes within the firm, such as service delivery, product development, and financial accountability.

Webster et al. (2005) discuss the results of a qualitative study on the decline and dispersion of marketing within firms. Their main contribution is that they conceptually synthesize the developments in marketing practice. They also stirred up renewed interest in the role of marketing. Verhoef and Leeflang (2009) empirically studied the role of marketing within Dutch firms. They studied three measure of influence: perceived MD influence, top management respect for the MD, and MD decision influence. Within Dutch firms they show that marketing has become mainly responsible for advertising, targeting, and positioning, and customer satisfaction measurement, while its influence on pricing, customer service, and product development and distribution decisions is limited. When comparing their results with Homburg et al. (1999) they indeed find some evidence for a declining influence of the marketing department.

In a cross-national follow-up study (Verhoef et al., 2010) they confirm these results in six additional Western countries, including the USA, Germany and the UK. In an exploratory analysis on the German, UK, and Dutch data they segment firms based on their influence in

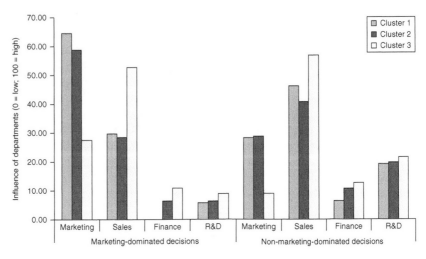

Figure 9.2   Clusters of firms based on influence of departments on marketing decisions

marketing-dominated marketing decisions (i.e., advertising) and non-marketing-dominated decisions (i.e., pricing). They find evidence for three clusters (see Figure 9.2). In one cluster comprising 46 percent of the included firms, marketing is the chief responsible department for the marketing-dominated functions, where sales has moderate influence and finance has no influence on these decisions. On non-marketing-dominated decisions, sales is the dominant department, marketing is the second important, and R&D and finance have limited influence. In the second cluster (37 percent) they find similar results. However, in this cluster finance also has some (marginal) influence on marketing-dominated decisions. Finally, in the third cluster (17 percent) their results show that the sales department is dominant for all studied marketing decisions. However, finance has the strongest influence in this cluster compared with the other two clusters. These results thus tend to show that finance in general is not the dominant department. It is either marketing or sales. So, probably the real battle is not between marketing and finance but between marketing and sales. This confirms remarks in the literature on ongoing conflicts between marketing and sales in many firms (Kotler et al., 2006). Having said this, finance has some influence in approximately 54 percent of the studied firms. Note, however, that in all the studied clusters R&D has a stronger influence than finance.

So, in sum, the above results suggest that although marketing has lost influence on some traditional marketing functions, it has mainly lost this influence to sales and finance cannot be blamed. This confirms the findings of Webster et al. (2005), which show a stronger emphasis on sales.

Consequences and Drivers of MD Influence

In general there is a normative idea that marketing losing its influence is not a good thing. It is generally believed that this is not good for the firm and that in the end it has a negative effect on (long-term) firm performance. This general idea is rooted in the fact that specialized knowledge present within the marketing department has important value for the firm. Moorman and Rust (1999) specifically argue that beyond the shared knowledge within firms on markets, reflected through an increased market orientation, more specialized knowledge is also required to create value. Moreover, marketing may have specific capabilities related to market sensing and market development, creating a competitive advantage and increased performance (Krasnikov and Jayachandran, 2008). Moorman and Rust (1999) indeed show that beyond market orientation the influence of the marketing department is positively related to business performance. Although, Verhoef and Leeflang (2009) cannot find evidence for a positive direct relationship between MD influence and business performance, they still plead for a strong marketing department, as weak marketing departments may lead to a weakened integration of marketing activities and the accumulated knowledge on customers within marketing departments may be lost. Webster et al. (2005) warn of weakened brands as marketing becomes less influential. In a broad sense they point to weakened market-based assets, which are known to create long-term firm value (Srivastava et al., 1998). In their cross-national follow-up study, Verhoef et al. (2011) derive the initial empirical generalization that MD decision influence and top management respect for the MD are positively related to business performance. Overall, the existing empirical evidence suggests that marketing departments create stronger business performance via two routes. First, there is a direct link. Second, strong marketing departments induce a stronger market orientation within firms. However, we note that there might be some dual causality in the relationship between MD influence and market orientation (Verhoef and Leeflang, 2009).

As stronger marketing departments are required within firms, it is undeniably important to understand what drives this influence and how firms can increase this influence. Homburg et al. (1999) looked at some internal and external contingency factors driving this influence. These include environmental turbulence, generic strategy, and presence of a CEO with a marketing background. Despite the effects of these factors on MD influence, Verhoef and Leeflang (2009) show that these types of factors only play a limited role. MD capabilities can be considered the main driver. Verhoef et al. (2010) distilled three major capabilities driving this influence: accountability, innovativeness of the marketing department, and customer connecting capabilities. Their results are pretty much in line with findings of Moorman and Rust (1999) and O'Sullivan and Abela (2007), suggesting that accountability and customer connection are major drivers. They also studied the impact of a good connection between marketing and other departments: finance, R&D, and sales. Importantly, they show that a good interface with finance improves top management respect and perceived MD influence. The effects of a good interface between marketing and sales and R&D on the studied influence variables are not so clear.

Considering these results in the context of this chapter, we can thus derive two major conclusions. First, from a general firm performance perspective finance should favor stronger marketing departments. Second, there are two important drivers of MD influence related to the marketing–finance interface: accountability and the quality of this interface!

Different Views on Marketing

To further understand the marketing–finance interface it is essential to understand the different views on marketing within top management. As noted, views in the management literature on perceptions of marketing within top management are rather negative. Verhoef et al. (2011) report differences in influence and perceptions on capabilities of marketing between finance executives (FEs), marketing executives (MEs), and CEOs. Their results are shown in Table 9.1. Interestingly, their results show that only the 'top management respect' perception shows significant differences. CEOs believe that marketing gets more top management respect than marketing and finance believe it gets. But in general differences are small, and there is no strong reason to assume that marketing is perceived as less influential between the considered functions.

With regard to the capabilities of the marketing department their results suggest some interesting differences. In general, MEs are more positive about their main capabilities then FEs and CEOs. Thus, this suggests that MEs may probably overvalue their own capabilities or that FEs and CEOs undervalue marketing's capabilities. Evidence within practice suggests that the latter may actually occur. Within General Electric the marketing department has actually started to communicate its activities to other departments within the firm in order to clearly show its value (Comstock et al., 2010). As can be observed from Table 9.1, Verhoef et al.'s (2010)

Table 9.1   Differences in average perceptions on MD influence and MD capabilities between marketing, finance, and CEOs

	Averages Per Function (Standard Deviation)			
	MEs (N = 870)	FEs (N = 262)	CEOs (N = 274)	p-value
Perceived influence	3.99	3.95	4.12	0.75
(1 = low, 7 = high)	(1.25)	(1.25)	(1.25)	
Top management respect	4.99	5.1	5.19	0.03
(1 = low, 7 = high)	(1.31)	(1.12)	(1.31)	
Decision influence	4.51	4.32	4.71	0.79
(1 = low, 10 = high)	(1.92)	(2.23)	(2.37)	
Accountability	4.72	3.92	4.54	0.00
(1 = low, 7 = high)	(1.29)	(1.31)	(1.37)	
Innovativeness of MD	3.35	2.86	2.92	0.00
(1 = low, 7 = high)	(2.53)	(2.31)	(2.39)	
Customer connection	5.21	4.74	4.89	0.00
(1 = low, 7 = high)	(1.08)	(1.16)	(1.34)	
Creativity	3.55	3.62	3.54	0.15
(1 = low, 7 = high)	(1.35)	(1.24)	(1.35)	
Integration with finance	4.96	4.80	4.99	0.05
(1 = low, 7 = high)	(1.48)	(1.43)	(1.59)	
Integration with sales	4.92	4.93	5.24	0.01
(1 = low, 7 = high)	(1.54)	(1.40)	(1.54)	
Integration with R&D	4.87	4.75	5.05	0.01
(1 = low, 7 = high)	(1.40)	(1.41)	(1.53)	

Source: Verhoef et al. (2010).

study also considered differences in perceptions on the integration between marketing and other departments. Given the focus of this chapter, we only discuss the finance interface. FEs tend to be a bit more negative about this integration then MEs and CEOs, suggesting some divergence in opinions about this interface.

Not only differences in perceptions were studied, but Verhoef et al. (2010) also investigated whether determinants of MD influence differed between FEs, MEs, and CEOs by running separate regression models per groups of executives. They could not provide evidence for strong differences in determinants between the three groups. Thus, all three groups have very similar views on how marketing could increase their influence: improve accountability, improve innovativeness, and improve customer connecting capabilities.

CROSS-FUNCTIONAL INTERFACE PERSPECTIVE

So far, we have mainly discussed the marketing–finance interface from a marketing influence perspective. In doing so we discussed the net influence of marketing departments within firms and also considered the influence of the finance department on marketing decisions. We already briefly discussed how the interface between marketing and finance affects the power of marketing departments within firms. In this section, we aim to provide a deeper discussion of this interface.

Within the marketing strategy literature there has been extensive research on marketing's interfaces with both R&D and sales (e.g., Griffin and Hausser, 1996; Kotler et al., 2006; Homburg and Jensen, 2007). One of the key assumptions in the literature on marketing interfaces is that a good interface improves the performance of the firm, as more knowledge is shared between departments. This leads to strong interfunctional coordination and more value creation towards customers (e.g., Narver and Slater, 1990). Research has, for example, shown that an improved interface between marketing and R&D improves innovation performance. Despite this rather positive view, recent research suggests that the interface should not only be characterized by having good relationships and having a cooperative culture. Instead, Luo et al. (2006) show that an interface should include both good cooperation and competition. They refer to this as cross-functional coopetition, which they define as the joint occurrence of cooperation and competition across functional areas within a firm. The underlying rationale for this finding is that as noted, cooperation is required for sharing knowledge between departments. However, competition forces departments to perform better (i.e., develop stronger proposals for obtaining budgets), as they have to compete with other departments within the firm to gain power. Luo et al. (2006) show that cross-functional coopetition between marketing and R&D is positively related to customer and business performance. Market learning, however, mediates this relationship.

If one does a search on the marketing–finance interface, the vast majority of articles focus on marketing's contribution to firm performance and shareholder value. This is also reflected in the contents of special issues devoted to the marketing–finance interface. In a special issue of the *Journal of Business Research* (Zinkhan and Verbrugge, 2000) six of the ten published papers focus on marketing's contribution to firm performance, while there is no attention to the organizational interface. Only one article studied the organizational marketing–finance interface. De Ruyter and Wetzels (2000) study determinants of the relational attitude in this interface. In their study relational attitudes consist of four dimensions: trust, bonding, reciprocity, and empathy. Their findings show that resource dependence and procedural fairness are positively related to relational attitudes and interfunctional rivalry is negatively related to relational attitudes. They do not study performance consequences, although based on the relationship marketing literature they tend to assume that stronger relational attitudes should be beneficial for the firm in some way. In a more recent special issue on this interface in the *Journal of the Academy of Marketing Science* (Hyman and Mathur, 2005) all published articles focus on the link between marketing and firm performance/shareholder value. Finally, in the special issue on 'Marketing meets Wall Street' in the *Journal of Marketing* (Hanssens et al., 2009) only articles on marketing's impact on shareholder value metrics are published.

Thus, we conclude that within the marketing–finance interface literature, studies on this specific cross-functional interface are almost lacking. As noted we could only find one single study specifically focusing on this cross-functional interface (De Ruyter and Wetzels, 2000). Beyond this, the studies executed by Verhoef and colleagues have considered the marketing–finance interface as an antecedent of MD influence. Their results suggest that improving this interface could potentially improve MD influence. However, overall there is a lack of cross-functional research on the marketing–finance interface.

Interdepartmental Integration

The marketing–finance interface is reflected in interdepartmental integration. Various definitions of interdepartmental integration have been developed in the literature. Moenaert and Souder (1990, p. 95) view integration, which they refer to as the strategic linking of functionally specialized groups while preserving their individual orientations, as 'the symbiotic interrelating of two or more entities that results in the production of net benefits to them, with these benefits exceeding the sum of the net benefits they would produce in a nonsymbiotic relationship.' Here we discuss two dimensions of integration: interaction and collaboration. Ruekert and Walker (1987) describe interaction based on a transaction dimension, which involves the flow of resources, work, and assistance and the amount and difficulty of communication. Kahn and Mentzer (1998, p. 54) define interdepartmental interaction as 'the information exchange process between departments,' in the form of meetings and information flows. We argue that interdepartmental integration is not only determined by interaction. Marketing and finance are expected to transfer information. In order to reach agreement to execute its projects marketing needs to justify its expenditures. The departments depend on each other's resources; finance provides the total marketing budget and marketing needs to communicate performance data to finance. The success of one department depends in part on the other department. A certain level of collaboration between marketing and finance is crucial. Collaboration reflects integration with teams, working together, and resource sharing. Certain firm-level characteristics may improve interdepartmental integration. Moenaert and Souder (1990) suggest that there are three major categories of mechanisms for integration: task specification, organization structure design, and organizational climate methods. The implementation of these mechanisms leads to integration.

One important discussion is, however, whether a strong marketing–finance interface is indeed beneficial for firms. Do firms having such a strong interface indeed perform better? And does this only occur in the short term or also in the long run? Clearly more research is required here.

DIFFERENT THOUGHT WORLDS

Within cross-functional research one of the crucial assumptions is that two departments have different thought worlds. Following Homburg and Jensen (2007) one could argue that these different thought worlds related to the orientation of marketing vs finance and the competences of marketing vs finance (see Table 9.2). Marketing is generally more oriented towards customers and brands/products. Finance has a stronger orientation towards shareholders (De Ruyter and Wetzels, 2000; Lehmann, 2004). Beyond that one could argue that there are differences in the long-term orientation of marketing and finance. Finance might also focus more on risks and costs, while marketing is generally more interested in revenue creation. Where marketing aims to create long-term value through building up customer and brand equity, finance is usually considered to have a short-term focus. Empirical evidence is, however, lacking. Moreover, one could argue that due to a wide adoption of market orientation within firms, differences in these orientations should have become smaller.

Marketing and finance could also have different competences. Marketing competences may concern market and customer knowledge, product knowledge, and execution of marketing campaigns. Finance competences may concern risk management, cost accounting, managing investor relations and so on.

Beyond differences in orientation and competence other differences could be mentioned. One important difference concerns the metrics used. Lehmann (2004) clearly shows that marketing is generally interested in product market metrics, such as market share and brand sales, while

Table 9.2   Different thought worlds of marketing vs finance

	Marketing	Finance
Orientation	Customers, channels	Shareholders, owners
	Products and brands	Corporate image
	Revenues	Risk and costs
	Long term	Short term
Competences	Market and customer knowledge	Financial market knowledge
	Creation and execution of marketing campaigns	Financial planning, controlling
Metrics	Perceptual metrics (i.e., brand awareness/attitudes)	Financial metrics (i.e., ROI, ROA, NPV)
	Sales metrics, market share	Firm value metrics (Tobin's Q, stock price)
	Market asset metrics (i.e., brand equity, customer equity)	

finance is more interested in financial metrics, such as ROA, ROI or market value and risk-adjusted return. Beyond that marketing might think in market-based asset metrics, such as brand equity, whereas finance has difficulties in understanding these metrics (De Ruyter and Wetzels, 2000; Srivastava and Wiesel, 2010).

Accountability

One potential way to overcome the potential differences between marketing and finance is a stronger focus on accountability. Moorman and Rust (1999) consider accountability as the linch pin between marketing and finance and this is essentially what multiple authors in the marketing literature have pleaded for (e.g., Lehmann, 2004; Rust et al., 2004). Marketing departments' accountability can be defined as the extent to which the marketing department can convincingly link its activities to financial outcomes up front when setting up the marketing plan and ex post when evaluating the marketing action (e.g., O'Sullivan and Abela, 2007; Verhoef and Leeflang, 2009). O'Sullivan and Abela (2007) label accountability as marketing performance measurement. They show that marketing performance measurement is positively related to firm performance.

Within the marketing literature there has been extensive attention paid to accountability. For years, the Marketing Science Institute has put forward accountability as one of its top research priorities. This has resulted in many studies on the effect of marketing actions on firm performance with lately a specific focus on the impact on shareholder value metrics (e.g., Srinivasan and Hanssens, 2009). Although, these studies are very valuable for the marketing discipline, they are less likely to be valuable for the individual marketing employee trying to become more accountable. Frequently, marketers work on specific product markets and their contribution to performance of the whole firm is rather vague. Imagine, for example, a marketing employee at P&G introducing a new version of Ariel washing powder. The contribution to firm value of this new introduction is not of much interest to this employee, although they might understand that innovations are a key driver for creating long-term firm value (Pauwels et al., 2004). Their main focus in marketing plans will be on how the proposed introduction strategy of this new version affects consumer behavior. Metrics that will be used concern distribution intensity, new product trials, market share, brand awareness and so on (Lehmann, 2004).

For many marketers, how they can become more accountable is still a problem. One of the general proposed solutions is that the right metrics should be chosen and that these metrics should be measured (Farris et al., 2006). Subsequently, links between marketing actions and marketing metrics should be sought. For example, marketers want to know how advertising affects brand awareness and sales over time (e.g., Hanssens, 2009). However, having the right metrics in place will be an insufficient condition for accountability. Firms should also have to gain access to the right capabilities to link actions with metrics. For that purpose econometric skills are of huge importance. For example, market response models required for understanding the impact of advertising on sales are usually far from simple (Leeflang et al., 2000). Though conceptually easy to understand, customer equity models for calculating the return on investment of marketing strategies require good econometric skills (Rust et al., 2004). Traditional marketing employees are not sufficiently equipped with these skills given the importance of more qualitative reasoning within marketing education. Beyond that, marketing employees might naturally be more interested in how they can create value by developing attractive marketing campaigns, building strong brands, and so on. The latter remark also refers to a required change of culture within marketing departments. Beyond good marketing intuition, fact-based reasoning also becomes very important (Davenport and Harris, 2006). Experiences within the Dutch Telco company (Verhoef and Lemon, 2011) KPN suggest that this change should be driven by top management and it may induce more intuition-oriented marketers to leave the firm. Also investments in IT and systems to collect metrics and visualizing these metrics on a day-to-day basis are probably required. In this respect marketing dashboards have received considerable attention (e.g., Pauwels et al., 2009).

Within the literature there is a lack of research on how marketing can indeed become more accountable. Important research questions are the following: What are actually drivers of accountability? What hinders marketing from becoming accountable? And how can marketing become accountable with a limited access to data and metrics?

A STAKEHOLDER PERSPECTIVE

Customer Perspective

The marketing–finance interface also impacts relationships with customers. We distinguish two perspectives: (1) how firms value customers and (2) how customers value the firm.

To overcome the gap between marketing and finance, marketing should adopt metrics that finance understands. Within finance, net present value (NPV) is a well-known metric. In the last decade marketing and especially customer relationship management researchers have embraced customer lifetime value (CLV) as a metric to evaluate customers. CLV is usually defined as the net present value of all future earnings from a customer. Based on CLV, customers are segmented. Marketing resources can be allocated across the resulting CLV segments (Venkatesan et al., 2007). For example, one can decide to re-allocate marketing resources in such a way that less marketing budget is allocated to low CLV segments, while more marketing budget is allocated to high CLV segments. Importantly, Kumar and Shah (2009) also show that by applying CLV-based valuations and resource allocation strategies firm value can be increased. Hence, not only CLV links to NPV, but also CLV is clearly related to firm value (see also Gupta et al., 2004). Rust et al. (2004) also use CLV as a metric to evaluate marketing initiatives. One potential problem with the CLV metric is that the focus on the customer becomes finance-oriented. Marketers then seem to be solely interested in the value of (current) customers and the bottom-line and may neglect growth opportunities, network effects and so forth (Leone et al., 2006). This may also result in undervaluation or overvaluation of customers. For example, the traditional CLV metric does not account for the network value of customers (i.e., opinion leaders) or customers' contribution to value creation (i.e., through co-creation) (Kumar et al., 2010; Hoyer et al., 2010; van Doorn et al., 2010).

From the second perspective (value to customer), a strong focus on CLV and other financial metrics may also potentially create a mechanistic relationship orientation, neglecting the fact that in a relationship relational attitudes, such as trust, commitment, reciprocity, and so on, are also important. Potentially firms may believe that they are customer-centric (i.e., through a strong focus on behavioral value metrics), but this may, however, attract attention away from how they can create value for customers. In general a strong focus on optimizing financial metrics such as shareholder value may be destructive for a customer focus and the creation of value for customers. For example, within mobile telecoms multiple firms have developed smart pricing mechanisms (i.e., one-minute billing) aiming to optimize the value of the customer base. They, however, forget that these smart pricing mechanisms may also backfire, as they may create strong negative emotions (i.e., belief that the firm is dishonest) leading to postings on blogs, which results in potentially weakened relationships and brands (van Doorn et al., 2010). In the same vein, there are numerous examples in which firms aiming to optimize shareholder value, have put too much emphasis on short-term earnings (i.e., through reducing service levels, higher prices), without looking at customer interests in the context of long-term negative effects for the firm. For example, forced by the Ahold holding company, Dutch retailer Albert Heijn systematically increased prices to contribute to shareholder value in the short term, damaging its price image. At some point this backfired on Albert Heijn severely, which forced it to start a costly and enduring price war (van Heerde et al., 2008).

Channel Perspective

The way marketers organize contract relationships within the channel can have profound impact on the financial performance of the firm. Contract relationships determine both the level of the cash flows generated as well as the volatility in these cash flows, both of which drive shareholder value (i.e., net present value of the firm). The focus on cash flow volatility has been a key focus in finance since it is associated with higher costs of accessing external capital and lower average levels of investment in capital expenditures, R&D, and advertising (Minton and Schrand, 1999). Marketing activities can reduce the volatility of cash flows, effectively lowering the firm's cost of capital and reducing its working capital (cash) needs (Rao and Bharadwaj, 2008). This lower cost of capital increases the firm's net present value and hence improves shareholders' wealth. By lowering its cash needs, the firm can return freed-up working capital to its shareholders for reinvestment purposes (ibid., p.17). Reducing cash flow volatility is key for any firm; the recent economic crisis shows that (lowering) the risk-adjusted cost of capital by means of reducing net cash flow volatility is necessary for survival. This has been recognized by the finance discipline, which has begun investigating other ways in which firms can reduce cash flow volatility and increase shareholder wealth. Bodnar et al. (2003), for example, demonstrate how firms can use financial facilitating services, such as derivatives, to reduce cash flow volatility. In particular, finance research has focused on the relationship between derivative usage and debt levels, dividend policy, the holding of liquid assets, and capital structure (Bartram et al., 2009; Pennings and Garcia, 2011). Such services may reduce cash flow volatility in a more direct way than 'traditional' marketing activities – such as increasing customer satisfaction (Gruca and Rego, 2005) or loyalty (Reichheld, 1996) – may accomplish. Whereas recent marketing–finance studies have shown how marketing spending (Fischer et al., 2009) and customer satisfaction (Gruca and Rego, 2005) impact cash flow volatility and hence shareholder value, it has not been established how a focus on shareholder value should alter the marketing decisions of line managers and how these decisions *directly* influence cash flow volatility.

In a recent study Pennings et al. (2010) focus on the role of futures contracts as an example of financial facilitating services (e.g., marketing instruments) that marketers can use. Hedging is the practice of offsetting the price volatility inherent in any cash contract relationship (i.e., cash market position) by taking an equal but opposite position in the futures market. Futures contracts are standardized with respect to characteristics of the product covered by the contract, time, and place of delivery of the product, and they are traded under the rules of an organized exchange. In general terms, a hedging service can be defined as 'a service through which a channel member is offered the opportunity to buy or sell products forward at a fixed price, thereby not restricting the channel member to engage in a cash contract relationship' (Pennings and Leuthsid, 2000, p. 875). The futures contract serves as the medium through which the hedging service is delivered. Pennings et al. (ibid.) show that these market instruments can help to establish satisfying channel relationships, even if partner companies start from different contract relationship preferences and can help marketers to manage cash flow volatility and hence contribute to shareholder value.

CONCLUSION

In this chapter we discussed the marketing–finance interface from a mere organizational perspective. One of our key questions was: what strategies does marketing have available to improve the marketing–finance interface and to regain its influence? Using our three-way perspective framework – influence/power, cross-functional, and stakeholder perspective – we make some recommendations.

The influence/power perspective shows that sales are becoming more dominant because of firms' focus on short-term earnings. While one may debate whether the short-term focus is beneficial for (long-term) value creation, marketing can play an important role when it teams up with finance. Marketing together with finance affects the short-term earnings by means of managing costs (marketing expenditures) as well as revenues in terms of levels and volatility. Finance can help marketing in better understanding the impact of marketing activities on short-term earnings and the volatility in them and hence marketing can better target the tools available. From a long-term perspective, marketing is said to induce market orientation and innovation. Here too, the finance department can facilitate marketing by providing financial data, methodology, and metrics to provide insights on the return of being market oriented and innovative and as such the finance department can help marketing to become accountable.

The cross-functional interface perspective suggests that interaction and collaboration are important for having a marketing–finance interface that contributes to firm performance. Interdepartmental integration reflects this interface. Interdepartmental integration and the benefits from it, may be enhanced by information sharing and degree of common knowledge such that information becomes meaningful for both departments.

Using a stakeholder perspective, focusing on the customer and marketing channel, allows the marketer to directly impact the value of the firm. A focus on customer lifetime value allows the marketer to make a better cost–revenue tradeoff when investing in the customer relationship. A focus on contract relationship management in the marketing channel, which includes financial facilitating services such as futures, allows marketers to directly influence the volatilities in cash flows and hence the value of the firm. This latter perspective is not entirely new: early marketing literature paid attention to the use of such services (Hoos, 1942; Working, 1954), although not in connection with a focus on shareholder value. Interestingly, marketing has lost the knowledge of these marketing instruments and marketing institutions and the finance field claimed them as its domain. While the finance discipline has focused on how to price these marketing instruments, the role of how these instruments can directly create value for the firm has been neglected. A similar pattern is found in practice; while the finance department is concerned with dealing with these marketing instruments from an accounting perspective, the crucial element is how these instruments complement channel relationships, a task that is managed by the marketer. Hence, the stakeholder perspective seems to suggest that marketing and finance have a shared responsibility in managing firms' relationships and by doing so, can directly impact the financial performance of the firm.

In sum, for marketers to capitalize on the marketing–finance interface, understanding finance is crucial. Many authors argued that marketing needs to develop financial metrics to demonstrate its value. While having these metrics is useful it does not provide the sufficient conditions for marketing to regain its value within the firm. Only when marketers are able to truly understand finance can interdepartmental integration be successful and by means of that integration marketing can reclaim its important role in the firm.

REFERENCES

Baker, S. and S. Holt (2004), 'Making Marketers Accountable: A Failure of Marketing Education?' *Marketing Intelligence and Planning*, **22** (5).

Bartram, S.M., G.W. Brown, and F. Fehle (2009), 'International Evidence on Financial Derivatives Usage,' *Financial Management*, **38** (1), 185–206.

Bodnar, G.M., A de Jong, and V. Macrea (2003), 'The Impact of Institutional Differences on Derivatives Usage: A Comparative Study of US and Dutch Firms,' *European Financial Management*, **9** (3), 271–97.

Comstock, B., R. Gulati, and S. Liguori (2010), 'Unleashing the Power of Marketing,' *Harvard Business Review*, **90** (8), 90–98.

Davenport, T.H. and J.G. Harris (2006), *Competing on Analytics*, Boston, MA: Harvard Business School Press.

De Ruyter, K. and M. Wetzels (2000), 'The Marketing–Finance Interface: A Relational Exchange Perspective,' *Journal of Business Research*, **50** (2), 209–15.

Farris, P., N.T. Bendle, P.E. Pfeifer, and D.J. Reibstein (2006), *Marketing Metrics: Fifty+ Metrics Every Marketer Should Know*, Philadelphia: Wharton School Publishing.

Fischer, M., H. Shin, and D.M. Hanssens (2009), 'Marketing Spending and the Volatility of Revenue and Cash Flows,' Working Paper, UCLA Anderson School of Management.

Griffin, A. and J.R. Hauser (1996), 'Integrating R&D and Marketing: A Review and Analysis of the Literature,' *Journal of Product Innovation Management*, **13** (3), 191–215.

Gruca, T.S. and L.L. Rego (2005), 'Customer Satisfaction, Cash Flow, and Shareholder Value,' *Journal of Marketing*, **69** (3), 115–30.

Gupta, S., D.R. Lehmann, and J.A. Stuart (2004), 'Valuing Customers,' *Journal of Marketing Research*, **41** (1), 7–18.

Hanssens, D.M. (2009), 'Advertising Impact Generalizations in a Marketing Mix Context,' *Journal of Advertising Research*, **49** (2), 127–9.

Hanssens, D.M., R.T. Rust, and R.K. Srivastava (2009), 'Marketing Strategy and Wall Street: Nailing Down Marketing's Impact,' *Journal of Marketing*, **73** (6), 115–18.

Homburg, C. and O. Jensen (2007), 'The Thought Worlds of Marketing and Sales: Which Differences Make a Difference?' *Journal of Marketing*, **71** (3), 124–42.

Homburg, C., J.P. Workman, and H. Krohmer (1999), 'Marketing's Influence Within the Firm,' *Journal of Marketing*, **63** (2), 1–17.

Hoos, S. (1942), 'Futures Trading in Perishable Agricultural Commodities,' *Journal of Marketing*, **6** (4), 358–65.

Hoyer, W.D., R. Chandy, M. Dorotic, M. Krafft, and S.S. Singh (2010), 'Consumer Cocreation in New Product Development,' *Journal of Service Research*, **13** (3), 283–96.

Hyman, M.R. and I. Mathur (2005), 'Retrospective and Prospective Views on the Marketing/Finance Interface,' *Journal of the Academy of Marketing Science*, **33** (4), 390–400.

Kahn, K.B. and J.T. Mentzer (1998), 'Marketing's Integration with Other Departments,' *Journal of Business Research*, **42** (1), 53–62.

Kotler, P., N. Rackham, and S. Krishnaswamy (2006), 'Ending the War Between Sales and Marketing,' *Harvard Business Review*, **84** (7–8), 68–78.

Krasnikov, A. and S. Jayachandran (2008), 'The Relative Impact of Marketing, Research-and-Development, and Operations Capabilities on Firm Performance,' *Journal of Marketing*, **72** (4), 1–11.

Kumar, V. and D. Shah (2009), 'Expanding the Role of Marketing: From Customer Equity to Market Capitalization,' *Journal of Marketing*, **73** (6), 119–36.

Kumar, V., L. Aksoy, B. Donkers, R. Venkatesan, T. Wiesel, and S. Tillmanns (2010), 'Undervalued or Overvalued Customers: Capturing Total Customer Engagement Value,' *Journal of Service Research*, **13** (3), 297–310.

Leeflang, P.S.H., D.R. Wittink, M. Wedel, and P.A. Naert (2000), *Building Models for Marketing Decisions*, Dordrecht: Kluwer Academic Publishers.

Lehmann, D.R. (2004), 'Metrics for Making Marketing Matter,' *Journal of Marketing*, **68** (4), 73–5.

Leone, R.P., V.R. Rao, K.L. Keller, A.M. Luo, L. McAlister, and R. Srivastava (2006), 'Linking Brand Equity to Customer Equity,' *Journal of Services Research*, **9** (2), 125–38.

Luo, X., R.J. Slotegraaf, and X. Pan (2006), 'Cross-functional "Coopetition": The Simultaneous Role of Cooperation and Competition Within Firms,' *Journal of Marketing*, **70** (2), 67–80.

McGovern, G.J., D. Court, J.A. Quelch, and B. Crawford (2004), 'Bringing Customers Back into the Boardroom,' *Harvard Business Review*, **82** (11), 70–80.

Moenaert, R.K. and W.E. Souder (1990), 'An Information Transfer Model for Integrating Marketing and R&D Personnel in New Product Development Projects,' *Journal of Product Innovation Management*, **7** (2), 91–107.

Minton, B.A. and Schrand, C. (1999), 'The Impact of Cash Flow Volatility on Discretionary Investment and the Costs of Debt and Equity Financing,' *Journal of Financial Economics*, **54** (3), 423–60.

Moorman, C. and R.T. Rust (1999), 'The Role of Marketing,' *Journal of Marketing*, **63** (4), 180–97.

Narver, J.C. and S.F. Slater (1990), 'The Effect of a Market Orientation on Business Profitability,' *Journal of Marketing*, **54** (4), 20–35.

Nath, P. and V. Mahajan (2008), 'Chief Marketing Officers: A Study of their Presence in Firms' Top Management Teams,' *Journal of Marketing*, **72** (1), 65–81.

O'Sullivan, D. and A.V. Abela (2007), 'Marketing Performance Measurement Ability and Firm Performance,' *Journal of Marketing*, **71** (2), 79–93.

Pauwels, K.H., J. Silva-Risso, S. Srinivasan, and D. Hanssens (2004), 'New Products, Sales Promotions, and Firm Value: The Case of the Automobile Industry,' *Journal of Marketing*, **68** (4), 142–56.

Pauwels, K., T. Ambler, B.H. Clark, P. LaPointe, D. Reibstein, B. Skiera, B. Wierenga, and T. Wiesel (2009), 'Dashboards as a Service: Why, What, How, and What Research is Needed?' *Journal of Service Research*, **12** (2), 175–89.

Pennings, J.M.E. and P. Garcia (2011), 'Risk & Hedging Behavior: The Role and Determinants of Latent Heterogeneity?' *The Journal of Financial Research*, **33** (4), 373–401.

Pennings, J.M.E. and R.M. Leuthold (2000), 'The Motivation for Hedging Revisited,' *Journal of Futures Markets*, **20** (9), 865–85.

Pennings, J.M.E., B.C. Wansink, and W.O. Hoffmann (2010), 'Marketing Activities & Risk Adjusted Cost of Capital: A Marketing–Finance Approach Linking Channel Contracting to Shareholder Value,' Maastricht University, Working Paper, Marketing–Finance Research Lab.

Rao, R.K.S. and N. Bharadwaj (2008), 'Marketing Initiatives, Expected Cash Flows, and Shareholders' Wealth,' *Journal of Marketing*, **72** (1), 16–26.

Reichheld, F.F. (1996), *The Loyalty Effect: The Hidden Force Behind Growth, Profits and Lasting Value*, Boston, MA: Harvard Business School Press.

Ruekert, R.W. and O.C. Walker (1987), 'Marketing's Interaction with Other Functional Units: A Conceptual Framework and Empirical Evidence,' *Journal of Marketing*, **51** (1), 1–19.

Rust, R.T., K.N. Lemon, and V.A Zeithaml (2004), 'Return on Marketing: Using Customer Equity to Focus Marketing Strategy,' *Journal of Marketing*, **68** (1), 109–27.

Schultz, D.E. (2003), 'Marketing Gets No Respect in the Boardroom,' *Marketing News* (24 November), 9.

Sheth, J.N. and R.S. Sisodia (2005), 'Does Marketing Need Reform?' *Journal of Marketing*, **69** (4), 10–12.

Srinivasan, S. and D.M. Hanssens (2009), 'Marketing and Firm Value: Metrics, Methods, Findings, and Future Directions,' *Journal of Marketing Research*, **46** (3), 293–312.

Srivastava, R.K. and T. Wiesel (2010), 'Brand Platform as Strategic Investments: Leveraging Customer Connections to Manage Profitability, Growth, and Risk,' in S. Wuyts, M.G. Dekimpe, E. Gijsbrechts, and R. Pieters (eds), *The Connected Customer – The Changing Nature of Consumer and Business Markets*, London: Routledge, Taylor and Francis Group.

Srivastava, R.K., T.A. Shervani, and L. Fahey (1998), 'Market-based Assets and Shareholder Value: A Framework for Analysis,' *Journal of Marketing*, **62** (1), 2–18.

Van Doorn, J., K.N. Lemon, V. Mittal, S. Nass, D. Pick, P. Pirner, and P.C. Verhoef (2010), 'Customer Engagement Behavior: Theoretical Foundations and Research Directions,' *Journal of Service Research*, **13** (3), 253–66.

Van Heerde, H., E. Gijsbrechts, and K. Pauwels (2008), 'Winners and Losers in a Major Price War,' *Journal of Marketing Research*, **45** (5), 499–518.

Venkatesan, R., V. Kumar, and T.R. Bohling (2007), 'Optimal CRM Using Bayesian Decision Theory: An Application for Customer Selection,' *Journal of Marketing Research*, **44** (4), 579–94.

Verhoef, P.C. and P.S.H. Leeflang (2009), 'Understanding the Marketing Department's Influence Within the Firm,' *Journal of Marketing*, **73** (2), 14–37.

Verhoef, Peter C. and Katherine N. Lemon (2011), 'Key Lessons from Customer Value Management Research,' in *Fast Forward Series*, Boston: Marketing Science Institute.

Verhoef, P.C., P.S.H. Leeflang, J. Reiner, M. Natter, W. Baker, A. Grinstein, A. Gustafson, and J. Saunders (2011), 'A Cross-national Investigation into the Marketing Department's Influence within the Firm: Towards Initial Empirical Generalizations,' *Journal of International Marketing*, **19** (3), 59–86.

Webster, F.E., A.J. Malter, and S. Ganesan (2005), 'The Decline and Dispersion of Marketing Competence,' *MIT Sloan Management Review*, **46** (4), 35–43.

Working, H. (1954), 'Whose Markets? Evidence on Some Aspects of Futures Trading,' *Journal of Marketing*, **19** (1), 1–11.

Zinkhan, G.M. and J.A. Verbrugge (2000), 'Special Issue on the Marketing/Finance Interface,' *Journal of Business Research*, **50** (2), 139–42.

10 Corporate financial policy and marketing strategy: the case of IPOs and SEOs
Didem Kurt and John Hulland

INTRODUCTION

Previous research on the marketing–finance interface has focused primarily on studying the direct market value consequences of changes in specific marketing elements such as advertising, customer satisfaction, and branding (e.g., Pauwels et al., 2004; Gruca and Rego, 2005; Mizik and Jacobson, 2008; Joshi and Hanssens, 2009; Luo, 2009; Srinivasan et al., 2009). Related research has examined how changes in corporate strategy (e.g., mergers and acquisitions) affect both marketing strategy and shareholder value (e.g., Bahadir et al., 2008; Swaminathan et al., 2008). One major impetus behind much of this work is the realization that marketing's influence within the firm has declined over the past few decades (e.g., see Brown et al., 2005; Webster et al., 2005; Verhoef and Leeflang, 2009), particularly in the boardroom (Sheth and Sisodia, 2006; Nath and Mahajan, 2008).

As an additional step in enhancing our understanding of the interaction between marketing and finance, scholars have started to examine the interaction between corporate financial policy and marketing strategy and its impact on firm value (e.g., Mizik and Jacobson, 2007; Luo, 2008; Kurt and Hulland, 2010). This growing body of literature offers valuable insights into managerial decisions for firms that routinely consider various forms of financing in order to make appropriate marketing decisions. In particular, it has become increasingly clear that equity financing plays a crucial role in supporting major increases in marketing spending. For example, Garmaise (2009, p. 325) notes that 'marketing assets are typically financed with equity.'[1] Thus, a better understanding of the connection between marketing strategy and firms' acquisition of equity capital through initial public offerings (IPOs) and seasoned equity offerings (SEOs) is critical to longer-term success. Such an understanding is also needed to help marketers achieve a more equal footing with other members in the boardroom.

Although firms' capital structures exhibit considerable cross-sectional variation, a large number of firms find it necessary at some point to access public equity. IPOs take place when firms seek equity investment from the public for the first time. SEOs, on the other hand, involve the issuance of additional equity by public companies to raise capital. Both IPOs and SEOs play a critical role in enhancing firms' competitive positions in product markets since issuers can raise significant amounts of funds through these offerings (Akhigbe et al., 2003; Hsu et al., 2010). The key questions of interest for marketers related to equity offerings fall into three broad categories:

1. To what extent do firms change their marketing expenditures in the pre-offering period? And, how do pre-offering marketing efforts affect the trading activity around the offering and the amount of capital raised by the offering firms?
2. Do pre-offering changes in marketing expenditures also impact long-term firm value?
3. To what extent do firms change their marketing efforts during the post-offering period (as a result of raising significant amounts of capital), and how does this change in marketing strategy affect subsequent firm value?

The goal of this chapter is to review the growing literature examining the questions listed above, discuss the managerial implications of the current findings, and offer directions for future research.[2] In our review, we distinguish between the pre-offering period and post-offering period since there are notable differences between the two. First, equity issuance (especially IPOs) can signal a change in the outlook of an industry as a whole, leading to increased investor attention during the post-offering period as compared to the pre-offering period (Akhigbe et al., 2003). Second, equity issuing firms raise significant amounts of cash that can be used to finance new projects, altering competitive dynamics in the industries wherein they operate (Hsu et al., 2010). Third, equity offerings also reduce the firms' financial leverage (i.e., the ratio of debt to total capital) and thus, the risk of bankruptcy, allowing greater flexibility in their investments. Finally, in the case of IPOs, changes in the ownership and governance structure of offering firms generally impact corporate-level decision-making (e.g., the management team needs to convince a larger group of investors that their projects are worth investing in; Chemmanur and Fulghieri, 1999).

To help organize the discussion that follows, we propose the framework shown in Figure 10.1. The top portion of this figure (shown within the dotted rectangle) represents most of the traditional work looking at the marketing–finance interface. In contrast, this chapter focuses on the work to date that has investigated: (1) how marketing strategy affects and is affected by corporate financial policy, and (2) how corporate financial

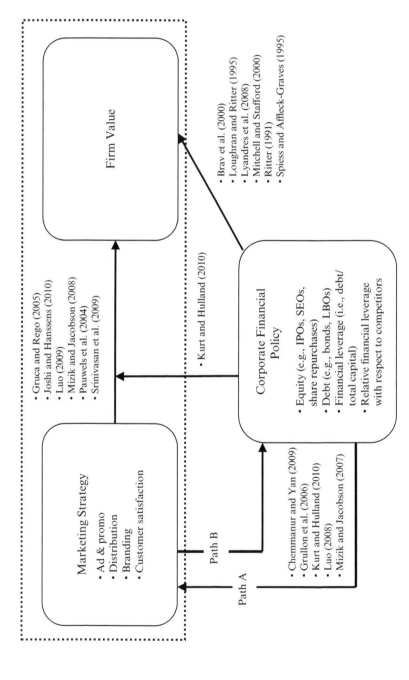

Figure 10.1 Corporate financial policy and marketing strategy: a framework

Firm Value

• Brav et al. (2000)
• Loughran and Ritter (1995)
• Lyandres et al. (2008)
• Mitchell and Stafford (2000)
• Ritter (1991)
• Spiess and Affleck-Graves (1995)

• Gruca and Rego (2005)
• Joshi and Hanssens (2010)
• Luo (2009)
• Mizik and Jacobson (2008)
• Pauwels et al. (2004)
• Srinivasan et al. (2009)

• Kurt and Hulland (2010)

Marketing Strategy

• Ad & promo
• Distribution
• Branding
• Customer satisfaction

Corporate Financial Policy

• Equity (e.g, IPOs, SEOs, share repurchases)
• Debt (e.g., bonds, LBOs)
• Financial leverage (i.e., debt/ total capital)
• Relative financial leverage with respect to competitors

Path B

Path A

• Chemmanur and Yan (2009)
• Grullon et al. (2006)
• Kurt and Hulland (2010)
• Luo (2008)
• Mizik and Jacobson (2007)

policy decisions of firms and their industry rivals moderate the link between marketing strategy and firm value.

The balance of this chapter is organized as follows. First, we present a summary of the work that has been done to date looking at the link between marketing strategy and corporate financial policy. Next, we discuss key methodological approaches that have been used to investigate these relationships. Finally, we propose a research agenda and discuss the managerial implications of this work.

MARKETING–FINANCE INTERFACE AROUND EQUITY OFFERINGS: WHAT WE KNOW

Background

Most businesses start out as small private firms that obtain initial funding from a single or small group of investors. However, as companies prosper and require additional capital, at some point in their growth they often find it desirable to go public and raise equity capital by selling shares to outside investors. This process is referred to as initial public offering (IPO), through which privately held entities transform into publicly held companies with shares traded on stock exchanges such as New York Stock Exchange (NYSE) and NASDAQ. An IPO is a very visible activity, marking an important turning point in the life of a firm. The act of going public itself focuses a spotlight on the firm and generates attention among not only its potential investors but also its customers.

In fact, IPOs play an important role in the growth of the US economy, representing $293 billion raised via more than 1300 offerings during the last decade.[3] Successful IPOs provide issuing firms with various benefits, including substantial equity capital, increased public recognition, and heightened financial analyst interest. IPOs also reduce information asymmetries between managers and investors since public firms must file quarterly/annual financial reports and regularly disclose information to the public regarding their operations and financial performance.

IPOs not only satisfy the immediate capital requirements of offering firms but also provide access to public equity capital, thereby decreasing the cost of funding the firms' current operations and future investments. The process of selling additional shares by a firm that is already publicly traded is called follow-on offering or seasoned equity offering (SEO), as contrasted with an unseasoned equity offering (i.e., IPO). SEOs are an important source of external funding for public companies; over the past decade, the number of SEOs was more than double the number of

IPOs issued. Furthermore, the size of an average SEO during the period 1980–2003 was 21 percent larger than that of an average IPO ($86 vs $68 million; Eckbo et al., 2007).

Both IPOs and SEOs alter firms' ownership and capital structures. However, these effects are more pronounced in the case of IPOs, when the ownership rights of a company can be bought and sold through stock trading for the first time, resulting in a more dispersed ownership structure. Accordingly, the process of valuing IPOs and SEOs is quite different. The valuation of IPOs, particularly young firms, is often difficult due to the uncertainties about future cash flows. In fact, one of the most commonly documented empirical regularities related to IPOs is that when companies go public, their shares tend to be underpriced in that their stock prices increase significantly on the first day of trading relative to their offering prices. Historically, the average underpricing of US firms has been around 18 percent (e.g., Ritter and Welch, 2002; Ritter, 2003), suggesting that IPO firms leave large sums of money on the table. On the other hand, after a firm goes public, the price at which its equity is sold becomes publicly observable. Hence, the valuation of SEOs is relatively easier in that offer prices are primarily based on firms' current market prices. However, previous research has also shown that SEOs, on average, are underpriced by about 2 percent (e.g., Corwin, 2003; Altinkilic and Hansen, 2003). As a result, effectively communicating the true value of their firms' equity to potential investors and thereby reducing the amount of money left on the table is an important task for managers of both IPO and SEO firms. In the next section, we review two recent studies examining how the use of marketing resources can help managers reduce equity underpricing, as well as enhance the trading of their stocks on the offering day.

Marketing Strategy in the Pre-offering Period and Firm Value at the Offering

Researchers have started to examine how the marketing strategies of equity issuing firms prior to the offering affect financial performance. For instance, Luo (2008) examines whether pre-IPO marketing expenditures impact how investors respond to IPOs. Specifically, he argues that managers of IPO firms can better convey their firm's intrinsic value and future prospects to potential investors by using product market advertising, enabling them to enhance trading volumes, reduce IPO underpricing (i.e., the extent to which the offering price is lower than the closing price at the end of the first trading day) and thereby raise more capital. By using a sample of 1981 IPOs issued between 1996 and 2005, he finds that IPO firms with higher pre-IPO marketing expenditures underprice less and have higher trading volume and that these effects are more pronounced for firms with higher cost reduction efficiency, as well as those operating in industries with a smaller number of historical IPOs. Thus, in addition to documenting the crucial role of marketing resources on the outcomes of firms' financing decisions, these findings provide evidence for a potential 'contingency theory of marketing–finance interface' (ibid., p. 107), which suggests the impact of marketing actions on shareholder wealth is heterogeneous across firms and market conditions.

Furthermore, Chemmanur and Yan (2009) investigate how firms' advertising strategies could impact and also be affected by the prospect of an upcoming IPO or SEO. They show that in equilibrium, the firm uses a combination of advertising and equity underpricing to convey its true product quality and intrinsic value to consumers and potential investors. Their model yields two testable predictions: (1) a firm advertises more when it is planning to issue equity versus when it has no plan to raise equity, and (2) advertising and equity underpricing are substitutes in terms of signaling the intrinsic value of the firm to potential investors. The authors test their predictions separately for samples of 884 IPOs and 663 SEOs issued between 1990 and 2000. Consistent with their first prediction, Chemmanur and Yan find that both IPO and SEO firms spend more on advertising in the year of their equity offering relative to other, non-offering years. In addition, providing support for their second prediction, Chemmanur and Yan find that offering firms with higher advertising spending underprice their equity less. Although the findings of Luo (2008) and Chemmanur and Yan (2009) demonstrate the direct impact of marketing resources on equity financing, these studies do not examine the feedback impact of equity financing on future marketing spending. That is, increased marketing efforts help firms raise higher amounts of capital at the offering, but to what extent do the offering firms allocate funds raised through the offering to finance future marketing projects? We address this question below. However, before we review the studies examining the marketing–finance interface in the post-offering period, we discuss the long-run valuation impact of pre-offering marketing spending in the next section.

Marketing Strategy in the Pre-offering Period and Firm Value in the Long Run

Mizik and Jacobson (2007) argue that managers of SEO firms may actually have incentives to cut their firms' marketing expenditures during the pre-offering period, enabling them to report higher pre-offering earnings. Assuming that the stock market is not efficient in terms of seeing through this real earnings management (through reduction of marketing expenditures), SEO firms can boost their pre-SEO stock prices as a result of higher earnings, and thereby raise more capital at the offering.[4] This argument is consistent with the misvaluation hypothesis proposed by Teoh et al. (1998) and Rangan (1998), who argue that investors are misled by SEO firms' discretionary accounting practices used to report higher earnings prior to the offering. Mizik and Jacobson (2007) use a sample of 2238 SEOs issued between 1970 and 2001 to test their prediction. They find that the proportion of firms that experience unexpectedly positive earnings in the year of the SEO coupled with a decrease in marketing spending (labeled by Mizik and Jacobson as 'myopic' SEO firms) is 36.4 percent, versus 29.2 percent during non-SEO years. Furthermore, Mizik and Jacobson show that SEO firms myopically cutting their marketing spending during the pre-SEO period experience poorer stock performance in the long run (i.e., four years following the offering) when compared with SEO firms that do not decrease their marketing spending prior to the offering. In a related study, Cohen and Zarowin (2010) also find that SEO firms engage in real earnings management by reducing their discretionary expenditures (i.e., SG&A, advertising, and R&D spending) in the year of the SEO. They find that the post-SEO decline in operating performance of offering firms is more closely linked to pre-SEO cuts in discretionary expenditures than to accounting-based earnings management.

Mizik and Jacobson's (2007) finding that SEO firms myopically reduce their marketing expenditure to boost earnings in the SEO year seems to contradict Chemmanur and Yan's (2009) finding that SEO firms increase their advertising spending during the same period. This seemingly inconsistent result can be attributed to differences in the sample periods and econometric approaches employed across the two studies.[5] First, Chemmanur and Yan examine SEOs issued over the period 1990–2000, whereas Mizik and Jacobson's sample covers the period between 1970 and 2001. Thus, the firm characteristics of both samples may differ significantly (e.g., the SEO sample of the 1990s may be dominated by high-tech firms). Also, macroeconomic conditions and availability of financing differ considerably during the 1970s versus 1990s, which may impact to what extent (and in what direction) firms change their marketing spending around equity offerings. Second, while Mizik and Jacobson employ a fixed-effects multivariate time-series panel data estimation technique to identify myopic firms, Chemmanur and Yan examine yearly changes in offering firms' advertising spending as compared to their industry-size-sales-matched peers. Accordingly, Mizik and Jacobson base their conclusion on the finding that the percentage of firms experiencing an abnormal negative shock in their marketing expenditures increases significantly in the SEO year as compared to non-SEO years. However, since they do not provide mean or median change in the level of marketing expenditure (or intensity), it is not possible to directly compare their results to those of Chemmanur and Yan who report changes in the level of advertising intensity. Overall, apparent differences in the estimation and presentation of empirical results between two papers prevent us from finding a common ground to make meaningful comparison of the documented findings. However, beyond the differences in the empirical approach, the two papers are in sharp contrast in terms of theoretical background. While Mizik and Jacobson argue that managers try to fool investors who naively extrapolate pre-SEO earnings without fully adjusting for the impact of myopic management, Chemmanur and Yan maintain that managers use product market advertising to signal the true value of their firms' projects to potential investors, allowing investors to correctly price the firms' equity in the equilibrium.

Marketing Strategy in the Post-offering Period and Firm Value

Previous research has also investigated how firms use the funds obtained from equity offerings. Studies have shown that in the post-offering period, both IPO and SEO firms significantly increase their investment in physical assets such as new machines and equipment (e.g., Jain and Kini, 1994; Chemmanur et al., 2010; Fu, 2010). However, excessive capital expenditures by issuing firms can result in the deterioration of operational performance. Consistent with this view, Jain and Kini (1994) find that while IPO firms significantly increase their post-offering capital expenditures, their profitability typically declines significantly. Similarly, Chemmanur et al. (2010) show that the total factor productivity and sales growth of manufacturing firms issuing IPOs decline steadily in the years following the offering, while their capital expenditures exhibit a consistently increasing pattern over the same period.

Furthermore, Loughran and Ritter (1997) report that SEO firms have higher ratios of capital expenditures plus R&D to assets than non-issuers in the years following equity issuance. More importantly, they show that the issuers' operating performance decreases significantly following the offering. For example, the median profit margin of issuers during the post-SEO period decreases from 5.4 percent (year 0) to 3.3 percent (year +2), whereas the median profit margin of matched non-issuers decreases from 3.9 percent to 3.7 percent during the same period. More recently, Fu (2010) has shown that when an SEO firm over-invests, there is a negative relationship between the firm's investment and its operating performance. Thus, simply raising capital through IPO and SEO issues does not guarantee superior subsequent firm performance. In fact, much of this literature indicates the opposite.

Recently, researchers have examined whether firms that raise equity increase their investments in marketing during the post-offering period (Grullon et al., 2006; Kurt and Hulland, 2010). Grullon et al. (2006) find that firms significantly increase their advertising spending after they decrease their financial leverage through equity financing. However, in their study, the source of equity financing (i.e., IPO or SEO) is not specified as they identify their sample firms through investigation of Compustat firms that have altered their capital structure with a significant change in net financing (i.e., equity issuance net of repurchases plus debt issuance net of debt retirements divided by total assets). Their study also does not examine how post-offering changes in marketing strategy affect firm value. A recent study by Kurt and Hulland (2010) addresses these questions. The authors report that both IPO and SEO firms significantly increase their marketing expenditures (relative to their industry peers) in the two years following the offering, though this effect is more pronounced in the case of IPO firms. They also find that enhanced marketing efforts of IPO and SEO firms dissipate after these initial two years.

More importantly, Kurt and Hulland (2010) examine investors' responses to increased marketing efforts of offering firms. Theories of market-based assets (Srivastava et al., 1998) and customer equity (Rust et al., 2004) suggest that increased marketing spending helps firms generate valuable assets such as strong brands and loyal customers, creating entry and switching barriers. Marketing activities can also help firms increase their value by enhancing cash flows, accelerating the receipt of cash flows, and reducing firm vulnerability to cash flow variability (Srivastava et al., 1999). In addition to both larger margins and more rapid cash flow, past work also suggests that marketing can have a direct and positive effect on productivity (Rao and Bharadwaj, 2008) and stock market returns (Srinivasan et al., 2009; Joshi and Hanssens, 2010). However, extending previous studies, Kurt and Hulland (2010) propose that the impact of marketing on firm value is heterogeneous across firms and market situations. They maintain that the post-offering period is potentially different from non-offering periods, for several reasons. First, equity offerings, particularly IPOs, can signal a change in the outlook of an industry as a whole, leading to increased investor attention for both issuers and their rivals (Akhigbe et al., 2003). Second, equity issuing firms raise significant amounts of cash that can be used to finance new projects and thus gain a temporary competitive advantage over rivals (Hsu et al., 2010). Third, an equity offering recapitalizes the firm in a way that significantly decreases its debt-to-equity ratio, leading to a major and rapid shift in its relative financial leverage versus rivals.

Furthermore, Kurt and Hulland (2010) maintain that not all firms are expected to benefit from pursuing an aggressive marketing strategy follow-ing equity issuance. They argue that the capital structure of offering firms relative to their industry rivals moderates the link between firms' market-ing expenditures and financial performance. Specifically, they propose that marketing expenditures result in higher firm value for issuing firms facing industry rivals with relatively high financial leverage (i.e., they have a high percentage of debt versus equity financing in their capital structures), but not for those facing rivals with relatively low leverage. They built their prediction on both the theoretical and empirical literature that examines the link between firms' financial strength and product market behavior (e.g., Telser, 1966; Bolton and Scharfstein, 1990; Chevalier, 1995; Phillips, 1995; Fresard, 2010). Using datasets of 1581 IPOs and 1729 SEOs issued between 1970 and 2004, Kurt and Hulland find that the stock market reacts favorably to an aggressive marketing strategy initiated by issuers competing against relatively highly leveraged rivals, whereas increased marketing expenditures do not translate into higher firm value when rivals are less leveraged. Consistent with their conjecture, the authors also show that the interactive influence of marketing expenditures and relative finan-cial leverage of rivals on firm value is more pronounced in the two-year period immediately following an offering than in other periods.

The Role of Firms' and Their Rivals' Corporate Financial Policy

As shown by Kurt and Hulland (2010), the capital structure of firms relative to their industry peers is a significant moderator of the link between marketing actions and firm value. Thus, in this section, we briefly review the literature on capital structure, financial strength, and product market competition. We believe this stream of literature is of significant importance to researchers studying the marketing–finance interface. As Srivastava et al. (1998, p. 2) point out: 'market-based assets arise from the commingling of the firm with entities in its external environment.'

The connection between financial markets and product markets has been extensively studied in the finance literature (e.g., Bolton and Scharfstein, 1990; Chevalier, 1995; Phillips, 1995; Campello, 2006; Matsa, 2009). Telser's (1966) 'long-purse' theory of predation describes how cash-rich firms drive their financially weak competitors out of the market by adopting aggressive product market strategies that reduce competitors' cash flows. Relatedly, Bolton and Scharfstein (1990) argue that financial constraints imposed on rival firms (by their external financiers) encour-age deep-pocketed firms to engage in predatory behavior and force these financially weak rivals out of business.

A number of studies provide empirical support for the 'long-purse' argument. For instance, Chevalier (1995) finds that highly leveraged supermarkets compete less aggressively and are subject to aggressive competitive behavior (e.g., market expansion) by less leveraged firms. In a related study, Khanna and Tice (2000) find that large and more profitable firms (versus highly leveraged firms) respond more aggressively (i.e., invest more) to the entry of Wal-Mart as a competitor. Furthermore, Phillips (1995) shows that leveraged recapitalization (i.e., changing capital structure by significantly increasing debt) of the leading firm in an industry leads to softened product market competition (in the form of higher industry prices and decreased industry output). Kovenock and Phillips (1997) also find that a firm is more likely to close plants and less likely to make major new investments following leveraged recapitalization. Recently, Fresard (2010) documents that firms with larger cash reserves relative to their rivals experience systematic future market share gains at the expense of their rivals and that this effect is more pronounced when rivals face tighter financing constraints.

This limited competitive ability of highly leveraged firms stems in part from the fact that they are often cash constrained because they must use funds generated from operations to service their debt loads. As a result, highly leveraged firms can find themselves in a situation where they must limit their investment, cut discretionary expenses, and reduce the quality of their products and services. For instance, Matsa (2009) finds that high leverage and limited corporate liquidity are associated with more frequent stockouts and lower product quality in the supermarket industry.

Even in situations where expenses do not need to be cut, high-leverage firms are often constrained in their ability to raise additional debt capital since they have already used most of the credit lines available to them. In addition, their cost of equity is high due to increased riskiness associated with large debt on their balance sheet, limiting their access to equity financing. Furthermore, highly leveraged firms may be reluctant to make major marketing investments due to the intangible and non-transferable nature of marketing assets (Srivastava et al., 1998; Grullon et al., 2006). Since marketing assets cannot be liquidated in the case of financial distress (or bankruptcy) and since leverage increases the probability of financial distress, highly leveraged firms are more likely to limit their marketing expenditures.

METHODOLOGICAL ISSUES

This section briefly discusses the methodological issues that need to be taken into account while conducting research on the marketing–finance interface around corporate financing events. (For a broader review of related methodological issues, see Mitchell and Stafford, 2000; Kothari and Warner, 2007; Srinivasan and Hanssens, 2009.) Our review focuses on two main issues: (1) measuring marketing investments and (2) measuring changes in firm value.

Measuring Marketing Investments

Previous studies have primarily used one of two measures as a proxy for firms' investments in marketing (i.e., selling, general, and administrative [SG&A] expenditure minus R&D expenditure, or advertising expenditure), both constructed using data obtained from the Compustat database. The first measure – SG&A expenditure minus R&D expenditure (scaled by total assets or sales) – has been commonly employed in the literature (Mizik and Jacobson, 2007; Luo, 2008; Kurt and Hulland, 2010). However, the main disadvantage of this measure is that it includes non-marketing expenses such as general overhead and legal expenditures. The second measure – advertising expenditure (scaled by total assets or sales) – is a less coarse measure of investment in marketing. However, this measure may underestimate firms' marketing efforts as it does not include marketing expense items such as sales force expenditures and promotions. Furthermore, this item is available for a smaller number of firms in Compustat than are the SG&A and R&D items.

The issue of whether researchers should use the observed level of expenditures or the (unanticipated) change in marketing expenditures as the independent variable in their models depends on the nature of the dependent variable under study (e.g., equity underpricing, trading volume, abnormal stock return). For instance, Luo (2008) and Chemmenur and Yan (2009) use the level of marketing and advertising intensity, respectively, in their models examining the cross-sectional determinants of equity underpricing.[6] On the other hand, researchers who examine the impact of marketing on stock return performance need to adjust their marketing expenditure measures so as to reflect unanticipated changes in firms' marketing strategy. This is because, as implied by the efficient markets hypothesis (Fama, 1970, 1991), the stock market reacts only to unexpected information and thus, independent variables predicting changes in stock returns should reflect unanticipated changes. Previous research (Mizik and Jacobson, 2007; Mizik, 2010; Kurt and Hulland, 2010) suggests two main ways in which unanticipated changes in firms' marketing expenditures can be calculated: (1) using a time-series estimation approach (e.g., first-order autoregressive model) and (2) using a cross-sectional estimation approach model.

Under the time-series approach, researchers usually estimate the following first-order autoregressive model using panel data (with all the available firm-year observations), and then use the residuals obtained from the model as a measure of unanticipated marketing expenditures of sample firms:

$$MKT_{it} = \beta_0 + \beta_1 MKT_{it-1} + \eta_{it} \qquad (10.1)$$

where, MKT_{it} is the marketing intensity (e.g., marketing expenditure divided by total assets) for firm i in year t; β_1 is the first-order autoregressive coefficient indicating the persistence of marketing expenditure intensity. Although not shown in equation (10.1), this model can be augmented with year and industry dummies to control for year- and industry-specific effects. Unanticipated change in marketing intensity is calculated by subtracting the estimated level of marketing intensity (i.e., $\hat{\beta}_1 * MKT_{it-1}$) from the actual level of marketing intensity (i.e., MKT_{it}).

However, as noted by Mizik (2010), in the presence of fixed effects (i.e., using panel data), the estimated coefficient on MKT_{it-1} will be biased. She suggests applying the Anderson and Hsiao (1982) procedure, which involves first-differencing demeaned variables and then using instruments for the first-differenced MKT_{it-1} measure to obtain consistent estimates. However, this procedure requires the use of MKT_{it-2} and MKT_{it-3} to create an instrument for the first-differenced MKT_{it-1}. In the case of IPOs (but not SEOs), applying this procedure for the pre-IPO and immediate post-IPO period is not possible since accounting/marketing data for most IPO firms are not available in the years preceding the IPO year. An alternative method to the instrumental variable approach is to estimate the first-order autoregressive model by using firm fixed effects (e.g., Flannery and Rangan, 2006). This method involves adding a dummy variable to equation (10.1) for each firm in the sample to control for firm-specific factors.

The cross-sectional approach is also commonly employed in the literature (e.g., Roychowdhury, 2006; Cohen and Zarowin, 2010; Kurt and Hulland, 2010). Under this approach, the 'normal' level of marketing expenditures can be expressed as a linear function of lagged sales and scaled lagged assets:

$$MKT_{it} = \beta_0 + \beta_1 \frac{1}{Assets_{i,t-1}} + \beta_2 \frac{Sales_{i,t-1}}{Assets_{i,t-1}} + v_{it} \qquad (10.2)$$

For each year, equation (10.2) is estimated for each industry (generally classified using two-digit SIC codes) using observations for all the firms in that industry. These estimations generate industry-specific betas that vary across time. The 'normal' level of marketing expenditure (*NMKT*) for each firm is then calculated as follows:

$$NMKT_{it} = \hat{\beta}_0 + \hat{\beta}_1 \frac{1}{Assets_{i,t-1}} + \hat{\beta}_2 \frac{Sales_{i,t-1}}{Assets_{i,t-1}} \qquad (10.3)$$

Finally, the unanticipated change in marketing expenditure is the difference between actual marketing expenditure in year t and the fitted 'normal' marketing expenditure for the same year (i.e., $U\Delta MKT_{it} = MKT_{it} - NMKT_{it}$).

Measuring Changes in Firm Value

Researchers who examine the valuation impact of marketing actions often use abnormal stock returns (i.e., realized return minus expected return) as a measure of changes in firm value.[7] Previous literature suggests a number of ways to calculate abnormal stock returns and discusses the advantages/disadvantages of these alternative methods (e.g., Barber and Lyon, 1997; Kothari and Warner, 1997; Lyon et al., 1999; Mitchell and Stafford, 2000). Our goal is not to provide an in-depth review of each method used in the literature. Rather, we summarize the methods employed by researchers who have examined the marketing–finance interface around corporate financing decisions and provide a methodological guideline for future studies on this topic.[8]

The reference portfolio approach (e.g., market index, size, and book-to-market decile portfolios), the matched control firm approach, the Fama and French (1993) three-factor model, and the Carhart (1997) four-factor model are all commonly used to measure abnormal stock return performance. Under the reference portfolio approach, an abnormal stock return is defined as the difference between the firm's realized return in a given time period minus the return on its respective reference portfolio for the same period. For instance, Kurt and Hulland (2010) calculate the market-adjusted abnormal stock return as follows. First, for each firm, they calculate the annual stock return for a given year following the equity offering by compounding the monthly stock returns for 12 months. They then subtract the corresponding annual market return (i.e., the CRSP NYSE/AMEX/NASDAQ value-weighted market index) from this computed value to obtain abnormal stock returns.

However, it is important to note that using the reference portfolio approach may yield test statistics that are severely mis-specified over longer time horizons (e.g., 60 months). Accordingly, Mizik and Jacobson (2007) – who examine the impact of pre-SEO changes in marketing expenditures on long-run financial performance – use a size and book-to-market matched control firm approach. Under this approach, each event firm is matched to a non-event control firm with similar pre-event size and book-to-market characteristics. The abnormal stock return for the event firms is then calculated by subtracting the stock return of the control firm for a given period from that of the event firm. The main disadvantage of this approach is that it does not take into account the cross-sectional dependence in sample observations, which may again lead to poorly specified test statistics.

To correct for potential problems associated with the cross-sectional dependence, researchers also use the calendar-time portfolio approach (e.g., Sorescu et al., 2007; Jacobson and Mizik, 2009; Kurt and Hulland, 2010). This approach, first introduced by Mandelker (1974) and Jaffe (1974), was designed to mitigate potential inference problems arising from measuring abnormal returns for events clustered in time. Since, under this approach, the standard errors of the abnormal return estimates of portfolios are calculated using inter-temporal variation of monthly stock returns rather than cross-sectional variance, and given that monthly stock returns are not serially correlated (Campbell et al., 1997), the calendar-time portfolio methodology is well-specified and statistical inferences are more accurate. However, as pointed out by Jacobson and Mizik (2009), the calendar-time portfolio approach overlooks the fact that the portfolio risk factor loadings may change over time. Thus, they propose a time-varying portfolio approach and outline the details of this estimation procedure in their study.

MANAGERIAL IMPLICATIONS AND A RESEARCH AGENDA

Managerial Implications

The framework summarized in Figure 10.1 represents a starting point for managers considering how to best finance their firms' investments in marketing, or debating how to most effectively use funds raised through IPOs or SEOs. The preceding review suggests that equity funds are often used most effectively – at least in part – to invest in intangible marketing assets. Furthermore, the framework points to the important moderating effect of relative leverage of industry rivals on the linkage between offering firms' marketing investments and subsequent financial performance.

The value-increasing role of marketing investments around equity offerings
Increased investments in marketing during the period prior to an equity offering can help firms enhance their trading volumes on the day of the offering (Luo, 2008) and underprice their equity less (Luo, 2008; Chemmanur and Yan, 2009), enabling them to raise higher amounts of capital. Conversely, attempts by offering firms to manipulate earnings in the pre-issue period by cutting marketing expenditures have been shown to have a negative impact on long-term stock return performance (Mizik and Jacobson, 2007). These results point to the importance of continued strong marketing effort and investment in the pre-offering period.

Once funds are received from IPO and/or SEO issues, substantial past work in the finance field shows that firms' operational performances are likely to diminish due to inefficient investments made (in physical assets) with the raised capital. However, Kurt and Hulland (2010) show that firms that allocate IPO/SEO funds to adopt a more aggressive marketing strategy enhance their post-offering financial performance, though this effect is not observed for those firms facing relatively less leveraged industry rivals. Thus, offering firms need to understand that investing capital raised through IPOs and SEOs solely in physical assets (e.g., new plant, new stores, machinery, and equipment) is likely to have a detrimental impact on firm value. However, allocating a sufficiently large portion of these proceeds to marketing resources may result in a more positive investor reaction during the post-offering period.

The importance of relative financial leverage
Recognizing the above, managers must also be aware that increased marketing spending does not unconditionally have a positive impact on firm value. In the case of issuers competing against relatively less leveraged rivals, unwise use of marketing capital can erode or even destroy shareholder value. Findings from Kurt and Hulland (2010) suggest that issuers' aggressive marketing strategies backfire when their rivals have higher financial flexibility and a motivation to respond. Furthermore, managers need to recognize that the impact of marketing spending depends on market conditions. That is, the positive effects of increased marketing spending are greatest in the two-year period immediately following equity issuance than at other times. The reasons for this are several. First, equity offerings (especially IPOs) result in heightened investor attention. Second, because equity offerings significantly deleverage issuers and generate large amount of funds in a short period of time, they enhance the competitive position of issuers over rivals. However, this competitive advantage of issuers does not last forever, and dissipates relatively quickly as the

offering proceeds are depleted. As a result, managers must act quickly if they want to take advantage of this opportunity.

A Research Agenda

Our proposed framework (Figure 10.1) suggests that marketing investment decisions and capital structure decisions are intertwined. This is a rich area of research inquiry that to date has received limited attention from marketing researchers. Although previous studies have started to enhance our understanding of the interaction between marketing and finance around equity offerings, how these two management functions interact around other forms of corporate financing events (e.g., debt offerings, leveraged buyouts) is not known.

IPOs and SEOs – the focus of this chapter – are leverage-decreasing financing events. It would be interesting to examine how leverage-increasing events such as debt offerings (capital inflow) or share repurchases (capital outflow) affect marketing strategy and how investors respond to changes in firms' marketing expenditures around these events. Recently, Anderson and Mansi (2009) examined whether firms' customer satisfaction ratings impact their credit ratings and cost of debt financing. They found that lower customer satisfaction is associated with lower credit ratings and a higher cost of debt financing. However, their study does not examine whether firms that raise debt capital change their marketing investments around the debt offering and the valuation impact, if any, of these changes. Relatedly, leveraged buyouts (LBOs) also provide an interesting setting within which to examine the marketing–finance interface, since by using LBOs, public companies become privately owned entities, and thereby lose the benefits gained via IPOs, including public recognition and investor attention. In addition, LBOs are heavily debt-financed and therefore represent an extreme example of a leverage-increasing event. One might wonder why firms would go private and forego the benefits of being a publicly traded company. Previous research (e.g., Lehn and Poulsen, 1989; Fox and Marcus, 1992) suggests that successful LBOs provide several benefits including reduced incentives for wasteful spending, lower agency costs, and increased efficiency/profitability. Another advantage of being private is not having to file reports with the Securities and Exchange Commission (SEC). Relatedly, although researchers' ability to collect marketing and accounting data during the post-LBO period is limited as LBO firms discontinue public disclosures of company information, they can still examine the valuation impact of changes in marketing expenditures prior to the LBO. Furthermore, many LBO firms return to the equity markets in subsequent years. The financial reports of these 'reverse LBOs' may allow researchers to extend their analysis to the post-LBO period as well.

Share repurchases also provide an interesting setting to examine the marketing–finance interface. One of the most commonly cited reasons for share repurchases is the signaling to the market of an undervaluation of firms' equity (e.g., Lakonishok and Vermaelen, 1990; Comment and Jarrell, 1991). Previous research (e.g., Louis and White, 2007) document that managers sometimes use discretionary accounting practices to supplement this undervaluation signal conveyed through the repurchase. One related question for marketing researchers is whether managers use marketing resources (e.g., advertising expenditures) around share repurchases to reinforce the undervaluation signal sent to investors. If this is the case, one would expect to see that repurchasing firms increase their marketing expenditures prior to the repurchase. However, if managers are concerned with minimizing the cost of repurchase (as well as generating additional funds to finance the repurchase) rather than signaling undervaluation, they may be inclined to cut marketing expenditures prior to the repurchase. Future research should explore these questions, which would enhance our understanding of the interaction between marketing and finance resources around corporate financing events.

CONCLUSION

Luo (2008) has proposed that marketing researchers need to develop and use a 'contingency theory of marketing–finance interface' that goes beyond looking at simple main effects. He notes (p. 107) that 'to date the extant literature in the marketing–finance interface seems to have paid scant attention to moderated relationships.' The framework proposed here explicitly incorporates both corporate financial policy and competitors' financing policies (in the form of relative financial leverage). If marketing wants to share meaningfully in boardroom discussions and to guide corporate investment decisions, it will be crucial for researchers to gain a better understanding of the nature of the links between the constructs in our framework.

NOTES

1. Gatchev et al. (2009) demonstrate that firms prefer equity financing over debt financing to fund their investments in advertising. Specifically, to finance a $1 investment in

advertising (or R&D), firms in their sample issued $0.80 of equity, whereas debt issuance represented only $0.20 of the financing package.
2. There is a large body of finance literature on IPOs and SEOs (for reviews see Ritter, 2003; Eckbo et al., 2007). It is beyond the scope of this chapter to review this broad literature, as we focus on only IPO/SEO studies examining the link between marketing and equity financing. Furthermore, our review excludes studies focusing on investment bankers' efforts to market the offerings that they undertake (e.g., Cook et al., 2006; Gao and Ritter, 2010).
3. Retrieved from Jay Ritter's website on 16 July, 2010: http://bear.warrington.ufl.edu/ritter/IPOs2009Factoids.pdf.
4. However, this argument ignores the possibility that lower marketing expenditures are associated with lower offering price (Luo, 2008; Chemmanur and Yan, 2009), which in turn reduces the amount of capital raised by the firm.
5. Mizik and Jacobson (2007) note that they obtain similar results when they use advertising spending instead of marketing spending in their analyses, suggesting that the inconsistency of results documented by the two studies cannot be attributed to the fact that they use different empirical measures.
6. Luo (2008) also tests the robustness of his results by examining the link between changes in pre-IPO marketing expenditures and underpricing (as well as trading volume).
7. As an alternative, researchers also use Tobin's Q (i.e., the ratio of the market value of the firm to the replacement cost of its assets; see Srinivasan and Hanssens, 2009 for a review), although this metric is not suitable for studies examining the valuation impact of discrete events (e.g., new product announcement). Jacobson and Mizik (2009) provide a detailed discussion of problems associated with working with Tobin's Q instead of stock returns.
8. Luo (2008) does not use abnormal stock returns as a dependent variable in his study. Rather, he uses two new metrics: equity underpricing and trading volume on the day of the offering.

REFERENCES

Akhigbe, Aigbe, Stephen F. Borde, and Ann Marie White (2003), 'Does an Industry Effect Exist for Initial Public Offerings,' *Financial Review*, **38** (4), 531–51.
Altinkilic, Oya and Robert Hansen (2003), 'Discounting and Underpricing in Seasoned Equity Offers,' *Journal of Financial Economics*, **69** (2), 285–323.
Anderson, Eugene W. and Sattar A. Mansi (2009), 'Does Customer Satisfaction Matter to Investors? Findings from the Bond Market,' *Journal of Marketing Research*, **46** (5), 703–14.
Anderson, T.W. and Cheng Hsiao (1982), 'Formulation and Estimation of Dynamic Models Using Panel Data,' *Journal of Econometrics*, **18** (1), 47–82.
Bahadir, S. Cem, Sundar G. Bharadwaj, and Rajendra K. Srivastava (2008), 'Financial Value of Brands in Mergers and Acquisitions: Is Value in the Eye of the Beholder?,' *Journal of Marketing*, **72** (6), 49–64.
Barber, Brad M. and John D. Lyon (1997), 'Detecting Long-run Abnormal Stock Returns: The Empirical Power and Specification of Test Statistics,' *Journal of Financial Economics*, **43** (3), 341–72.
Bolton, Patrick and David S. Scharfstein (1990), 'A Theory of Predation Based on Agency Problems in Financial Contracting,' *American Economic Review*, **80** (1), 93–106.
Brav, Alon, Christopher Geczy, and Paul A. Gompers (2000), 'Is the Abnormal Return Following Equity Issuances Anomalous?' *Journal of Financial Economics*, **56** (2), 209–49.
Brown, Stephen W., Frederick E. Webster Jr., Jan-Benedict E.M. Steenkamp, William L.

Wilkie, Jagdish N. Sheth, Rajendra S. Sisodia, et al. (2005), 'Marketing Renaissance: Opportunities and Imperatives for Improving Marketing Thought, Practice, and Infrastructure,' *Journal of Marketing*, **69** (4), 1–25.

Campbell, John Y., Andrew W. Lo, and A. Craig MacKinlay (1997), *The Econometrics of Financial Markets*, Princeton, NJ: Princeton University Press.

Campello, Murillo (2006), 'Debt Financing: Does it Boost or Hurt Firm Performance in Product Markets?' *Journal of Financial Economics*, **82** (1), 135–72.

Carhart, Mark M. (1997), 'On the Persistence in Mutual Fund Performance,' *Journal of Finance*, **52** (1), 57–82.

Chemmanur, Thomas and Paolo Fulghieri (1999), 'A Theory of the Going-public Decision,' *Review of Financial Studies*, **12** (2), 249–79.

Chemmanur, Thomas and An Yan (2009), 'Product Market Advertising and New Equity Issues,' *Journal of Financial Economics*, **92** (1), 40–65.

Chemmanur, Thomas, Shan He, and Debarshi K. Nandy (2010), 'The Going-public Decision and the Product Market,' *Review of Financial Studies*, **23** (5), 1855–908.

Chevalier, Judith A. (1995), 'Capital Structure and Product-market Competition: Empirical Evidence from the Supermarket Industry,' *American Economic Review*, **85** (3), 415–35.

Cohen, Daniel A. and Paul Zarowin (2010), 'Accrual-based and Real Earnings Management Activities Around Seasoned Equity Offerings,' *Journal of Accounting and Economics*, **50** (1), 2–19.

Comment, Robert and Gregg A. Jarrell (1991), 'The Relative Signalling Power of Dutch-auction and Fixed-price Self-tender Offers and Open-market Share Repurchases,' *Journal of Finance*, **46** (4), 1243–71.

Cook, Douglas O., Robert Kieschnick, and Robert A. Van Ness (2006), 'On the Marketing of IPOs,' *Journal of Financial Economics*, **82** (1), 35–61.

Corwin, Shena (2003), 'The Determinants of Underpricing of Seasoned Equity Offers,' *Journal of Finance*, **58** (5), 2249–79.

Eckbo, B. Espen, Ronald W. Masulis, and Oyvind Norli (2007), 'Security Offerings,' in B. Espen Eckbo (ed.), *Handbook of Corporate Finance: Empirical Corporate Finance*, Vol. 1, Amsterdam: Elsevier-North-Holland.

Fama, Eugene F. (1970), 'Efficient Capital Markets: A Review of Theory and Empirical Work,' *Journal of Finance*, **25** (2), 383–417.

Fama, Eugene F. (1991), 'Efficient Capital Markets II,' *Journal of Finance*, **46** (5), 1575–617.

Fama, Eugene F. and Kenneth R. French (1993), 'Common Risk Factors in Returns to Stocks and Bonds,' *Journal of Financial Economics*, **33** (1), 3–56.

Flannery, Mark J. and Kasturi P. Rangan (2006), 'Partial Adjustment Toward Target Capital Structures,' *Journal of Financial Economics*, **79** (3), 469–506.

Fresard, Laurent (2010), 'Financial Strength and Product Market Behavior: The Real Effects of Corporate Cash Holdings,' *Journal of Finance*, **65** (3), 1097–122.

Fox, Isaac and Alfred Marcus (1992), 'The Causes and Consequences of Leveraged Management Buyouts,' *The Academy of Management Review*, **17** (1), 62–85.

Fu, Fangjian (2010), 'Overinvestment and the Operating Performance of SEO Firms,' *Financial Management*, **39** (1), 249–72.

Gao, Xiaohui and Jay R. Ritter (2010), 'The Marketing of Seasoned Equity Offerings,' *Journal of Financial Economics*, **97** (1), 33–52.

Garmaise, Mark J. (2009), 'Marketing Issues in Corporate Finance,' *Journal of Marketing Reaearch*, **46** (3), 324–6.

Gatchev, Vladimir, Paul A. Spindt, and Vefa Tarhan (2009), 'How Do Firms Finance Their Investments? The Relative Importance of Equity Issuance and Debt Contracting Costs,' *Journal of Corporate Finance*, **15** (2), 179–95.

Gruca, Thomas S. and Lopo L. Rego (2005), 'Customer Satisfaction, Cash Flow, and Shareholder Value,' *Journal of Marketing*, **69** (3), 115–30.

Grullon, Gustavo, George Kanatas, and Piyush Kumar (2006), 'The Impact of Capital

Structure on Advertising Competition: An Empirical Study,' *Journal of Business*, **79** (6), 3101–24.

Hsu, Hung-Chia, Adam V. Reed, and Jorg Rocholl (2010), 'The New Game in Town: Competitive Effects of IPOs,' *Journal of Finance*, **65** (2), 495–528.

Jacobson, Robert and Natalie Mizik (2009), 'The Financial Markets and Customer Satisfaction: Reexamining Possible Financial Market Mispricing of Customer Satisfaction,' *Marketing Science*, **28** (5), 809–18.

Jaffe, Jeffrey F. (1974), 'Special Information and Insider Trading,' *Journal of Business*, **47** (3), 410–28.

Jain, Bharat A. and Omesh Kini (1994), 'The Post-issue Operating Performance of IPO Firms,' *Journal of Finance*, **49** (5), 1699–726.

Joshi, Amit M. and Dominique M. Hanssens (2009), 'Movie Advertising and the Stock Market Valuation of Studios: A Case of "Great Expectations?"' *Marketing Science*, **28** (2), 239–50.

Joshi, Amit M. and Dominique M. Hanssens (2010), 'The Direct and Indirect Effects of Advertising Spending on Firm Value,' *Journal of Marketing*, **74** (3), 20–33.

Khanna, Naveen and Sheri Tice (2000), 'Strategic Responses of Incumbents to New Entry: The Effect of Ownership Structure, Capital Structure and Focus,' *Review of Financial Studies*, **13** (3), 749–79.

Kothari, S.P. and Jerold B. Warner (1997), 'Measuring Long-horizon Security Performance,' *Journal of Financial Economics*, **43** (3), 301–39.

Kothari, S.P. and Jerold B. Warner (2007), 'Econometrics of Event Studies,' in B. Espen Eckbo (ed.), *Handbook of Corporate Finance: Empirical Corporate Finance*, Vol. 1, Amsterdam: Elsevier-North-Holland, pp. 3–36.

Kovenock, Dan and Gordon M. Phillips (1997), 'Capital Structure and Product Market Behavior: An Examination of Plant Exit and Investment Decision,' *Review of Financial Studies*, **10** (3), 767–803.

Kurt, Didem and John Hulland (2010), 'Changing the Rules of the Game: The Impact of Firm Value of Adopting an Aggressive Marketing Strategy Following Equity Offerings,' Working Paper, Katz Graduate School of Business, University of Pittsburgh.

Lakonishok, Josef and Theo Vermaelen (1990), 'Anomalous Price Behavior Around Repurchase Tender Offers,' *Journal of Finance*, **45** (2), 455–77.

Lehn, Kenneth and Annette Poulsen (1989), 'Free Cash Flow and Stockholder Gains in Going Private Transactions,' *Journal of Finance*, **44** (3), 771–87.

Loughran, Timothy and Jay Ritter (1997), 'The Operating Performance of Firms Conducting Seasoned Equity Offerings,' *Journal of Finance*, **52** (5), 1823–50.

Louis, Henock and Hal White (2007), 'Do Managers Intentionally Use Repurchase Tender Offers to Signal Private Information? Evidence from Firm Financial Reporting Behavior,' *Journal of Financial Economics*, **85**, 205–33.

Luo, Xueming (2008), 'When Marketing Strategy First Meets Wall Street: Marketing Spendings and Firms' Initial Public Offerings (IPOs),' *Journal of Marketing*, **72** (5), 98–109.

Luo, Xueming (2009), 'Quantifying the Long-term Impact of Negative Word of Mouth on Cash Flows and Stock Prices,' *Marketing Science*, **28** (1), 148–65.

Lyandres, Evgeny, Le Sun, and Lu Zhang (2008), 'The New Issues Puzzle: Testing the Investment-based Explanation,' *Review of Financial Studies*, **20** (6), 2825–55.

Lyon, John D., Brad M. Barber, and Chih-Ling Tsai (1999), 'Improved Methods for Tests of Long-run Abnormal Stock Returns,' *Journal of Finance*, **54** (1), 165–201.

Mandelker, Gershon (1974), 'Risk and Return: The Case of Merging Firms,' *Journal of Financial Economics*, **1** (4), 303–35.

Matsa, David A. (2009), 'Running on Empty? Financial Leverage and Product Quality in the Supermarket Industry,' Working Paper, available at SSRN: http://ssrn.com/abstract=970790; accessed 9 December 2011.

Mitchell, Mark L. and Erik Stafford (2000), 'Managerial Decisions and Long-term Stock Performance,' *Journal of Business*, **73** (3), 287–329.

Mizik, Natalie (2010), 'The Theory and Practice of Myopic Management,' *Journal of Marketing Research*, **47** (4), 594–611.

Mizik, Natalie and Robert Jacobson (2007), 'Myopic Marketing Management: Evidence of the Phenomenon and its Long-term Performance Consequences in the SEO Context,' *Marketing Science*, **26** (3), 361–79.

Mizik, Natalie and Robert Jacobson (2008), 'The Financial Value Impact of Perceptual Brand Attributes,' *Journal of Marketing Research*, **45** (1), 15–32.

Nath, Pravin and Vijay Mahajan (2008), 'Chief Marketing Officers: A Study of Their Presence in Firms' Top Management Teams,' *Journal of Marketing*, **72** (1), 65–81.

Pauwels, Koen, Jorge Silva-Risso, Shuba Srinivasan, and Dominique M. Hanssens (2004), 'New Products, Sales Promotions and Firm Value, with Application to the Automobile Industry,' *Journal of Marketing*, **68** (4), 142–56.

Phillips, Gordon M. (1995), 'Increased Debt and Industry Product Markets: An Empirical Analysis,' *Journal of Financial Economics*, **37** (2), 189–238.

Rangan, S. (1998), 'Earnings Management and the Performance of Seasoned Equity Offerings,' *Journal of Financial Economics*, **50** (1), 101–22.

Rao, Ramesh K.S. and Neeraj Bharadwaj (2008), 'Marketing Initiatives, Expected Cash Flows, and Shareholders' Wealth,' *Journal of Marketing*, **72** (1), 16–26.

Ritter, Jay (1991), 'The Long-run Performance of Initial Public Offerings,' *Journal of Finance*, **46** (1), 3–27.

Ritter, Jay R. (2003), 'Investment Banking and Securities Issuance,' in George Constantinides, Milton Harris, and Rene Stulz (eds), *Handbook of the Economics of Finance*, Amsterdam: North-Holland, pp. 253–304.

Ritter, Jay R. and Ivo Welch (2002), 'A Review of IPO Activity, Pricing, and Allocations,' *Journal of Finance*, **57** (4), 1795–828.

Roychowdhury, Sugata (2006), 'Earnings Management Through Real Activities Manipulation,' *Journal of Accounting and Economics*, **42** (3), 335–70.

Rust, Roland T., Tim Ambler, Gregory S. Carpenter, V. Kumar, and Rajendra K. Srivastava (2004), 'Measuring Marketing Productivity: Current Knowledge and Future Directions,' *Journal of Marketing*, **68** (4), 76–89.

Sheth, Jagdish N. and Rajendra S. Sisodia (2006), *Does Marketing Need Reform? Fresh Perspectives on the Future*, Armonk, NY: M.E. Sharpe.

Sorescu, Alina, Venkatesh Shankar, and Tarun Kushwaha (2007), 'New Product Preannouncements and Shareholder Value: Don't Make Promises You Can't Keep,' *Journal of Marketing Research*, **44** (3), 468–89.

Spiess, Katherine D. and J. Affleck-Graves (1995), 'Underperformance in Long-run Stock Returns Following Seasoned Equity Offerings,' *Journal of Financial Economics*, **38** (3), 243–67.

Srinivasan, Shuba, and Dominique M. Hanssens (2009), 'Marketing and Firm Value: Metrics, Methods, Findings, and Future Directions,' *Journal of Marketing Research*, **46** (3), 293–312.

Srinivasan, Shuba, Koen Pauwels, Jorge Silva-Risso and Dominique M. Hanssens (2009), 'Product Innovations, Advertising and Stock Returns,' *Journal of Marketing*, **73** (1), 24–43.

Srivastava, Rajendra K., Tasadduq A. Shervani, and Liam Fahey (1998), 'Market-based Assets and Shareholder Value: A Framework for Analysis,' *Journal of Marketing*, **62** (1), 2–18.

Srivastava, Rajendra K., Tasadduq A. Shervani, and Liam Fahey (1999), 'Marketing, Business Processes and Shareholder Value: An Organizationally Embedded View of Marketing Activities and the Discipline of Marketing,' *Journal of Marketing*, **63** (Special Issue), 168–79.

Swaminathan, Vanitha, Feisal Murshed, and John Hulland (2008), 'Value Creation Following Merger and Acquisition Announcements: The Role of Strategic Emphasis Alignment,' *Journal of Marketing Research*, **45** (1), 33–47.

Telser, Lester G. (1966), 'Cutthroat Competition and the Long Purse,' *Journal of Law and Economics*, **9** (2), 259–77.

Teoh, Siew Hong, Ivo Welch, and T.J. Wong (1998), 'Earnings Management and the Underperformance of Seasoned Equity Offerings,' *Journal of Financial Economics*, **50** (1), 63–99.
Verhoef, Peter C. and Peter S.H. Leeflang (2009), 'Understanding the Marketing Department's Influence Within the Firm,' *Journal of Marketing*, **73** (2), 14–37.
Webster, Frederick E., Alan J. Malter, and Shankar Ganesan (2005), 'The Decline and Dispersion of Marketing Competence,' *MIT Sloan Management Review*, **46** (6), 35–43.

PART III

MARKETING ACTIONS AND VALUE DESTRUCTION

11 Putting the cart before the horse: short-term performance concerns as drivers of marketing-related investments
Anindita Chakravarty and Rajdeep Grewal

The year 2002 was recognized as a time of far-reaching corporate reform, with the enactment of the Sarbanes-Oxley Act on 30 July (Pub. L. 107-204, 116 Stat. 745). The act was designed to protect investors by tightening accounting standards and reducing management flexibility with regard to reporting of financial metrics. Cohen et al. (2011) suggest that since 2002, accounting report credibility has increased, and the practice of exploiting accounting methods (or accrual-based earnings management) to misrepresent actual performance has declined.

However, post–Sarbanes-Oxley, such accounting-based earnings management practices have been substituted for a gradual rise in a tactic called real activities management (REAM) that is of direct concern to marketing professionals and academics (Schipper, 2003; Cohen et al., 2011). In the context of marketing, REAM refers to the practice by which managers deviate from their planned marketing-related expenditures to deliver current period earnings that maintain or increase stock prices. Roychowdhury (2006) and Gunny (2010) list multiple forms of REAM, two of which are directly relevant to marketing. First, REAM practices might accelerate the timing of sales by instituting increased sales promotions and lenient credit terms to downstream channel partners. Lodish and Mela (2007) and Mela et al. (1998) have warned repeatedly that accelerating sales through such price discounts dilutes brand equity and customer loyalty over time. Moreover, the Securities and Exchange Commission (SEC) has investigated several firms, including Coca-Cola, that report high earnings due not to increased sales but rather to accelerated sales to downstream bottlers after price promotions (SEC Litigation Release No. 21599, 2010). Second, REAM might encompass sudden or unexpected changes in marketing spending, such as advertising, R&D, or sales, general, and administration (SG&A) costs, that boost current period earnings, perhaps at the cost of product market advantage (e.g., Srivastava et al., 1998).

Although in both these forms, REAM inflates current period earnings, the short-term inflationary effects are usually misleading, because REAM might negatively affect long-term cash flow and revenues.[1] For example, unplanned reductions in R&D budgets might delay product development cycles, reduce the speed of product launches, and affect the predictability of future revenue streams (see Kessler and Chakrabarti, 1996). If REAM takes the form of reduced customer-centric investments, such as advertising and loyalty programs, it might harm customer loyalty (e.g., Bell et al., 2005), which could affect predictions of customer demand. As a result, REAM gradually may lead to less predictable production cycles and inventory management (e.g., Bharadwaj et al., 2007), all of which might jeopardize future cash flows. Thus, REAM may potentially destroy shareholder value over time. Of additional concern is that the managerial motivations for unexpected changes in real activities, such as marketing, are difficult to detect. Furthermore, unanticipated reductions in marketing-related activities often result in higher current period earnings and cash flows (Roychowdhury, 2006), which may distract the investor community from probing the motivations for unexpected changes in real activities (e.g., Dechow, 1994; Healy and Palepu, 2001).

Marketing academics attribute managerial readiness to engage in REAM to marketing myopia (e.g., Mizik, 2010), as induced by accounting standards set by the Financial Accounting Standards Board. These standards treat current period marketing activities as expenses to be justified in the short run, rather than as investments that create assets with value that gets appropriated over time (e.g., Henrikson and Van Breda, 1992; Canibano et al., 2000). In a bid to appease investors by avoiding negative current earnings or reporting higher than expected current earnings (e.g., Abarbanell and Bernard, 1992; Burgstahler and Dichev, 1997), managers may work to reduce expenses without immediate monetary payoffs. The prevalence of unanticipated reductions in marketing-related activities, especially advertising, R&D, and SG&A, confirms the sense that managers ignore the long-term implications of these reductions, whether because they are unaware or unable to quantify the consequences of disrupting customer-oriented activities.

In an effort to quantify the financial payoffs of marketing-related activities, Srivastava et al. (1998) have paved a thoughtful path for marketing research at the interface of marketing and finance. Influenced by their research, several studies have theoretically and empirically demonstrated to managers how increased marketing activities related to brand management (e.g., Rao et al., 2004), customer satisfaction (e.g., Anderson et al., 2004), customer satisfaction heterogeneity (e.g., Grewal et al., 2010), product quality (e.g., Tellis and Johnson, 2007), technology adoption (e.g., Lee and Grewal, 2004), product development pipeline (e.g., Grewal et al., 2008), and product innovation (e.g., Sorescu and Spanjol, 2008) directly affect investor perceptions of a firm's long-term cash flows and revenues. Consequently, marketing-related activities create shareholder value and even reduce the risk of buying and holding on to the firm's stock for shareholders (e.g., Rego et al., 2009; Tuli and Bharadwaj, 2009).

Yet the valuable extant marketing literature at the interface of marketing and finance is not directly relevant to REAM. First, with the exception of a few studies (e.g., Mizik and Jacobson, 2007; Gunny, 2010; Mizik, 2010), it does not investigate the shareholder value effects of not investing in or curtailing marketing-related activities. However, negative firm consequences, whether short or long term, related to unexpected reductions in budgets allocated to marketing-related activities (i.e., REAM practices) should constitute a direct caution for both managers and investors about the value-destroying potential of REAM practices. Second, for scholars to show the negative consequences of REAM, they must identify those practices, first by theoretically demonstrating managerial motivations for inflating current earnings and stock prices, and then by empirically showing the causal relationship between those managerial motivations and unexpected changes in marketing-related activities. In essence, any investigation of REAM and its consequences for the firm requires a perspective unlike that of existing literature at the interface of marketing and finance: it must ask, 'Do short-term concerns for shareholder value drive marketing activities?' rather than 'Do marketing activities drive shareholder value?'

With the goal of adopting this different perspective and thus cautioning both principals (i.e., investors) and agents (i.e., managers) about the value-destroying potential of REAM, in this chapter we investigate the point of view of a standard setter that wishes to reduce the incidence of REAM and therefore needs to address three substantive problems: (1) why and when managers want to inflate current period earnings and influence stock prices, (2) the different ways marketing-related activities get adjusted to inflate current period earnings, and (3) the short- and long-term impacts of REAM on firm cash flows and revenues and thus on shareholder value. To probe these substantive problems, we first review current literature relevant to each problem, then suggest multiple research questions that cumulatively may help set standards for marketing valuation and reporting. We conclude by laying out theoretical and methodological challenges associated with academic research on REAM.

MOTIVATIONS FOR INFLATING CURRENT PERIOD EARNINGS

Managers may seek ways to adjust current period earnings, primarily to enable their firms to access funds from capital markets, meet the capital market expectations of firm performance, and fulfill personal motivations.

Acquiring Funds from Capital Markets

Initial public offerings (IPOs) and seasoned equity offerings (SEOs) constitute typical ways to raise capital from equity markets. Whether in the context of a first initiative to expand ownership to the public or an initiative for an already publicly traded company to raise funds from the equity market again, firms that report stronger earnings just prior to the event usually signal better potential for future financial growth and thus raise funds more successfully (Ritter, 1991; Yi, 2001). In turn, accounting literature reports unexpected accruals prior to both IPOs (e.g., Teoh et al., 1998; Aharony et al., 2000) and SEOs (e.g., Teoh et al., 1998; Kim and Parka, 2005). These earnings components are not reflected in current cash flows, and a great deal of managerial discretion goes into their construction. For example, Teoh et al. (1998) report that unexpected accruals represent earnings management, because after an equity offering, firms tend to report actual earnings, which disappoints investors and leads the stock price to drop. Similarly, Mizik and Jacobson (2007) identify an SEO as an event that gives managers an incentive to reduce advertising budgets unexpectedly to inflate earnings in advance of the offering.

Other evidence indicates that some firms, when they acquire a target firm through a stock swap method, tend to overstate earnings in the quarter preceding the stock swap announcement (e.g., Rau and Vermaelen, 1998; Louis, 2004). For example, Louis (2004) detects overstated earnings in the form of unexpected accruals, calculated on the basis of net income and operating cash flows, as well as evidence of post-merger reversals of the stock price. Evidence in merger documents (e.g., DeAngelo, 1990) reveals the importance of current earnings for appraising the price of an acquiring firm's stock. When this price increases at the time of the acquisition, the number of shares that must be issued to purchase the target firm decreases (e.g., Erickson and Wang, 1999). However, the acquiring firm's incentive to manage earnings depends on the relative sizes of the acquiring and target firms; as the size of the target firm decreases relative to that of the acquiring firm, the economic benefits from increasing stock price through managed earnings decreases.

For managers, an upcoming IPO or SEO or impending stock swap merger thus are important events that make current period earnings critical, such that they prompt strategies such as REAM that can boost current period earnings. Some resultant research questions include the following:

1.   Does REAM occur during IPOs and SEOs? Are some firms (characterized in terms of size, leverage, liquidity, market orientation, customer orientation, or competitor orientation) more likely to engage in

REAM during IPOs and SEOs than others? Do industry-level factors, such as competitive intensity, technological intensity, market turbulence, and technological turbulence, affect the incidence of REAM during SEOs and IPOs?

2. Does REAM occur during mergers and acquisitions? Does the type of merger or acquisition (i.e., cash based, stock swap based, or a combination) matter in terms of the occurrence and level of REAM? Does the strategic purpose of the merger or acquisition determine the incidence or level of REAM? For example, is a firm motivated by product and technology complementarities to acquire a target in a related business prone to less REAM (i.e., manipulating marketing-related activities might compromise the synergy between the acquirer's and target's market-based assets) than a firm motivated to diversify its business in unrelated markets?

3. What other events related to raising funds from capital markets might drive managers to manage real activities, such as marketing, in an attempt to inflate current period earnings?

Meeting the Capital Market Expectations of Firm Performance

Capital market expectations of firm performance often rely on past stock returns (i.e., past performance) and security analysts' forecasts of financial metrics such as future earnings or revenues. In terms of past stock returns, Markovitch et al. (2005) find that pharmaceutical firms whose past stock returns underperformed industry returns (relative to those that exceeded industry returns) are more likely to acquire firms and change product portfolio and distribution strategies. In applying prospect theory, these authors theorize that managers in underperforming firms are likely to be in the domain of losses and thus seek more risk than managers in overperforming firms, who are likely to be in the domain of gains.

Furthermore, both naive individual investors and institutional investors, such as brokerage houses, depend on analyst forecasts to make their trading decisions (e.g., Barber et al., 2001). Following these forecasts, investors might penalize firms that fail to meet a consensus forecast, such as the average forecast issued by all analysts that follow the firm (e.g., Bartov et al., 2002). In August 2010, Cisco posted a quarterly result that missed analyst expectations by only 0.5 percent; in response, the stock price of this multibillion-dollar company sank 10.0 percent – a 'pounding' by the stock market, in analyst terms (WSJ.com, 2010).

Yet it is acknowledged in the prior research that analysts do not use rational models to arrive at their forecasts and are susceptible to human judgment biases that emanate from overreactions to information (e.g.,

Abarbanell and Bernard, 1992), herding tendencies (e.g., Clement and Tse, 2005), and affiliations with biased brokerage houses (e.g., Eames et al., 2002). Managers still seem strongly motivated to meet these earnings thresholds, according to evidence that shows managers use accounting strategies such as accruals to meet and sometimes beat consensus analyst forecasts (e.g., Bartov et al., 2002). When earnings do not meet analyst forecasts, investors question managers' competency and downgrade stock prices (e.g., Barth et al., 2001). In addition, analyst forecasts include managerial expectations of firm performance (e.g., Ruland et al., 1990). If managers announce their earnings expectations, which prompts the announcement of analyst forecasts, managers then may feel bound to meet those forecasts to avoid investor-initiated litigation (e.g., Kasznik, 1999), whiplash in the stock market (e.g., Barth et al., 2001), or the loss of personal and organizational reputation (e.g., Francis et al., 2008).

The pressure on managers also might derive from analyst stock recommendations (e.g., buy, hold, or sell for a stock). Abarbanell and Lehavy (2003) use analyst stock recommendations to predict the direction of earnings management. They find that firms that receive buy recommendations are more likely to manage earnings than are those that receive sell recommendations.

In summary, for managers, prior period financial performance, consensus analyst forecasts, and analyst trading recommendations offer important benchmarks of performance that may drive practices such as REAM, designed to boost current period earnings. The related research questions include the following:

1. Do managers use past stock performance metrics (e.g., past stock returns) as stringent performance benchmarks for the current period that they must achieve, perhaps through the use of REAM? What role does stock volatility play in driving managers to engage in REAM? Firms might forgo investments related to marketing to lower short-term cash flow volatility, while ignoring the need to smooth volatility over the long term (Minton and Schrand, 1999). Therefore, do managerial concerns for cash flow volatility and stock volatility drive REAM?

2. How do analyst forecasts of cash flow, revenues, and earnings influence REAM? With what frequency do managers engage in REAM to meet analyst expectations – once every couple of years, once every few fiscal quarters, or more often? Does the degree of analyst following influence whether and how managers engage in REAM?

3. Do firms that receive buy recommendations from analysts manage their marketing activities differently than firms that receive sell rec-

ommendations? After receiving a certain recommendation, do some firms adjust their budgets for marketing-related activities to maintain the buy recommendation or change the sell recommendation? Which adjustments fall under the purview of REAM, and which may be construed as genuine efforts to gain a product market advantage?

Personal Motivations of Managers

Compensation plans may give managers incentives to adjust firm earnings. For example, Guidry et al. (1999) find that business managers of a prominent multinational firm likely defer income if they are entitled to the maximum bonuses permitted under their compensation plans. Other studies show that when caps exist on bonus awards, relative to no caps, executives likely defer some current period revenues and only report that deferred portion in the following period (e.g., Healy, 1985; Holthausen et al., 1995). Furthermore, bonuses tend to increase management incentives to focus exclusively on short-term, year-end performance goals (e.g., Fisher and Govindarajan, 1992; Veliyath, 2002).

Scholars also criticize stock options as 'an increasing part of executive compensation,' such that 'as managers who made great fortunes on options became the stuff of legends . . . the preservation and enhancement of short-term stock prices became a personal (and damaging) priority for many CEOs and CFOs' (Fuller and Jensen, 2010, p. 42). Both Bergstresser and Philippon (2006) and Beneish and Vargus (2002) find that periods of high accruals coincide with high levels of CEO option exercises. Bergstresser and Philippon (2006) also cite Xerox as an example of a company whose executives exercised large numbers of stock options and caught the attention of the SEC. In 2002, after the SEC sued Xerox for manipulating reported earnings and revenues, the company restated earnings that were $1.4 billion lower than those previously declared for the period 1997–2001. Dechow and Sloan (1992) suggest that in their final years in office, executives have little incentive to develop intangible assets and therefore reject investments with positive net present value, such as R&D, in favor of investments with immediate payoffs that affect their compensation.

Thus, different forms of managerial compensation provide incentives to manage current period earnings, which could drive strategies such as REAM that can boost current period earnings. As a result, several research questions arise:

1. Do top management compensation schemes influence the incidence and level of REAM related to marketing activities? Is the influence

on marketing activities a direct effect, or do compensation schemes moderate the extent to which managers engage in REAM while raising funds from capital markets or attempting to meet performance benchmarks?

2.   Do characteristics of the executive team such as its tenure, experience, and functional (e.g., finance, accounting, marketing) representation moderate the extent to which executive compensation schemes influence REAM related to marketing activities?

3.   Compensation concerns may increase near the end of a fiscal year with the revelation of private knowledge about actual performance from production-related activities. Most compensation schemes are based on year-end performance. Are executives thus more likely to engage in REAM in the fourth fiscal quarter than in other quarters?

MARKETING AND INFLATED EARNINGS

In Table 11.1, we summarize some ways scholars have demonstrated the existence of REAM. Early evidence in the context of marketing came from Bushee (1998), who shows that managers are more likely to decrease R&D budgets relative to the prior year's R&D budget when a firm's institutional ownership is transient rather than dedicated. The earnings motivations become clear by comparing the level of cuts across firms with (1) small decreases, (2) large decreases, and (3) increases in earnings before R&D and taxes, relative to the prior year (ibid.). Considering that prior years' earnings performance is often a benchmark for current performance (Burgstahler and Dichev, 1997), firms with larger declines in earnings before R&D and taxes should be more likely to reduce current R&D budgets to meet earnings targets.

Through extensive interviews and surveys of chief financial officers, Graham et al. (2005), report managerial inclinations toward earnings management strategies. Specifically, 80 percent of managers would decrease advertising and R&D budgets if faced with a possible failure to achieve quarterly earnings targets, and approximately 55 percent of them said that they would postpone new product projects, even with the explicit understanding that a delay could lead to lost future value. Finally, 39 percent of the managers surveyed said they would increase promotional incentives for customers in the current quarter.

Roychowdhury (2006) reports further evidence of price discounts to boost current sales, as well as reductions to discretionary expenses, to avoid reporting negative earnings. In particular, the reductions in discretionary expenses in suspect years – defined as years in which firms report

Table 11.1 Demonstrations of REAM in prior literature

Article	Measuring Marketing-related Activities	Do Marketing-related Activities Represent REAM?
Bushee (1998)	Levels of R&D budget decreases by firm f from period $t-1$ to t, i.e., $$R\&D_{ft} - R\&D_{ft-1} < 0$$	The author compares levels of R&D budget decreases across three samples of firms with (1) small decreases in earnings before R&D and taxes relative to the prior year, (2) large decreases in earnings before R&D and taxes relative to the prior year, and (3) increases in earnings before R&D and taxes relative to the prior year. The author infers REAM when larger decreases in earnings before R&D and taxes relative to prior year are accompanied by larger reductions in R&D budgets
Roychowdhury (2006)	Unexpected changes in marketing-related activities (discretionary expenses) of firm f at period t are deviations from industry forecasts where the industry forecast model is $$\frac{DE_t}{A_{t-1}} = \alpha_0 + \alpha_1\left(\frac{1}{A_{t-1}}\right) + \beta\left(\frac{S_{t-1}}{A_{t-1}}\right) + \varepsilon_t,$$ where DE_t is discretionary expenditures of the specific industry at time t (i.e., sum of industry R&D, advertising, and SG&A expenses at time t). A is total industry assets, and S is total industry sales	The author compares unexpected changes in discretionary expenses of suspect firm years (years in which firms report net income greater than zero but less than 0.005) to other firm years. The author infers REAM when unexpected changes in discretionary expenses in suspect firm years are negative
Mizik and Jacobson (2007)	Unexpected changes in marketing intensity (measured as difference in SG&A and R&D) at period t are deviations from the cross-sectional forecasts, as follows: $$Mktg_{ft} - \overline{Mktg_t} = \alpha_{mf} + \phi_1(ROA_{ft-1} - \overline{ROA_{t-1}})$$ $$+ \phi_2(ROA_{ft-2} - \overline{ROA_{t-2}}) + \phi_3(Mktg_{ft-1} - \overline{Mktg_{t-1}})$$ $$+ \phi_4(Mktg_{ft-2} - \overline{Mktg_{t-2}}) + \varepsilon_{ft}$$	The authors demonstrate REAM at the time of an SEO when the proportion of firms with unexpected changes in $ROA_{ft} > 0$ and unexpected changes in $Mktg_{ft} < 0$ is significantly greater at the time of an SEO than at other periods. Unexpected changes in ROA_{ft} are calculated from a forecast model similar to that of marketing intensity

Table 11.1 (continued)

Article	Measuring Marketing-related Activities	Do Marketing-related Activities Represent REAM?
	where ROA_{ft}, ROA_{ft-1}, ROA_{ft-2} are returns on assets of firm f at time t, $t-1$ and $t-2$, respectively; $\overline{ROA}_{t-1}$, $\overline{ROA}_{t-2}$ are economy-wide means of returns on assets at time $t-1$ and $t-2$, respectively; $Mktg_{ft}$, $Mktg_{ft-1}$, $Mktg_{ft-2}$ represent marketing intensity of firm f at time t, $t-1$, and $t-2$, respectively; and $\overline{Mktg}_{t-1}$, $\overline{Mktg}_{t-2}$ represent economy-wide means of marketing intensity at time $t-1$ and $t-2$, respectively	
Moorman and Spencer (2008)	The pattern of innovation introductions in each of the four quarters of year t. A new product is an innovation if it fits into the following categories: packaging innovation, merchandising innovation, formulation innovation, positioning innovation, market innovation, or technological innovation	The authors estimate a latent class growth model on the number of innovation introductions by a panel of firms. The model shows that one group of firms begin innovation introductions late in the year and exhibited increasing innovation levels over time. A second group exhibited an early increase in the number of innovations, followed by a steep fall off. A third group innovated at a consistently low level. The authors infer that group 1 engages in REAM (i.e., is strategically managing innovation introductions over a year), because the yearly abnormal returns of group 1 are significantly greater than the abnormal returns of other groups
Cohen et al. (2009)	Unexpected changes in advertising outlay of firm f in month t are residuals of the following model: $$E(ADV_{ft}) = \theta_1 * (ADV_{ft-1} - ADV_{ft-13}) + \varepsilon_t$$ where $E(ADV_{ft})$ is the expectation of advertising (ADV) outlay of firm f in month t	The authors compare unexpected changes in advertising outlay of suspect firms – including those (1) whose quarterly earnings before extraordinary items scaled by total assets are between 0 and 0.00125, (2) whose quarterly change in earnings compared with same quarter the previous year is between 0 and 0.005, and (3) that just met earnings per share consensus

Mizik (2010)

Unexpected changes in marketing intensity and R&D budgets of firm f at period t are deviations from the time-series forecasts of the following models:

$$Mktg_{ft} = \alpha_{mktg,f} + \phi_{mktg}*Mktg_{ft-1} + \sum_{t=1}^{T} \partial_{mktg,t}*year_t + \sum \lambda_{mktg,sic}$$

$$*SIC_{sic} + \varepsilon_{mktg,ft}$$

$$R\&D_{ft} = \alpha_{R\&D,f} + \phi_{R\&D}*R\&D_{ft-1} + \sum_{t=1}^{} \partial_{R\&D,t}*year_t + \sum \lambda_{R\&D,sic}$$

$$*SIC_{sic} + \varepsilon_{R\&D,ft}$$

where $Mktg_{ft}$ is the marketing intensity (measured as difference in SG&A and R&D) of firm f at year t, $R\&D_{ft}$ is R&D budget of firm f at year t, $Mktg_{ft-1}$ is lagged marketing intensity, $R\&D_{ft-1}$ is lagged R&D budget, SIC_{sic} represent dummy variables that take a value of 1 if the firm belongs to a specific SIC code or 0 otherwise, and $year_t$ is a dummy for the year

analyst forecast by $0.0.1 – with non-suspect firms (i.e., all other firms). The authors infer REAM when unexpected changes in advertising outlay in suspect firms are negative

The authors infer REAM if all of the following are true for firm f at time t: unexpected change in $ROA_{ft} > 0$, unexpected change in $Mktg_{ft} < 0$, and unexpected change in $ROA_{ft} < 0$. Unexpected change in ROA_{ft} calculated from a forecast model similar to that of marketing intensity

Table 11.1 (continued)

Article	Measuring Marketing-related Activities	Do Marketing-related Activities Represent REAM?
Chapman and Steenburgh (2011)	Marketing activities measured as dummy variables that represent special prices, feature advertisements, and aisle displays	The authors estimate the following sample equation: $Mktg\ Activity_{fst} = \alpha + \beta_1 Qend_{fst} + \beta_2 Yend_{fst} + \beta_3 MPQeps_{fst}*Qend_{fst} + \beta_4 MPQeps_{fst}*Yend_{fst} + \sum_{j=1}^{12} \gamma_{1j} Month_{fstj} + \varepsilon_{fst}$ where $Mktg\ Activity_{fst}$ is the dummy for a specific marketing activity of firm f in store s at quarter t, $Qend$ is a dummy for quarter-end, $Yend$ is a dummy for year-end, MPQ_{eps} is 1 if in the previous quarter the firm had achieved an earnings per share (EPS) about 80–100% of the EPS achieved in the same quarter last year (else 0), and month is a dummy for the jth month. The authors infer REAM when β_3 is significantly positive, because marketing actions occur more frequently at the fiscal quarter-end following quarters of slightly lower EPS. The authors also infer REAM if β_4 is significantly positive, because marketing activities occur more frequently at the fiscal year-end following quarters of slightly lower EPS

Chakravarty and Grewal (2011)

Unexpected changes in marketing budgets and R&D budgets of firm f at period t are deviations from the time-series forecasts of the following models:

$$\frac{Mktg_{ft}}{Sales_{ft}} = \phi_{f,mktg} + \phi_{Mktg} Mktg_{f(t-4)}/Sales_{f(t-4)} + \sum_{t=1}^{T} \partial_{mktg,t} Time_t$$
$$+ \sum \delta_{mktg,ind} Ind + \varepsilon_{mktg,ft}$$

$$\frac{R\&D_{ft}}{Sales_{ft}} = \phi_{f,R\&D} + \phi_{R\&D} R\&D_{f(t-4)}/Sales_{f(t-4)} + \sum_{t=1}^{T} \partial_{R\&D,t} Time_t$$
$$+ \sum \delta_{R\&D,ind} Ind + \varepsilon_{R\&D,ft}$$

where $Mktg_{ft}$ is the quarterly marketing budget of firm f; $R\&D_{ft}$ is the quarterly R&D budget of firm f; $Sales_{ft}$ refers to net sales of firm f at quarter t; $Time_t$ is a set of dummy variables for the year of the observation; and Ind is a set of dummy variables representing the four-digit SIC codes of the firms

The authors estimate a Bayesian VAR model and infer REAM when the coefficient for the effect of prior period stock returns on unexpected changes in current period R&D and advertising budgets is statistically significant. The model also shows causality from prior period stock volatility to unexpected changes in current period R&D and advertising budgets

281

zero or nearly zero earnings (i.e., net income scaled by total assets is greater than zero but less than 0.005) – are significantly higher than those in other years. Firms appear to manage their earnings to avoid reports of negative earnings.

Mizik and Jacobson (2007) also show that a greater proportion of firms than is typical report higher than normal earnings and lower than normal marketing intensity (i.e., the difference between SG&A and R&D expenses, scaled by total assets) at the time of their SEO. According to Moorman and Spencer (2008), some public firms slow down their new product introductions early in a year and then increase introductions later to better manage stock market expectations and earn high abnormal returns. Chapman and Steenburgh (2011) also show that soup manufacturers double the frequency of their marketing promotions (e.g., special prices, feature advertisements, aisle displays) at the end of a fiscal quarter, which boosts quarterly earnings by almost 5 percent. As a further demonstration of REAM activities, Mizik (2010) cites firm years in which the returns on assets are greater than normal but R&D and advertising budgets are lower than normal.

Finally, Chakravarty and Grewal (2011) show that in a bid to maintain prior gains in stock prices and stabilize current stock prices, some high-technology firms unexpectedly reduce R&D spending and increase advertising and promotional spending; however, as firm size and industry concentration increase, the tendency to engage in REAM decreases.

In summary, prior literature suggests that advertising, R&D, SG&A, and sales promotions get adjusted to manage earnings. However, marketing comprises a gamut of activities, only some of which are represented by the practices summarized in this literature review. We focus on these specific marketing activities primarily because of the lack of publicly available information about other marketing activities, such as brand and customer relationship management (CRM). Yet research questions arise about what other measurable marketing activity might be managed, as well as what other ways marketing activities might be adjusted to manage current earnings. Some related research questions include the following:

1. Are budgets for activities such as CRM unexpectedly reduced to meet current period performance benchmarks such as earnings? Because customer relationship management activities should influence the rate and magnitude of receivables, such as payment for goods sold and the rate of inventory outflow to customers and level of inventory, they could be measured by proxies provided in income statements and balance sheets. Can CRM thus be investigated for unexpected changes in response to performance benchmarks?

2. Because organizational budgets are limited, managers might have to trade off budgets across multiple activities to allocate funds and thereby achieve important performance targets. Do managers trade off budgets among marketing activities? With what frequency are budgets designated to marketing activities, such as CRM, reallocated to activities such as rebates and sales promotions that yield financial payoffs faster? The frequency of tradeoffs matters, because one-time reallocations might not have long-term negative performance consequences.

3. What, if any, is the degree of real activity manipulation? Unexpected reductions in a single marketing-related activity may represent the lowest degree of REAM, whereas unexpected tradeoffs in marketing budgets in favor of non-marketing activities represent a moderate degree of REAM, and simultaneous unexpected reductions in multiple marketing-related activities could represent the highest degree.

PERFORMANCE CONSEQUENCES OF REAM

Aaker (2001) notes the practice of 'milking' brand equity by reducing brand-building investments and instead increasing sales promotions. He considers this practice myopic, because managers might immediately improve sales, but the potential decline in brand equity is not immediately visible. Hauser et al. (1994) observe that managers usually focus on short-term performance and frequently confront a dilemma about how to allocate their efforts across activities that influence current versus future sales.

Lodish and Mela (2007) also note that managers can tie sales to price promotions using store scanner data. Because it is easy to measure immediate sales spikes, managers push promotions that look highly profitable. In the process, consumer willingness to pay higher prices decreases, which gradually dilutes brand equity. Mizik and Jacobson (2007) also categorize firms into four groups according to their abnormal returns on assets and abnormal (i.e., unexpected) marketing intensity at the time of their SEO. Across all groups, only firms with higher than expected returns on assets and lower than expected marketing intensity exhibit a systematic adjustment in stock market valuation a year after their SEO. The adjustment arrives in the form of 17.9 percent underperformance compared with matched counterparts. The differential is almost 39 percent lower four years after the SEO. Related to post-SEO stock underperformance, Kurt and Hulland (2009) show that some firms increase their marketing investments after their SEO to recover from post-SEO stock underperformance.

For soup brands, Chapman and Steenburgh (2011) also find that price promotions that run for a week and offer a 33 percent discount increase current quarterly revenues by approximately 11 percent and current quarterly earnings per share by 5.5 percent. However, the post-promotion dip in the next quarter is 7.5 percent of net income. Finally, Mizik (2010) benchmarks the current and future period abnormal stock returns of firms that unexpectedly reduce advertising and R&D outlays, which achieve unexpected increases in their returns on assets compared with (1) all firms with any other combination of unexpected returns on assets, R&D, and advertising outlays; (2) firms with unexpected increases in return on assets; and (3) firms with unexpected decreases in returns on assets. Relative to the benchmark firms, the focal firms exhibit higher abnormal stock returns in the current year but lower abnormal stock returns over four following periods.

Literature on the performance consequences of REAM is sparse but emerging, perhaps because of the predominance of studies that investigate whether increasing investments in marketing activities lead to greater shareholder value. However, in the context of REAM, firms do not increase but rather decrease or trade off budgets among marketing activities or in favor of other activities. Therefore, extant literature is perhaps less relevant than studies that show how the short- and long-term financial performance of a firm is affected by REAM. We then pose the following research questions that pertain to the financial consequences of REAM:

1. How does REAM influence current period earnings and shareholder returns, as well as future period earnings and shareholder returns?
2. How does REAM affect current period and future period cash flows? How is cash flow volatility affected by REAM? Considering that idiosyncratic risk reflects uncertainties in cash flows, does REAM influence long-term idiosyncratic risk?
3. Does REAM have long-lasting effects on a firm's vulnerability to market movements (especially downturns), that is, does it influence long-term systematic risk?
4. Although adjusting real activities such as marketing is not illegal, the SEC investigates instances of REAM if it suspects reported earnings are being inflated. For example, the SEC recently alleged that Dell's strong earnings reports from 2002 to 2006 were supported mainly by rebate-related cash infusions from its main chip supplier Intel rather than any product market advantage Dell had claimed (SEC Litigation Release No. 21599, 2010). In this context, how do shareholders react to public investigations of REAM? If shareholder reactions are negative, does REAM fail to create value and instead destroy value for the firm?

THEORETICAL CHALLENGES

The key theoretical challenge in this field is understanding how events (e.g., IPOs, SEOs), performance benchmarks (e.g., analyst forecasts, prior performance), and management compensation schemes cause managers to assess the potential costs and benefits of REAM. The costs include the potential negative effects of REAM on long-term financial performance; the gains are its potential positive effects on short-term or current period financial performance. In effect, theory should be able to explain whether and how a specific managerial motivation to manage earnings leads to short-sightedness or myopia, to the extent that managers forgo value-creating activities. We discuss some preliminary theoretical predictions of agency theory that might provide valuable insights, though we provide only a glimpse of how it might explain and predict managerial myopia, because our intention is to suggest one of multiple directions for theoretical discourse on REAM.

Agency theory implies that principals, such as shareholders, can diversify their wealth, whereas managers are agents who have invested most of their human capital in one firm. The resulting risk differential can lead to conflicts of interest between principals and agents, because agents choose actions that maximize their personal utility (Jensen and Meckling, 1976). Furthermore, information asymmetry between shareholders and managers makes it difficult for shareholders to monitor managerial actions. Instead, shareholders may resort to outcome monitoring and scrutinize only the performance results, such as earnings, that managers reveal. In turn, when managers are under pressure to improve immediate outcomes, they may weigh the possible long-term costs of earnings management (e.g., through REAM, which managers likely do not reveal) much less than the immediate benefits of demonstrating their ability to increase firm earnings and avoid shareholder-initiated replacements of the executive team.

Agency theory also suggests that agency costs can be reduced by aligning managerial interests with those of shareholders. Increasing managerial ownership of a firm's stocks (Eisenhardt, 1988) is one method for achieving such alignment, though scholars debate the viability of this approach (e.g., Denis et al., 1999; Zhang et al., 2008). Managerial ownership of equity, such as stock options, puts their short-term managerial compensation and wealth at risk by tying them closely to firm performance (Jensen and Murphy, 1990; Denis et al., 1999). Stock-based incentives, which relate directly to firm financial performance, create compensation risk for managers (Zhang et al., 2008) and thus could lead to excessive managerial concerns about short-term stock returns. That is, stock-based incentives for managers might disrupt the alignment of managerial interests and shareholder interest and induce managerial myopia, as manifested in actions such as REAM that can improve short-term earnings and stock returns.

Finally, agency theory suggests that agency costs decrease when shareholders are motivated to reduce the information asymmetry between themselves and managers. Shleifer and Vishny (1986) demonstrate that dominant shareholders (i.e., with more than 5 percent equity ownership of a firm) monitor management disclosures more closely than shareholders with smaller equity stakes. Because these shareholders hold large blocks of shares, they cannot easily sell off their holdings for short-term gains (Holderness and Sheehan, 1988), and it is in their long-term interest to scrutinize management disclosures and challenge them if necessary to ensure long-term value creation. This line of thought then suggests that if a majority of shareholders are non-dominant (i.e., each hold less than 5 percent equity), they can trade the company's stock easily and may be interested only in short-term gains. In this case, a firm's inability to attain performance benchmarks, such as earnings, could lead to mass stock sales by smaller shareholders. Managers of firms with a majority of non-dominant shareholders thus may weigh the benefits of earnings management (e.g., through REAM) more than its costs. Abrahamson and Park (1994) provide some support for this reasoning by showing that managers of firms with a majority of non-dominant shareholders conceal negative organization outcomes from those shareholders.

METHODOLOGICAL CHALLENGES

The main methodological challenges pertain to understanding the association between motivations for earnings management and unexpected marketing budget changes (i.e., REAM). To demonstrate REAM, it is important to establish causality, from the motivations for earnings management to unexpected changes in budgets for marketing-related activities. Only after establishing this causality is it possible to state conclusively that unexpected changes in budgets for marketing-related activities constitute REAM, because they are motivated by earnings management intentions rather than intentions to enhance product market advantages. Demonstrating such causality is methodologically challenging due to endogeneity issues. For example, analyst forecasts of current period earnings are based on public knowledge of prior period strategies related to marketing, innovation, and operations, so it becomes a challenge to assess whether unexpected budget changes represent responses to analyst forecasts or prior period firm strategies. Some methods used to demonstrate REAM (see Table 11.1) in existing literature circumvent this endogeneity issue by avoiding regressions in which earnings management motivations are independent constructs and unexpected changes in budgets for marketing-related activities are dependent constructs. However, such methods only indirectly demonstrate the association between the relevant constructs, without directly establishing causality. We therefore propose two techniques that may address endogeneity issues in a direct regression setting: vector autoregression (VAR) models and instrumental variable approaches that explicitly account for endogeneity.

The VAR procedure not only measures the lagged effects of variables but also incorporates complex feedback loops among all endogenous variables in the system. For example, a simple VAR model with j lagged periods may be represented as:

$$\begin{bmatrix} \Delta MKTG_{ft} \\ \Delta PB_{ft} \end{bmatrix} =$$

$$\begin{bmatrix} C_{\Delta MKTG,0} \\ C_{\Delta PB,0} \end{bmatrix} + \sum_{j=0}^{J} \begin{bmatrix} b_{11,j} & b_{12,j} \\ b_{21,j} & b_{22,j} \end{bmatrix} \begin{bmatrix} \Delta MKTG_{f(t-j)} \\ \Delta PB_{f(t-j)} \end{bmatrix} + \begin{bmatrix} \varepsilon_{\Delta MKTG,ft} \\ \varepsilon_{\Delta PB,ft} \end{bmatrix}, \quad (11.1)$$

where $f = 1, 2, \ldots, F$ firms; $t = 1, 2, \ldots, T_f$ refers to the observation period of firm f; the lag $j = 0, 1, 2, 3, \ldots, J$ is empirically determined; $\Delta MKTG_{ft}$ is the unexpected change in budget for some marketing-related activity; and ΔPB_{ft} is the shortfall compared with the performance benchmark. For example, the difference between analyst forecasts of the earnings per share of firm f for period t (performance benchmark) and the declared earnings per share of firm f in period $t - 1$ (expected earnings per share) could offer a possible measure of the degree of expected shortfall from the performance benchmark of firm f in period t. Finally, $\varepsilon_{\Delta MKTG,ft}$ and $\varepsilon_{\Delta PB,ft}$ are normally distributed errors, and b and c are coefficients.

In the VAR procedure, $b_{11,0}$ and $b_{22,0}$ must be constrained to 0 because the dependent and independent variables are the same for these coefficients. Similarly, $b_{11,1}$ and $b_{11,2}$ should be constrained to 0 because changes in marketing budgets at t are unanticipated and cannot be predicted by prior period unanticipated changes in marketing budgets. We do not constrain the b_{11} coefficients further back in time (i.e., $t - 3$ or further), because the effects of unanticipated budget changes three periods back on current period unanticipated budget changes are likely negligible. The VAR procedure estimates the effect $(b_{12,0})$ of a shortfall from a performance benchmark at t (ΔPB_{ft}) on unexpected changes in budgets for marketing-related activities at t $(\Delta MKTG_{ft})$. Further details of the application of VAR to other marketing problems appear in Pauwels et al. (2004) and Dekimpe and Hanssens (1999), among others.

For instrumental variable approaches, we consider the general method of moments procedure prescribed by Arellano and Bond (1991) for addressing endogeneity:

$$\Delta MKTG_{ft} = c_0 + \Delta PB_{ft} + \Delta MKTG_{ft-1} + \varepsilon_{ft}, \tag{11.2}$$

where $\Delta MKTG_{ft}$, ΔPB_{ft}, c, and ε have the same definitions as in equation (11.1). Thus, equation (11.2) depicts a panel data model that suggests the unexpected marketing budgetary changes of firm f in period t ($\Delta MKTG_{ft}$) are influenced by shortfalls from firm performance benchmarks for period t (ΔPB_{ft}) and prior period ($t-1$) unexpected marketing budgetary changes ($\Delta MKTG_{ft-1}$). Endogeneity arises because the shortfall from the performance benchmark (ΔPB_{ft}) depends partially on the lagged values of the dependent variable in equation (11.2). Arellano and Bond (1991) further indicate that $\Delta MKTG_{ft-1}$ in equation (11.2) should be replaced by instruments that reflect other lagged values, such as $MKTG_{ft-2}$ and $MKTG_{ft-3}$, thereby avoiding the expected correlation between ε_{ft} and ε_{ft-1}. Tuli and Bharadwaj (2009) provide a marketing application of the Arellano and Bond (1991) procedure.

CONCLUSION

Emerging evidence of marketing-related real activities management (REAM) calls for a thorough study of the practice to understand when and why it occurs, in what way it occurs, and its impact on short- and long-term firm financial performance. Answers to the proposed research questions can not only caution managers about REAM but also warn investors about when and how REAM is most likely to occur. Furthermore, for standard setters, academic research into the REAM phenomenon could suggest appropriate corporate governance policies that increase transparency and disclosures in marketing-related budgets. These disclosures would provide better information to investors as they attempt to predict a firm's future cash flows and earnings (e.g., Lang and Lundholm, 1996; Leuz and Verrechia, 2000). Finally, systematic research into REAM might provide the impetus the SEC needs to track and record marketing-related budgetary practices that are not transparent but that attempt to boost the firm's near-term valuation, at the expense of its fundamentals.

NOTE

1. We note that REAM is rational behavior by managers, because it is driven by managerial concerns about firm performance. However, REAM may not be optimal behavior, because it might negatively affect long-term revenues and cash flows – a major concern of shareholders. This potential negative effect on long-term firm performance is supported by some studies discussed in this chapter (e.g., Gunny, 2010; Mizik, 2010). However, since REAM can take numerous forms (see 'Marketing and Inflated Earnings' section), potential long-term negative performance consequences of different forms of REAM must be investigated, as we discuss subsequently (see 'Performance Consequences of REAM' section).

REFERENCES

Aaker, David A. (1991), *Managing Brand Equity*, New York: Free Press.

Abarbanell, Jeffery S. and Victor L. Bernard (1992), 'Tests of Analysts' Overreaction/ Underreaction to Earnings Information as an Explanation for Anomalous Stock Price Behavior,' *Journal of Finance*, **47** (3), 1181–207.

Abarbanell, Jeffery and Reuven Lehavy (2003), 'Can Stock Recommendations Predict Earnings Management and Analysts' Earnings Forecast Errors?,' *Journal of Accounting Research*, **41** (1), 1–31.

Abrahamson, Eric and Choelsoon Park (1994), 'Concealment of Negative Organizational Outcomes: An Agency Theory Perspective,' *Academy of Management Journal*, **37** (5), 1302–34.

Aharony, Joseph, Chi-Wen Lee Jevons, and T.J. Wong (2000), 'Financial Packaging of IPO Firms in China,' *Journal of Accounting Research*, **38** (1), 103–26.

Anderson, Eugene W., Claes Fornell, and Sanal K. Mazvancheryl (2004), 'Customer Satisfaction and Shareholder Value,' *Journal of Marketing*, **68** (4), 172–85.

Arellano, Manuel and Stephen Bond (1991), 'Some Tests of Specification for Panel Data: Monte Carlo Evidence and an Application to Employment Equations,' *Review of Economic Studies*, **58** (2), 277–97.

Barber, Brad, Reuven Lehavy, Maureen Nichols, and Brett Trueman (2001), 'Can Investors Profit from the Prophets? Security Analyst Recommendations and Stock Returns,' *Journal of Finance*, **56** (2), 531–63.

Barth, Mary E., Ron Kasznik, and Maureen F. McNichols (2001), 'Analyst Coverage and Intangible Assets,' *Journal of Accounting Research*, **39** (1), 1–34.

Bartov, Eli, Dan Givoly, and Carla Hayn (2002), 'The Rewards to Meeting or Beating Earnings Expectations,' *Journal of Accounting and Economics*, **33** (2), 173–204.

Bell, Simon J., Seigyoung Auh, and Karen Smalley (2005), 'Customer Relationship Dynamics: Service Quality and Customer Loyalty in the Context of Varying Levels of Customer Expertise and Switching Costs,' *Journal of the Academy of Marketing Science*, **33** (2), 169–83.

Beneish, Messod D. and Mark E. Vargus (2002), 'Insider Trading, Earnings Quality, and Accrual Mispricing,' *Accounting Review*, **77** (4), 755–91.

Bergstresser, Daniel and Thomas Philippon (2006), 'CEO Incentives and Earnings Management,' *Journal of Financial Economics*, **80** (3), 511–29.

Bharadwaj, Sundar, Anandhi Bharadwaj, and Elliott Bendoly (2007), 'The Performance Effects of Complementarities Between Information Systems, Marketing, Manufacturing and Supply Chain Processes,' *Information Systems Research*, **18** (4), 437–53.

Burgstahler, David and Ilia Dichev (1997), 'Earnings Management to Avoid Earnings Decreases and Losses,' *Journal of Accounting and Economics*, **24** (1), 99–126.

Bushee, Brian J. (1998), 'The Influence of Institutional Investors on Myopic R&D Investment Behavior,' *Accounting Review*, **73** (3), 305–33.

Canibano, Leandro, Manuel Garcia-Ayuso, and Paloma Sanchez (2000), 'Accounting for Intangibles: A Literature Review,' *Journal of Accounting Literature*, **19** (1), 102–30.

Chakravarty, Anindita and Rajdeep Grewal (2011), 'The Stock Market in the Driver's Seat! Implications for R&D and Marketing,' *Management Science*, **57** (9), 1–16.

Chapman, Craig J. and Thomas J. Steenburgh (2011), 'An Investigation of Earnings Management Through Marketing Action,' *Management Science*, **36** (3), 762–84.

Clement, Michael and Senyo Y. Tse (2005), 'Financial Analyst Characteristics and Herding Behavior in Forecasting,' *Journal of Finance*, **60** (1), 307–41.

Cohen, Daniel, Aiyesha Dey, and Thomas Lys (2011), 'Real and Accrual Based Earnings Management in the Pre and Post Sarbanes Oxley Periods,' *Accounting Review*, **24** (1).

Cohen, Daniel, Raj Mashruwala, and Tzachi Zach (2009), 'The Use of Advertising Activities to Meet Earnings Benchmarks: Evidence from Monthly Data,' *Review of Accounting Studies*, **15** (4), 808–32.

DeAngelo, Linda Elizabeth (1990), 'Equity Valuation and Corporate Control,' *Accounting Review*, **65** (1), 93–112.

Dechow, Patricia M. (1994), 'Accounting Earnings and Cashflows as Measures of Firm Performance: The Role of Accounting Accruals,' *Journal of Accounting and Economics*, **18** (1), 3–42.

Dechow, Patricia M. and Richard G. Sloan (1992), 'Executive Incentives and the Horizon Problem: An Empirical Investigation,' *Journal of Accounting and Economics*, **14** (1), 51–89.

Dekimpe, Marnik G. and Dominique M. Hanssens (1999), 'Sustained Spending and Persistent Response: A New Look at Long-term Marketing Profitability,' *Journal of Marketing Research*, **36** (4), 397–412.

Denis, David J., Diane K. Denis, and Atulya Sarin (1999), 'Agency Theory and the Influence of Equity Ownership Structure on Corporate Diversification Strategies,' *Strategic Management Journal*, **20** (11), 1071–6.

Eames, Michael, Steven M. Glover, and Jane Kennedy (2002), 'The Association Between Trading Recommendations and Broker-analysts' Earnings Forecasts,' *Journal of Accounting Research*, **40** (1), 85–104.

Eisenhardt, Kathleen M. (1988), 'Agency- and Institutional-theory Explanations: The Case of Retail Sales Compensation,' *Academy of Management Journal*, **31** (3), 488–51.

Erickson, Merle and Shiing-wu Wang (1999), 'Earnings Management by Acquiring Firms in Stock for Stock Mergers,' *Journal of Accounting and Economics*, **27** (2), 149–76.

Fisher, Joseph and Vijay Govindarajan (1992), 'Profit Center Manager Compensation: An Examination of Market, Political and Human Capital Factors,' *Strategic Management Journal*, **13** (3), 205–17.

Francis, Jennifer, Allen H. Huang, Shivaram Rajgopal, and Amy Y. Zang (2008), 'CEO Reputation and Earnings Quality,' *Contemporary Accounting Research*, **25** (1), 59–63.

Fuller, Joseph and Michael C. Jensen (2010), 'Just Say No to Wall Street: Putting a Stop to the Earnings Game,' *Journal of Applied Corporate Finance*, **22** (1), 59–63.

Graham, John R., Campbell R. Harvey, and Shiva Rajgopal (2005), 'The Economic Implications of Corporate Financial Reporting,' *Journal of Accounting and Economics*, **40** (1–3), 3–73.

Grewal, Rajdeep, Murali Chandrashekharan, and Alka V. Citrin (2010), 'Customer Satisfaction Heterogeneity and Shareholder Value,' *Journal of Marketing Research*, **47** (4), 612–26.

Grewal, Rajdeep, Anindita Chakravarty, Min Ding, and John Leichty (2008), 'Counting Chickens Before the Eggs Hatch: Associating New Product Development Portfolios with Shareholder Expectations in the Pharmaceutical Sector,' *International Journal of Research in Marketing*, **25** (4), 261–72.

Guidry, Flora, Andrew J. Leone, and Steve Rock (1999), 'Earnings-based Bonus Plans and Earnings Management by Business-unit Managers,' *Journal of Accounting and Economics*, **26** (1–3), 113–42.

Gunny, Katherine A. (2010), 'The Relation Between Earnings Management Using Real

Activities Manipulation and Future Performance: Evidence from Meeting Earnings Benchmarks,' *Contemporary Accounting Research*, **27** (3), 855–88.

Hauser, John R., Duncan I. Simester, and Berger Wernerfelt (1994), 'Customer Satisfaction Incentives,' *Marketing Science*, **13** (4), 327–50.

Healy, Paul M. (1985), 'The Effect of Bonus Schemes on Accounting Decisions,' *Journal of Accounting and Economics*, **7** (1–3), 85–107.

Healy, Paul M. and Krishna G. Palepu (2001), 'Information Asymmetry, Corporate Disclosure, and the Capital Markets,' *Journal of Accounting and Economics*, **31** (1), 405–40.

Henrikson, Eldon S. and Michael F. Van Breda (1992), *Accounting Theory*, New York: McGraw-Hill Companies, Inc.

Holderness, Clifford G. and Dennis P. Sheehan (1988), 'The Role of Majority Shareholders in Publicly Held Corporations: An Exploratory Analysis,' *Journal of Financial Economics*, **20** (1–2), 317–46.

Holthausen, Robert W., David F. Larcker, and Richard G. Sloan (1995), 'Annual Bonus Schemes and the Manipulation of Earnings,' *Journal of Accounting and Economics*, **19** (1), 29–74.

Jensen, Michael C. and William H. Meckling (1976), 'Theory of the Firm: Managerial Behavior, Agency Costs and Ownership Structure,' *Journal of Financial Economics*, **3** (4), 305–60.

Jensen, Michael C. and Kevin J. Murphy (1990), 'Performance Pay and Top-management Incentives,' *Journal of Political Economy*, **98** (2), 225–64.

Kasznik, Ron (1999), 'On the Association Between Voluntary Disclosure and Earnings Management,' *Journal of Accounting Research*, **37** (1), 57–81.

Kessler, Eric H. and Alok K. Chakrabarti (1996), 'Innovation Speed: A Conceptual Model of Context, Antecedents, and Outcomes,' *Academy of Management Review*, **21** (4), 1143–91.

Kim, Yongtae and Myung Seok Parka (2005), 'Pricing of Seasoned Equity Offers and Earnings Management,' *Journal of Financial and Quantitative Analysis*, **40** (2), 435–63.

Kurt, Didem and John Hulland (2009), 'Marketing to the Rescue: The Critical Role of Marketing Resources in Ameliorating the Underperformance of Seasoned Equity Offerings (SEOs),' Working Paper, University of Pittsburgh.

Lang, Mark H. and Russell J. Lundholm (1996), 'Corporate Disclosure Policy and Analyst Behavior,' *Accounting Review*, **71** (4), 467–92.

Lee, Ruby P. and Rajdeep Grewal (2004), 'Strategic Responses to New Technologies and Their Impact on Firm Performance,' *Journal of Marketing*, **68** (4), 157–71.

Leuz, Christian and Robert E. Verrechia (2000), 'The Economic Consequences of Increased Disclosure,' *Journal of Accounting Research*, **38** (Supplement), 91–124.

Lodish, Leonard and Carl F. Mela (2007), 'If Brands are Built Over Years, Why are they Managed Over Quarters?,' *Harvard Business Review*, July–August, 102–12.

Louis, Henock (2004), 'Earnings Management and the Market Performance of Acquiring Firms,' *Journal of Financial Economics*, **74** (1), 121–48.

Markovitch, Dmitri G., Joel H. Steckel, and B. Young (2005), 'Using Capital Markets as Market Intelligence: Evidence from the Pharmaceutical Industry,' *Management Science*, **21** (10), 1467–80.

Mela, Carl F., Sunil Gupta, and Gupta Jedidi (1998), 'Assessing Long-term Promotional Influences on Market Structure,' *International Journal of Research in Marketing*, **15** (2), 89–107.

Minton, Bernadette A. and Catherine Schrand (1999), 'The Impact of Cash Flow Volatility on Discretionary Investment and the Costs of Debt and Equity Financing,' *Journal of Financial Economics*, **54** (3), 423–60.

Mizik, Natalie (2010), 'The Theory and Practice of Myopic Management,' *Journal of Marketing Research*, **47** (4), 594–611.

Mizik, Natalie and Robert Jacobson (2007), 'Myopic Marketing Management: Evidence of the Phenomenon and its Long Term Performance Consequences in the SEO Context,' *Marketing Science*, **26** (3), 361–79.

Moorman, Christine and Fredrika Spencer (2008), 'Innovation and the Ratchet Effect: How Firms Tradeoff Value Creation in Financial and Product Markets,' in *MSI Report*, 8th edition, Vol. 08–116.

Pauwels, Koen, Jorge Silva-Risso, Shuba Srinivasan, and Dominique M. Hanssens (2004), 'New Products, Sales Promotions, and Firm Value: The Case of the Automobile Industry,' *Journal of Marketing*, **68** (4), 142–56.

Rao, Vithala R., Manoj K. Agarwal, and Denise Dahloff (2004), 'How is Manifest Branding Strategy Related to the Intangible Value of a Corporation?,' *Journal of Marketing*, **68** (4), 126–41.

Rau, P. and T. Vermaelen (1998), 'Glamor, Value and the Post-acquisition Performance of Acquiring Firms,' *Journal of Financial Economics*, **49** (2), 223–53.

Rego, Lopo L., Matthew T. Billett, and Neil A. Morgan (2009), 'Consumer-based Brand Equity and Firm Risk,' *Journal of Marketing*, **73** (6), 47–60.

Ritter, Jay R. (1991), 'The Long-run Performance of Initial Public Offerings,' *Journal of Finance*, **46** (1), 3–27.

Roychowdhury, Sugata (2006), 'Earnings Management Through Real Activities Manipulation,' *Journal of Accounting and Economics*, **42** (3), 335–70.

Ruland, William, Samuel Tung, and Nashwa E. George (1990), 'Factors Associated with the Disclosure of Managers' Forecast,' *Accounting Review*, **65** (3), 710–21.

Schipper, Katherine (2003), 'Principles-based Accounting Standards,' *Accounting Horizons*, **17** (1), 61–72.

Shleifer, Andrei and Robert W. Vishny (1986), 'Large Shareholders and Corporate Control,' *Journal of Political Economy*, **94** (3), 461–88.

Sorescu, Alina B. and Jelena Spanjol (2008), 'Innovation's Effect on Firm Value and Risk: Insights from Consumer Packaged Goods,' Journal of Marketing, **72** (2), 114–32.

Srivastava, Rajendra K., Tasadduq A. Shervani, and Liam Fahey (1998), 'Market-based Assets and Shareholder Value: A Framework for Analysis,' *Journal of Marketing*, **62** (1), 2–18.

Tellis, Gerard J. and Joseph Johnson (2007), 'The Value of Quality,' *Marketing Science*, **26** (6), 758–73.

Teoh, Siew Hong, Ivo Welch, and T.J. Wong (1998), 'Earnings Management and the Long-run Market Performance of Initial Public Offerings,' *Journal of Finance*, **53** (6), 1935–74.

Tuli, Kapil and Sundar G. Bharadwaj (2009), 'Customer Satisfaction and Stock Returns Risk,' *Journal of Marketing*, **73** (6), 184–97.

Veliyath, Rajaram (2002), 'Top Management Compensation and Shareholder Returns: Unravelling Different Models of the Relationship,' *Journal of Management Studies*, **36** (1), 123–43.

WSJ.com (August 5, 2010), 'For Cisco, a Tailored Approach to Markets,' available at: http://online.wsj.com/article/SB10001424052748704023404575428904279878536.html; accessed 16 December 2011.

Yi, Jong-Hwan (2001), 'Pre-offering Earnings and the Long-run Performance of IPOs,' *International Review of Financial Analysis*, **10** (1), 53–67.

Zhang, Xiaomeng, Kathryn M. Bartol, Ken G. Smith, Micheal D. Pfarrer, and Dmitry M. Khanin (2008), 'CEOs on the Edge: Earnings Manipulation and Stock-based Incentive Misalignment,' *Academy of Management Journal*, **51** (2), 241–58.

12 Product-harm crisis management and firm value
Yong Liu, Yubo Chen, Shankar Ganesan and Ronald Hess

INTRODUCTION

Product-harm crisis occurs when a product fails to meet a mandatory safety standard, contains a defect that could cause substantial harm to consumers, creates an unreasonable risk of serious injury or death, or fails to comply with a voluntary standard adopted by the specific industry (Mullan, 2004). As one of the most damaging incidents that the firms have to cope with, product-harm crises span a wide variety of product categories and, once occurred, usually cause a significant amount of media attention, policy scrutiny, and public outcry.

Many of the crises have led to well-publicized product recalls. For example, Bridgestone Corporation of Japan recalled 6.5 million Firestone brand tires on 7 August, 2000, which were reportedly exhibiting tendencies to come apart at high speed, causing vehicles to roll over (Govindaraj et al., 2004). In 2007, Mattel issued more than ten toy recalls for problems such as lead paint hazard and the magnets being too small and likely to detach from the toy. From the end of 2009 to early 2010, Toyota, a company that has been long acclaimed for product quality, was involved in three major recalls involving floor mats and accelerator pedals. Unfortunately, some of the recalls were issued after serious injuries and/or death to consumers. As an example, Playskool recalled about 255 000 of its Tool Bench toys only after receiving the death reports of two toddlers (CPSC, 2006).

The consequences of product-harm crisis are multidimensional. In general, firms suffer both direct and indirect costs. While the literature differs in terms of how specific costs are categorized, in general, direct costs can be broadly defined as the expenses of the crisis event and the product itself. These include the expenses related to the communication with various parties who are affected (particularly consumers), handling the product recall process, product repair and replacement costs, lost sales of the unsold inventory, and litigation and legal expenses. A detailed list of direct costs is provided by Berman (1999).

On the other hand, indirect costs are mostly long-term costs that are particularly linked to the recalled product. For instance, product crises could damage brand equity, spoil quality perceptions, and tarnish the company's reputation (e.g., Sullivan, 1990; Siomkos and Kurzbard, 1994; Laufer and Coombs, 2006; Rhee and Haunschild, 2006; Van Heerde et al., 2007). Based on an empirical analysis of Kraft peanut butter recall in Australia, Heerde et al. (2007) show that the incidence of product-harm crisis may lead to a 'quadruple jeopardy.' That is, in addition to a loss in baseline sales of the product (direct cost), the recalling firm may experience three other indirect costs, that is, a reduced effectiveness of the firm's marketing activities, an increased responsiveness to competitors' marketing activities, and a decreased impact of the firm's marketing activity on the sales of competing brands that are not affected by the recall. Collectively, the magnitude of indirect costs can be very high. The specific company involved in product-harm crises, as well as other companies in the industry, often face a heightened level of scrutiny and often incur higher operational expenses to comply with new, or revised, regulations.

Direct and indirect costs lead to reduced revenue and higher expenses both in the short and long term. As a result, product-harm crises have the potential to damage the confidence of investors in the firm's profitability and long-term viability in the marketplace. This may cause either a decline in the financial value of publicly traded firms or the unwillingness of investors to continue funding private firms (Chen et al., 2009). On 30 September, 2004, Merck recalled its once popular arthritis treatment drug Vioxx, which had been marketed in 80 countries and used by 84 million people worldwide. Merck's stock price plummeted from $45.07 to $33.00 on the same day. Topps, one of the largest makers of frozen hamburgers in the United States, went bankrupt after it was forced to recall 21.7 million pounds of frozen hamburger on 29 September, 2007.

In this chapter, we focus on the impact of product-harm crises on firm value. The remaining sections are organized as follows. We first examine the recent trends of product-harm crises and factors contributing to these trends. We also document the processes that are followed when product recalls are issued. Then we survey existing studies from a number of disciplines such as finance, management, and marketing to discuss whether and how product-harm crises could influence the investors and firm value. Finally, we discuss firm strategies before, during, and after product-harm crises. In these discussions we highlight what we believe are promising opportunities for future research. The chapter ends with discussions about two particular issues that call for further investigation – consumers' reaction versus investors' reaction to product-harm crises and firms' strategies in handling them, and the role of media during product-harm crises.

PRODUCT-HARM CRISES AND PRODUCT RECALLS

The prevalence of product-harm crises in the United States has grown sporadically over the past ten years as depicted in Figure 12.1. Specifically, the number of safety-related recalls mostly grew since year 2000, with dips from 2002 to 2003 and from 2008 to 2009. Although these recalls only cover voluntary recalls from the US Consumer Protection and Safety Commission (CPSC), we believe they are representative of a broader trend. In the next section we offer several potential reasons for this trend.

Why Product-harm Crises are Rising

We believe there are four main reasons behind the growing trend of product-harm crises and product recalls. First, outsourcing and globalization of production have made the task of quality control more challenging. When a product is designed in one place, its parts manufactured in a different country, assembled in yet another country, and the final products sold worldwide, it is often difficult to maintain and enforce a consistent safety standard. The globalization also makes it challenging to identify the exact source problems in the supply chain resulting in an unsafe product. For instance, after Mattel ordered three high-profile recalls in the summer of 2007 involving more than 21 million Chinese-made toys, public attention was focused on what really happened in the manufacturing process

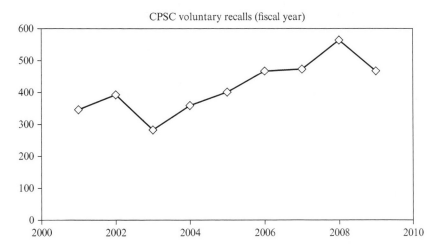

Source: Mullan (2010).

Figure 12.1   Trends of US product recalls by CPSC

and who should primarily be responsible for those defects. As the debate heated up on the specific source of problems in these recalls, Thomas A. Debrowski, Executive Vice President of Worldwide Operations at Mattel, acknowledged in a public announcement that the 'vast majority of those products that were recalled were the result of a design flaw in Mattel's design, not through a manufacturing flaw in Chinese manufacturers.'[1]

Second, as the market evolves and new technologies are being employed, many consumer products have become more complex in terms of their functionality. This inevitably leads to complicated designs and sophisticated manufacturing processes, which tend to increase the likelihood of safety issues occurring. They also make safety control a more challenging task.

Third, over time consumers have increasingly demanded higher product quality and safety standards. At the same time, newly conducted scientific studies have indicated that some products that were previously regarded as safe may not be that safe. For instance, when it was discovered that high-temperature plastic vent (HTPV) pipes attached to gas or propane furnaces or boilers could crack or separate at the joints and leak carbon monoxide gas, 250 000 of the pipes were recalled in 1998 (Berman, 1999).

Finally, both firms and government agencies have stepped up their effort to monitor product safety and pushed for newer (and higher) safety standards (ibid.). As a result, safety-related defects are more likely to be detected, resulting in a greater number of product-harm and recall events.

Detecting Safety Hazard and Announcing Product Recalls[2]

Product safety is overseen by several federal government agencies in the US. The CPSC is responsible for the product safety of most 'consumer products.' These include products used in household, outdoor, sports and recreation, and by children. The National Highway Traffic Safety Administration (NHTSA) is responsible for safety issues related to motor vehicles and related equipment, child safety seats, and tires. The Food and Drug Administration (FDA) has jurisdiction over safety recalls involving foods, drugs, medical devices, cosmetics, as well as pet food and animal feed. The Environmental Protection Agency (EPA) has jurisdiction over recalls involving pesticides, rodenticides, fungicides, and vehicle emission testing.

Chen et al. (2009) provide a detailed description of the recall process for most product categories, using CPSC as an illustration. The process starts with either the firm or CPSC receiving information from consumers or distribution channel members about the potential hazard of a product. Very often such information comes from consumer complaints either directly to the firm or to the federal agency. For example, CPSC receives about 400000 calls annually from consumers through its 24-hour hotline (Schoem, 2001). A firm has the obligation to report to CPSC within 24 hours if it receives information or evidence that 'reasonably supports the conclusion' that safety issues exist (Mullan, 2004).

CPSC and the firm are then involved in 'risk analysis' to identify patterns or data that suggest the product 'creates a substantial product hazard.' If a product is identified as potentially harmful and it is determined that a recall is in order, the firm and CPSC could decide to issue a recall at any time. A firm can also issue a 'fast track' recall without waiting for the risk analysis to be completed. In either case, CPSC initiates an official recall announcement jointly with the firm in a standard format. The firm is not allowed to provide its own news release prior to the CPSC announcement. Such recalls are 'voluntary' recalls.

In very rare cases, the firm does not agree with the agency's decision that a recall is warranted. The agency then needs to decide whether to impose a mandatory (i.e., involuntary) recall. Since mandatory recalls often require elaborate legal proceedings before an administrative judge, which can be lengthy, costly, and involve uncertain outcomes, it is usually in the interest of the agency and the firm to cooperate in the recall process. For example, in the case of CPSC, almost all recalls are voluntary recalls. On average the mandatory recall process is used less than once a year (ibid.).

Regardless of the type of recall, the main purpose is to locate and remove all defective products as quickly as possible from consumers and channel members, and to give the public, in a timely manner, accurate and understandable information about the product defect, the extent of hazard it poses, and the firm's corrective plan (CPSC, 1999). In the next section, we review the literature concerning the impact of product-harm crises on firm value.

IMPACT OF PRODUCT-HARM CRISES ON FIRM VALUE

Quantifying the impact of product harm-crises on firm value is critical to understanding the importance of such incidents, and motivating the firms to pay greater attention to safety issues and be socially responsible. As suggested by Jarrell and Peltzman (1985) and Bromiley and Marcus (1989), it is important to examine whether the stock market reaction represents a sufficient deterrent to dubious corporate behavior including reneging on safety standards.

Extant studies on the impact of product-harm crises on the stock market have mainly focused on product recall incidents since the data are more readily available for publically announced recalls. For the ease of exposition, we will follow this approach and examine the findings and issues surrounding product-harm crises using product recalls, noting that product-harm crises are potentially broader in scope and do not always lead to recalls.

A Conceptual Framework

Figure 12.2 presents the key factors and considerations on how product-harm crises, and the likely consequence of product recalls, may influence firm value. Direct and indirect costs both influence sales and profits of the firm involved in the recall. The premise is that these expense items play a central role in how the investors would perceive the cash flow and the profitability of the firm, and thus its equity value.

Note that although direct costs are clearly associated with a particular product being recalled, investors usually make estimations of these expenses when the recall news is leaked to the public. Therefore, direct costs can be either actual or based on speculation, depending on the extent to which the operations of the firm are known to the investors and the complexity of the recalls.

It is also important to note that when product quality is unobservable, a recall event can be particularly detrimental since consumers and/or investors can use the recall as a signal of inferior quality. Such perceptions would have important implications for future sales.

Besides direct and indirect costs, Figure 12.2 also includes three additional factors that may influence the impact of product recalls on firm value – firms' product recall handling strategies, media coverage of the recall event, and several potential moderators including firm reputation, firm size, and the degree of business diversification of the firm. In the remainder of this section, we discuss the impact of product recalls on firm value based on these variables.

Do Recalls Affect Firm Value?

A number of studies have examined the impact of product recalls on firm value (e.g., Jarrell and Peltzman, 1985; Hoffer et al., 1988; Davidson and Worrell, 1992; Thomsen and McKenzie, 2001). Most of these studies employ the event study approach (e.g., MacKinlay, 1997) to quantify the abnormal returns associated with a firm's stock on, and surrounding, the date when the recall was announced.

The studies vary in terms of the product category examined, and present a mixed set of findings. Table 12.1 summarizes these studies by industry and product category, sample size, and key conclusions.

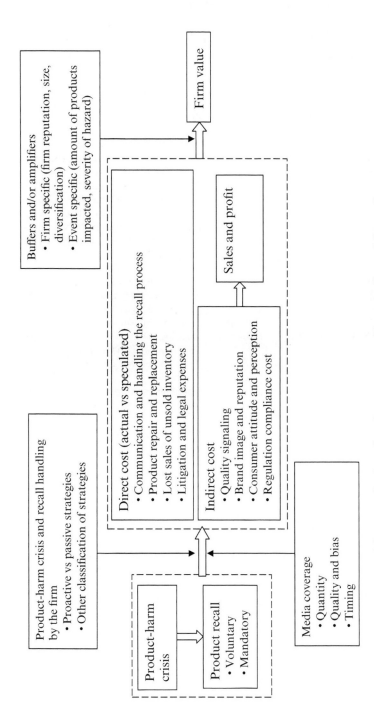

Figure 12.2   A conceptual framework of product-harm crisis, product recalls, and firm value

Table 12.1 Studies on the effects of product recalls on firm value

Study	Industry/ Category	Sample Size	Findings
Jarrell and Peltzman (1985)	Automobiles, pharma-ceuticals	32, 116	Recalling firms suffer a loss greater than direct costs and social costs
Pruitt and Peterson (1986)	Non-automobile	156	Firm value drops for about two months after the recall news. Indirect costs are important drivers of equity decline
Hoffer et al. 1988)	Automobiles	66	There is almost no firm value loss associated with automobile recalls
Bromiley and Marcus (1989)	Automobiles	91	Stock market reactions vary substantially across time and companies. No clear evidence that the stock market punishes companies for recalls
Davidson and Worrell (1992)	Non-automobile	133	Product recall announcements caused decreases in firm value, and this effect is greater when the products are replaced than when they are checked and repaired
Dowdell et al. (1992)	Pharma-ceuticals	29	Recalling firm suffered significant firm value loss. Other firms in the industry had declining share price during the subsequent regulation proceedings, not when the recall occurred
Salin and Hooker (2001)	Food	4	Mixed findings: firm value fell in some recall cases but not in other incidents
Thomsen and McKenzie (2001)	Food (meat and poultry)	79	Firm value dropped due to recall, but only for recalls involving serious food safety hazards
Wang et al. (2002)	Food	5	Initial recall caused decline in firm value, but repeated recalls by the same company do not cause such effect
Govindaraj et al. (2004)	Automobile – tires	1	Firm value drops as the stock market overreacts to recall news, and this drop is based on all potential losses associated with the recall. The overreaction is corrected as information on actual costs becomes available
Chu et al. (2005)	Non-automobile	269	Firm value drops on, and one day prior to, the recall announcement date. Drugs/ cosmetics firms suffer more significant equity losses than other firms
Chen et al. (2009)	Non-automobile	153	Proactive recall strategies have a more negative effect on firm value than passive strategies

A commonly used data source of recall information is *The Wall Street Journal* and/or *The Wall Street Journal Index* (e.g., Pruitt and Peterson, 1986; Davidson and Worrell, 1992; Chu et al., 2005). Researchers have also consulted other sources, such as trade publications and the records of government agencies that oversee recall activities in a certain industry, to obtain recall information. For instance Jarrell and Peltzman (1985) obtained their drug recall sample from the weekly reports of FDA Recalls and Court Actions in the *Food, Drug and Cosmetic Law Reporter*, an industry newsletter. Chen et al. (2009) obtained their non-automobile recall sample from the recall database maintained by the CPSC. Many of these databases are in the public domain. Extensive federal recall records can be searched and downloaded from the website www.recalls.gov, which maintains recalls in the categories of consumer products, motor vehicles, boats, food, medicine, cosmetics, and environmental products. These recalls were issued by a variety of government agencies including the CPSC, the FDA, the NHTSA, and the EPA.

It should be noted that the automobile industry is where many of the product recalls have occurred. It is, therefore, not surprising that several of the studies have used the automobile industry as the research context. For the same reason, it is also not surprising that several other studies have intentionally focused on non-automobile recalls, since looking at a sample of automobile and non-automobile recalls will likely be skewed by the dominant proportion of automobile cases.

Jarrell and Peltzman (1985) contributed the earliest study on how product recalls may influence firm value. Based on data from automobile and drug product recalls, they conclude that the stock market penalizes the firm far more than the direct cost of the recall. The decrease in shareholder value exceeds the costs attributable specifically to the recalled product, and spills over to the firm's 'goodwill.' Such goodwill can be linked to several factors in Figure 12.2, such as brand image, firm reputation, and product quality. The authors also show that the spillover even extended to competitors in the industry. An interesting implication of this study is that, since the penalty on firm value is severe, the stock market can function as an effective tool to motivate firms to heighten safety standard and tighten quality control. This is consistent with the view that the stock market has the governance role of monitoring and disciplining corporate behavior (Samuel, 1996).

In a follow-up study to Jarrell and Peltzman (1985), Hoffer et al. (1988) re-examined the automobile industry using the same data but with several modifications (e.g., excluding non-recall events such as extended warranties on air conditioning equipment). They found that recall announcements did not significantly affect firm value.

In yet another re-examination of the automobile industry, Bromiley and Marcus (1989) studied the recalls on a more disaggregate basis with longer event windows and some refined assumptions about investor behavior. They show that the stock market's response to recalls varies significantly across time and companies, and that the change in stock returns is no greater than the direct costs of recall. 'If one examines the market's reactions to recalls on an event-by-event basis, asking of each event "did the market react in a significantly negative way," one finds little basis for thinking that the market punishes companies for recalls' (p. 248). This study seems to provide pessimistic evidence on the socially desirable role of the stock market as a governance mechanism of firm behavior since the stock market cannot act as a deterrent if managers do not perceive the market losses to be severe.

In another study of the automobile industry, Govindaraj et al. (2004) focus on the recall event of Firestone tires. What makes this recall incidence unique is that although many vehicles used Firestone tires, it was only the popular Ford Explorer SUV that consistently displayed tendencies to roll over, pointing to potential design problems of the vehicle. As a result, examining the effect of the tire recall on both Bridgestone and Ford was particularly interesting. The authors find that both firms lost substantial market value during the recall, and the losses far exceeded the direct costs of the recall. They conclude that 'these additional losses in capitalization are approximately equal to, and can be explained by factoring in and adding to the direct costs the estimates of the almost worse-case costs of litigation in the future, the loss of reputation, and the regulation compliance costs' (p. 47). This result is broadly consistent with the conclusion of Jarrel and Peltzman (1985). However, different from Jarrel and Peltzman, they find that the competing tire and auto firms benefited from the recall.

Several other studies have looked at non-automobile recalls in industries such as food, pharmaceuticals, electronics, and toys. Pruitt and Peterson (1986) find that firm value continues to drop after the recall announcement for about two months. However, they find no relationship between such decline and the direct costs of recalls and conclude that indirect costs are important drivers of stock market reaction. Dowdell et al. (1992) examine the pharmaceutical recalls and find significant firm value decrease. Other firms in the industry also experienced declining share prices. However, this occurred during the subsequent regulation proceedings, not when the recall was announced. This finding emphasizes the industry-wide uncertainty that could result from a recall event. Examining food recalls, Salin and Hooker (2001) find that firm value fell in some cases, but there was no discernable drop in other incidents.

Finally, a few extant studies have found moderating effects in how product recalls would influence firm value. Davidson and Worrell (1992) examine recalls in multiple, non-automobile categories. They conclude that recall announcements reduce firm value, and this effect is greater when the products need to be replaced than when they can be checked and repaired. Thomsen and McKenzie (2001) and Wang et al. (2002) both study food-related recalls. Thomsen and McKenzie (2001) find significant shareholder losses when publicly traded food companies were involved in recalls. However, this effect is only significant for recalls involving serious food safety hazards. Wang et al. (2002) find that, when there are a series of recalls for a firm, firm value fell at the first recall but repeated recalls by the same company do not cause such an effect.

Summarizing the literature on the impact of product recalls on firm value, the following observations can be made. First, there is a mixed set of results on whether the impact is significant. The studies on automobile-related recalls are particularly divergent on their findings, while those on the recalls in food and other product categories have generally found a significant impact. It might be useful to consolidate the findings and determine how and why different product categories result in dissimilar stock market responses to product recalls. As Figure 12.2 shows, the extent to which the direct and indirect costs can be observed and/or estimated in a particular case could be a contributing factor.

Second, many studies have used the event study approach. How rigorously this approach is applied could generate different results. For instance, it is critical to carefully screen out events with confounding issues and to ensure that events collected are cleanly and consistently defined (Hoffer et al., 1988). Without doing so, the findings from an event study that relies heavily on attributing the stock market reaction to a particular event would be ambiguous.

McWilliams and Siegel (1997) explicitly discuss the impact of confounding events on the validity of event studies. They highlighted four useful methods of Foster (1980) to control for confounding events: to eliminate firms that have confounding events, to partition the sample by grouping firms that have experienced the same confounding events, to eliminate a firm from the sample on the day that it experiences a confounding event, and to subtract the financial impact of the confounding event when calculating abnormal returns. When studying the impact of product recalls on firm value, extra precaution is needed to identify firms experiencing multiple recalls in a relatively short period of time in addition to other events that might have occurred during the event window.

Third, it is important to examine potential moderators of how product recalls might influence firm value. As Figure 12.2 suggests, these moderators could include both firm-specific and event-specific factors. Firm-specific factors, such as firm reputation, firm size, the degree of business diversification, the level of financial liability (long-term and short-term debt), and whether the recalled product uses the company name in its brand or carries an individual brand name, could either amplify or buffer the impact of product recalls on investors. These variables may influence the stock market reactions to product recalls in different ways. Strong firm reputation, as well as a larger firm size, may help buffer the firm from negative events such as product recalls (Siomkos and Kurzbard, 1994; Ahluwalia et al., 2000; Dawar and Pillutla, 2000). A high level of financial liability may make the firm more susceptible to the consequence of product-harm crises. Finally, the branding strategy adopted by a firm is relevant since it captures the potential spillover effect especially if the recalled product used the company name in its brand (Sullivan, 1990).

Event-specific factors could also moderate the impact of product recalls on firm value. For instance, a large volume of recalled products usually implies higher direct and indirect expenses. The severity of the hazard may also matter. As an example, CPSC classifies product safety hazards into three classes – Class A hazard, Class B hazard, and Class C hazard. The risk of death or grievous injury or illness ranges from likely or very likely for Class A hazard to not likely but possible for Class C hazard.

FIRM STRATEGIES BEFORE, DURING AND AFTER PRODUCT-HARM CRISES

Given the increase in the number of product-harm crises and their potential impact on consumers and firm value, it is important to examine what strategies the firm should adopt to reduce the chance of these crises from happening, to manage them efficiently and appropriately, and to learn from them after the events. How to manage product-harm crises effectively has become a top priority for many firms. In this section we discuss the strategic choices and implications of managing product-harm crises. It should also be noted that in general, there is a lack of empirical research in this area. As we discuss later, most published works with such a strategy angle are conceptual and aim at providing a practical guide to firms (e.g., Smith et al., 1996; Berman, 1999).

Preventing and Preparing for Product-harm Crisis

Both Berman (1999) and Smith et al. (1996) provide a list of tasks firms should accomplish to prevent product-harm crises from happening. These tasks also help the firm get ready to handle the crisis if product recalls do occur. For instance, Berman (1999) highlights the importance of designating the responsibility for a product recall to specific persons in the company, as well as designing and maintaining effective product and customer databases. Smith et al. (1996) provide a broader range of tasks, ranging from promoting quality control processes and explicitly considering product safety issues in new product development to testing product traceability through the distribution channels.

Given the critical importance of 'getting ready' for product-harm crises, two particular issues should be examined to provide guidance on these strategies. First, it is important to examine the effectiveness of different strategies provided by various lists in *reducing* the occurrence of product-harm crises. This could be analyzed by relating the number of recall events of a firm in a particular time period to what preventive strategies the firm has adopted before (and during) that time period. If there is sufficient variance in the recalls, such as the severity of the hazards and the voluntary vs mandatory nature of recalls, it is also possible to examine how different preventive strategies could influence the recalls that have occurred.

Second, it will be useful to study whether different preventive strategies have received attention from investors. Are there significant abnormal returns associated with the *announcement* of a particular type of preventive strategy before any product-harm crisis occurs? If a recall still occurs, does the preventative strategy have an impact on firm value?

A frequently applied methodology to examine whether a strategy has an impact on certain performance measures is to estimate a cross-sectional model. In the case of whether a particular strategy would influence abnormal returns (AR), the following specification can be used:

$$AR_i = \alpha_0 + \alpha_1 START_i + \alpha_2 X_i + \varepsilon_i \qquad (12.1)$$

where $STRAT_i$ is a binary variable denoting whether the firm has adopted the strategy of concern. X_i includes firm- and event-specific variables that may influence stock market reactions.

A methodological issue that requires particular attention when estimating equation (12.1) deals with endogeneity. As Chen et al. (2009) indicate, it is possible that firms may choose a particular strategy based on their characteristics. If there are firm characteristics that are unobservable to the researcher but affect both market outcomes and firm strategy, the problem of self-selection bias may arise in the estimation of the impact of strategies on performance measures (Shaver, 1998; Greene, 2000; Hamilton and Nickerson, 2003).

The Heckman two-step estimation is an effective approach to checking and correcting for potential self-selection bias and endogeneity (Heckman, 1979). The first stage of the Heckman process involves estimating a probit model on the choice of particular strategies:

$$Prob(START) = \gamma'\mathbf{Z}_i + \varepsilon_i \qquad (12.2)$$

where vector Z_i includes the intercept and firm-specific and event-specific variables, with γ being the parameters to be estimated. The inverse Mills ratio λ, which serves as the self-selection correction parameter in the Heckman model, is constructed using the probit estimates.

The second stage then includes OLS regressions of performance measures (e.g., abnormal returns) on the explanatory variables plus λ, separately, for different subsamples of firms that have adopted the strategy and those that have not adopted it:

$$AR_i(STRAT = 1) = \beta_1'W_i + \beta_{\lambda 1}\lambda_1 + \varepsilon_{i1}, \qquad (12.3)$$

$$AR_i(STRAT = 0) = \beta_0'W_i + \beta_{\lambda 0}\lambda_0 + \varepsilon_{i0}, \qquad (12.4)$$

where W_i includes the intercept and the exogenous variables that may influence the performance measure *PERF*. λ_1 and λ_0 are inverse Mills ratios for each observation in different subsamples. They are calculated as follows:

$$\lambda_1 = \phi(\gamma'Z)/\Phi(\gamma'Z), \lambda_0 = -\phi(\gamma'Z)/[1 - \Phi(\gamma'Z)] \qquad (12.5)$$

where φ and Φ are the probability density function and cumulative distribution function of the standard normal distribution.

The key to the Heckman estimation is that the significance of the inverse Mills ratio terms reflects the degree of self-selection bias. If $\beta_{\lambda 1} = 0$ and $\beta_{\lambda 0} = 0$, self-selection bias is not a concern for the cross-sectional regression of the performance measures in equation (12.1).

In the following sections, we discuss how firms can most effectively handle a product-harm crisis before, during, and after the event to minimize the negative impact on firm value.

Managing Product Recalls During Crisis

Should a product recall occur, what will be the most effective strategy to handle it? Berman (1999) proposes several strategies that enable firms to manage the product recall process more effectively. These strategies are related to specific tasks in the process of 'conducing comprehensive safety analysis, estimating the product recall budget, informing intermediaries and final consumers, recovering the recalled products, and developing procedures to ensure that recalled products can be repaired or replaced in a timely manner' (p. 73). Smith et al. (1996) provide a similar list of tasks, such as to establish a recall response team and determine the seriousness of recall, to decide type of recall and scale of response, and to select media and decide on messages.

Beyond the literature on the impact of product recall itself on firm value, which we reviewed earlier in this chapter, there is very limited work on how alternative product recall strategies might influence the stock market. As Chen et al. (2009) suggest, different firms may respond to product-harm crises and product recalls along a 'company response continuum.' At one extreme, firms forsake (or try to forsake) any responsibility for the defective product by denying culpability and delaying the recall process. At the other extreme, firms respond to consumer complaints early, issue speedy voluntary recalls, communicate extensively with consumers and other stakeholders, and often provide additional compensation beyond the legal requirement. Thus, a major distinction among various product recall strategies is whether the firm acts passively and defensively, or proactively and responsibly (Siomkos and Kurzbard, 1994). A fundamental question is whether a proactive strategy would help attenuate the effects of product recalls on firm value.

Chen et al. (2009) tackle this question using CPSC recalls over a 12-year period from 1996 to 2007. They apply an event study and show that regardless of firm and product characteristics, proactive strategies have a more *negative* effect on firm value when compared to more passive strategies. One explanation for this surprising result is that proactive strategies are interpreted by the stock market as a signal of substantial financial losses to the firm. When a firm proactively manages a product recall, the stock market infers that the consequence of the product-harm crisis is sufficiently severe that the firm had no choice but to act swiftly to reduce potential financial losses. Therefore firms dealing with product recalls need to be sensitive to how investors may interpret a proactive strategy and be aware of its potential drawbacks.

There are other ways of categorizing product recall strategies adopted by firms in addition to them being proactive or passive. For instance, the firm's recall efforts and remedy measures may have important effects on consumers and investors, and thus firm value (Zivan, 2002). Future research could focus on different aspects of these strategies and examine how they might influence the investors and the stock market.

Managing After the Occurrence of Product-harm Crises

Once a particular product-harm crisis is over and most if not all involved products have been recalled, do firms learn a lesson and implement additional safety measures and additional mechanisms for crisis prevention and response? Examining organizational learning in the context of product-harm crisis has the potential to generate useful managerial and public policy guidelines. Such an investigation would require historical data on particular firms regarding their recall history and any changes in their strategies.

First, are there major strategy changes before and after a recall event? The strategy list provided by Berman (1999) and Smith et al. (1996) could serve as the pool of possible strategies, and a study can be conducted by comparing the strategies a firm adopts before and after the event. Second, what is the trend in a company's recall history? Does the frequency of recalls become less over time? Does the severity of recalls exhibit some patterns over time? For firms that do not effectively learn from experience, public policy and regulations should be utilized to enforce strategy modifications.

CONSUMER REPONSES VS INVESTOR RESPONSES TO PRODUCT RECALLS

The investigation of the impact of product recalls on firm value relies on the basic premise of efficient markets. As McWilliams and Siegel (1997) indicate, the methodology of event studies is based on the assumption of efficient markets. Investors in the stock market receive information that is indicative of the cash flow and profitability of the firm. They then act upon the information and make trading decisions. In other words, stock prices, and the change in stock prices, incorporate all the relevant information that is available to market traders. In the context of product recalls, this implies that investors would form expectations about the severity and potential impact of a product recall on the firm, and react accordingly to buy or sell stocks. As Figure 12.2 and the literature we reviewed earlier suggest, such expectations are formed largely on the basis of the estimated direct and indirect costs associated with the recall.

Note that much of the direct and indirect costs of product recalls are the consequence of consumer reaction to recalls. For instance, the number of consumers who respond to recalls and bring their products for repair and replacement would directly influence the direct expense. To what extent a product recall signals problems in product quality also matters because it implies whether consumers will continue to purchase the product. Similarly, brand image, reputation, and consumer attitude and perceptions are all related to consumer reactions. As a result, as investors try to estimate the magnitude of direct and indirect costs, consumer reaction should be an important factor. Several existing studies have attempted to estimate the direct costs of a recall in order to examine whether the change in firm value is about equal to, or much larger than, the direct costs (Jarrell and Peltzman, 1985; Pruitt and Peterson, 1986; Govindaraj et al., 2004). However, no research has directly measured overall consumer reaction quantified by both direct and indirect costs, and whether investor behavior is consistent with such reaction.

In terms of firm strategies, the same rationale suggests that consumer and investor reactions to product recall strategies should be broadly consistent. Again, such consistency has not been addressed in extant research. Extant research has investigated consumer reactions and investor reactions (i.e., firm value) to product recall strategies separately, but not together. More importantly, existing studies suggest that these two reactions may not always be consistent.

Take the proactive versus passive strategies as an example. On the one hand, a limited number of studies have investigated the impact of product recall strategies by focusing on consumer evaluations of products and services (e.g., Ahluwalia et al., 2000; Dawar and Pillutla, 2000). Most of these studies are conducted in a laboratory setting and indicate that a proactive strategy may have positive consequences on consumer perceptions. For example, firms acting in a socially responsible manner are perceived to be of a higher quality by consumers (Siegel and Vitaliano, 2007). More active responses by the firm help reduce the negative impact of product-harm crises on consumers' perception of the firm and their future purchase intentions (Siomkos and Kurzbard, 1994). Furthermore, the negative effect on brand equity and consumer perceptions can be reduced when a firm accepts the responsibility for its product recall (e.g., Siomkos and Kurzbard, 1994; Dawar and Pillutla, 2000). Finally, a proactive strategy can be interpreted as an indication that the firm is trustworthy and cares about its consumers. Therefore, consumers tend to use a firm's recall strategy as a signal of its quality and trustworthiness; they are thus likely to respond positively to proactive product recall strategies.

On the other hand, it is likely that the stock market and investors would perceive the implications of a proactive product recall strategy differently from consumers. As Chen et al. (2009) suggest, the stock market is very sensitive to news and signals about a firm's financial prospects (Ross, 1977). By observing that the firm is moving quickly and early to initiate the recall and managing it in a proactive manner, investors could speculate that the financial consequences are severe and the firm had no other choice but to act proactively to reduce the potential impact. In other words, the investors are likely to interpret proactive actions as a signal for severe financial loss. Chen et al. (2009) thus hypothesize that a proactive strategy will receive greater investor attention and be interpreted by the stock market as a signal for significant financial losses. Firm financial value, in turn, will be affected more negatively when the recall strategy is proactive rather than passive. As we discussed earlier, they find empirical support for this hypothesis, that is, proactive strategies have a more negative effect on firm value when compared to more passive strategies. This indicates that in product recalls, overtly socially responsible behavior by a firm that may generate positive responses from consumers could be interpreted by the stock market in a negative manner. Therefore, when initiating proactive recalls, it is important for those financially sound firms to disclose more information behind their recall strategies to differentiate themselves in the minds of investors. Public policy-makers also can mandate more information disclosure in this case to correct the potential market failure to discourage socially responsible corporate behavior.

At a more general level, the similarity and differences between consumers and investors should be studied to fully understand the impact of product-harm crises. This calls for an integration of research in the marketing and finance disciplines, as they focus on consumers and investors, respectively.

THE ROLE OF MEDIA IN PRODUCT PRODUCT-HARM CRISES

Media plays a unique yet influential role during product crises. As Figure 12.2 indicates, media coverage of a crisis event could directly influence consumers and other stakeholders affected by the recall. This, in turn, will influence the direct and indirect expenses of the recall. For instance, Smith et al. (1988) found that media coverage following the milk recall in Oahu, Hawaii in 1981 had a significant impact on milk purchase and that negative coverage had a larger effect than positive coverage.

Research in media and public communications generally suggest three key dimensions of media coverage: quantity, quality, and timing. Quantity relates to the number of media reports on the event, the number of pages in newspapers and magazines, the amount of airtime on radio and television, and so on. Quality refers to the positive or negative opinions expressed in reporting, and whether the reporting takes a prominent position in the media, such as the cover page of a newspaper. Timing relates to the timeliness of reporting; whether the media breaks the news, or reports the event when it is already well-known. All three aspects of media coverage could influence the impact of product-harm crisis on firm value. It will be interesting to examine how media coverage, via the three dimensions, might moderate the impact of product recalls on firm value.

It is important to note that media coverage of a particular event is usually not 100 percent objective. The media, based on its own interests and reader base, could focus on different aspects of the crisis. Given the perceivable impact of media coverage, it might be quite valuable to study what factors of a product-harm crisis are the main drivers of media behavior. In doing so, it is useful to account for the two-sided business model of most media. That is, they try to attract advertisers through increased reader base and subscription base. Such a business model has direct implications for media coverage of the crisis. For example, product-harm crises that exhibit salient and controversial aspects are more likely to be reported. In the case of Mattel toy recalls in 2007, the fact that the country-of-origin of these toys is China has induced many media to give extensive coverage of the incident. Similarly, the recalls of a number of Toyota models in 2009 and 2010 have generated more media coverage than what is typically observed during automobile recalls by a domestic producer such as GM and Ford.

OTHER FUTURE RESEARCH OPPORTUNITIES

At the end of this chapter we highlight several other issues that represent promising research opportunities. First, most of the current research on how product-harm crises management affects firm value focuses on the US market. The investors' behavior in other countries and their preferences on corporate social responsibility might be different from US investors. It will thus be interesting to examine how global investors respond to firm product-harm crisis management in an era of globalization. In addition, different countries have different regulations towards product safety issues. Future research can examine how product-harm crises management affects firm value in other countries, and show whether the extant findings in the US markets can be generalized to international markets.

Second, related to the deceptive marketing literature (e.g., Johar, 1995; Darke and Ritchie, 2007; Tipton et al., 2009), the relevance of corporate social responsibility in managing product-harm crises can be broadened to include whether firms would employ a strategy of being honest with errors and mistakes, or trying to cover them up and mislead the consumers and investors. The behavior literature in marketing has identified a number of conditions (such as consumer involvement) under which consumers are likely to be deceived. It will be interesting to examine whether the investors are more or less likely to be deceived by tactics that are potentially deceptive or misleading when handling product-harm crises. A recent study by Tipton et al. (2009) shows that incidents of exposed deceptive marketing are associated with significant, negative abnormal returns amounting to a drop of 1 percent, which translates into a wealth loss of $86 million for the median-sized firm in their sample.

Third, and related to firm strategies in managing product-harm crises, future studies could take a longer-term perspective and examine how the stock market reacts when further information about the crises events and firm behavior is disclosed after an extended period of time. For instance, will the stock market react when it becomes clear why some firms had behaved passively during a past recall and whether they had intentionally covered up the problem?

Lastly, investment decisions and firm value are often based on the assessment of future profits and cash flow. Given that any forecast and estimation needs to take into consideration risk and uncertainty, it will be interesting to examine the role of firm risk during product-harm crisis. However, almost all extant studies on the impact of product-harm crises have looked at either sales effect or stock return effect, but not firm risks. Furthermore, some extant research has also explicitly treated firm risks as components of shareholder value. For instance, Osinga et al. (2011) include stock return, systematic risk, and idiosyncratic risk in shareholder value, and examine the effects of direct-to-consumer advertising and direct-to-physician marketing on these three components. Thus, the impact of product-harm crises on firm risks is a promising issue for future research.

NOTES

1. MSNBC, 'Mattel apologized to China over recalls: Firm takes blame for design flaws, says it pulled more toys than needed,' 21 September, 2007 (Associated Press).
2. All phrases in quotation marks in this section reflect the terminology specified by CPSC in its recall procedures.

REFERENCES

Ahluwalia, Rohini, Robert E. Burnkrant, and H.R. Unnava (2000), 'Consumer Response to Negative Publicity: The Moderating Role of Commitment,' *Journal of Marketing Research*, **37** (2), 203–14.

Berman, Barry (1999), 'Planning for the Inevitable Product Recall,' *Business Horizons*, **42** (2), 69–78.

Bromiley, P. and A. Marcus (1989), 'The Deterrent to Dubious Corporate Behavior: Profitability, Probability and Safety Recalls,' *Strategic Management Journal*, **10** (3), 233–50.

Chen, Yubo, Shankar Ganesan, and Yong Liu (2009), 'Does a Firm's Product Recall Strategy Affect Its Financial Value? An Examination of Strategic Alternatives during Product-harm Crises,' *Journal of Marketing*, **73** (6), 214–26.

Chu, T., C. Lin, and L. Prather (2005), 'An Extension of Security Price Reactions Around Product Recall Announcements,' *Quarterly Journal of Business and Economics*, **44** (3/4), 33–49.

CPSC (1999), *Recall Handbook*, Bethesda, MD: US Consumer Product Safety Commission, Office of Compliance, Recalls and Compliance Division, available at: http://www.cpsc. gov/BUSINFO/8002.html; accessed 14 December 2011.

CPSC (2006), 'Playskool Voluntarily Recalls Toy Tool Benches after the Death of Two Toddlers,' available at: http://www.cpsc.gov/cpscpub/prerel/prhtml06/06266.html; accessed 14 December 2011.

Darke, Peter and Robin Ritchie (2007), 'The Defensive Consumer: Advertising Deception, Defensive Processing, and Distrust,' *Journal of Marketing Research*, **44** (1), 114–27.

Davidson, Wallace III and Dan Worrell (1992), 'The Effect of Product Recall Announcements on Shareholder Wealth,' *Strategic Management Journal*, **13** (6), 467–73.

Dawar, Niraj and Madan M. Pillutla (2000), 'Impact of Product-harm Crises on Brand Equity: The Moderating Role of Consumer Expectations,' *Journal of Marketing Research*, **37** (2), 215–26.

Dowdell, T., S. Govindaraj, and P.C. Jain (1992), 'The Tylenol Incident, Ensuing Regulation, and Stock Prices,' *Journal of Financial and Quantitative Analysis*, **27** (2), 283–301.

Foster, G. (1980), 'Accounting Policy Decisions and Capital Market Research,' *Journal of Accounting and Economics*, **2** (1), 29–62.

Govindaraj, S., B. Jaggi, and B. Lin (2004), 'Market overreaction to product recall revisited – the case of Firestone tires and the Ford Explorer,' *Review of Quantitative Finance and Accounting*, **23** (1), 31–54.

Greene, William (2000), *Econometric Analysis*, New Jersey: Prentice-Hall.

Hamilton, Barton and Jackson Nickerson (2003), 'Correcting for Endogeneity in Strategic Management Research,' *Strategic Organization*, **1** (1), 51–78.

Heckman, James (1979), 'Sample Selection Bias as a Specification Error,' *Econometrica*, **47** (1), 153–61.

Hoffer, George, Stephen Pruitt, and Robert Reilly (1988), 'The Impact of Product Recalls on the Wealth of Sellers: A Reexamination,' *Journal of Political Economy*, **96** (3), 663–70.

Jarrell, Gregg and Sam Peltzman (1985), 'The Impact of Product Recalls on the Wealth of Sellers,' *Journal of Political Economy*, **93** (3), 512–36.

Johar, Gita (1995), 'Consumer Involvement and Deception from Implied Advertising Claims,' *Journal of Marketing Research*, **32** (3), 267–79.

Laufer, Daniel and W. Timothy Coombs (2006), 'How Should a Company Respond to a Product Harm Crisis? The Role of Corporate Reputation and Consumer-based Cues,' *Business Horizons*, **49** (5), 379–85.

MacKinlay, A. Craig (1997), 'Event Studies in Economics and Finance,' *Journal of Economics Literature*, **35** (1), 13–39.

McWilliams, Abagail and Donald Siegel (1997), 'Event Studies in Management Research: Theoretical and Empirical Issues,' *The Academy of Management Journal*, **40** (3), 626–57.

Mullan, J. Gibson (2004), 'Reporting Safety Problems: U.S. Perspective,' available at: www. icphso.org/oldfiles/international/2004Euro/2004/London1.pdf; accessed 14 December 2011.

Mullan, J. Gibson (2010), 'Recall Effectiveness', ICPHSO Symposium.

Osinga, Ernst, Peter Leeflang, Shuba Srinivasan, and Jaap Wieringa (2011), 'Why Do Firms

Invest in Consumer Advertising with Limited Sales Response? A Shareholder Perspective,' *Journal of Marketing*, **75** (1), 109–24.

Pruitt, Stephen W. and David R. Peterson (1986), 'Security Price Reactions around Product Recall Announcements,' *Journal of Financial Research*, **9** (2), 113–22.

Rhee, Mooweon and Pamela R. Haunschild (2006), 'The Liability of Good Reputation: A Study of Product Recalls in the U.S. Automobile Industry,' *Organization Science*, **17** (1), 101–17.

Ross, Stephen A. (1977), 'The Determination of Financial Structure: The Incentive-signaling Approach,' *The Bell Journal of Economics*, **8** (1), 23–40.

Salin, Victoria and Neal Hooker (2001), 'Stock Market Reaction to Food Recalls,' *Review of Agricultural Economics*, **23** (1), 33–46.

Samuel, Cherian (1996), 'Stock Market and Investment: The Governance Role of the Market,' March, the World Bank Policy Research Working Paper.

Schoem, Marc (2001), 'Product Safety Enforcement and Recalls in the United States,' available at: http://www.konsumentverket.se/; accessed 12 December 2011.

Shaver, J. Myles (1998), 'Accounting for Endogeneity When Assessing Strategy Performance: Does Entry Mode Choice Affect FDI Survival?' *Management Science*, **44** (4), 571–85.

Siegel, Donald S. and Donald F. Vitaliano (2007), 'An Empirical Analysis of the Strategic Use of Corporate Social Responsibility,' *Journal of Economics & Management Strategy*, **16** (3), 773–92.

Siomkos, George and Gary Kurzbard (1994), 'The Hidden Crisis in Product-harm Crisis Management,' *European Journal of Marketing*, **28** (2), 30–41.

Smith, Mark, Eileen Ravenswaay, and Stanley Thompson (1988), 'Sales Loss Determination in Food Contamination Incidents: An Application to Milk Bans in Hawaii,' *American Journal of Agricultural Economics*, **70** (3), 513–20.

Smith, N.C., R.J. Thomas, and J.A. Quelch (1996), 'A Strategic Approach to Managing Product Recalls,' *Harvard Business Review*, **74** (5), 102–12.

Sullivan, Mary (1990), 'Measuring Image Spillovers in Umbrella-branded Products,' *Journal of Business*, **63** (3), 309–29.

Thomsen, Michael and Andrew McKenzie (2001), 'Market Incentives for Safe Foods: An Examination of Shareholder Losses from Meat and Poultry Recalls,' *American Journal of Agricultural Economics*, **82** (3), 526–38.

Tipton, Martha, Sundar Bharadwaj, and Diana Robertson (2009), 'Regulatory Exposure of Deceptive Marketing and its Impact on Firm Value,' *Journal of Marketing*, **73** (6), 227–43.

Van Heerde, Harald, Kristiaan Helsen, and Marnik Dekimpe (2007), 'The Impact of a Product-harm Crisis on Marketing Effectiveness,' *Marketing Science*, **26** (2), 230–45.

Wang Zijun, Victoria Saline, Neal Hooker, and David Leatham (2002), 'Stock Market Reaction to Food Recalls: A GARCH Approach,' *Applied Economics Letters*, **9** (15), 979–87.

Zivan, David (2002), 'The Playskool Travel-Lite Crib,' Center for Decision Research at University of Chicago Case, available at: http://www.chicagocdr.org/cases/; accessed 14 December 2011.

Index